We Are All Priests

We Are All Priests

The Ecclesiological Boundaries and Horizons of Martin Luther's Common Priesthood

Roger Whittall

LEXINGTON BOOKS/FORTRESS ACADEMIC
Lanham • Boulder • New York • London

Published by Lexington Books/Fortress Academic
Lexington Books is an imprint of The Rowman & Littlefield Publishing Group, Inc.
4501 Forbes Boulevard, Suite 200, Lanham, Maryland 20706
www.rowman.com

86-90 Paul Street, London EC2A 4NE, United Kingdom

Copyright © 2024 by The Rowman & Littlefield Publishing Group, Inc.

All rights reserved. No part of this book may be reproduced in any form or by any electronic or mechanical means, including information storage and retrieval systems, without written permission from the publisher, except by a reviewer who may quote passages in a review.

British Library Cataloguing in Publication Information Available

Library of Congress Cataloging-in-Publication Data

Names: Whittall, Roger, 1980– author.
Title: We are all priests : the ecclesiological boundaries and horizons of Martin Luther's common priesthood / Roger Whittall.
Description: Lanham : Lexington Books, [2023] | Includes bibliographical references and index. | Summary: "In this book, Roger Whittall argues that Luther's teaching on the common priesthood (the "priesthood of believers") was a persistent element of Luther's ecclesiology and closely related to his understanding of the church as the communion of saints"—Provided by publisher.
Identifiers: LCCN 2023037004 (print) | LCCN 2023037005 (ebook) |
 ISBN 9781978715424 (cloth) | ISBN 9781978715431 (epub)
Subjects: LCSH: Pastoral theology—History of doctrines—16th century. | Priesthood, Universal—History—16th century. | Luther, Martin, 1483–1546.
Classification: LCC BR333.5.P32 W49 2023 (print) | LCC BR333.5.P32 (ebook) | DDC 253—dc23/eng/20231024
LC record available at https://lccn.loc.gov/2023037004
LC ebook record available at https://lccn.loc.gov/2023037005

*This work is dedicated to the memory of Lena Elizabeth Whittall,
truly one of Christ's saints
and his priest as well
(Revelation 5)*

Contents

Acknowledgements	ix
Abbreviations	xi
Introduction	xiii
Chapter 1: Church and Priesthood in Luther's First Lectures	1
Chapter 2: Luther's Early Ecclesiology, Its Substance and Form	23
Chapter 3: Luther's Early Teaching on the Common Priesthood, to 1525	37
Chapter 4: The Biblical Data for the Common Priesthood	57
Chapter 5: Luther's Ecclesiology and the Challenge of Reform, from 1524	77
Chapter 6: The Response to Rome: Next Instalment	97
Chapter 7: The Common Priesthood in Luther's Old Testament Writings, 1524–1546	119
Chapter 8: The Common Priesthood in Luther's New Testament Preaching, 1522–1546	153
Chapter 9: Summary Conclusions	181
Bibliography	201
Index to Luther's Works for Church and Priesthood	209
Index	213
About the Author	227

Acknowledgements

This book originated as my doctoral thesis, completed in 2021, at Australian Lutheran College, Adelaide, under the auspices of the University of Divinity, Melbourne. It has been the work of many years, and is now offered with revisions to its introduction and conclusions. As a study of the common priesthood in Luther's ecclesiology, its immediate context is the Lutheran Church of Australia and New Zealand (LCANZ) and reflects some of the challenges currently facing that church community, but as will become clear to the reader its roots extend deep within the theological conundrums that have occupied all the evangelical churches ever since their reformatory origins in the early sixteenth century.

With gratitude and thanks I acknowledge the direction, guidance, and scholarly expertise of my supervisors in Adelaide, Jeffrey Silcock and Wendy Mayer, with Jo Laffin and Stefan Gigasz, without whom this project would have been neither begun nor continued, and certainly not completed—especially I must thank Jeff, whose keen scholarship and knowledge of reformational theology has been invaluable, and insistence on detail indispensable. Additional thanks are now due to Wendy and Peter Lockwood for their encouragement and help in the work needed for a thesis to become a book and to Wendy (again) for pointing me in the direction of its eventual publisher. My gratitude is also due to Professors Cheryl Peterson and Robert Kolb who as the readers appointed by the University of Divinity provided a wealth of critical evaluation, with scholarly insights into the substance of Luther's teaching on the church and its priesthood.

Similarly, I thank the library staff at the Löhe Memorial Library of Australian Lutheran College for their dedicated attention to my many needs over many years, given with unwavering cheerfulness and professionalism.

Further thanks are due to the staff, faculty, and especially the principal of Australian Lutheran College, Pastor James Winderlich, for facilitating and supporting my lengthy time of study in North Adelaide, and for providing the opportunities both formal and informal for the presentation and discussion of my research, and the invitation to join in the life and work of this community of learners and teachers. Beyond Adelaide, the Research Office of the University of Divinity resourced, enabled, supported and encouraged my study in many ways, and I thank Dr. Suman Kashyap and Associate Professor Liz Boase for everything that they provided for me and all their students. Particularly, I want to thank the university for the grant that enabled my participation in the Luther Research Congress at Wittenberg in 2017, providing needed inspiration and stimulus for the completion of this project. A further grant made it possible to engage the professional editorial services of Margaret Gaskin, whose careful attention to my draft copy greatly enhanced the syntax and readability of the final text—thank you Margaret.

Most of all, my love and gratitude to Lois for her patience, encouragement, love, and forbearance almost beyond words. Thank you!

Abbreviations

MARTIN LUTHER'S WRITINGS

LW	*Luther's Works* ("American Edition")
WA	D. Martin Luthers Werke (Weimar Ausgaber)
WA, Br	D. Martin Luthers Werke. Briefwechsel
WA, DB	D. Martin Luthers Werke. Die Deutsche Bibel
WA, TR	D. Martin Luthers Werke. Tischreden

REFERENCE WORKS

Brecht, *Luther* 1	Brecht, Martin. *Martin Luther: His Road to Reformation 1483–1521*
Brecht, *Luther* 2	*Martin Luther: Shaping and Defining the Reformation 1521–1532*
Brecht, *Luther* 3	*Martin Luther: The Preservation of the Church 15321546*
CCML	*The Cambridge Companion to Martin Luther* (ed. Donald K. McKim)
BOC	*The Book of Concord* (eds. Robert Kolb and Timothy J. Wengert)
DLLT	*Dictionary of Luther and the Lutheran Traditions* (ed. Timothy J. Wengert)
OEML	*The Oxford Encyclopedia of Martin Luther* (ed. Derek R. Nelson)

OHE	*The Oxford Handbook of Ecclesiology* (ed. Paul D. L. Avis)
OHMLT	*The Oxford Handbook of Martin Luther's Theology* (eds. Robert Kolb, Irene Dingel, and L'ubomir Batka)
TRE	*Theologische Realenzyklopädie*

Introduction

It would please me very much if this word "priest" were used as commonly as the term "Christians" is applied to us. For priests, the baptised, and Christians are all one and the same.

—Martin Luther on 1 Peter 2:9

Theologians continue to debate the church, its ministry and mission, often in terms of the boundaries—real or imagined—between clergy and laity. At issue here is not just personal ministry style, or a quarrel about importing secular democratic principles into the church, but convictions about the nature of the church itself. For me, those convictions are heavily influenced by Martin Luther and his teaching that the church is first of all the communion of saints, all those called and gathered as Christ's people by the work of the Spirit. Prompted by forty or so years of pastoral and teaching ministry, further reading has suggested that the in-depth study of Luther's common priesthood yields transformative insights into the church and the fullness of its ministry, as the basis for an ecclesiology that embraces the participation of all Christians in the community of faith—people and pastors alike.[1] This understanding of Christian priesthood stands apart from the individualism of "the priesthood of all believers" on the one hand, and encourages a more purposed understanding of the "communion of saints" on the other.

This study, therefore, offers a comprehensive account of Martin Luther's teaching on the common priesthood, arguing for its place as a persistent element of Luther's ecclesiology *in its own right*, as an important expression of his work as a biblical theologian. While the common priesthood is not Luther's primary insight or teaching, its full significance is worth pursuing because of the richness it brings to his theological narrative, and not least because it continues to be misrepresented on a number of levels.[2]

Because Luther produced no unified account of his own theology, it is possible to approach his work from many different perspectives. However, the simple structure of the Apostles' Creed, used consistently in his catechetical and confessional writings, does suggest a theological framework within which the essential elements of his teaching (word and promise, Christ and salvation, sin, grace, Spirit, and faith) were consistently treated by Luther himself.[3] In this way Luther's ecclesiology, with its setting in the Third Article of the Creed ("I believe in the Holy Spirit, the holy Christian church"), is to be seen in relation to this theological core, as well as its development in his thought. Therefore, it is possible to approach Luther systematically, to take account of this creedal perspective, and to evaluate teachings such as the common priesthood in the same manner. This requires a more rigorous method than one that seeks a simple answer to the question, "What does Luther say about the church, and its priesthood?" The aim here is to move through the collection of sources and quotations into analysis and synthesis, to show how the nature and purpose of Christian priesthood are presented throughout Luther's writings in their historical context and according to their theological purpose(s). And, of course, the complicating factors of Luther's extravagant rhetoric and polemic, together with his personal worldview shaped on the cusp of the transition from late medieval to early modern times, always need to be considered.[4]

Accordingly, Luther's teaching on the priesthood throughout his career as a reforming teacher and pastor is being identified and evaluated here, utilizing both systematic and historical perspectives. First taking account of the development of Luther's understanding of the church in the years leading up to his theological breakthrough (*circa* 1518), and in relation to the initial events of the German Reformation (1519–1523), I then show how his early teaching on the church and its priesthood was incorporated into his theological discourse from 1524 onwards, with the developments that led to the establishment of the churches that came to bear his name. The book concludes by summarising the extent of Luther's teaching, with some thoughts on its significance for today's church and the possibilities ("horizons") it offers for future expressions of Christian community.

THE CHALLENGE OF THE COMMON PRIESTHOOD

This priesthood had been acknowledged by theologians for many centuries prior to Luther's controversial use of it in the reformation debate about the nature of the church.[5] In the *City of God* Augustine had written that "as we call all believers Christians on account of the mystical chrism, so we call all priests because they are members of the One Priest."[6] But Luther's teaching still polarizes theological opinion, and for well over a century the "priesthood of all believers" has been a focal element in a Lutheran debate over the authority and status of the church's public ministry.[7] On the one side is the proposition that Luther taught that the church's public ministry is derived ("delegated" or "transferred") from its priesthood and is dependent on it. This is seen to varying degrees, for example, in the work of German theologian Paul Althaus, and his students Hellmut Lieberg and Harald Goertz.[8] On the other hand, an influential study by Timothy Wengert has dismissed the priesthood of all believers—as seen in its later development by Lutheran pietists, and then in its popular usage today—as a "pious myth" uncritically adopted by the editors of the *Weimar Edition* of Luther's works.[9] Writing to address the North American church situation, he argues that Luther's refiguring of priesthood was chiefly a metaphorical device used against the Roman hierarchy in his early reformational writings, affirming the spiritual equality of all God's people but without relevance for the debates over ministry and church order.[10] Wengert's reservations resonated deeply with those of many other Lutheran writers who argue for the unique status of the ordained ministry. Alternatives to his dismissal of the common priesthood regard it as a staging post, a preliminary step on Luther's journey to a more settled view of the church's public ministry; or as an another expression of Luther's theology of Christian vocation.[11] By those who seek to maintain its importance, sometimes it is embraced as the basis for a congregational church order and for the freedom of the laity from clerical control; or more moderately as an affirmation of lay involvement in the church's mission to the world.[12] Perhaps because of its contentious character, some recent studies of the church bypass or ignore this aspect of Luther's ecclesiology.[13]

Whatever the case, by isolating, constraining or minimizing Luther's teaching on the common priesthood, its significance for his theology as a whole is thereby diminished. None of these approaches adequately expresses its importance for the life of the church and its gathered people. And when resolving a perceived conflict between priesthood and public ministry becomes the chief aim—giving precedence to either side of the equation—both suffer as the consequence. In many cases, these conclusions rely on a selective reading of a small number of Luther's reformatory works, ignoring his later writings and without consideration of the broader ecclesiological context.[14]

A wide reading of Luther reveals that throughout his writing and preaching he makes no distinction between clergy and laity when he expresses what it means to be a Christian, and to live a Christian life.[15] This spiritual equality is one of the foundations of the common priesthood and depends on the context that connection may be articulated, but sometimes it is not. The unifying thread remains the way in which Luther upholds God's word of promise in Christ as the basis for the life of faith, worship, and service of all Christians, regardless of the context in which he is teaching, or the texts that he expounds.

In seeking to demonstrate the importance of the common priesthood for Luther's ecclesiology, I have endeavored to keep my own preconceptions around church and ministry in check, not least by a careful engagement with his consistent use of key biblical texts in the formation, development, and consolidation of this teaching.[16] The texts which shaped Luther's ecclesiology from the very beginning are chiefly from the Pauline writings and include (variously, according to context) verses from Romans 12, 1 Corinthians 10, 12 and 14, Ephesians 4, and Galatians 3. In this study, they are presented in terms of four interrelated themes: unity and community; equality and participation. To these will be added the related texts and themes that speak specifically to Luther's understanding of priesthood, 1 Peter 2:4–10, Romans 12 (again) and Psalm 110. The final goal, I believe, is more than worthwhile: to show that a Christian's priesthood is expressed by their deep and vital engagement with the work of the word in the church, and rather than serving as representations of "metaphorical language" these priestly activities form the very heart of a common life of worship and service. When Luther proposes that "we are all priests" he is urging Christians to embrace the spiritual reality of the church as the *communion of saints*, and to discover their own place within it.

Luther's Interpreters

The work of several major theologians has informed the approach taken in this book, although (in my evaluation) none of them provides a fully-rounded picture of Luther's teaching. For this introduction, the Luther-studies of Paul Althaus and Hans-Martin Barth serve as significant expositions of the whole range of Luther's theology that offer an integrated understanding of church and priesthood at the same time as they set the stage for my detailed investigation of Luther's writings. Both Althaus and Barth emphasise the importance of Christ's own priesthood—and a Christian's baptism into Christ—as Luther's basis for the common priesthood.[17] The overall influence of Paul Althaus is seen where I follow him in his insistence that Christian priesthood is to be located within Luther's understanding of the church as the communion of saints, the people of God who hear and speak Christ's word.[18] Less helpful is the undifferentiated way in which he then argues that the church's public ministry is directly derived from the priesthood and its grounding in the gospel. The more recent work of Hans-Martin Barth also strongly affirms Luther's teaching as a highly significant reformational insight, connected to his teaching on justification, baptism and the church. *The Theology of Martin Luther* incorporates these findings from his earlier study on the common priesthood, *Einander Priester Sein*.[19] However, Barth's consideration of Luther's later writings is substantially limited in both studies, and he is critical of Luther's failure to realise the full potential of the common priesthood after the early years of the Reformation. I am seeking to provide a more nuanced—and optimistic—version of those events, based on both early and later writings.

More broadly, I am also utilizing the work of Bernhard Lohse, who examined the content and development of Luther's theology, using a historical-systematic methodology. Here, I am adapting that methodology to show the interrelated development of Luther's use of the biblical themes for church and priesthood by surveying the length and breadth of Luther's writing, and their context(s) in his career as a reforming teacher and pastor of the church.[20] In addition, the historical and biographical work of Martin Brecht still provides the most complete modern evaluation of Luther in his many contexts, and this is supported here by the earlier work of Heinrich Bornkamm who also investigated the important dimensions of Luther as a biblical theologian.[21] Further perspectives are provided by, for example, Heinz Schilling's biography of Luther, as an important account of Luther's life that brings into view the results of contemporary scholarship in relation to his medieval roots. Other recent biographies provide further perspectives on Luther's life and significance, including those of Scott Hendrix and Lyndal Roper.[22] The wide-ranging work of Robert Kolb is noted at several key points, for his insights into the context(s) of Luther's theology. Readers will also notice the influence of Oswald Bayer's understanding of the critical issue of Luther's theological breakthrough in terms of God's word of promise in Christ, of great significance to his ecclesiological development.[23] Engagement with these and other important works is apparent throughout this book and its notes, especially in its earlier chapters. The anniversary year of 2017 unleashed a wealth of writing about the impact of Luther and his theology that has scarcely abated and requires careful assessment.[24] Unfortunately there is still no definitive, substantial account of Luther's ecclesiology, although I have been able to make use of several important studies in this area.[25] But—with some trepidation—this book, based on my doctoral thesis, breaks new ground in that it offers (in English) a detailed account of Luther's common priesthood. I am arguing for the overall consistency of Luther's ecclesiology while acknowledging its necessary developments and changing emphases, including his prioritising of the *Predigtamt* as a key component of his ecclesiastical order for the emerging churches. Tracking his persistent use of a series of key biblical texts, I show that the changes did not lead to the inevitable disappearance of his teaching on the common priesthood from his teaching and preaching, even though its application was then more carefully delineated. But Luther's later emphasis on the public ministry is scarcely a surprise: already in the reformation treatises Luther taught that while all Christians are priests, it remains true that "we cannot all publicly minister."[26]

By accepting the tensions inherent in Luther's approach, and giving voice to the common priesthood on its own terms, my aim is to explore the boundaries and horizons of a reformational ecclesiology in which this priesthood and the ordained public ministry can be seen as complementary partners in the life and ministry of the Christian church. Because of this, this study can also have relevance for other churches in the Protestant and Evangelical traditions for whom the priesthood of believers has an enduring significance. And given the circumstances at the heart of the Lutheran reformation, it provides an interesting contrast to the renewed ecclesiology of Roman Catholic theology, following the Second Vatican Council.[27]

The Basis for the Common Priesthood According to Paul Althaus and Hans-Martin Barth

Paul Althaus' aim was to allow Luther to speak for himself, in a systematic manner, and he quotes extensively from a wide range of Luther's works. Historical context does not play a large role in his methodology, and neither does he engage with the ongoing debates in Luther studies.[28] In contrast, Hans-Martin Barth engages more critically with Luther, and goes much further than many other theologians in pointing out deficiencies and inconsistencies in Luther's thought, particularly in relation to contemporary questions. But, he says, "[t]hose who occupy themselves with Luther get to the center of Christian theology."[29]

Althaus considers Luther's view of the church in three chapters. Following a preliminary chapter on "The People of God," he considers the church as the "Community of Saints" (*Gemeinde der Heiligen*). This shows Luther's understanding of *communio* with his early emphasis on the sharing (*Gemeinschaft*) of faith and love among these saints on earth.[30] Althaus further explores Luther's understanding of the community as "Gift and Task,"[31] and this provides the context for the subsections entitled "The Evangelical Priesthood" and "The Sacrament of Communion."[32] These three are closely related, and give a strong indication of the significance awarded to the concept of priesthood by Althaus.

Priesthood is in itself a way, says Althaus, in which Luther can express this understanding of the church as *communio sanctorum*. This is because, Althaus says, the "church is founded on Christ's priesthood," and Christ's unique priestly work—bearing the burden of sin, and intercession for others—flows on into the ways in which Christians serve one another.[33] This latter point is strongly emphasised, in contradistinction to "religious individualism." Priesthood is "the reality of the congregation as a community."[34]

When the individual comes before God, in prayer on behalf of others, they do so in a representative capacity.[35] This is because "the priesthood is the inner form of the community of saints," and expresses its living connection with—and dependence on—the life and work of Christ himself.[36] A life of priestly sacrifice and self-offering characterises Christ, his Christians, and thus also his church. For Althaus, this is a key insight into Luther's thinking, and his approach gives prominence to the priesthood of believers in the reformer's ecclesiology.

In *The Theology of Martin Luther* Hans-Martin Barth similarly gives a central role to what he characterises as "the universal, mutual, and common priesthood of the faithful."[37] Barth's use of the term "mutual" is a significant addition to the usual designation. The three elements, Barth says, provide the full emphasis to how Luther understood this priesthood. This priesthood figures repeatedly in Barth's introductory material, and then significantly in the three chapters entitled "Dialectics: Freedom and Limitation."[38] "Complementarity: Word and Sacrament."[39] and "Struggle: Between the 'True' and the 'False' Church."[40] This latter chapter has sections titled, "Church as "Creature of the Word," "Communion of Saints," "Universal, Mutual, and Common Priesthood," "Ministry and Orders," and then a "Critical Evaluation" which includes a section "Tragedy of the Common Priesthood?"[41]

For Barth's evaluation of Luther, the priesthood serves both a "church-critical" purpose, in the anti-Roman polemics, but then also makes clear its "constructive ecclesiological impetus" within Luther's overall theology.[42] He asserts that while biblical passages such as 1 Peter 2:9 are important for Luther, the common priesthood is affirmed by "the whole biblical witness." It is based in baptism, as a call to freedom and responsibility, and then also in Luther's Christology and his teaching on justification. These points mirror his presentation of its "grounding" in *Einander Priester Sein*, where he states that all of this means that

> Luther's understanding of the common priesthood is neither an isolated theologumenon nor can it be derived from individual theological insights. Rather, it corresponds to his overall conception of the Christian faith and of the nature of the Christian church.[43]

In *The Theology of Martin Luther*, Barth reaches a similar conclusion on the significance of the common priesthood, that "The [mutual] priesthood of believers to one another, grounded in Christ and filled with life and spiritual dynamism, is thus acknowledged as the life-principle of the church of Christ."[44] No other contemporary theologian—including those whose accounts of Luther's theological development are being utilised here—affords such a level of importance to the common priesthood or places it in such a close relationship with Luther's ecclesiology.[45] However (as will become clear), while agreeing with Barth's overall approach, I am also arguing for the importance of a specific group of biblical texts for church and priesthood that greatly influenced and shaped Luther's teaching.

The Use of Luther's Early Writings by Althaus, Barth, et al.

As a general rule, discussions of Luther's common priesthood focus on the major reformation treatises as the primary source for this teaching.[46] For his examination of Luther's teaching, Althaus begins with the *To the Christian Nobility of the German Nation* (1520) and *The Babylonian Captivity of the Church* (1520).[47] He also notes an earlier reference to the foundational text from 1 Peter 2:9 ("You are a royal priesthood"), in the *Commentary on Galatians* (1519).[48] For its grounding in Christ's priesthood, Althaus uses four particular sources. These are passages from a *Sermon on Mark 7:31–36* (1522);[49] from Luther's 1523 opinion on the rights of a Christian congregation;[50] from the *Exposition of First Peter* (1523);[51] and the 1525 postil sermon on the key text, *Romans 12:1–6*.[52] Apart from the *Exposition of First Peter*, these significant examples are seldom noted in the literature and that may partly explain how the importance of the Christ-connection can be missed.

Althaus also supports his presentation with references to the sections which focus on "Christ as priest" in *The Freedom of a Christian* (1520), and also Luther's exploration of the work of priesthood in *Concerning the Ministry* (1523).[53]

Barth's presentation in *Einander Priester Sein* is also based on his examination of the chief reformational texts, *To the Christian Nobility* and the *Babylonian Captivity*, for their critical attack on the Church of Rome but also their constructive program of reform.[54] *The Freedom of a Christian* further embodies this positive approach for Barth, and provides the important link to Luther's teaching on justification. Along with *Concerning the Ministry*,[55] Barth adds supporting references from a selection of other works (largely identical to those used by Althaus) but none of these has the same significance as he places on the major treatises.[56] In *The Theology of Martin Luther* he tends to present brief quotations within his detailed topical discussions, and does not repeat his analysis of the works themselves.

The Content of the Priesthood of Believers in Luther's Theology

After establishing the context for priesthood, grounded in relationship to Christ, Althaus then focuses on "two manifestations" of this priesthood. They are, he says, "the preaching of God's word," and the "administration of absolution and discipline."[57] Expressed in these terms, these are contentious areas, as will be seen in the review of his later chapter on "The Office of the

Ministry." The terminology that Althaus uses here is already that of the public ministry ("preaching" and "administration"), and his narrative does not suggest any development on these points, and a subsequent emphasis on the ordained ministry. Here, Althaus' particular focus is on the community of the church, and the responsibilities of each member of that community in regard to speaking God's word.

With references to *The Freedom of a Christian*, *That a Christian Assembly has the Right to Judge and to Call*, and the *Exposition of First Peter*, Althaus emphasises that for Luther here the priesthood of all believers "means" (not just includes) "the right and duty to confess, to teach, and to spread God's word."[58] This embraces what Luther calls the "highest office in the church," but Althaus also notes that *public* preaching of the word is a task only for those called to do so by the church, except in situations involving mission, or a failure in regular ministry.[59]

The Christian community is shaped and defined by its message. It can be noted that throughout these pages, Althaus reflects Luther's preference in referring to the "community"(*Gemeinde*) rather than "church." Its message is proclaimed to the world, and among its members it is spoken to one another with the consolation of the word. Proclamation of the gospel is the community's "power . . . [its] unlimited authority and duty." His other references for this section include two early sermons, the later *Sermons on John 14–16* (1537), as well as Luther's writings on the Psalms.[60] The wide range of references here indicates the significance Althaus sees here, and that he considers this to be Luther's consistent teaching, and feels no need to offer any historical differentiation. This approach needs to be evaluated in relation to the evidence supplied by Martin Brecht, as he traces the development in Luther's understanding, from his advocacy of the congregation's "right and power to judge and to call" in 1523, through to its limitation in the circumstances surrounding, for example, the writing of *Infiltrating and Clandestine Preachers* in 1532.[61] Barth, like Brecht, makes that work a definitive marker for a shift in Luther's teaching in the direction of the public ministry.[62]

In the final paragraphs of this section, Althaus presents the proclamation of forgiveness, through confession and absolution (the office of the keys), as the specific concern of the Christian community as a whole, people and pastors alike.[63] This is not treated in any detail in his next chapter on "The Office of the Ministry," even though he characterises this forgiveness, with absolution, as a particular form of preaching the gospel. Neither does it receive further consideration in the chapters on the sacraments. For Luther it is, Althaus repeats, a community possession, its greatest, exclusive gift. The key texts, Matthew 16:19 and 18:18, are considered by Luther to be words for the whole community, and each member.[64] And Althaus sees this as a point at which, in Luther's ecclesiology, the effectual presence of the common priesthood can be assumed, even where it is not directly named. He therefore includes here Luther's words from the 1519 *Sermon on Penance*, "The whole church is full of the forgiveness of sins," even though that sermon does not explicitly name the common priesthood.[65] This is the case for a number of these references: Althaus recognises that for Luther the words that mandate forgiveness and comfort in Christ's name ("the Keys"), are addressed to the whole church and to each and every Christian, so that they serve as priests for one another.

Similarly, Hans-Martin Barth in his *Theology* draws on a range of Luther's writings on this topic, following on from *Einander Priester Sein*. Where Luther claims the common possession and use of the gifts of grace for all Christ's people, there the work of priesthood can be implied. Barth strongly emphasises the value Luther places on mutual confession. He draws on statements on Christian kinship from the *Babylonian Captivity* and *To the Christian Nobility*, but also has in view the examples drawn from Luther's 1522 sermons (noted above), as well as *Von der Beichte* (1521).[66]

Barth then includes the postil sermon *On Confession and the Sacrament* (1524), which affirms the responsibility of Christian sisters and brothers to comfort one another with God's absolution, alongside the role of the appointed priest.[67] Martin Brecht helpfully traces the earlier development of these issues around penitential practices, which ultimately related to the indulgence question itself, and the implementation of the Reformation in Wittenberg.[68] Like Althaus, Oswald Bayer highlights the importance of this mutual sharing of forgiveness for Luther, with references to the catechisms, and then also to the later sermons on *Matthew 18* (1537).[69] Barth also notes the catechetical material, including the importance of the *Our Father* as a basic confession of sins for Luther.[70]

Althaus sees this practice of confession as a highly significant expression of priesthood for Luther. Unlike the regulations governing traditional practices, there are no laws here because this (says Althaus), is "an indispensable form of the gospel," and a priestly service that I may request from any brother.[71] Luther's assumption is that in normal circumstances Christians seek out their pastor for this assurance of forgiveness. But Althaus stresses that for Luther the called ministers are (in this respect, at least) regarded as the brothers in Christ of those they serve. And it is a profound priestly insight, originating with Christ himself, that the confessor also shares the burden of sin.[72] Althaus' concluding words to this section on the evangelical priesthood reveal the heart of his insight into what could be called "Luther's pastoral ecclesiology":

> This seems to be the greatest thing about the community for Luther: God's word, the gospel, is always near and present to me so that I am everywhere

surrounded by its sound and do not need to ask for it. It is close to me in every brother, for he may, in God's name, speak it to me in my trouble.[73]

Althaus' chapter on the church as the community of saints concludes with a section on the sacrament of communion.[74] It is one of his rare accounts of Luther's historical development. To explore the focus on community, he presents Luther's sermon, *The Blessed Sacrament of the Holy and True Body of Christ and the Brotherhoods*, from 1519.[75] The theme of participation is very clear, as Luther shows how the communicant shares both in Christ's priestly sacrifice, and in the mutual life and love of the community. This sermon, and the others from the same year, are for Althaus important stepping stones in the development of the common priesthood. Likewise for Hans-Martin Barth, Luther's "great themes" in his early work on the Eucharist are "communion with Christ and the communion of believers with one another."[76]

Althaus notes, with regret, the loss after 1524 of this communal emphasis in Luther's teaching on the lord's supper, a loss he connects to the dispute about the real presence.[77] Summarising the chapter on "Church as Communion," he does so in terms of the presence of Christ. Christ is present in the word, in the mutual service of the community for one another, and in its loving service of those in need.[78] Keeping this largely separate from his discussion of the public office, but seeing connections to the emphasis on communion and community, Barth likewise explores the "Constructive Ecclesiological Elements" of Luther's teaching. Within everyday relationships (e.g., in the family), Luther sees Christians teaching one another, sharing forgiveness and prayer, and growing in their knowledge of the Bible. In all of this it is the gifts of Christ that are being shared, for all Christians. This is not just the prerogative of the ordained. It leads to social action to alleviate poverty, and to promote education which includes enabling the public role of women.[79] For these developments, Barth draws on material on the spiritual kinship of the baptised from *The Babylonian Captivity of the Church*,[80] and from *To the Christian Nobility of the German Nation*,[81] making a unique connection to *Persons . . . Forbidden to Marry* (1522).[82] For the need for public education, seen in the aftermath of Luther's abolition of the separate spiritual estate, Barth uses *To the Councilmen of Germany* (1524).[83] This is another example of how the pervasive themes of spiritual equality in Luther's thought can be shown to function as otherwise unseen dimensions of the common priesthood; they will continue to be pursued and examined in more detail in the chapters that follow.[84]

The Challenge of the Common Priesthood and Its Relation to the Office of the Ministry

The priesthood of believers remains prominent in Althaus' chapter on "The Office of the Ministry."[85] He begins its first section ("Basis and Content"), with a reference to the [third part] from *On the Councils and the Church*, noting that, for Luther, public "offices" (*Die Ämter*) are among the "marks" by which the church is recognised. These offices, with people to perform them, are necessitated by the first four marks, the Word, Baptism, the Lord's Supper, and the Keys. Luther, he says, "describes a double basis for the necessity and authority of this official ministry," first in the priesthood of believers, but then also through Christ's institution of the apostolic ministry.[86] The challenge faced by Althaus et al. is to give each of these its appropriate weight, and to provide an account of their relationship which does not favour the one, at the expense of the other.[87] One difficulty is that Luther can here be quoted against himself, because he rarely acknowledges the tension inherent in this duality. The usual solution is to suggest a clear progression of developmental stages in Luther's thinking: first (to 1524), Luther proposes that the public office is delegated by authority from the congregation, on the basis of the priesthood of all believers; then, in the following years, he emphasises the unique character of the public preaching office, instituted by Christ alone. But Althaus presents this evidence as he finds it, with the "two lines of development" for the public office, differentiated by content but not (it seems) by context or chronology.

Althaus asserts that "Luther without hesitation co-ordinates these two derivations of the office of the ministry": the one from "below" and the other from "above." Luther, he claims, sees no contradiction in them. Further, "In the first, he bases the office on the presupposition of the universal priesthood and thus describes it as a mediated office. In the second, he derives it directly from its institution by Christ without any reference to the universal priesthood."[88] However, Althaus has opened the door to contradiction and confusion by again using terminology more appropriate to the public office in relation to the priesthood of believers. He begins by stating, "By the power of the priesthood they are authorised and called to serve through the word and sacrament," adding that to avoid confusion, this is committed to one person "for the sake of and in the name of the church."[89]

But to speak of "power," "authorisation," and "call" is not helpful at this point, especially as Althaus continues that, "[t]he necessity and authority of this office is however 'much more' derived from its institution by Christ." For this latter point the biblical reference is Ephesians 4:4–8, utilised by Luther in, for example, *On the Councils and the Church*.[90] Luther writes that God himself has "commanded, instituted, and ordered" the office of preaching,

Introduction xxv

which continues from the time of the apostles.[91] This extensive work from 1539 is the major source for a consideration of Luther's mature ecclesiology, although Althaus does not present it here in those terms. Althaus' other references to support Luther's view of the ministry's institution by Christ are taken from the *Confession Concerning Christ's Supper* (1528); his *Admonition Concerning the Sacrament of the Body and Blood of Our Lord* (1530); on *The Private Mass and the Consecration of Priests* (1533); and a sermon from January 1534 on *The Conversion of St Paul*.[92]

For Althaus, it is the common priesthood that has the priority, and any progression in Luther's thinking on the ministry does not alter his view. He argues, "[Luther] must provide a foundation of the special office which takes the universal office into account. *He does this by deriving the special office from the universal.*"[93] According to Althaus, the authority for ministry is thus delegated to one who is the representative of "the entire community." He does not fully consider how the language of "delegation" sits uneasily with Luther's emphasis on "divine institution." Rather, Althaus states that the special office remains necessary for the sake of good order, and here he identifies the text used by Luther as 1 Corinthians 14:40. It can be noted that Althaus' students, Lieberg and Goertz, also use the language of "delegation" or "transfer" by the congregation.[94] For this derivation of the ministry "from below" Althaus' references are chiefly from the earlier Reformation period.[95] They are: *To the Christian Nobility of the German Nation* (1520); *The Babylonian Captivity of the Church* (1520); *Concerning the Ministry* (1523); *That a Christian Assembly . . . has the Right to Call* (1523); but also (appearing in both lists), *The Private Mass and the Consecration of Priests* (1533).

Taking a moment to consider how other writers deal with this issue, it is not surprising to find that the same Luther texts used by Althaus commonly appear wherever the relationship between priesthood and ministry is explored. Lohse's use of the sources is the most comprehensive, and he makes more of the historical context. Barth has in view the present-day church situation, as does Oswald Bayer.[96] But these writers do not attempt the same in-depth analysis as Althaus (or Lieberg and Goertz), and perhaps for that reason find it easier to avoid the difficulties inherent in reconciling Luther's statements on the ministry. Barth sees it this way: "the common priesthood was in the foreground during his early period, but with the consolidation of the Reformation congregations the ordered ministry tied to ordination came more to the fore."[97] Lohse begins by exploring the divergent views of Luther scholars, since the mid-1800s onwards.[98] For Lohse himself, the resolution of this dilemma lies chiefly in taking account of the differing contexts into which Luther first wrote, and then the development of Luther's views on an ordered ministry.[99] He states that even in the early writings, Luther insisted that only those appointed to ministry were authorised to preach publicly.

Lohse moves on to suggest, in effect, that the priesthood of believers was a theological construct, teaching the equality of Christians and the freedom of the individual from spiritual control, but concludes that "at no time did [Luther] draw consequences for congregations from his doctrine."[100] He thus avoids the suggestion that the ministry is derived from the priesthood, but also implicitly downplays other aspects of the common priesthood.

While Bayer presents less source material than Lohse and Barth, his conclusions are more helpful in providing a broader context for the relationship between priesthood and ministry in Luther. It is important to note that the subdivisions within his chapter on the church begin with "The Office of the Word" rather than "The Office of the Ministry." This is followed by a section on "The Marks of the Church" which follows the sequence in *On the Councils and the Church*. "The Office Connected with Ordination" is therefore treated within that listing, following the sacraments. It is here that he distinguishes the priesthood of believers from the public ministry, and then follows with a section on "The Other Offices," which is a description of the work of the church through its baptised people, embracing the other marks of prayer, worship, and cross. His point is that the pastoral office cannot be isolated from the other ministry carried out in the Christian community, and neither does that office take precedence over the word itself. First, Bayer affirms that "[t]he institution by God does not stand for Luther in contradiction to the installation by the congregation and its representatives."[101] Barth also notes that for Luther the preaching of God's word is preeminent, and while the office is one, those who work in it may fulfil different functions. And the unordained in the priesthood also play their parts in this, each in her or his own sphere, but together when gathered around pulpit and altar.[102]

It is under "The Other Offices," drawn from *On the Councils and the Church*, that Bayer explores further the implications of the common priesthood within the church community. He lists the texts used by Luther: Ephesians 4:11–12 for the public office's institution, and 1 Corinthians 12–14 and Romans 12 for the Pauline image of the body of Christ. Helpfully, this gives the wider context for ministry and priesthood, in the prayer and praise of congregation, the "great ecclesiastical meaning" of the Lord's Prayer, the use of the catechism in the home, in music, and the work of deacons, together with the mutual conversation of believers, all given to strengthen others in the faith. One of Luther's central passages is Matthew 18:19–20, on the presence of Christ with those gathered in his name.[103] Brecht has noted that early on, in Luther's *The Estate of Marriage* (1522), he is already proposing that parents have the role of "apostles, bishops, and pastors" in teaching the gospel to their children.[104] This teaching on parents' spiritual responsibility is consistent throughout Luther's career.

These ideas are not foreign to Althaus, and his chapter does not end with the statement on a derived connection given above. He continues at some length, exploring particularly the common content of both priesthood and ministry, cooperatively shared. This includes the way in which Christ is represented in pastoral relationships and in those between Christian individuals.[105] Christ's own authority is operative in both situations. For Luther, he says, the only distinction "is the public character of the official ministry of the word and sacrament to the entire community." The individual is entrusted with responsibility to represent Christ to the neighbour; all Christians can in this way exercise the "highest office in the church," the ministry of the word.[106]

However, Althaus' positive views need to be tempered—once again—with Brecht's appraisal of the historical reality in 1528–1530, where Luther's hopes had not only been thwarted by the widespread activities of the enthusiasts, but also close to home by the indifference of the congregation in Wittenberg. He writes that "Evangelical preaching was not producing the expected fruit," and that included the assumption of Christian responsibilities by those whom Luther had intended to know themselves to be members of the priesthood of believers.[107] Barth's judgement is more pointed: "The Reformation model of the church is demanding . . . the self-criticism required by the Reformation, especially after 1527/28, caused the aspect of a communion of believers and, parallel to it, the idea of the universal, mutual, and common priesthood to retreat—an irrecoverable loss."[108] In *Einander Priester Sein*, Barth is forthright in his conclusion that even allowing for an inherently complex situation, Luther himself was responsible for this outcome.[109]

Althaus then ends this section by contrasting Luther's view of priesthood with the Roman teaching and practice. Luther argues that in accordance with New Testament usage, the name of "priest" ought not be limited to a particular office in the church, because it is held by all Christians in common. Here, once again, Althaus refers to the Reformation treatises. Properly, the public office is designated by the terms "minister" or "servant." Therefore, there is no special status for the ministers; they have received no indelible, sacramental character. The most that can be said of ordination is that it is the church rite by which the calling of a preacher of the gospel is publicly acknowledged.[110] The call to serve the community is all important.[111] Brecht adds a historical perspective here. Already in 1524, Luther saw ordination as a means of controlling unauthorised preachers, and maintaining order in a time of transition and reform. It was to function, not as a sacramental separation from the priesthood of believers, but as "a human election and commission to the church's service."[112]

In exploring "Ministry," Barth comments on the ambiguity of Luther's use of the language of priest and priesthood, and its lukewarm reception by lay people in the church. He sees the tension inherent in Luther's search for a new terminology for the public office—speaking positively of Christ as priest and negatively of the medieval priesthood.[113] This, again, for Barth is an aspect of the critical flaw that Luther did not satisfactorily resolve in his reformational journey. So Barth can still affirm the new vision for congregational worship that Luther introduced, while questioning the extent to which he allowed laity the expression of their spiritual gifts:

> Ministers and laity stand facing one another on the ground of their common priesthood. The ministry serves the laity through preaching in worship and the celebration of the sacraments; the laity sustain the ministry through their prayers and support it by their participation in spiritual tasks within their own sphere . . . [but] not in view is the understanding that charisms [Romans 12:6–8] may be alive in the congregation and awaiting their development for the good of the whole.[114]

This is a historical judgement, and it requires us to balance Luther's personal experiences and his reactions to, for example, his colleague Karlstadt's more thoroughgoing approach to reform, to account for his own more cautious approach to ordering the church and his desire to protect those who were challenged by the sudden impact of change. The political considerations, including Luther's dependence on his "princes" also played a significant part in the progress of reform, as did the more general social realities of the time. It is apparent that Luther (with many other colleagues, including Melanchthon) chose to follow the more ordered approach, and prioritized the provision of authorised preachers for the church. But none of this prevents Luther's teaching on the common priesthood from its subsequent application in our own radically different social and ecclesiological contexts.

We Are All Priests: What Does This Mean?

The review of Luther's interpreters provides the groundwork for this book's chief task: establishing the extent, persistence and essential purpose(s) of Luther's teaching of the common priesthood. Despite its deficiencies, I have found the work of Paul Althaus most helpful in establishing the parameters of the common priesthood, its grounding in Christ's own priesthood and its close connection to the communion of saints. This is matched by Hans-Martin Barth's exploration of "the universal, mutual, and common priesthood of the faithful" and by his critical engagement with Luther's implementation of his reforms. Martin Brecht's historical analysis and Oswald Bayer's insights into the ministry of the word add further important elements, together with Bernhard Lohse's insistence on taking account of Luther's historical and systematic contexts. To these findings I am adding my own particular perspective that brings an emphasis on the importance of Luther's later writing on the common priesthood, and also its consistent basis in his biblical thought. I have come to believe that it is essential not to force Luther to say too much on the issue of priesthood and ministry—that is, to find unwarranted meanings and connections in his words in order to achieve systematic conclusions that remove all tensions and inconsistencies from his thought. This, I think, is the trap that Althaus and his students fall into, as do others who attempt to reach a fully-configured doctrine of the "holy ministry" from Luther's writings.

Therefore, in negotiating a path through the narrative that limits the significance of this teaching to the issue of laity ("congregation") *versus* clergy, my reading of Luther suggests that the more fruitful lines of investigation are those which clarify and bring to the fore his understanding of word, worship, ministry, and sacramental competence; the role of faith and the relationship between its personal and corporate expressions; and then also the purpose(s) of ordination, of church order, and the office of the keys. I have also found that it is worth paying attention to the way Luther uses the concepts of "emergency situations" and the right to judge doctrine; and (by no means least) his struggle with the status and role of women in the church, through which his biblical convictions continued to trouble his innate social conservatism. All of these can help to achieve the goal of a more rounded presentation of the common priesthood, and they will be variously considered in the chapters that follow.

And as it reaches its conclusion(s), this study will pay close attention to a number of questions as it clears the ground to reveal the common priesthood's meaning and purpose.

The first concerns the basic issue of the status of Luther's teaching on the common priesthood, and its later relevance. How did it figure in his theology after 1523, and to what extent (if any) was it subject to change and development? And if so, what factors influenced the changes and how are they reflected in his later ecclesiology, before and after 1530?

Secondly, is it correct, with Hans-Martin Barth, Martin Brecht and Bernhard Lohse, to characterise the common priesthood as a "missed opportunity" for Luther's reformation, and did that "failure" impact other aspects of his reform agenda?

The third question revisits the attempts to harmonize Luther's teachings on priesthood and ordained ministry. Is this possible or does this pairing represent an unresolved tension in his ecclesiology and an unsolvable theological conundrum for the churches?

And then finally moving beyond the constraints of its historical boundaries, and embracing this task of discerning, developing and applying Luther's insight that *we are all priests*, how can the full ecclesiological horizons of the common priesthood be realized, so that people, pastors and bishops become communities of faith and love that truly worship and work together in the church and the world as servants of Christ and bearers of his word?

NOTES

1. Typically designated "the priesthood of all believers" (*das priestertum aller Gläubigen*), this has been understood to be one of Luther's chief insights, and a distinctive doctrine of Protestant theology (see n2). However, that terminology is of later provenance, although Luther does very occasionally come close to it. Except in quotations, or where referring to other works, this study uses "common priesthood" (*allgemeines Priestertum*) as a more neutral term used by many theologians, including Paul Althaus, Oswald Bayer and Bernhard Lohse. It also reflects the core of Luther's teaching, that this priesthood represents what is held in common by all Christians and in the New Testament there is only one "special priest," Christ himself. Often, Luther uses the simple phrase adopted for the title of this book, "we are all priests," e.g., LW 12:289 (WA 40/2:595), *Commentary on Psalm 45*, (1533–1534).

2. There is no commonly accepted definition of the priesthood of [all] believers, and often what is written bears little resemblance to Luther's teaching. For example, the *Oxford Dictionary of the Christian Church*, Third rev. ed. (OUP, 2007), 1348, suggests that the three characteristic teachings of "Protestantism" are "The Bible as the sole source of revealed truth, the doctrine of justification by faith alone, and the universal priesthood of all believers . . . [that] has led protestants to reject any kind of two-tier spirituality, and [hold to] lay spirituality based upon Bible reading and a high standard of personal morality . . . [with] the development of the principle of private judgement in interpreting the Bible which, in turn, has often encouraged an intense individualism." Alternatively, "the priesthood of all believers was a key doctrine that Martin Luther used in anti-Catholic polemics, especially attacking the validity of the papacy," in *New Dictionary of Theology,* second edition, ed. David F. Wright (Downers Grove: Inter-Varsity Press, 2016), 704–705. The diverse Lutheran views appear below, in "The challenge of the common priesthood" (nn8–13).

3. See, for example, LW 37:360–372 (WA 26:499–509) *Confession Concerning Christ's Supper* (1528), Third Part. Luther's "Creedal Faith" is explored in Robert Kolb, *Martin Luther: Confessor of the Faith*, Christian Theology in Context (Oxford; New York: Oxford University Press, 2009), 59–64.

4. See: Thomas Kaufmann, "Luther as Polemicist" in OEML, 3:110–127; Harold Ristau, *Understanding Martin Luther's Demonological Rhetoric in His Treatise Against the Heavenly Prophets (1525): How What Luther Speaks Is Essential to What Luther Says* (Lewiston: Edwin Mellen Press, 2010); Eike Wolgast, "Luther's Treatment of Political and Societal Life" in OHMLT, 397–413.

5. For the common priesthood's early church background and theological development, see: Yves Congar, *Lay People in the Church*, trans. Donald Attwater (London: Geoffrey Chapman, 1965), 121–233; Cyril Eastwood, *The Royal Priesthood* (London: Epworth Press, 1963).

6. Augustine, *City of God*, trans. Marcus Dods (New York: Modern Library, 1993), Book 20,10.

7. See: Bernhard Lohse, *Martin Luther's Theology: Its Historical and Systematic Development*, trans. and ed. Roy A. Harrisville, (Minneapolis: Fortress Press, 1999), 286–287. Lohse identifies the nineteenth-century roots of this "extraordinary controversy." For an informative study that provides further historical context for current debates over Lutheran church structures, see Walter Sundberg, "Ministry in Nineteenth-Century European Lutheranism" in *Called and Ordained: Lutheran Perspectives on the Office of the Ministry* (Minneapolis: Augsburg Fortress, 1990), 77–92. And similarly helpful is John Reumann, *Ministries Examined: Laity, Clergy, Women, and Bishops in a Time of Change* (Minneapolis: Augsburg Publishing House, 1987).

8. For this account of the background to the study of the common priesthood, I am using Althaus' wide-ranging analysis that locates the priesthood within Luther's ecclesiology, Paul Althaus, *The Theology of Martin Luther*, translated by Robert C. Schultz (Philadelphia: Fortress Press, 1966), first published as *Die Theologie Martin Luthers* (Gutersloh: Gerd Mohn, 1962). Hellmut Lieberg and Harald Goertz were Althaus' students who considered in some depth the relationship of the priesthood to the public ministry. See Lieberg, *The Office and Ordination in Luther and Melanchthon*, trans. Matthew Carver (St Louis: Concordia Publishing House, 2020), originally published as *Amt und Ordination bei Luther und Melanchthon* (Gottingen: Vandenhoeck & Ruprecht, 1962); Harald Goertz, *Allgemeines Priestertum und Ordiniertes Amt Bei Luther* (Marburg: N.G.Elwert Verlag, 1997). Like Althaus, neither Lieberg nor Goertz pay much attention to historical context or development. Lieberg works very hard to make Luther's statements on the common priesthood ("the embodiment of the office") become the basis for a functional framework for the ordering of public ministry; Goertz also fits Luther's teaching into a systematic framework, summarised in TRE 27:402–409. I think that the approach of both writers makes Luther's teaching more complex—and more "complete"—than it actually is. For an analysis of Goertz that questions his argument that Luther uses a threefold "priestly metaphor" while affirming his other conclusions, see Martin Krarup, *Ordination in Wittenberg: Die Einsetzung in Das Kirchliche Amt in Kursachsen Zur Zeit Der Reformation* (Tübingen: Mohr Siebeck, 2007). I also find Goertz's proposal regarding Luther's use of metaphor to be flawed because (as he says), "Priesthood describes aspects of the Christian life that . . . are intrinsically proper to it," *Allgemeines Priestertum*, 323 (see also n10).

9. Timothy J. Wengert, "The Priesthood of All Believers and Other Pious Myths," chapter 1 in *Priesthood, Pastors, Bishops: Public Ministry for the Reformation and Today* (Minneapolis: Fortress Press, 2008). For Wengert the "myth" is first of all the wording itself, "the priesthood of all believers," and then its use to claim Luther's sanction for congregational autonomy to the detriment of pastoral authority in the church. For a review that challenges Wengert's methods and his conclusions, see Dorothea Wendebourg, "Review of Wengert, 'Priesthood, Pastors, Bishops: Public Ministry for the Reformation & Today'" *Lutheran Quarterly* 23:348–351 (2009). She comments on the "uproar" that Luther's teaching actually caused, in comparison with

the "undisputed banality" with which Wengert presents it. For a response that leaps to the defence of the priesthood of believers, generating more heat than light, see Kristian T. Baudler, *Martin Luther's Priesthood of All Believers: In an Age of Modern Myth* (New York: Oxen Press, 2016).

10. As noted (n8), Harald Goertz also describes Luther's teaching as a "metaphor" but gives these figures particular meaning: they are not "improper speech." Rather, "from their New Testament background, metaphorical statements (about Christ and the faithful) are the most precise and substantial ways of speaking about priests and priestly service from a Christian perspective" (TRE 27:408, my translation). So while Wengert uses "metaphor" to downplay the importance of Christian priesthood, Goertz's conclusions are diametrically opposite. To be a priest, writes Goertz, "is to be a Christian" (*also Christ zu sein*)—with all that is implied by that spiritual status (TRE 27:409). Here again, Goertz himself shows that the term "Christian priesthood" represents more than a metaphor for the Christian life because it encompasses actual priestly activities—prayer, teaching, worship, and sacrifice of self.

11. For an account that describes the common priesthood in terms of Christian vocation, see András Korányi, "Universal priesthood of all believers: unfulfilled promise of the Reformation" in *Reflecting Reformation and the Call for Renewal in a Globalized and Post-Colonial World* (Neuendettelsau: Erlanger Verlag für Mission und Ökumene, 2018), 69–84. A similar approach is taken in Dave Daubert, *Reclaiming the 'V' Word: Renewing Life at Its Vocational Core* (Minneapolis, MN: Augsburg Fortress, 2009).

12. The debate over the priesthood of believers and its relation to the public ministry is represented by this selection of articles, and others are included in the notes to later chapters. For its earlier stages among Lutheran theologians in the United States, see L.W. Spitz, "The Universal Priesthood of Believers with Luther's Comments" *Concordia Theological Monthly* 23 (1952): 1–15; Brian A. Gerrish, "Priesthood and Ministry in the Theology of Luther," *Church History: Studies in Christianity and Culture* 34:4, 404–422 (1965); Lowell Green, "Change in Luther's Doctrine of the Ministry," *Lutheran Quarterly* 18:174–179 (1966); Robert Fischer, "Another Look at Luther's Doctrine of the Ministry," *Lutheran Quarterly* 18:3, 260–271 (August 1966). Herman A. Preus, "Luther on the Universal Priesthood and the Office of the Ministry" *Concordia Journal* 5, no. 2 (1979), 55–62.

For arguments against the use of Luther's teaching in relation to the church's ministry, see, for example, David S. Yeago, "'A Christian, Holy People': Martin Luther on Salvation and the Church," *Modern Theology* 13:1 (January 1997): 101–120; Norman Nagel, "Luther and the Priesthood of All Believers," *Concordia Theological Quarterly*, 61:4 (October 1997); David Daniel, "A Spiritual Condominium: Luther's Views on Priesthood and Ministry with Some Structural Implications" *Concordia Journal* 14 (1988): 266–282; William Weinrich, "Should a Layman Discharge the Duties of the Ministry?" *Concordia Theological Quarterly* 68:3 (July 2004): 207–229; John Stephenson, "Reflections on the Holy Office of the Ministry for the Scandinavian Diaspora, *Logia* 15:1 (2006): 43–47; Ken Schurb, "Church and Ministry," *Logia* 16:3, (2007):25–29; Albert Collver, "Origin of the term laity," *Logia* 19:4 (2010): 5–12.

For positive views of the priesthood, see, for example, Eugene F. A. Klug, "Luther on the Ministry," *Concordia Theological Quarterly* 47:4, 293–303 (October 1983); Cameron A. Mackenzie, "The 'Early' Luther on Priesthood of All Believers, Office of the Ministry, and Ordination," accessed 17 October, 2017, http://www.ctsfw.net/media/pdfs/ mackenzieearlyluther.pdf; Joel Lehenbauer, "The priesthood of all saints," *Missio Apostolica* 9:1,4–17 (2001); Gilberto da Silva, "The Lutheran Church as a Church of Mission against the background of the Priesthood of all believers," *Missio Apostolica* 14:1, 21–27 (2006); Charles Lindquist. "The Priesthood of All Believers: Making Room for the Gift," *Missio Apostolica* 17, no. 1 (2009): 31–37. Justo L. González, "The Universal Priesthood of Believers," *Lutheran Quarterly* 31, no. 3 (2017): 328–329; Shauna Hannan, "That All Might Proclaim: Continuing Luther's Legacy of Access," *Dialog* 56, no. 2 (2017), 169–175, https://doi.org/10.1111/dial.12320.

13. For example, Cheryl Peterson, *Who is the Church?* (Minneapolis: Fortress Press, 2013), does not include the common priesthood in her review of Luther's teaching on the church as she argues for an ecclesiology that "starts with the Spirit" for a revitalisation of the church and its missional task.

14. For a more comprehensive survey of Luther's writings, see Thomas Winger, "We Are All Priests: A Contextual Study of the Priesthood in Luther," *Lutheran Theological Quarterly* 2 (1992): 129–156. However, Winger (like Timothy Wengert et al.) is most concerned to uphold the special character of the church's public ministry. He concludes: "The priesthood was fulfilled when the laity heard God's Word with faith and responded in prayer and praise, and sacrificial living in their vocation." See also chapter 7 n1.

15. This is expressed very clearly throughout *The Freedom of a Christian* (LW 31:333–377, WA 7:20–38).

16. See especially chapter 4; in addition, examples and discussion of Luther's use of particular texts figure throughout this book and in its conclusions.

17. For Althaus, see n8; Hans-Martin Barth, *The Theology of Martin Luther*, trans. Linda M. Maloney (Minneapolis: Fortress Press, 2013).

18. See also Paul Althaus, *Communio sanctorum: die Gemeinde im lutherischen Kirchengedanken* (Munchen: Chr. kaiser, 1929).

19. Hans-Martin Barth, *Einander Priester Sein: Allgemeines Priestertum in Ökumenischer Perspektive* (Göttingen: Vandenhoeck & Ruprecht, 1990).

20. Lohse, *Martin Luther's Theology*, 3–10. Lohse proposes that only by utilising what he calls a "historical-genetic" approach in conjunction with the systematic presentation of Luther's thought can the imposition of a writer's own theological preconceptions be kept in check. His opening chapter is a useful brief survey of Luther interpretation from Theodosius Harnack until his own day. Lohse's work requires careful study, as the connections between part two (Historical Development) and part three (Systematic Context) are not cross-referenced or indexed; there are no index entries to Luther's writings. See also Bernhard Lohse, *Martin Luther: An Introduction to His Life and Work,* trans. Robert C. Schultz (Philadelphia: Fortress Press, 1986).

21. Martin Brecht, *Martin Luther: His Road to Reformation, 1483–1521*, trans. James L. Schaaf, (Philadelphia: Fortress Press, 1985) [Brecht, *Luther* 1]; *Martin*

Luther: Shaping and Defining the Reformation 1521–1532, trans. James L. Schaaf, (Minneapolis: Fortress Press, 1990) [Brecht, *Luther* 2]; *Martin Luther: The Preservation of the Church, 1532–1546*, trans. James L. Schaaf, (Minneapolis: Fortress Press, 1993) [Brecht, *Luther* 3]. Brecht's strength is his consideration of Luther's theological output in its personal, social, and historical context. His focus "lies in the specifically religious experiences of the reformer and their theological explication" (*Luther* 1, xi–xiii). See also Heinrich Bornkamm, *Luther in mid-Career*, trans. E. Theodore Bachmann (Philadelphia: Fortress Press, 1983).

22. Heinz Schilling, *Martin Luther: Rebel in an Age of Upheaval* (Oxford: Oxford University Press, 2017); Scott H. Hendrix, *Martin Luther: Visionary Reformer* (New Haven: Yale University Press, 2016); Lyndal Roper, *Martin Luther: Renegade and Prophet* (London: The Bodley Head Ltd., 2016). Hendrix illuminates Luther's life and work with his detailed accounts of key incidents, while Roper writes a biography that while acknowledging his many achievements also presents a psychoanalytical portrait of Luther as a character who was "deeply flawed"—she highlights, for example, his virulent hatred of the pope, the peasants, and the Jews, 381–396. See Hendrix, 278, for an explanation for Luther's "harsh language" that stops short of justifying it.

23. Oswald Bayer, *Martin Luther's Theology: A Contemporary Interpretation*, trans. Thomas H. Trapp (Grand Rapids: W. B. Eerdmans, 2008). Bayer acknowledges the difficulty of systematising Luther's thought, and finds his key to understanding Luther by engaging in depth with the central themes of Luther's theological breakthrough in a variety of representative texts, to reach a "contemporary interpretation" (*Theology*, xv–xxi).

24. For a wide-ranging survey, see Harmut Lehmann, "New Publications for the 500th Anniversary of the Reformation," *Lutheran Quarterly*, 32 (2018): 307–355.

25. See the literature on Luther's ecclesiology listed in chapters 2 and 5.

26. "Although we are all equally priests, we cannot all publicly minister and teach. We ought not do so even if we could," LW 31:356 (WA 7:58), *The Freedom of a Christian*. See also LW 44:145 (WA 6:408), *To the Christian* Nobility and LW 36:116 (WA 6:564) *The Babylonian Captivity*, where Luther insists that while there are different forms of service, those who teach and rule in the church do so "by common consent."

27. See Dennis M. Doyle, *Communion Ecclesiology: Vision and Versions* (Ossining, NY: Orbis Books, 2000); Heinrich Holze, *The Church as Communion: Lutheran Contributions to Ecclesiology,* (Lutheran World Federation, 1997); *Communio Sanctorum: The Church as the Communion of Saints*, Unitas Books (Collegeville, MN.: Liturgical Press, 2005). The report of the Australian Lutheran-Roman Catholic Dialogue, *Communion and Mission* (Adelaide: 1995, 11–13), presents the concept of *communio* as central to the "recovery" of ecclesiology at the Second Vatican Council. This *communio* has Trinitarian, eucharistic, ecclesial, baptismal, and world-focused dimensions, and it is the fourth of these that most closely relates to Luther's understanding of the church as the communion of saints, although the other elements are present as well.

28. Althaus, *Theology*, v.

29. Barth, *Theology*, 8.

30. Althaus, *Theology*, 297–300.
31. Althaus, *Theology*, 304–313.
32. Althaus, *Theology*, (Priesthood) 313–318, and (Sacrament) 318–322.
33. Althaus, *Theology*, 313–314.
34. Althaus, *Theology*, 314.
35. Althaus, *Theology*, 314–315. For Hellmut Lieberg, "the primary element in the concept of the priesthood in Luther . . . remains the immediate access to God," *Office and Ordination*, 26. For Goertz, its "dignity" (*des Würde-Aspekts*) also rests in its "free 'priestly' access" to God for all, *Allgemeines Priestertum*, 325. It is interesting that neither Lieberg nor Goertz pay much attention to the ecclesiological foundations for the common priesthood, despite their particular focus on its integral relationship to the public ministry.
36. Althaus, *Theology*, 315.
37. Barth, *Theology*, 13, 267–291, "allgemeines, gegenseitiges und gemeinsames Priestertum."
38. Barth, *Theology*, 199–220. A study of *The Freedom of a Christian*, and *The Bondage of the Will.*
39. Barth, *Theology*, 221–275. The chapter begins, "How does anyone come to believe?"
40. Barth, *Theology*, 277–312
41. Barth, *Theology*, 301–302.
42. Barth, *Theology*, 287.
43. Barth, *Einander*, 35 (my translation).
44. Barth, *Theology*, 287–288. It should also be noted that Barth's "critical assessment" of Luther's theology employs insights from a variety of sources: theological, philosophical, psychological, and sociopolitical.
45. Bernhard Lohse treats "the universal priesthood" (*allgemeines Priestertum*) in his chapter on "Office and Ordination," following the "The Church," and covering similar ground to Althaus (*Theology*, 286–297). Contrasting Luther's view of the ministry with the traditional hierarchical approach to the church's "estates," Lohse notes the connections of priesthood to baptism, and especially to faith (*Theology*, 290–291). Oswald Bayer considers priesthood in relation to the church as the creation of the word in keeping with his overall approach, specifically in "Office Connected with Ordination" (*Theology*, 273–276). However, he includes Luther's emphasis that all Christians are to speak the word of Christ's forgiveness to one another, and he also briefly develops the implications of this priesthood for the life of the church (276–278). The theme of equality under the word persists throughout Bayer's exploration of Luther's reformational discovery. Martin Brecht highlights the priesthood of believers as an important aspect of Luther's early writings but, for Brecht, this disappears from view after 1530. Considering *A Treatise on the New Testament* (1520), Brecht unpacks how the application of promise and faith in relation to the Sacrament "show how Luther came to the understanding of the priesthood of believers." He summarises, "Faith is to be directed to Christ's sacrifice for us, which consecrates all believers as priests" (*Luther* 1, 381).

46. Lohse does not include *The Freedom of a Christian*, but otherwise largely covers the same material, excluding the sermons. Brecht is very comprehensive in his coverage, and has frequent references to Luther's early teaching on the priesthood of believers, its origins and its influence. Bayer uses *To the Christian Nobility* and *Concerning the Ministry* for his chief presentation in relation to the office of the ministry, but has other works in view for his wider consideration. These include *The Babylonian Captivity* and *The Freedom of a Christian*, as well as *On the Councils and the Church* (1539). *Theology,* 273–278. Neither Bayer, Lohse, nor Althaus refer to *The Misuse of the Mass* (1522), an important text for the development of Luther's understanding of eucharistic sacrifice in the context of priesthood. This is where Brecht's comprehensiveness is helpful: alone of the authors under review, he includes a detailed account of the content and context of that work (*Luther* 2,11). Other early works discussed by Brecht include *On the Papacy in Rome* (1520) and the *Answer . . . to the Book by Goat Emser* (1521). Both contain significant material but, again, these works do not figure in Althaus, Lohse, Bayer, or Barth in relation to the priesthood of believers.

47. LW 44:123–217 (WA 6:404–469), *To the Christian Nobility*; LW 36:11–126 (WA 6:497–573), *The Babylonian Captivity;* Althaus, *Theology,* 313–314.

48. LW 27:393 (WA 2:606); Althaus, *Theology,* 314–315nn86–91 for this and the next five citations from Luther.

49. *Sermons of Martin Luther*, ed. John N. Lenker (Grand Rapids: Baker Book House, 1983), 4:376–377 (WA 10/3:308–309), *Sermon on Mark 7:31–37.*

50. LW 39:309 (WA 11:411–412), *That a Christian Assembly or Congregation Has the Right and Power To Judge All Teaching and To Call, Appoint, and Dismiss Teachers, Established and Proven by Scripture.*

51. LW 30:53 (WA 12:308), *Exposition of First Peter.* "Christ is priest, and we are all priests."

52. LW 76:182 (WA 17/2:6), *Sermon on Romans 12:1–6.*

53. LW 31:352–353 (WA 7:56–57), *The Freedom of a Christian*; LW 40:20 (WA 12:179), *Concerning the Ministry.*

54. Barth, *Einander Priester Sein*, 38–39.

55. Ibid., 45–46.

56. Ibid. .

57. Althaus, *Theology*, 315.

58. Althaus, 315nn92–93.

59. Althaus, 315n94.

60. Althaus, 315–316nn95–96. WA 10/3:106–108, *Sermon on Psalm 22* (1522); WA 10/3:308–309, *Sermon on Mark 7:31–37* (1522); WA 10/3:394–399, *Sermon on Matthew 9:2–8*; LW 24:1–422 (WA 45:465–733), *Sermons on John 14–16* (1537); WA 40/3:342, *Psalm 130:1–2* (1534); LW 13:111 (WA 40/3:543), *Psalm 90:7* (1534). Also LW 69:430 (WA 49:139), *Sermon on John 20.*

61. Compare Brecht, *Luther* 2:69–70 and 2:73–74 (*Concerning the Ministry*) with Brecht *Luther* 2:447, LW 40:379–394 (WA 30/3:518–527), *Infiltrating and Clandestine Preachers).* See also Brecht *Luther* 2:338–339, on Luther's rejection of Anabaptist preachers, LW 13:39–72 (WA 31/1:189–218), *Psalm 82* (1530).

62. Barth, *Einander Priester Sein*, 48–52.
63. Althaus, *Theology*, 316–318.
64. Althaus, 316, also nn97–99. WA 7:219 (see LW 43:28–29 (WA 10/2:394), *Personal Prayer Book* (1522); WA 10/3:215–216, *Sermon on the Power of St Peter* (1522); WA 10/3:394–399, *Sermon on Matthew 9:2–8* (1522); LW 40:26–27 (WA 12:183–184), *Concerning the Ministry*.
65. Althaus, *Theology*, 316. LW 35:21–22 (WA 2:722), *The Sacrament of Penance* (1519).
66. This treatise on confession (*Von der Beichte*) is only otherwise discussed by Brecht, and cited by Althaus, but not by Bayer or Lohse. It contains the significant description of a Christian as *Beichtvater* ("Confessor"), which depends on the presence of Christ in the exchange between penitent and confessor, and not on clerical status. WA 8:129–204. See Barth, *Einander Priester Sein*, 40–41; *Theology*, 246–251, 289; WA 8:184, *Von der Beichte*: "Christ is there, and the Father hears"; for Luther's use of "Beichtvater" see WA 8:183. Brecht's lengthy account shows this to be an important treatise that aimed "at a changed [voluntary] practice of confession," *Luther* 2:18–21.
67. LW 76:437 (WA 15:487), *On Confession and the Sacrament* (1524). Published in the *Church Postil*.
68. See Brecht, *Luther* 1:359–360; Brecht 2:18–21.
69. Bayer, *Theology*, 269–270; 277, LW 67:407–408 (WA 47:298), *Sermons on Matthew 18*.
70. Barth, *Theology*, 249–251. Bernhard Lohse mentions some of this in passing; it appears only briefly in his developmental discussion of the sermons on the sacraments from 1519, and in his summary of the "universal priesthood." Lohse, *Theology*, 129, 291.
71. Althaus' words reflect the gendered language of his own day—and Luther's. In both cases it is clear that this ministry of forgiveness is for all Christians, without distinction.
72. Althaus, *Theology*, 317 (WA 8:184), *Von der Beichte*.
73. Althaus, *Theology*, 318. He notes Luther on "mutual consolation" in the *Smalcald Articles* (BOC 319).
74. Althaus, 318–322.
75. LW 35:45–73 (WA 2:742–758), *The Blessed Sacrament*.
76. Barth, *Theology*, 233–234.
77. Althaus, *Theology*, 321–322. I think, however, that the "fellowship" aspect of holy communion is not entirely absent; see, for example, Luther's sermon on "The Great Supper" (1535), discussed in chapter 5 at nn13–14.
78. Althaus, *Theology*, 322.
79. Barth, *Theology*, 288–291.
80. LW 36:99–100 (WA 6:547–548), *The Babylonian Captivity*.
81. LW 44:193 (WA 6:452), *To the Christian Nobility*.
82. LW 45:8 (WA 10/2:266), *Persons Forbidden to Marry*.
83. LW 45:371 (WA 15:47), *To the Councilmen of Germany*. Only Barth makes this connection.

84. See especially *Luther's Reforms as expressions of the common priesthood* in chapter 5 below.

85. Althaus, *Theology*, 323–332.

86. Althaus, *Theology*, 323.

87. See, for example, Lohse's account of the history of interpretation, *Theology*, 286–287.

88. Althaus, *Theology*, 324. This "bipolarity" (*Zweipoligkeit*) was suggested by Hellmut Leiberg, *Office and Ordination*, 205–207 (see above n8). See also Lohse, *Theology*, 286–287.

89. Althaus, *Theology*, 323.

90. LW 41:3–178 (WA 50:509–653), *On the Councils*.

91. Althaus, *Theology*, 324. LW 41:171 (WA 50:633).

92. Althaus, *Theology*, 324n5. LW 37:151–372 (WA 26:261–509), Luther's "Great Confession"; LW 38:91–137 (WA 30/2:595–626), *Admonition concerning the Sacrament*; LW 38:139–214 (WA 38:195–256), *The Private Mass*; WA 37:269–270, *Sermon on the Conversion of St Paul*.

93. Althaus, *Theology*, 325 (emphasis added).

94. Althaus, *Theology*, 325. "Die Befugnis und Beauftragung zur öffentlichen Ausubung bestimmter Dienste innerhalb der Christlichen Kirche wird durch Ordination auf dafür geeignete Personen ubertragen," Goertz, TRE 47, 409; "Whoever occupies the public office entered it by means of the congregation's *delegatio*," Lieberg, *Office and Ordination*, 69–72.

95. Provided as a group at Althaus, *Theology*, 325n11.

96. Lohse includes: *To the Christian Nobility of the German Nation; Concerning the Ministry; Psalm 82* (1530); *Sermon on Matthew 9:2; Exposition of First Peter; That a Christian Assembly . . . has the Right to Call; The Babylonian Captivity of the Church; On the Councils and the Church; Against Hans Wurst*. Bayer's more limited initial selection includes *To the Christian Nobility of the German Nation, Concerning the Ministry,* and *Psalm 82.*

97. Barth, *Theology*, 291.

98. Lohse, *Theology*, 286–287.

99. Lohse, *Theology*, 287–288. He proposes four stages, from the early development of the priesthood of believers to the "fixed contours" of the ministerial office after 1530.

100. Lohse, *Theology*, 290–291. But *That a Christian Assembly . . . has the Right to Call* (1523) and *Concerning the Ministry* (1523) appears to contradict that assertion.

101. Bayer, *Theology*, 276.

102. Barth, *Theology*, 294–296.

103. Bayer, *Theology*, 277. He references the sermons on Matthew from 1537–1540: LW 67:407–408 (WA 47:298).

104. Brecht, *Luther* 2:91–92. LW 45:11–49 (WA 10/2:267–304).

105. Althaus, *Theology*, 326–327.

106. Althaus, *Theology*, 327nn14–17. LW 40:23 (WA 12:181).

107. Brecht, *Luther* 2:292.

108. Barth, *Theology*, 301.

109. Barth, *Einander Priester Sein*, 52–53. "It will have to be admitted that Luther himself finally deprived his theology of the common priesthood of its assertiveness or at least severely impaired it" (my translation).

110. Also cited, LW 34:357 (WA 54:428), *Against the Thirty–Five Articles of the Louvain Theologians* (1545).

111. Althaus, *Theology*, 328–329. His final section (329–332), explores the call to ministry in more detail.

112. Brecht, *Luther 2*, 284.

113. Barth, *Theology*, 291–292.

114. Barth, *Theology*, 295–296; see also n112 above. I think that Barth's discussion at this point is compromised by his conclusion that the common priesthood had lost importance for Luther by 1530 ("Nur noch am Rande kommt der mittlere und spätere Luther darauf zu sprechen"), *Einander Priester Sein*, 48 (n50). He appears to have ignored *The Private Mass* and *The Sermons on Psalm 110* and other writings, and points only to *On the Councils and the Church*. From these writings, my conclusion is that Luther continued to place the common priesthood alongside of the public ministry in a mutually dependent relationship.

Chapter 1

Church and Priesthood in Luther's First Lectures

Christ is himself the Priest and the Sacrifice and our Altar, on which we are placed and offered to God the Father, and in him we offer all our sacrifices

—Martin Luther on Psalm 84:3

In order to ground the development of Luther's "common priesthood," this chapter traces the evolution of his ecclesiology in his early biblical lectures, with related elements of his theology, before and after the events of 1517 and his reformational "breakthrough."[1] Luther comments on church, and—to a lesser extent—its priesthood, as he engages with relevant biblical texts in the course of his teaching in *First Lectures on the Psalms*, and subsequent lectures on the Epistle to the Hebrews, followed by Paul's Letters to the Romans and Galatians. The themes that emerged in this teaching became integral to his ecclesiology and are closely related to his teaching on the common priesthood as it then appeared in his later writing and preaching. Rather than discovering (let alone inventing) a "priesthood of all believers" in 1520 as a response to his conflict with the Roman hierarchy, in this earlier period Luther is seen to be engaging with both Scripture and the tradition, as he works his way towards an ecclesiology that becomes an integral part of his reformational theology. This important description of the ecclesiological antecedents of the common priesthood is absent from most studies of Luther's teaching.[2]

LUTHER AS A STUDENT AND TEACHER OF HOLY SCRIPTURE

It was his commitment to biblical study and teaching that led to Luther's breakthrough understanding of the Gospel and faith, and it was how he articulated this doctrine in its unifying relationship to the others. The streams of biblical interpretation continued to flow through all of his activity.[3] As Martin Brecht says, "It is essential, as far as possible, to trace the connections that existed between the interpretation of the Bible and Luther's personal situation and entire existence."[4]

Luther's early biblical lectures contained the roots and seeds of the theology which included his approach to the question of the church and the place of the individual Christian within its fellowship.[5] They show how widely Luther had read in both Testaments, in the patristic authors and in contemporary commentators as well.[6] His teaching was shaped by his own spiritual struggle, and as he advanced beyond the theories and methods of scholasticism. As an Augustinian friar, he had been trained in the *Via Moderna* and the Occamist school.[7] Volker Leppin has also explained the significance of late medieval mysticism for Luther's development, and these influences are apparent in the lectures on the psalms.[8] However, Luther did not construct a formal ecclesiology from prior questions or theories about the church, although there is evidence of his Augustinian heritage.[9] His engagement with Scripture, aided by the resources of humanism's new learning, drew him into a re-evaluation of the church in his own context. That context included the development of the university and church in Wittenberg and Saxony, as well as events more widely in the German lands, Imperial Europe, and Rome.[10]

THE CHURCH IN THE FIRST LECTURES ON THE PSALMS, DICTATA SUPER PSALTERIUM (1513–1515)[11]

Christ, and the Word

In the daily life of the monastery, the Psalter was Luther's primary engagement with the scriptures, and his immersion in its text is evident in these lectures.[12] Unraveling the theology of the *Dictata* is a challenging task, as Luther was still engaging with the traditional fourfold exegesis on his journey to fresh understandings of both Scripture and theology.[13] The influences of Augustine, Bernard, and other writers are also evident throughout Luther's commentary.[14] The old and the new often appear side by side and it is easy to be misled by his early use of terms which will take on changed meanings after his breakthrough. At this early stage, his understanding of the word gives weight to its internal operation in the heart of the believer. Later, he fixes on the certainty of salvation given in the external word and promise of God, and this transformed his approach to the nature of faith also. His use of these and other key terms continued to develop, changing the way Luther presents the work of the Spirit in the life of the church.[15]

The question of Luther's theological development is important. In the early twentieth century, Karl Holl influentially argued that Luther's new understanding of the doctrine of justification can already be found in the *Dictata*. He also proposed that Luther's understanding of the church is fixed at this point, and is "that which he retained for the remainder of his life." Holl thus places an early date on these aspects of Luther's theology.[16] More recently, many Luther scholars have warned about the problem of seeking "Luther the Reformer" in his early writings. Bernhard Lohse points out that no developed ecclesiology is to be found in the text of these lectures, not least because Luther's concerns pointed him in other directions.[17] He helpfully proposes that the *Dictata* represents a "process of fermentation" at this time.[18] By 1520, a major shift will have occurred in Luther's theology, including his ecclesiology.

However, these first lectures reveal Luther's exegetical and hermeneutical priorities, which affect how he speaks of the church, even in passing. *Ecclesia* often figures as a voice in Luther's treatment of the psalms, but still influenced by medieval (Augustinian) understandings.[19] The recurrent themes indicate the direction his ecclesiology is ready to take, as the situation changes. Those themes are closely related. The first is the emphasis he places on a Christological understanding of the Psalter, which is closely related to the priority he gives to the word as the sole basis for theology. A third principle is his early distinction between the spirit and the letter.[20] This is significant for the way in which Luther presents "faith" at this time, emphasising the inner humility which—following Christ on the road of suffering and sacrifice—prepares the soul to receive God's word of righteousness both as judgement and mercy.[21]

Luther was developing a particular understanding of how the word is received in the lives of the faithful. The gospel, writes Luther, "comes inside and speaks of internal, spiritual, and true things."[22] There is a significant use here of John 6:45, Jesus' self-application of Isaiah 54:13, "you will all be taught by God."[23] Later, Luther will quote this same text to support the idea of the common priesthood, understanding it to refer to the necessity of the faithful hearing of God's promise of forgiveness by all God's people, as the external word of the gospel.[24] That will represent a major shift for Luther, closely related to his theological breakthrough after 1517.[25] In the *Dictata*, however, Luther's focus is on the necessity of entering into Christ's humility and suffering through receiving the internal word, which prepared and enabled the faithful to participate in the salvation offered through Christ alone. The church and its saints are hidden in Christ's wounds and thus share in his self-offering to the Father by their imitation of his self-sacrifice.[26]

For Luther, the traditional fourfold exegesis presupposed a Christocentric interpretation, and this governed his use of the allegorical method of expounding the text. His chief concern is with the spiritual life of the church, and of the faithful. To some extent, this use of allegory continued throughout Luther's teaching career, to assist in uncovering the heart of a text.[27] Here, Luther applies the text to Christ himself, to the church, and then to "any believer."[28] In the *Preface of Jesus Christ . . . To the Psalter of David* he writes,

> Whatever is said literally concerning the Lord Jesus Christ as to His person must be understood allegorically of a help that is like Him *and of the church conformed to Him in all things*. And at the same time this must be understood tropologically of any spiritual and inner man against his flesh and the outer man.[29]

This is by no means reformational theology, but it does indicate the direction for Luther's ecclesiology. Placing Christ at the centre of theology, and honoring him as head of the church, as well as prioritising the activity of the divine word for the life of faith of "any believer," all prefigure later developments.[30]

This focus on Christ and the word as the basis for Christian spirituality feeds into Luther's early understanding of ecclesiastical order, worship and the priesthood, the sacraments and sacrifice, and the nature of faith. The question continues to be posed as to how far Luther's later thought depends on these early insights, or if his conflict with Rome and his "discovery" of justification by faith were wholly instrumental in bringing about the developments that led to his mature theology.[31] However, it becomes apparent that delving into the complexities of Luther's development is usually best approached in terms of "both/and" rather than "either/or."

Luther's Acceptance—and Criticism—of the Established Church Order

Luther's lectures reflect his recognition of the existing church structures, together with the rejection of heretics who attempt to break the unity of the church.[32] At this stage he does not question the hierarchical nature of the Roman Church, with its dependence on the clerical structures of priesthood and episcopal oversight by the bishops. This includes upholding the position of the pope. The popes, he writes, "adorn . . . the universal church . . . the one church."[33] They are "the fathers of souls,"[34] and "the head of the church."[35] He relates three estates of the church (prelates, preachers and the religious) to the offerings in Psalm 66, especially the prelates ("rams") whose duty it is "to perform and offer masses."[36]

This was the reality of living and working within the received tradition of the medieval Catholic church. At the same time, Luther explored the spiritual life of that church. This was his chief concern, and reflected his reading in Augustine, other commentators, and also the mystics,[37] but especially it reveals his own perception of biblical texts as he explored the role of the church in nurturing faith. Writing on Psalm 71:6, the image of birth ("the womb") leads him from Christ and the Virgin, to the gospel and Scripture, mediated by those in authority, as the sources of spiritual life:

> Therefore an apostle or a teacher, who is the father of souls and begets children for Christ and raises up seed for his dead brother, that is, for Christ, has the gospel itself as a womb. In it he feeds and forms, bears and nourishes them. But the heretics attempt to ravish this womb.[38]

This Luther is not on the side of the heretics.[39] They occupy the "corners of the house of Christ" separated from the "bond of the communion of saints."[40] His reform agenda is several years away, but Luther does have a keen awareness of problems confronting the late medieval church. That reflects his growing status in the Augustinian order, and perhaps also his earlier visit to Rome.[41] He does not hold back criticism of a worldly church and those who rule it for their own ends. Commenting on Psalm 68:14, and the divine appointment of kings, he says,

> The superiors should be spiritually oriented and engaged in spiritual things, so that you do not think the rule of the church consists in a physical prelacy. Then indeed, if they would rule the church in this way, the church can make progress and be cleansed. But now they rule literally, but rarely in spiritual things and in particular. Because their only concern is to enlarge the church in earthly things, they are extremely foolish.[42]

The hierarchy was established for these spiritual ends, according to Luther. Their responsibility is to the word, and to Christ himself.[43] Not morality or works of piety, but faith itself is the focus of Luther's concern. To that end, his emphasis is already on the preached word, as the vehicle for the enduring rule of Christ in the church:

> The word of Christ is preached until now and will endure in the church always. . . . But the foundation of the church is Christ, that is, faith in Christ, on which the Most High, born in her, has founded her, that He might be a very firm rock for her. But also the leaders of the churches will never end.[44]

Jared Wicks suggests that Luther's critique derives from Bernard of Clairveux, who saw the history of the church in "three epochs." Following the early church's struggles in the face of persecution, and later against heresies, Luther perceived the late medieval church as mired in a period of prosperity, indifference and decay. Personal trials and suffering provide the best opportunity for the Christian to escape the corruptions of the age![45]

At the heart of Luther's criticism are those who seek to establish their own righteousness in God's sight, apart from Christ and his word. It is a sign of a weak, misplaced faith.[46] The specific fault of church leaders is a failure to preach Christ's word, to "lift up the gates" for the faithful people.[47] Or worse, to preach "the kind of Christ they dream about."[48] This failure will soon enough become the subject of Luther's full-blown attack on the Catholic hierarchy. But at this point, his understanding reflects the influence of writers like St Bernard, because the word effects an active participation in Christ's suffering.[49] Commenting on the "mystical sense" of sacrifice in Psalm 66 he writes that "the body itself, slaughtered and crucified through the word of God and kindled by the fire of divine love [is] thus offered to God through true thanksgiving."[50] This priestly offering reflects the true inner nature of the church itself. It is hidden from the "senseless," and "wicked." Luther says, "Christ's work and creation, the church, does not appear to be anything outwardly, but her entire structure is inward in the presence of God, invisible."[51] Here, he quickly moves beyond the outward structures of the church to a description of its inner community, as the body of Christ.

The Church as the People of God and the Body of Christ

Basic to Luther's understanding of the church in the *Dictata* are both the Old Testament image of the "people of God,"[52] and the New Testament, Pauline image of the "body of Christ." For the latter, the texts from 1 Corinthians 10 and 12, and especially Ephesians 4 are used.[53] This idea can also be expressed as "the congregation of the faithful people," in distinction to the synagogue which can be either Israel waiting for Christ, or the forces opposed to him.[54] These terms can reflect the opposition of the spiritual (or inner) church, and the worldly (or earthly) church, which relates to the nature of faith, as discussed above. Inevitably the church is a mixed body, with "true people" who are "foreigners and strangers of the world," and "Christians after the flesh" who are "strangers and visitors" in the holy city and ultimately will have no place among Christ's people.[55] Luther will continue to wrestle with this distinction between true and false Christians throughout his career, and his later use of the concept of the marks of the church reflects his search for more objective means to identify the presence of the true church, and its antithesis.[56]

Bernhard Lohse notes that in the *Dictata* Luther employs "the traditional figures of speech" for the church such as "God's temple" and "new Jerusalem," and still uses them after 1520.[57] But the psalms provided Luther with a whole host of images for the church, new and old. A passage commenting on Psalm 65:1 is a prime example of how his theological imagination is able to run riot while he works within his own biblical parameters. The picture of the river as the believers ("saints") born of God in the word is especially striking as baptismal imagery:

> The psalmist gives a number of names to the same church, such as *Zion, Jerusalem, courts, house, temple, earth, river, fields, wilderness, vales, sheep, field*—all because of the excellence of the glow and manifold strength in the church. "Zion," because it observes heavenly things; "Jerusalem," because it has peace and perceives it; "courts," because it is the preparation of future glory and the entrance to it; "house" of God, because God dwells in it; "temple," because God is worshiped in it; "earth," because it is a pilgrim in this life; "river" of God, because it gushes forth from God continually with ever new believers that are born. As from a fountain the waters flow forth constantly, so the saints are born of God in his word.[58]

When Luther speaks of the saints, he can be referring to people recognised for their particular holiness,[59] but also, as here, he often follows the Pauline understanding. Sometimes his use is ambiguous. But commenting on "die Heiligen" in Psalm 32:6 Luther notes that "the apostle always calls the Christians saints (Romans 1:7)," and it seems that by 1513 this is already his own preferred use.[60]

In contrast to the concerns that led Luther to consider distinctions between Christians, and a spiritual view of the church in contrast to its outward appearance, there is also an emphasis on the unity of the one church to be found in the *Dictata*. This closely relates his understanding of the *communio sanctorum*, explored further below. Here, commenting on the pictures of the "house of the Lord" and "Jerusalem" in Psalm 122:1, he draws together the content of the key Pauline texts in what will become his signature formulation:

> But if we are citizens of this city, behold, there is one bread, one cup, one faith, one Lord, and all things are one for us. But Christ is all things in us.[61]

In this way, Luther writes of the "bond of the communion of saints" which, while it describes the inner, spiritual character of the church, is nonetheless a present reality for Christians in the here and now, in "the midst of [God's] house."[62] This reality is the certainty of Christ's presence to faith, "But the dwelling places of Christ are His churches throughout the world, which are altogether one dwelling place."[63] "Christ," Luther writes, "is our one united whole, in whom we all share."[64] Commenting on Psalm 122:6 ("pray for the peace of Jerusalem") and the heretics who "fight against the church," he says, "This does not mean that Christ has two churches. One is his dove (Songs 6:8)."[65]

Luther makes little use of a sacramental emphasis in relation to this "communion."[66] Exploring the Melchizedek story in relation to Psalm 110, Luther bypasses a eucharistic interpretation, stating that "the spiritual bread and wine is Christ Himself, the Head and the whole Church. Thus the apostle says, 1 Cor. 10:17: 'We, being many, are one bread and one body.'" Only Christ as eternal priest could offer this bread—"the whole church"—to the Father. This lack of specific interest in the sacrament will shift, as Luther begins to reimagine how church and sacraments are to be reformed according to their biblical roots, and as a true communion.

References to other worship practices are rare in this commentary, as Luther focuses on a personal spiritual encounter through the word. He does discuss the superstitious use of a Scripture text relating to penance, noting that care needs to be taken that, "a person does not neglect the sacraments of the church, going to Confession and Communion, and receiving Unction." But straightaway he adds that "any word of God has this power . . . for the benefit of a soul even a Lord's Prayer will no doubt suffice."[67]

His chief concern remains his spiritual, Christological understanding of the psalms. In this way familiar Old Testament worship terms such as "altar," "sanctuary," "offering" and "sacrifice" play an important role in his discussion. These terms also appear in his early use of texts that will figure prominently when the common priesthood comes into view. Romans 12:1 ("present your bodies as a living sacrifice") is quoted here when Luther is describing the mystical goal of faith, the soul's ultimate surrender to God in and with Christ. And 1 Peter 2:5 will continue as one of its partners:

> For what else does the Gospel do but slaughter and kill us according to the flesh and thus offer us to God as made alive after the spirit? Rom. 12:1: "Present your bodies as a sacrifice"; and 1 Pet. 2:5: "To offer up spiritual sacrifices through Him." We are those sacrifices.[68]

Romans 12 also appears in connection with the burnt offerings of Psalm 66:15, "the body . . . kindled by the fire of divine love and thus offered to God with true thanksgiving."[69] In Psalm 81:1 there is a striking phrase typical of the character of Luther's theology of faith and humility at the time: "hate your soul so that you are worthy to be loved by him."[70] This is the "living, holy" sacrifice of Romans 12:1, as is that of Psalm 84:4 in which "our crosses and our sufferings and our altars" are where "we present our bodies as a living sacrifice."[71] And in Psalm 96:6 the images of the temple and the sanctuary bring 1 Corinthians 6:19 ("your body is a temple") into conjunction with the sacrifice and offering of Romans 12, together with that of John 17:9 in which the Lord speaks of "his own temple."[72] Here, our "living sacrifices" seek union with Christ's. Later, after 1520, they will be clearly delineated as faith's response to the word in worship or in a Christian's daily living.

The role of the clergy remains mostly unexamined in the *Dictata*, as does that of the Old Testament priesthood. They do figure as representatives of the high priest himself, who is Christ. Once again, Luther is concerned to offer a spiritual understanding of his text: "Christ is the first altar of all, for what he is for the whole church, his representatives are for the individual parts."[73] Christ is "himself the Priest and the Sacrifice and our Altar, on which we are placed and offered to God the Father, and in him we offer all our sacrifices."[74] The references to Hebrews and Christ as "eternal priest" are prominent in Psalm 110, once more in relation to Melchizedek.[75] This acknowledgement of Christ as high priest is important for the later understanding of the common priesthood, but as yet there is no examination of that priesthood in these texts. Even where Luther quotes 1 Peter 2:9 ("a royal priesthood") in his commentary on Psalm 114, he explores this no further than to state that this is a spiritual kingdom, in which "priests should rule."[76]

Brief Conclusions

Thus underlying Luther's early ecclesiology is the prominence he gives to Christ and the word, and their significance as the presuppositions which undergird his whole theology. The hierarchy of bishops and priests is not challenged, but their proper role as teachers and preachers of the word receives pointed emphasis. In the piety that Luther derives from the psalms themselves, it is the hiddenness of the true church and the humility of the faithful in the "communion of saints" that commands his theological attention. While he retains a traditional view of the church, and particularly its community, for Luther this is necessarily grounded only in the Pauline texts on the body of Christ. With the benefit of hindsight, these important themes and texts are the building blocks—or at least, the stepping stones—from which Luther's later ecclesiology will be approached, and then constructed. In a more limited sense, this is also true of the themes of priesthood and sacrifice.

THE CHURCH IN THE LECTURES ON
ROMANS, GALATIANS, AND HEBREWS[77]

Christ and the Word

This series of biblical lectures is considered together, because, as Bernhard Lohse states, ecclesiology "appears to have had less place [in them] than in the Psalms lectures." This is perhaps surprising, given how Luther made use of the Pauline writings in his early exegesis. Certainly, the language of the psalms lent itself to his earlier allegorical interpretations; perhaps the intensity of his concentration on the soteriological content of the Romans and Galatians is also part of the answer. But Luther's fundamental approach is confirmed in a marginal gloss to Romans 1:3. Its similarity to his stated aim in the *Preface of Jesus Christ . . . to the Psalter* in the *Dictata* is noteworthy:

> Here the door is thrown open wide for the understanding of Holy Scriptures, that is, that everything must be understood in relation to Christ, especially in the case of prophecy. But Scripture is completely prophetical, although not according to the superficial sense of the letter.[78]

The ecclesiological statements in these lectures have a Christological basis, but it often reflects Luther's prereformational portrayal of the Saviour Christ in terms of a guide and example. And as Lohse notes, the traditional descriptions of the church continued to appear in Luther's presentations.[79] In the Romans lectures, the church and its head are an "immortal body," one with Christ in his suffering. It is the "bride of Christ,"[80] established by the apostles who are themselves the "foundation of the church."[81] Similar phrases occur in the Galatians commentary.[82] The Hebrews lectures begin with an extended examination of the preeminence of the Christ, in the context of Old Testament prophecy, with references to a "spiritual people" and the "priestly kingdom" occurring in the discussion of 1:8.[83]

Just as significant is the primary place given to the word of God and its preaching, in the life of the church. During this period—at least until the later stages of the lectures on Hebrews—Luther's emphasis is still on the believer's progress in faithful adherence to Christ, and the salvation received through a life of penitence, and participation in the example of his suffering.[84] It is for this purpose that preachers perform the church's fundamental task, for it is "Christ who speaks in such men," and without this kind of faith in God there can be no "justification."[85] The word of God is "the church's first and greatest benefit"; its "first and greatest work."[86] It is a blessing from God, that "the church does not teach itself with its own doctrines," but that it "is taught by God, as Isaiah 54:13 states."[87] As noted in connection with Psalm 85:9, here Luther is using a favored text, which coupled with John 6:45, in later writings is consistently applied to the hearing of the word by all Christians. An example of his developing understanding is when Luther comments on Hebrews 8:10, in which the promise of the new covenant of Christ the High Priest is confirmed by Jeremiah 31:33, "I will put my laws in their minds and write them on their hearts." Luther explains, "therefore it happens in the New Testament that while the Word of life, grace, and salvation is proclaimed outside, the Holy Spirit teaches inside at the same time."[88] This is supported again by John 6:45, in which, Luther says, Christ refers to both Jeremiah and Isaiah (54:13). Then he links the outward processes of teaching, hearing, seeing, and then understanding the word "in the mind," with a spiritual love of God's word, which takes place, of necessity, "in the heart."[89]

But these lectures on Romans and Hebrews still contain echoes of the theological method and themes of the *First Lectures on the Psalms*. Luther continues to focus on the importance of humility and the self-emptying of faith which is able to receive Christ's righteousness, and justification. In effect, it is the tropological use of Scripture that dominates here, as Christians are urged to grow in personal faith. However, the role of the church in preaching the word that achieves this is also becoming more and more prominent. Commenting on Romans 10:15 ("how beautiful are the feet"), he says,

> Thus the feet of the church as it preaches are voices and words [*voces et verba*] by which it cuts and shakes up the people and "beats them to pieces." And the church does this with nothing else than with words and voices [*verbis et vocibus*]. But they are "beautiful" [*speciose*] and desirable to those whose consciences are pressed down by sins.[90]

Clearly, Luther does not here distinguish the word of grace from the word of judgement, as he does later, when the distinction between law and gospel is fully realised. But similar themes occur in the Hebrews lectures, delivered in the midst of the indulgence controversy, and at the time of his theological breakthrough. In Hebrews 1:8, Christ's ruling power is a "staff of justice," whose purpose is to destroy the "carnal and old man." But this power is "the Gospel itself" for "Christ rules the church with no other power than the word." Thus being born again to enter Christ's kingdom involves the destruction of the old, "until hatred of oneself utterly roots out love of self through faith in Christ."[91] So during this period from 1515–1518, Luther's view of the word and faith continues to develop, and both his old and new understandings can be seen, often side by side. Consequently, it is not surprising that his view of the church is also changing at this time, and he begins to place more emphasis on getting the externals into a proper order, elevating the significance of the preached word as the catalyst for the essential, inner work of the Spirit. But there is no suggestion that this happens anywhere other than in the community of the church, those who are responsible for the word and its preaching. This is the foundation from which he questions the papacy, and the hierarchical "structure" that surrounds it.

Luther's Changing View of the Established Church Order

In the *Dictata*, Luther's acceptance of the prevailing hierarchy was observed, and his criticisms were chiefly for heretics and those who failed in their responsibility to uphold Christ's word. The subsequent series of lectures also lack any detailed evaluation of the church's status quo, but the criticisms are more widespread, and are becoming more pointed.[92]

There are several examples of Luther's criticism of the church in his treatment of Romans 12:3–8, in a discussion of the gifts given to the "members of the body." These, he said, should be used for the benefit of those in need; in the church of his day, it is those in the higher positions who expect to be given all the more! This is a systemic criticism of the church's evolved culture, where "they have made a marketplace out of the worship and service of God."[93] It is no longer only about the greedy or self-righteous among the monks and priests, it is about all those who rule. To them, Ezekiel's words to the false shepherds can be applied, in both church and state: "But in our day he who rules, both spiritually as well as in the secular realm, does so in luxury, idleness, riches, pleasure, in glory and honor, in power and terror."[94]

For Luther, those holding office in the church are placed there for one reason only. His emphasis is consistently on ministry as service. Right at the beginning of the lectures, in the glosses on Romans 1:5 where Paul discusses his apostleship in terms of servanthood, Luther insists that "all ministry is for the benefit of all." As an apostle, Paul may hold the "highest ministry existing in the church," but he does so *"to bring about the obedience of faith*, not for the purpose of dominating and being overbearing, as now."[95] And commenting on the role of the high priest in Hebrews 5:1 ("to act on behalf of people in relation to God"), Luther both upholds the position of the priest, and then fills that position with its Christ-like imperative:

> Priests are reminded that, beyond other Christians, they are anointed on their fingers, not so much for the purpose of being worthy to touch the sacrament of the body of Christ [*sacramentum corporis Christi*] as to deal gently with the matter of the same sacrament, that is, with the people of Christ [*eiusdem sacramenti i.e. populum Christi*].[96]

In spite of the problems that he sees all around him, Luther also expresses the opinion in the first Galatians lectures that separation from the institutional church is not an option.[97] But there is a distinction to be made between the true church, and the false. In the Hebrews lectures, Pope Julius II is singled out as one who was "appointed on behalf of demons against Christ and the Christians."[98] By the time the Galatians lectures were published (1519), Luther has the Roman Curia firmly in his sights. He writes, "It is unable to hear and uphold the word of God so that it is taught purely."[99] The events of 1517–1518 brought into the foreground the question of ecclesiastical authority and this developed strongly during the subsequent conflict. It led to the distinction between Christ as head of the church and the pope as antichrist which emerges forcefully in Luther's Reformation writings of 1520. The interpretation of the Petrine text, Matthew 16:16–19, is not discussed by Luther before 1518, but he has already begun to question the nature of what is happening in Rome. Commenting on Galatians 5:10, where those who destroy Christian freedom are placed under God's judgement, he says,

> Heralds of the Antichrist babble that the pope has no judge on earth, and that Christ would not have provided adequately for his church if he had not assigned to a human being such great power as this man has.[100]

Here, Luther is drawing very near to a rejection of the Roman church's hierarchical system. He is already convinced that the church should remain close to its apostolic roots, and closer yet to Christ's prayer for God's kingdom.[101]

The Church as the Body of Christ, and Its Community

There is incremental development here, rather than sudden change in Luther's thinking. He uses the "traditional descriptions" of the church to speak of its relationship to Christ, rather than its institutional character, as Bernhard Lohse has noted. The image of the bride of Christ is used with Romans 8:26, the groaning of Christians waiting for grace, and for "the soul to be impregnated by the Spirit . . . [being] still."[102] The distinction between the outward and inner nature of the church is also apparent when Luther glosses Romans 6:12, "*Let not sin therefore reign*, although it is neither absent nor quiet, *in your mortal bodies*. This statement differentiates the physical from the mystical body, which is the church of Christ, an immortal body, as is the Head also."[103]

Romans 12 and its teaching on the body of Christ will become very prominent in Luther's writing on the church, including the common priesthood. In 1515–1516, it is clear that he already considers this text in conjunction with others such as Ephesians 4:4–6 ("There is one body and one Spirit"). Paul's descriptors for the church as the body of Christ flows through, and becomes Luther's composite language for the Christian community, its unity and its tasks. He writes, without need for a formal citation, "for although there is one faith, one Baptism, one church, one Lord, one Spirit, one God, nevertheless, there are various kinds of gifts in this faith, church, lordship, etc."[104]

Luther is now frequently using the scriptural definition of "saints" in relation to these Pauline writings and the psalms, and this influences how he understands the creedal phrase, *communio sanctorum*. In relation to Romans 12:13 ("contribute to the needs of the saints") he comments that, "by the term 'saints' in our day we understand those who are blessed or have been glorified, but the apostle [Paul], and indeed the whole Scripture, understands the term 'saints' to apply to all who are faithful believers in Christ." In the Bible, Luther has now noted, there is no spiritual elite.[105]

That sets the stage for a more radical Pauline emphasis on spiritual equality, which Luther relates to the hiddenness of the church. Social distinctions abounded, both in Paul's day and Luther's, but in Christ these lose their determinative significance. Galatians 3:28 ("There is neither Jew nor Greek") is another text freighted with meaning for Luther's enduring view of the church as a Christian community. Within its spiritual fellowship, the all-too-obvious distinctions around *persona* disappear, and this goes to the heart of what Luther means when he speaks of the church as "hidden." He writes,

> Scripture calls the church concealed and hidden [*abscondita et occulta*]; and one observes very well that as often as the righteous are described, they are described without any term for sect or status, as in Ps. 1:6: "For the Lord knows the way of the righteous."[106]

This emphasis did not change in Luther's understanding from the lectures in 1516–1517 to their publication in 1519, a period of significant developments in his thinking. Indeed, in the original marginal gloss he writes, "Therefore there is neither priest nor lay," but omits that notable coupling when the gloss was incorporated into the later edited publication.[107] Perhaps in 1519 he was still cautious about publicly challenging distinctions between the clergy and the laity? Whatever the case, the later version omits "neither priest nor lay." The comparative list is otherwise unchanged from the lectures, and still quotes Acts 10:34, to emphasise that in the church social and even religious distinctions should not apply:

> One must pronounce the same judgment concerning every other status, because God does not regard the person (Acts 10:34). Therefore there is neither rich nor poor, neither handsome nor ugly, neither citizen nor farmer, neither Benedictine nor Carthusian, neither Minorite nor Augustinian.[108]

In the intervening period when the lectures on Hebrews were delivered (1517–1518), Luther's focus on Christ's preeminence in the church is seen through the lens of worship, priesthood and sacrifice. As in a number of the psalms, the primary image is that of the high priest.[109] There is also the emphasis on the humanity of Christ, and his "brotherhood," which is about his relationship to the entire Christian family and not with a select band only.[110] In worship, through the "external word and sacrament," we "taste Christ in the things that are hidden." This entry into the Holy Place (Hebrews 9:2), which represents the church militant, is for every Christian, "because of his faith in Christ, in which he has all that is Christ's."[111]

Summarising Luther's Early Ecclesiology

From these early lectures it can be seen that Luther as a biblical theologian worked throughout this period to develop a consistent Christocentric hermeneutic for interpreting Scripture, and this fed into his discernment of its teaching on the church. This method did not begin with Luther, but the intensity of its application is unique to him. In his early teaching on the psalms, he follows, for example, Augustine and Bernard of Clairvaux, but he is not bound to them, not in the same way as he binds himself to Christ, and through Christ to the word of God.

On the basis of his studies, especially of the Pauline writings, Luther already teaches that the church is the New Testament people of God, which he identifies with the creedal "communion of saints." He understands—and experiences—the church as a spiritual communion, and wrestling with its weakness, he is led to conclude that the true church is essentially hidden in the world, known only to faith, and by faith. As the body of Christ, the church participates in all Christ's benefits, and shares in his priestly blessings as well as his self-offering. And likewise, the faithful share Christ's suffering and rejection. In this way also, the church is hidden with Christ under the appearance of the cross and sacrifice. This mirrors his own personal spiritual struggle.

Negatively, he criticises what he sees as a spirit of self-righteousness in the church, of self-serving pride and greed, and—among the hierarchy—a failure to preach the word. But, positively, he urges the spiritual equality of all believers, as baptised Christian people. While this equality has personal implications, it is not individualistic but places the Christian in a reciprocal relationship with other members of the community, those who together receive Christ's promised blessing through the word and the sacraments of grace.

He continues to uphold the legitimacy of the church's hierarchy, but already emphasises that in the New Testament authority is given by the call to serve the people of God. These offices are instituted for the purpose of the ministry of the word, they are not about personal status or the exercise of power. For Luther, the biblical office can never be a platform for lordship and exploitation. But at first he does not explore the full nature of priesthood or ministry in the church, except that they are to be seen as grounded in the work of Christ who is High Priest, and the servant Lord of the church. However, the priestly themes of offering and sacrifice are certainly present, from his study of the psalms onwards.

During this period, therefore, even before the controversy over indulgences, Luther has developed the understanding that it is the nature of the church as *communio*, a fellowship of believers united in Christ and his word and sharing these as common spiritual possessions, that claims first place. Everything—everyone—is to be judged on the basis of this relationship to Christ that includes Christ's role as the preeminent high priest for God's people. This relationship in its turn must determine, shape and legitimise the institutional character of the church, its offices and traditions, its worship and its religious practices, rather than vice-versa.[112] These are the ecclesiological themes with their biblical presuppositions and imperatives out of which grew and emerged Luther's understanding of Christian priesthood as a common value shared by all believers.

NOTES

1. For discussion of the date and nature of the breakthrough see Lohse, *Theology*, 85–95. I am following Oswald Bayer's proposal of 1518 for Luther's breakthrough understanding of the performative nature of God's promise(s) in Christ as an external, orally proclaimed word of comfort. Bayer, *Theology*, 44–50. Scott Hendrix, *Martin Luther*, 50–52, points to Luther's preparations for his lectures on Romans (1515), and the importance of his reading of Augustine's *On the Spirit and the Letter*. For more on Luther's breakthrough, see Jeffrey Silcock, "A New Look at the Theology of the Cross" in *Luther@500 and Beyond: Martin Luther's Theology Past, Present and Future*, edited Stephen Hultgren, Stephen Pietsch and Jeffrey Silcock (Adelaide: ATF Press, 2019), 75–104.

2. But see Christine Helmer, ed., *The Medieval Luther*, Spätmittelalter, Humanismus, Reformation / Studies in the Late Middle Ages, Humanism, and the Reformation (Tübingen, Germany: Mohr Siebeck GmbH & Co. KG, 2020). Helmer states that "This volume's goal is to explicitly situate Luther's doctrines of Christ, salvation, and priesthood in continuity with medieval and late medieval ideas," 2–3.

3. Scott Hendrix, *Luther*, (Nashville: Abingdon Press, 2009), 4. See also: Jaroslav Pelikan, *Luther the Expositor* (St. Louis: Concordia Publishing House, 1959), 32–47. For a more recent study, see Robert Kolb, *Martin Luther and the Enduring Word of God: The Wittenberg School and Its Scripture-Centred Proclamation* (Grand Rapids: Baker Academic, 2016).

4. Brecht, *Martin Luther*, 1:83. See also Oswald Bayer, "Luther as an interpreter of Holy Scripture" (CCML), 73–85.

5. David Daniel, "Luther on the Church," OHMLT, 337. Daniel discerns "five phases in Luther's formulation and application of his ecclesiology." The first, "preliminary phase," is 1513–1517.

6. Jared Wicks, *Man Yearning for Grace* (Washington, D.C.: Corpus Publications, 1968), 3–8. Erik Herrmann, "Luther's Absorption of medieval biblical interpretation and his use of the church fathers," OHMLT, 71–90. Alister McGrath, *Luther's Theology of the Cross*, revised ed. (Chichester: John Wiley & Sons Ltd., 2011), 96–99.

7. Heiko Oberman, *Luther: Man between God and the Devil* (New York: Image Books, 1992), 113–150; Gerhard Müller, "Luther's transformation of medieval thought," OHMLT, 105–114; Pekka Kärkkäinen, "Nominalism and the Via Moderna" in OEML, 2:696–708.

8. Volker Leppin, "Luther's roots in monastic-mystical piety," OHMLT, 49–61.

9. Oberman, *Luther: Man between God and the Devil*, 270. He argues that Luther followed Augustine on the epochs of church history, and the triumph of God's reformation.

10. Robert Rosin, "Humanism, Luther, and the Wittenberg Reformation," OHMLT, 90–104. See also Brecht, *Martin Luther* 1:288. Heinz Schilling's opening chapter ("New departures for Christendom") serves to locate Luther's life in its broader sociopolitical context, *Martin Luther Rebel*, 9–38.

11. LW 10 and 11 (WA 3:11–652 and 4:1–717; revised WA 55/1 and 55/2), *First Lectures on the Psalms ("Dictata")*.

12. Brecht, *Martin Luther* 1:130–131; Hendrix, *Martin Luther*, 48–50, provides additional background to these first lectures.

13. Wicks, *Man Yearning for Grace*, 51–54, on the primacy of the tropological (moral) sense for Luther at this stage.

14. Herrmann, "Luther's absorption of medieval biblical interpretation," 73; McGrath, *Luther's Theology of the Cross*, 100–119.

15. Hendrix, *Ecclesia in Via: ecclesiological developments in the medieval Psalms exegesis and the Dictata super Psalterium (1513–1515) of Martin Luther*, (Leiden: Brill, 1974), 1–5. See also Brecht, *Martin Luther*, 1:130.

16. Hendrix, *Ecclesia in Via*, 143–54. He discusses the debate on Luther's early ecclesiology.

17. Lohse, *Theology*, 51–67.

18. Lohse, *Theology*, 53.

19. Hendrix, *Ecclesia in Via*. 284–287, "Conclusions."

20. Lohse, *Theology*, 51–53. See also Phillip Anderas, "Augustinianism, and Augustine," OEML, 71–85.

21. Lohse, *Theology*, 59–61.

22. LW 11:160 (WA 4:9), *Dictata*, Psalm 85:9.

23. LW 11:161 (WA 4:10), *Dictata*. See also LW 10:293 (WA 3:347), Psalm 60:6. LW 11:364 (WA 4:231), Psalm 110:4.

24. See chapter 4, *The Word and The Priesthood*.

25. See n1 above. Also: Wicks, *Man Yearning for Grace*, 8–15. Wicks, like Bayer, delineates the fundamental change that occurred in Luther's theology after 1517.

26. LW 11:142 (WA 3:647), *Dictata*, Psalm 84:4, "to make a nest of the wounds of Christ for oneself."

27. Herrmann, "Luther's Absorption of Medieval Biblical Interpretation," OHMLT, 80–84. See also Heinrich Bornkamm, *Luther and the Old Testament,* translated by Eric W. and Ruth C. Gritsch (Philadelphia: Fortress Press, 1969), 89–96. Further perspectives are supplied by Volker Leppin, *Martin Luther: A Late Medieval Life* (Grand Rapids: Baker Academic, 2010), 21–22. Leppin suggests that in effect Luther conflated the fourfold into a double use, emphasising the text's direct address to the believer (*pro nobis, pro me*), as well as its Christological thrust.

28. Wicks, *Man Yearning for Grace*, 41.

29. LW 10:7 (WA 3:13), *Dictata* (emphasis added).

30. Wicks, *Man Yearning for Grace*, 42–45. He states that Luther's Christocentric approach intensifies that of the medieval commentaries.

31. Hendrix, *Ecclesia in Via*, 143–154; Heribert Smolinsky, "Luther's Roman Catholic Critics," OHMLT, 509–510; Theo Bell, "Roman Catholic Luther Research in the Twentieth Century," OHMLT, 584–597. For a recent positive Catholic assessments of Luther's significance for the church, see Walter Kasper, *Martin Luther: An Ecumenical Perspective* (New York: Paulist Press, 2016); Franz Posset, "Our Martin: Catholic Sympathisers of Martin Luther Yesterday, Today and Tomorrow," in *Luther@500 and Beyond*, 51–73.

32. LW 11:545 (WA 4:404), *Dictata*, Psalm 122, the "church militant" has been arranged in "orders and ranks."

33. LW 11:328 (WA 4:180), *Dictata*, Psalm 104:10.

34. LW 10:385 (WA 3:442), *Dictata*, Psalm 70:1.

35. LW 10:297 (WA 3:349), *Dictata*, Psalm 60:7.

36. LW 10:320 (WA 3:381). *Dictata*, Psalm 66:13–15

37. Volker Leppin, "Luther's Transformation of Medieval Thought," OHMLT, 115–124.

38. LW 10:397 (WA 3:454) *Dictata*. For more womb imagery see LW 10:143 (WA 3:170), Psalm 31:18, also LW 11:367–368 (WA 4:234), Psalm 110:2.

39. See also LW 10:144 (WA 3:171), *Dictata*, Psalm 30:20.

40. LW 11:292 (WA 4:139), *Dictata*, Psalm 101:7. See also LW 11:470 (WA 4:345), Psalm 118:79, the Bohemians' attack on the sacrament and the primacy of the Roman Church.

41. Brecht, *Luther* 1:98–103, and 1:155–161.

42. LW 10:331 (WA 3:395) *Dictata*. See also LW 10:361 (WA 3:424), Psalm 69:5, the misuse of indulgences.

43. LW 11:141 (WA 3:645), *Dictata*, Psalm 84:3, with Christ they are the "altars of the church."

44. LW 11:477 (WA 4:350), *Dictata*, Psalm 119:89–90.

45. Wicks, *Man Yearning for Grace*, 56–57. Compare n9 above, the suggestion by Heiko Oberman that Luther follows Augustine here, and how this relates to Luther's teaching on the "true and false church."

46. Lohse, *Theology*, 65–67.
47. LW 11:176 (WA 4:25), *Dictata*, Psalm 87:2. Luther says Christ "called himself a door."
48. LW 11:54 (WA 3:576), *Dictata*, Psalm 78:18. See also LW 10:330 (WA 3:395), Psalm 68:14, "Now they rule literally, but rarely in spiritual things."
49. Leppin, "Luther's Roots in Monastic-Mystical Piety," OHMLT, 50–55.
50. LW 10:320 (WA 3:380), *Dictata*. See also LW 11:142 (WA 3:646), Psalm 84:4, "the word of God is the knives with which [Christ] slaughters"; also LW 10:232 (WA 3:282), Psalm 50:5, "We are those sacrifices."
51. LW 11:229 (WA 4:81), Psalm 92:6.
52. See, for example, LW 11:124 (WA 3:632), *Dictata*, Psalm 83:9.
53. LW 10:330 (WA 3:395), *Dictata*, Psalm 68:14; LW 11:369 (WA 4:234), Psalm 110:4; LW 11:341 (WA 4:190), Psalm 104:24, citing Ephesians 4:15–16, Christ as "head of the body." See also LW 10:52 (WA 3:46), Psalm 4:2, a general reference to the church as Christ's body.
54. LW 10:434 (WA 3:494), *Dictata*, Psalm 74:2.
55. LW 11:124 (WA 3:632), *Dictata*, Psalm 83. See also LW 11:372 (WA 4:239), Psalm 110:1, "outside the church no confession can please God."
56. On the "marks of the church," see chapter 2 (n29) and chapter 6 (nn27, 41, 51), *On the Councils and the Church* (1539).
57. Lohse, *Theology*, 63.
58. LW 10:314 (WA 3:372–373), *Dictata*, Psalm 65:1.
59. See LW 11:139 (WA 3:645), *Dictata*, Psalm 84:3, "the example of Christ and the saints"; LW 11:143 (WA 3:647), Psalm 84:4, "any saint is anyone's patron . . . whose intercession he makes his votive offerings."
60. LW 10:151 (WA 3:178) *Dictata*. See also LW 10:156 (WA 3:184), Psalm 33:7. Luther says "a saint calls another saint to the inner things of faith." See discussions of the identification of the "sancti" with the "fideles" in Hendrix, *Ecclesia in Via*, for example, 157–158.
61. LW 11:540 (WA 4:401) *Dictata*. See chapter 2 below for Luther's use of this synthesis of Pauline texts. (*Christian Community and Unity in Christ*). Its use here suggests that Luther has taken up these phrases even before 1513.
62. LW 11:291 (WA 4:138), *Dictata*, Psalm 101:6.
63. LW 11:136 (WA 3:643), *Dictata*, Psalm 84:1.
64. LW 11:541 (WA 4:401), *Dictata*, Psalm 122:3. See also LW 10:330 (WA 3:395), the different gifts given "for the edifying of his body," (Ephesians 4:12; 1 Corinthians 12:4).
65. LW 11:548 (WA 4:406) *Dictata*.
66. Luther refers to the mass only thirty times in the *Dictata*: Lohse, *Theology*, 57–58.
67. LW 11:401 (WA 4:268), *Dictata*, Psalm 116:16.
68. LW 10:232 (WA 3:282), *Dictata*, Psalm 50:5, "[the saints] who set his covenant before sacrifices."
69. LW 10:320 (WA 3:380) *Dictata*.
70. LW 11:103 (WA 3:614) *Dictata*.

71. LW 11:142 (WA 3:646) *Dictata*. This imagery figures extensively in this commentary on Psalm 84.
72. LW 11:261 (WA 4:109) *Dictata*.
73. LW 11:141 (WA 3:646) *Dictata*. Psalm 84:4.
74. LW 11:141 (WA 3:646) *Dictata*.
75. LW 11:368 (WA 4:234) *Dictata*. Psalm 110. Also LW 11:28 (WA 3:542), Psalm 77:13, quoting from Hebrews 13:11, the blood brought into the sanctuary by the high priest.
76. LW 11:393 (WA 4:260) *Dictata*.
77. LW 25:1–132 (Glosses), 133–524 (Scholia) (WA 56:3–154 (Glosses), 161–528 (Scholia)), *Lectures on Romans* (1515–1516); WA 57(2):5–49 (Glosses), 53–108 (Scholia), *Luthers erste Vorlesung über den Galaterbrief* (1516–1517); LW 27:153–410 (WA 2:445–618), *Lectures on Galatians* (1519); LW 29:107–241 (Scholia only) (WA 57/3:3–91 (Glosses), 97–238 (Scholia)), *Lectures on Hebrews* (1517–1518).
78. LW 25:4 (WA 56:5), *Romans* c.f. LW 10:6–7 (WA 3:12–13) *Dictata*.
79. Lohse, *Theology*, 81.
80. LW 25:368 (WA 56:379), Romans 8:26.
81. LW 25:124 (WA 56:144), Gloss on Romans 15:20.
82. LW 27:166 (WA 2:454), Galatians 1:1–2.
83. LW 29:117 (WA 57/3:107–108), *Hebrews*, Exodus 19:5–6, 1 Peter 2:9, God's throne representing a spiritual kingdom.
84. Wicks, *Man Yearning for Grace*, 127–128.
85. LW 25:242 (WA 56:251), Romans 3:22.
86. LW 27:165 (WA 2:454), Galatians 1:1; LW 27:396 (WA 2:608), Galatians 6:6.
87. LW 29:183 (WA 57/3:183), Hebrews 6:7.
88. LW 29:198 (WA 57/3:196), *Hebrews*.
89. LW 29:198 (WA 57/3:196), *Hebrews*.
90. LW 25:417 (WA 56:426) *Romans*. Also LW 29:164–165 (WA 57/3:161–162), Hebrews 4:12, the two-edged sword of God's word as God's wrath.
91. LW 29:118–119 (WA 57/3:108–109), *Hebrews* (translation modified).
92. Lohse, *Theology*, 81–84.
93. LW 25:450 (WA 56:458) *Romans*.
94. Ibid.
95. LW 25:5 (WA 56:6), *Romans* (emphasis in original).
96. LW 29:170 (WA 57/3:167–168), *Hebrews*.
97. LW 27:169 (WA 2:456), *Galatians*, "One should not withdraw and cause a schism."
98. LW 29:170–171 (WA 57/3:168), on Hebrews 5:1 the appointment of the High Priest. Julius II was pope from 1503–1513, when Luther visited Rome. Luther's developing awareness of the papacy—well before his condemnation by Rome—cannot be ignored, when assessing Luther's increasingly antagonistic responses to its corrupt behaviour.
99. LW 27:398 (WA 2:609), *Galatians*, on slavery to the ceremonial law (Galatians 4:10).
100. LW 27:342 (WA 2:571–572), *Galatians*.

101. LW 27:169 (WA 2:456), *Galatians*, quoting Augustine, "The church which no longer says 'forgive us our debts'."

102. LW 25:368 (WA 56:379), *Romans*.

103. LW 25:52 (WA 56:60), *Romans*.

104. LW 25:444 (WA 56:451), *Romans*.

105. LW 25:461 (WA 56:469), *Romans*; LW 29:184 (WA 57/3:184), Hebrews 6:10, "the love you showed in serving the saints." Brecht, *Luther* 1:210–211, discusses Luther's attitude to "the saints." For his earlier use, see nn59–60 above.

106. LW 27:280 (WA 2:530), *Galatians*. See WA 58:85 for the gloss.

107. WA 57:28, *Galatians*, "Ergo non est sacerdos neque laicus."

108. LW 27:281 (WA 2:530), *Galatians* (1519).

109. LW 29:188–98 (WA 57/3:187–196) *Galatians*. See especially LW 29:189 (WA 57/3:188).

110. LW 29:134 (WA 57/3:126–127), Hebrews 2:14, "the children share in flesh and blood." Also LW 29:157 (WA 57/3:153), Hebrews 3:14. Luther says that Christians by faith are united with Christ and in this way "partake" of Christ.

111. LW 29:200–202 (WA 57/3:197–201) *Hebrews*.

112. So Luther did not reach this conviction about the church casually but from deep biblical study, his personal experience (including leadership in the Augustinian community) and after prolonged engagement with the teaching and methodologies of the medieval schools. The contention that Luther abandoned an acceptance of the church's dual nature chiefly because of reactions to his reforming agenda after 1517–1518 is thereby challenged. It is Luther's emergence as a fully *biblical* theologian that is the decisive factor here, and his commitment to the Pauline texts that shaped his understanding of the church as the communion of saints.

Chapter 2

Luther's Early Ecclesiology, Its Substance and Form

> *I believe that throughout the whole wide world there is only one holy, universal, Christian church, which is nothing other than the community or congregation of saints*
>
> —Martin Luther, *A Short Form of the Creed*, 1520

Luther's view of the church had evolved through his major exegetical work on Psalms and also Romans, Galatians and Hebrews, and by his experience of leadership at a local level. While still affirming the traditional hierarchy and structures of the late medieval church, his interest lay in grasping what he perceived to be the true nature of Christian life and faith within the community of the church. His Christology, soteriology, and also his ecclesiology all stand in a relationship derived from their (chiefly) Pauline roots.[1] In Luther's developed understanding the true church is made up of faithful believers, redeemed by Christ to be a community gathered around the word, and this became his natural reference point for his evaluation and proposed reform of the institutional church. How did he reach this understanding?[2]

Early on, Luther's interpretation of Scripture had focused on the tropological or moral use, the work of word and Spirit in the heart and life of the believer. Later, he taught that the external word, proclaiming the unique work of Christ, holds the central place in Christian theology, and is the object of faith. This changed his understanding of the believers' relationship to Christ, the nature of justifying faith and the certainty of salvation. This, in turn, affected the way he viewed the church as the people of God and the body of Christ. In the church, Christ's saving work was enacted, and the life of faith was nurtured through the work of the word. From an emphasis on the (mystical) relationship between the word and faith in the heart, Luther moved to teach faith's reception of the external (preached) word. From understanding faith as *imitatio Christi*, and spiritual progress, he taught that faith is a simple trust in Christ's promise of salvation. Likewise, he now views participation in Christ's salvation as an effectual blessing which is freely received and then shared in the community, rather than as the self-emptying and inner humility of the believer which elevates them with Christ on the cross. This change in Luther's Christology, and the nature of faith, is then also reflected in a related understanding of the church, its ministry, and its sacraments. An evolutionary shift occurs from a focus on the church's fellowship of faith and love to a strong emphasis on the church as the word's "creature," a listening community living out their calling to be the communion of saints.[3]

Significant texts from Romans, 1 Corinthians, Ephesians and Galatians, already used by Luther before 1520, become prominent in his writing during the period of early reform to 1525.[4] Their unifying theme of "one body in Christ" underpins his presentation of the church in its true colours as the people of God, with Christ as their head, and gathered into community by the Spirit of Christ. These texts help shape his assessment that the phrase "communion of saints" was a later addition to the Apostles' Creed as a clarification of "the holy Christian church."[5] His use of these texts (discussed below) reflects the themes of unity and community, together with equality and participation. In these ways he explored the meaning of *communio sanctorum* as the present reality for the whole church on earth, not only in heaven. Rather than comprising a remote, heavenly elite, accessible only to privileged intercession, this communion embraces all God's people, both living and dead. It also then provides the natural context for his presentation of Christian priesthood.[6]

This identification of the entire church with the communion of saints is commonly accepted as the basis for Luther's concept of the church. There are, of course, differences of emphasis among his interpreters.[7] But all of them would agree, to a greater or lesser degree, with Oswald Bayer's proposal that Luther envisaged a "communion of hearers" gathered around the word in worship.[8] Luther used further texts to identify the church as the creation ("creature") of the word, and its servant, including, for example, John 6:45; Romans 10:14–15,17; and 1 Peter 1:23.

All of these significant texts, and their interrelated themes of the body of Christ, the communion of saints, and their life of worship, provide the link between what Luther says more broadly about the church, and his explicit characterisation of all Christians as priests. At that point, Luther is also drawn to 1 Peter 2:1–10 and Revelation 5:9–10, which he recognises as consistent with this foundational ecclesiological framework. This is not least because 1 Peter also presents the church as a spiritual community in Christ, a "priestly kingdom" (1 Peter 2:9), "a spiritual house" (2:4), and as people born anew "through the living and abiding word of God" (1:23).

THE FORMATIVE THEMES: COMMUNITY AND UNITY, EQUALITY AND PARTICIPATION

Christian Community and Unity in Christ

An early example of Luther's close amalgamation of the texts from Romans 12, Ephesians 4, and 1 Corinthians 12 was seen in his scholia on Psalm 122:1. There he concluded that "Christ is all things in us . . . the cause of all concord, peace, friendship, life and the communion of saints."[9] And in his subsequent lectures and sermons before 1520, characterisation of the church as a united body under Christ's headship predominates. This helps to confirm that well before the conflict with Rome (1518 onward), a key aspect of Luther's concept of the church was its suprainstitutional character.[10]

Certainly, as the conflict over the sale of indulgences began after October 1517, he employs the texts that speak of "one body" as he promotes a more inclusive view of the church in defending his theses. He uses the significant "one bread" image from 1 Corinthians 10:17 in his defense of the *Ninety-Five Theses*, arguing that all Christians already receive the benefits of Christ and the church, even without letters of indulgence.[11] He refers to Paul's understanding of the church in 1 Corinthians 12:12 ("one body, many members"), then adds "and in other places, where he describes the church as one body, one bread, we are altogether in Christ, members one of another."[12]

And as Luther emphasises this unity in Christ, he takes up the "one flesh" text from Genesis 2:24 to bring into consideration the marriage imagery from Ephesians 5:32, the mystery that "means Christ and the church."[13] This image appears to be used here for the first time by Luther, perhaps unexpectedly in connection with the issue of indulgences.[14] Marriage imagery also figures prominently in *The Freedom of a Christian* (1520) where Luther says, regarding "Christ and the soul," that "everything they have they hold in common, the good as well as the evil."[15] This is the work of the word and faith, and while this tract emphasises the personal nature of the union between Christ and the believer, its corporate character is never far from view either. Intrinsic to Christian freedom is willing service, each of the other. The work of Christ, his servant kingship and priesthood, is shared in this spiritual marriage with those whose sin he has assumed into his own flesh.[16] The church community that Luther thus envisages is able to incorporate, and then transcend, the bonds of our closest human relationships.

In 1519, as the dispute with Rome intensified, Luther published German sermons on penance, baptism, and holy communion, explaining their significance from the perspective of the word and faith.[17] For the third of these, he grounds this in his understanding of *communio*, translated as *Gemeinschaft*, fellowship. "Christ and all saints" he says, "are one spiritual body, just as the inhabitants of a city are one community and body."[18] Quoting 1 Corinthians 10:17 ("one bread and one body"), he proposes that the external elements of the sacrament are therefore the "sure sign of this fellowship and incorporation with Christ and all saints."[19] This sacramental sign of the communion fellowship of the community is an emphasis characteristic of Luther in this early period, but then (largely) disappears after 1524 as the dispute over the real presence comes to the fore.[20]

Rejecting the flawed brotherhood of the Roman lay sodalities and other highly individualistic uses of the sacrament, Luther argues in *The Blessed Sacrament of the Holy and True Body of Christ and the Brotherhoods* (1519) for a fellowship in Christ's body that embraces the whole Christian community. It calls forth the mutually beneficial fruits of faith and love. The use of the key Pauline texts is expanded here to the fullest extent as Luther urges his point about true unity. The addition of "one sacrament, one food" to the more standard formulations is a good example of how Luther often draws together related biblical phrases relevant to his theme:[21]

> In this [fellowship] we are all brothers and sisters, so closely united that a closer relationship cannot be conceived. For here we have one baptism, one Christ, one sacrament, one food, one gospel, one faith, one Spirit, one spiritual body, and each is a member of the other. No other kinship is so close and strong.[22]

This accent on the fellowship of hearts and minds represents an important stage in Luther's development as we consider how he then began to give prominence to the common Christian priesthood in his teaching. To be able to call on the church as a community united in Christ ("one spiritual body") becomes highly significant as he wrestles with the reality that the institutional, hierarchical church has left far behind its New Testament roots. However, the prime significance of Christ's words of institution as the chief thing in the Supper begins to be seen more and more clearly in the decisive writings of 1520–1524. This becomes Luther's distinctive approach to the sacraments.[23]

In *To the Christian Nobility of the German Nation* (1520), Luther brings his biblical insights to bear as he argues for reform. He states that the secular authorities have a responsibility to act, transcending any false division of the church into its lay and religious members. Appealing to their unity in Christ, he writes:

This is the teaching of St. Paul in Romans 12 and 1 Corinthians 12 and in 1 Peter 2, as I have said above, namely, that we are all one body of Christ the Head, and all members one of another. Christ does not have two different bodies, one temporal, the other spiritual. There is but one Head and one body . . . just as all the members of the body serve one another.[24]

This is a prime example from that early reformational period which employs the central ecclesiological texts in proximity to the proposal that "we are all priests." As Christ is, so are his Christians, in one body with him. References now increase to Christ as the true head of the church, and also to the service that its members render to one another. Luther is arguing for a wholesale reform, to restore the word to its rightful place in the church. The sacraments also needed to be rescued from their "captivity" to clerical control, which denied the laity free access to their benefits.[25] Reform required clergy and bishops who served the body of Christ as ministers of the word, rather than ruling as lords over God's people, enjoying the status of a spiritual elite. This went far beyond the usual calls for a reform of clerical sexual morality, and the eradication of superstitious practices.[26] For Luther, Scripture, supported by the historical evidence and contemporary experience, clearly demonstrated that this was no longer tenable.

The contemporary opposition that Luther aroused is hardly surprising, not least when he included the papacy in the call for radical reform. Writing *On the Papacy in Rome, Against the Most Celebrated Romanist in Leipzig*, in May 1520, he explores three levels of meaning for an understanding of the church ("Christendom," *Christenheit*).[27] The first, true biblical meaning is that of a spiritual community, gathered in faith, and among whom "everyone is equal" and to whom the name Christian should apply without any distinctions (Galatians 3:28). Secondly, there are the physical manifestations of the church, its outward forms, and the people who are mistakenly called (says Luther) the "spiritual estate," elevated in popular consciousness because of the trappings of power and wealth. For Luther, the papacy has become the supreme example of this false, antiscriptural view of the nature of the church and its priesthood. And thirdly there are the buildings called churches, and all the goods which pertain to them. These are also falsely called "spiritual" in Luther's evaluation. But only faith, he says, is the basis for what is truly spiritual. Here, the ecclesiological texts have been condensed to one essential element:

Therefore, whoever does not want to err should remember clearly that Christianity is a spiritual assembly of souls *in one faith*, and that no one is regarded as a Christian because of his body. Thus he should know that the natural, real, true, and essential Christendom exists in the Spirit and not in any external thing, no matter what it may be called.[28]

Writing at the same time his *Answer to the Book of our Esteemed Master Ambrosius Catherinus, the Keen Defender of Sylvester Prierias* (1521), in response to a defense of papal supremacy, Luther had proposed an understanding of the church's presence recognised by the necessary signs (*signum necessarium*) of "baptism, bread, and most of all the gospel. These three are the symbols, tokens, and characteristics of the Christian people [*Christianorum symbola, tesserae et carateres*]." Where they are present, there is the church, as Paul says in Ephesians 4:5, "one faith, one baptism, one Lord." This, says Luther, "is the unity of spirit, which Paul commands us to preserve, not a unity of places, persons, things, or bodies."[29] Luther then continued with his rebuttal of papal authority: "whoever teaches the gospel is pope, Peter's successor; whoever does not teach it is Judas, Christ's betrayer."[30]

Then, in his *Defence and Explanation of all Articles* (1521), Luther challenges the pope to explain his control of the sacrament of penance, misappropriating the "office of the keys" as a vehicle for oppressing God's people rather than serving them with Christ's absolution.[31] The validity of the sacraments does not depend on the person administering them. Ephesians 4:5 states that there is "[o]ne Lord, one faith, one baptism" and therefore "if all baptisms and all masses are equally valid, wherever and by whomever they are administered, then the absolution also is equally valid wherever and by whomever it is pronounced."[32] But there is more. Quoting 1 Corinthians 10:17 ("one bread, one body"), and stating that all those who are Christians are to receive the bread and the cup, he asks "Why, then, does the pope want to segregate them and allow only the priests to be Christians?"[33] This argument is intensified in *Receiving Both Kinds in the Sacrament* (1522), where Luther states that a Christian is "sanctified by the word, as well as the sacrament is" because this means that "a Christian is holy in body and soul, whether [she] be layperson or priest, woman or man."[34] This understanding goes to the heart of his argument for the declaration of a common Christian priesthood, as will be seen in the next chapter.

In *Concerning the Ministry* (1523), Luther repeats his summary of the key texts to support the priesthood of Christ and his Christians. He writes that "many similar expressions indicate our oneness with Christ—one loaf, one cup, one body, members of his body, one flesh, bone of his bone, and we are told we have all things in common with him."[35]

These New Testament texts, which speak inclusively of "one body, one faith (etc.) in Christ," resonated strongly with Luther as he taught the scriptures. Emerging from the failure of the monastic disciplines to provide him with a path to spiritual peace, and then in the midst of the conflict with Rome, he embraced an inclusive message which rejected the elitism prevalent within the church, and this became a fundamental principle of his call for reform. This "unity in Christ" is one of the building blocks of Luther's teaching on the common priesthood. For him, it is fundamental to the nature of the church's spiritual fellowship as *communio sanctorum*.

Equality in the Body and Participation in the Gospel

Developing his understanding of the texts which taught the church's unity in Christ, Luther taught that, in the church, all share and participate equally in its gifts and blessings. Commenting on Galatians 3:28, he states that, "In Christ, however, all things are common to all."[36] Equality and mutual participation is the reality of the promise that all of Christ's gifts are held in common in the church, and that through faith in Christ all things are possible for those who believe. This is at the heart of Luther's argument in the *Ninety–Five Theses* and in the subsequent *Explanations of the Ninety–Five Theses* (1518). There are spiritual blessings and privileges which a Christian possesses by personal right, apart from any priestly regulation. They cannot be bought and sold in the church; there is no "treasury of merits" at the hierarchy's disposal.[37] Thesis 37 affirms that this *possessio* is fundamental to Christian existence, and that the believer in fact "possesses Christ" and all his benefits, as a member of Christ's body:

> *Any true Christian, whether living or dead, participates in all the blessings of Christ and the church; and this is granted him by God, even without indulgence letters.* It is impossible for one to be a Christian unless he possesses Christ. If he possesses Christ, he possesses at the same time all the benefits of Christ. ... [I]n I Cor. 12 [Paul] says, "You are not your own, but individually members of the body." And in other places, where he describes the church as one body, one bread, we are altogether in Christ, members one of another. ... And in Rom. 8[:32] he says, "Will he not also give us all things with him?"[38]

By 1519, Luther's consideration of the theology around indulgences, penance and absolution had led him to explore further what this common participation involves. He addresses what will become a key reformatory question: Where does the right (and authority) to exercise the power of the keys reside? Basic to his understanding is an interpretation of the key Matthaean texts proposing a representative role for Peter, rather than an exclusive one.[39] And, in Luther's view, neither do Christ's words in these texts necessitate a unique role for the clergy in the church. This is another building block for his understanding of the common priesthood, even before that concept is thoroughly explored.[40] In *A Sermon on the Sacrament of Penance* (October, 1519), Luther explains how the keys belong to all:

> But in the New Testament every Christian has this authority to forgive sins, where a priest is not at hand. And he has it through the promise of Christ, where he said to Peter, "Whatever you loose on earth shall be loosed in heaven" [Matt. 16:19]. Had this been said to Peter alone, then in Matthew 18[:18] Christ would not have said to all in general, "Whatever you loose on earth shall be loosed in heaven." There he is speaking to all Christendom, and to each [Christian] in particular.[41]

This had been dramatically argued by Luther in a sermon on Matthew 16 preached at the beginning of the Leipzig Debate, earlier in the year (June 1519). Luther's clarity on this issue is shown by the way in which he connects it to a primary concern for the individual's certainty of salvation: "It is true that the keys were given to St. Peter; but not to him personally, but rather to the person of the Christian church. They were actually given to me and to you for the comfort of our consciences."[42]

In the same year, 1519, in *The Blessed Sacrament of the Holy and True Body of Christ and the Brotherhoods*, he discusses the significance of the united community, as noted above. Having quoted 1 Corinthians 10:17 ("one bread, one body"), he then argues for the fellowship Christians experience in connection with receiving the sacrament to be considered a "sure sign" of incorporation into the community. He writes,

> This fellowship consists in this, that all the spiritual possessions of Christ and his saints are shared with and become the common property of him who receives this sacrament. Again all sufferings and sins also become common property; and thus love engenders love in return and [mutual love] unites.[43]

At an early stage, it appears that Luther was ready to regard this shared love as a "mark of the church." That was a transitional position, to be followed by the primacy of faith in its pre-Reformation dress of *imitatio Christi*. Finally, it is the word itself that is definitively seen both as the means and also the essential constituent for the life of the church, itself the source of both faith and love.[44] But equality and participation do not therefore disappear from Luther's ecclesiology. When *The Babylonian Captivity of the Church* (1520) sets about demolishing the Roman sacramental system (and the priestly elite that administered it) he continues to celebrate the goal of spiritual equality and freedom in Christ as the chief benefits of the church's reformation under the word:

> If this sacrament and this fiction ever fall to the ground, the papacy with its "characters" will scarcely survive. Then our joyous liberty will be restored to us; we shall realize that we are all equal by every right. Having cast off the yoke of

tyranny, we shall know that he who is a Christian has Christ; and that he who has Christ has all things that are Christ's, and can do all things [Philippians 4:13].[45]

The message of freedom in Christ, from Romans 8:21, 1 Corinthians 3:21–3, as well as the Philippians text, is also in view in the treatise on *The Freedom of a Christian* (1520), and shows how Luther's Christocentric understanding of justification and faith permeate his reformatory teaching. Christians freely participate in "all things":

All things are made subject to him and are compelled to serve him in obtaining salvation. Accordingly Paul says in Rom. 8, "All things work together for good for the elect," and in 1 Cor. 3, "All things are yours whether . . . life or death or the present or the future, all are yours; and you are Christ's."[46]

But shared possession was not only a theme for Luther's attack on the papacy or for the Latin writings aimed at promoting reform in the church at -large. Closer to home, when he begins to publish catechetical writings for educational use by the clergy, this understanding of the church as an equal community in Christ is very much to the fore. In his German explanation of *A Short Form of the Creed* (1520), Luther describes for the lay audience what it means to belong to the spiritual community of the church. Not just prayers, but also good deeds, ground the reality of this fellowship in the lived experience of its members:

I believe that throughout the whole wide world there is only one holy, universal, Christian church, which is nothing other than the community or congregation of saints [*die gemeine odder samlung der heiligen*]—pious believers on earth. This church is gathered, preserved, and governed by the same Holy Spirit and is given daily increase by means of the sacraments and the word of God . . .

. . . I believe that in this community or Christendom [*gemeine odder Christenheit*] all things are held in common; what each one possesses belongs also to others and no one has complete ownership of anything. Hence, all the prayers and good deeds of all the Christian community benefit, aid, and strengthen me and every other believer at all times, both in life and in death, and that each one bears the other's burden, as St. Paul teaches.[47]

Connecting these two paragraphs and their explanation of the third article of the Apostles' Creed is yet another version of the thematic Pauline texts from which Luther derived his understanding of the church. To confess "one holy Christian church, one communion of saints" includes the belief that "no one can be saved who is not in this gathering or community, harmoniously sharing the same faith with it, the same word, sacraments, hope, and love."[48]

And later, when problems arose with the process of reform in Wittenberg, Luther continued to urge the importance of this spiritual communion.[49] Writing on the *Adoration of the Sacrament* (1523), he brings into view yet another text from 1 Corinthians [9:22] ("I became all things to all people"), as part of his wide-ranging arsenal of Pauline resources to promote the understanding of the church as a community built on Christ, rather than on an ecclesiastical hierarchy. He writes,

> Christ has become all things to us; and we, if we are Christians, have become all things among ourselves, each to the other. What one has belongs to the other, and what one lacks is a matter of concern to each of the others as if he were lacking it himself.[50]

This shows how Luther uses his biblical witnesses as he urges his readers and hearers to broaden their understanding of what it means that the church is the communion of saints and "one body in Christ." In the sermons published as the *Exposition of First Peter* (1522), Luther returns to the final verses of Galatians 3[:27] for the image of the priestly garment given in baptism to all Christians without distinction. It is, in fact, the garment that is Christ's own self, the spiritual reality in which all Christians share and participate:

> Whoever is a Christian enters with the Lord Christ into a sharing of all His goods. Now since Christ is holy, that person also must be holy, or must deny that Christ is holy. If you have been baptized, you have put on the holy garment [*das heilig kleid*], which is Christ, as Paul says.[51]

Summarising the Formative Themes and the Common Priesthood

Luther's primary insight was that it is faith alone, born of the gospel, that is definitive for what it meant to be a spiritual person, a Christian ("justification by faith"). This faith, nurtured by an active engagement with Christ's word (*unity* and *communion* with Christ), remains essential to all those whose lives are joined in Christian community (*unity* and *communion* with fellow saints), those who as *equal* priests serve (*participate*) in Christ's church on the basis of their common possession of all of Christ's "goods." Seen in a close relationship to his creedal understanding that the church is the communion of saints, this is the foundation on which Luther will assert, throughout his life, "we are all priests."[52] It is also the way that the common priesthood expresses an individual's standing *coram Deo*, as well as the corporate character of God's people gathered for worship, prayer and mutual service in the church, those who are commissioned for service in God's world.

By 1520, this teaching has been drawn together as the form and substance of Luther's emerging ecclesiology, maintaining his understanding of the church as the communion of saints under the lordship of Christ. The community of the church and its priesthood will now appear in close proximity—released from the shackles of their scholastic, medieval interpretations—in the writings that relate to and follow on from Luther's "reform treatises." Underpinning it all is his teaching on justification by faith and the priority he gives to the work of God's word, and out of which have arisen the ecclesiological themes and presuppositions that lead to his understanding of the nature of Christian priesthood.

NOTES

1. Erik Herrmann, "Luther's Divine Aeneid. Continuity and Creativity in Reforming the Use of the Bible," in *Lutherjahrbuch* (Gottingen: Vandenhoeck & Ruprecht, 2018), 85–109.

2. For recent surveys of Luther's ecclesiology see David Daniel, "Luther on the Church," OHMLT, 333–352; Veli-Matti Kärkkäinen, *An Introduction to Ecclesiology*, second edition (Downers Grove, IL: IVP Academic, 2021), 43–52; Cheryl Peterson, "Ministry and Church," OELM, 542–554; Peterson, "Church," DLLT, 145–149.

3. This paragraph is my summary of Oswald Bayer's approach to Luther's "breakthrough" to an understanding of the promise of the gospel, leavened by, for example, Robert Kolb's proposal for Luther's "evangelical maturation," *Martin Luther: Confessor of the Faith*, 42–71.

4. Romans 10:12 ("there is no distinction"), 12:5 ("one body in Christ"); 1 Corinthians 10:16–17 ("one bread . . . one body"), 12:12–13 ("baptized into one body"); Ephesians 4:4–6 ("one Lord, one faith, one baptism"); Galatians 3:28 ("all one in Christ Jesus"); Colossians 3:11 ("Christ is all, and in all") and the other related texts discussed in this chapter, including 1 Peter 2:5–9 ("you are . . . a royal priesthood").

5. For the creedal addition of "communion of saints" see Althaus, *Theology*, 294n2; also BOC 437 n146.

6. Althaus, *Theology*, 298. "We are obligated to serve not those who are dead, but those who are living."

7. Althaus, *Theology*, 288. Together with those resources listed in the introduction, see also Heinrich Bornkamm, *Luther's World of Thought*, trans. Martin H. Bertram, (St. Louis: Concordia Publishing House, 1958), 144–145; Brecht, *Luther* 1:353; Daniel, "Luther on the Church," *OHMLT*, 333; Werner Elert, *The Structure of Lutheranism*, trans. Walter Hansen, (St. Louis: Concordia Publishing House), 259–260; Lohse, *Theology*, 278–279.

8. Bayer, *Theology*, 72. Dorothea Wendebourg says that "the declaration that the One, Holy, Catholic, and Apostolic Church is the communion of those who hear the gospel and believe in it" is the "one *cantus firmus* running through all of Luther's

statements about the church from his early period right to his end" ("The Church in the Magisterial Reformers," OHE, 219).

9. LW 11:540 (WA 4:401), *Psalm 122.*

10. Hendrix, *Ecclesia in Via*, 143–154. For the application of Hendrix's research, see Peterson, "Ministry and Church," OEML, 542–543.

11. LW 31:189–191 (WA 1:593), "Thesis Thirty–Seven," *Explanations of the Ninety–Five Theses* (1518).

12. LW 31:190 (WA 1:593).

13. LW 31:189 (WA 1:593).

14. In the *Dictata* Luther describes the church as the "bride of Christ" but does not explore this any further, LW 10:291 (WA 3:346), *Psalm 60*; LW 10:380 (WA 3:438), *Psalm 69*, "the wounded bride of Christ."

15. LW 31:351 (WA 7:54) *The Freedom of a Christian*. In the *Dictata*, these images reflect the influence of mysticism on Luther's Christology and soteriology. Here in 1520, salvation is solely the work of Christ, mediated through the spoken or preached word, to be received by faith.

16. LW 31:354–355 (WA 7:57) *The Freedom of a Christian*. See also LW 31:300 (WA 2:145), *Two Kinds of Righteousness* (1519), for another use of the imagery of marriage and shared possessions: "[T]hrough the first righteousness arises the voice of the bridegroom who says to the soul, 'I am yours,' but through the second comes the voice of the bride who answers, 'I am yours.' Then the marriage is consummated."

17. Brecht, *Martin Luther*, 1:358–365, "The First Form of the New Understanding of the Sacraments."

18. LW 35:51 (WA 2:745), *The Blessed Sacrament.*

19. Ibid. Lyndal Roper says that the practical expression of this teaching in Luther's demand that the laity should receive the whole sacrament ("both kinds") popularised his teaching in "parish after parish." *Martin Luther Renegade*, 142.

20. Althaus, *Theology*, 321–322. See also Dean Zweck, "The Communion of Saints," *Lutheran Theological Journal* 49:3 (2014), 116–125.

21. Other early examples of Luther's textual synthesis can be seen in, for example: LW 27:359 (WA 2:582–583), *Commentary on Galatians* (1519); LW 39:65 (WA 6:293), *On the Papacy at Rome* (1520); LW 30:42 (WA 12:297), *Exposition of First Peter* (1522); LW 30:124 (WA 12:379), *Second Peter* (1523); LW 35:285 (WA DB 11/1:397), *Prefaces to the Old Testament* (1523); LW 36:286 (WA 11:440), *Adoration of the Sacrament* (1523).

22. LW 35:70 (WA 2:756), *The Blessed Sacrament . . . and the Brotherhoods* (1519) (translation altered).

23. Bayer, *Theology,* 270–273; Lohse, *Theology*, 306.

24. LW 44:127 (WA 6:408) *To the Christian Nobility* (1520).

25. LW 36, 3–126 (WA 6:497–573), *The Babylonian Captivity of the Church* (1520). Denying the Communion cup to the laity was for Luther a prime example of clerical elitism and control, at odds with Christ's institution.

26. Brecht, *Luther* 1:349–388.

27. LW 39:65–69 (WA 6:292–296) *On the Papacy at Rome* (1520).

28. LW 39:68 (WA 6:296) (emphasis added).

29. WA 7:720–721, *Answer to the Book of our Esteemed Master Ambrosius Catharinus* (1521). Translation based on Gordon Lathrop and Timothy Wengert, *Christian Assembly Marks of the Church in a Pluralistic Age* (Minneapolis: Fortress Press, 2004), 26–28. This work, says Wengert, is Luther's first exploration and use of the "marks of the church." For their further use, see, for example, chapter 6 at nn27,41, (*The Private* Mass) and especially n51 (*On the Councils*).

30. WA 7:721, *Answer to Catharinus*. See also Brecht, *Luther* 1,430–432.

31. LW 32:3–98 (WA 7:308–357) *Defence of All Articles*.

32. LW 32:51 (WA 7:382), on "Penance."

33. LW 32:57 (WA 7:390), on "Both Kinds' in the Sacrament.

34. LW 36:244–245 (WA 10/2:20), *Receiving Both Kinds in the Sacrament* (1522), (translation modified).

35. LW 40:20 (WA 12:179) *Concerning the Ministry* (1523).

36. LW 27:280 (WA 2:530), *Galatians* (1519). Luther disallows all claims to spiritual status on the basis of religious observances.

37. For an account of Luther's meetings with Cardinal Cajetan, where Luther attempts to debate this issue, see Roper, *Martin Luther Renegade*, 115–120.

38. LW 31,189–190 (WA 1:593), *Explanations of the Ninety-Five Theses* (1518).

39. Matthew 16:19, "I will give you the keys of the kingdom of heaven"; and 18:18 "Whatever you bind on earth will be bound in heaven."

40. Althaus (e.g.) makes a close connection to the common priesthood here, because preaching and absolution are "manifestations of this priesthood" (*Theology*, 315). See further chapter 6 (*The Keys*) and chapter 8 (*Sermons on John 20:19–31*) below.

41. LW 35:22 (WA 2:722–723), *Sermon on Penance* (1519).

42. LW 51:59 (WA 2:248), *Sermon on Matthew 16:13–19 (Ss Peter & Paul,*1519). Luther continues, "The church is the woman and bride, whom he should serve with the power of the keys; just as we see in daily use that the sacrament is administered to all who desire it of the priests."

43. LW 35:51 (WA 2:743), *Sermon on Penance*.

44. Elert, Werner, *The Structure of Lutheranism*, trans. W. A. Hansen (St. Louis: Concordia Publishing House, 1962), 258–259. Luther's early "supraindividual communion" emphasises the hiddenness of the church in faith; his breakthrough leads him to emphasise the gospel as "the substance of the church."

45. LW 36:116 (WA 6:567), *The Babylonian Captivity*.

46. LW 31:353 (WA 57:4–8), *The Freedom of a Christian*.

47. WA 7:219, *Eine kurze Form des Glaubens* (1520); the translation is from LW 43:28 (WA 10/2:394), *Personal Prayer Book* (1522). This is an enduring statement by Luther of the nature of Christian community, bridging the earlier and later phases of his ecclesiology.

48. Ibid.

49. Brecht, *Luther* 2:25–45.

50. LW 36:286 (WA 11:441), *The Adoration of the Sacrament* (1523).

51. LW 30:32 (WA 12:287), *Exposition of First Peter* (1523) (translation altered), 1 Peter 2:16.

52. See the early occurrences of this expression given in chapter 3 (n4), and then later in, for example, LW12:289 (WA 40/2:595), *Commentary on Psalm 45* (1533–1534), chapter 7.

Chapter 3

Luther's Early Teaching on the Common Priesthood, to 1525

A Priest is not identical with Presbyter or Minister—for one is born to be priest, one becomes a minister.

—Martin Luther, *Concerning the Ministry*

FROM CAPTIVITY TO FREEDOM

In the three major reform writings of 1520, Luther attacked the medieval and scholastic foundations of the Church of Rome.[1] Following the indulgence controversy, and his examination before Cajetan in 1518, with the fallout from the Leipzig debate (1519) and his impending excommunication by Rome, Luther began to apply his fresh understandings of the Christian faith as he set out a program for the reform of the church, and to defend himself against the charge of heresy.[2]

On the basis of his prior understanding of the church, Luther proclaimed the equality of all Christians, under the word of God and the headship of Christ, opposing what he saw as spiritual elitism, and the illegitimate use of power by an entrenched hierarchy. Luther's argument was framed by the powerful metaphor of captivity and freedom that he used in these writings to describe the degraded state of the church, and its urgent need for reform. Rome's hierarchy, he said, had constructed three walls around itself, maintaining its usurped power and privilege, preserving its spiritual status, and upholding its sole right to act as interpreter and judge of Scripture. Moreover, its priesthood had taken the church captive under a falsely conceived sacramental system that removed the word of God from its proper use, and robbed that word of its necessary efficacy and power. Thus, the need for faith was also hidden, and held captive by the absence of the word. Only the Gospel's call to spiritual equality and liberty could break down the walls and set Christian people free for the true worship of God, and mutual love and service. Lyndal Roper characterizes the ideas unleashed by these writings as "audacious," but integral to them was Luther's understanding of the church's true character as one fellowship of believers under God's word.[3] This was expressed in each of the three treatises, and was the context in which he presented and applied his insight that according to the New Testament, "we are all priests."[4]

To the Christian Nobility of the German Nation

Setting out a program for reform, Luther argues against the traditional division of spiritual and secular estates and uses the common priesthood as the basis for his assertion that the political authorities can and should legitimately exercise Christian authority to bring about that reform.[5] It can be noted that this is in itself a quite limited use of the concept, primarily relevant to a late medieval sociopolitical context. However, the underlying theology is consistent with the understanding that Luther had derived from Scripture and then applied more broadly to the situation in the church. His use of the Pauline insight into the nature of Christendom noted in the previous chapter is fundamental here, as elsewhere: all Christians share in the same baptism, gospel and faith, which "alone makes us spiritual and a Christian people."[6] There is only one spiritual estate; there is no indelible priestly "character" which sets a priest apart from other Christians, for life. Differences may exist in church and society for the sake of the various offices which need to be exercised; but in spiritual terms, all Christians share the same status. This understanding breaks down the First Wall: "we are all consecrated priests [*zu priestern geweihet*]." This consecration takes place only in baptism, and Luther here refers his readers to 1 Peter 2:9 and Revelation 5:9–10.[7]

Addressing the leaders of the German people, he tells them that as baptized Christians this kind of intervention is their right and their responsibility, when those called to preach the word fail in their calling to uphold that same word in the life of the church. He then calls on the nobility to do all in their power to convene a council for the reform of abuses in the church (the Third Wall).[8] This is based on the God-given, priestly responsibility of all Christians in relation to God's word, and in judging doctrine; this is not a right that the papacy can claim exclusively for itself (the Second Wall).[9] So Luther's aim is not revolution, but reformation: the restoration of the word to its rightful place at the heart of Christian teaching, and in the lives of God's people. He writes,

No one can do this so well as the temporal authorities, especially since they are also fellow-Christians [*mitchristen*], fellow-priests [*mitpriester*], fellow-members of the spiritual estate [*mitgeistlich*], fellow-lords [*mitmechtig*] over all things. Whenever it is necessary or profitable they ought to exercise the office and work [*ampt und werck*] which they have received from God over everyone.[10]

The Babylonian Captivity of the Church

Here the reform imperative is lifted to a higher level, drawing together themes that Luther had already broached in the previous months, and now calling for the church to be set free from an oppressive system of seven sacraments, for the sake of the faith of its people.[11] Luther seeks to restore both the priesthood—which administered the sacraments—and the sacraments themselves, back to their proper biblical footing. The sacraments were not instituted for a select group in the church to enrich themselves and exercise power and control over God's people. Rather, the three true sacraments (baptism, the lord's supper, and absolution) are the gifts of God's promise, to be the means of salvation and not oppression. This goes to the very heart of the Reformation message.[12] The priests are appointed to serve the people, not act as spiritual lords over them. The other four sacraments of the Roman church (confirmation, marriage, ordination, and extreme unction) lacked the promise of grace, Christ's institution, and the work of faith. For Luther, they represent a misreading of Scripture, and ignorance of its central theme. In these ways, God's will for the church is being set aside, and the spiritual benefit of his people ignored.

Luther's chief concern was the mass, and he suggests three ways in which the church of his day held it captive.[13] First, they had changed Christ's institution and withheld the cup from the laity. Christ's words, "Drink of it, all of you" (Matthew 26:27), mean that the laity cannot be excluded from full participation. Then, the doctrine of transubstantiation had been introduced. Luther sees this as unhelpful philosophical wrangling, and again argues for acceptance of Christ's words alone. But it was the distorted view of sacrifice, represented by the words of the canon that for Luther was the main offence in the mass and also the heart of his attack on the clergy. The mass is Christ's testament, his gift, not a work of human devotion for the priests alone. Luther can even say that the laity have a right to receive the sacrament, it cannot be denied them. In his judgement, in obscuring the word of God and faith, the mass encapsulated all that was wrong with Rome, and was a key driver in his attempt to reclaim an authentic, biblical view of priesthood for the church. At this point in the treatise, there is no direct reference to the common priesthood, but it awaits, latent within his view of the church and the sacrament.

Luther says, "As far as the matter of the mass and sacrament is concerned we are all equals [*omnes sumus aequales*], whether we are priests or lay."[14]

Luther begins his treatment of baptism by giving thanks that—at least in its institution—it has not been corrupted in the church as have the mass and penance.[15] But he continues by stressing its proper meaning and use, which have been largely obscured. He emphasizes its permanent, sacramental character, and the need to cling to its promise by faith. Once again, it is God's work, not ours, and this knowledge frees us from the burden of any laws regarding its observation and practice. But this liberty is lost, and the captivity of the sacrament is apparent, when the leaders of the church replace the gospel with their own requirements. So in conclusion, he introduces the subject of religious vows, which have replaced baptism's simple vow to live as a Christian that embraces all.[16] So while we might be looking for a further explication of the connection between baptism and the common priesthood made in *To the Christian Nobility*, it does not occur here. Here, however, we do have reinforcement of a key principle that sits behind this idea of priesthood. In God's eyes, only faith counts, and in faith all works are "spiritual." This is embedded in the sacrament of baptism, given to all. There is no spiritual status in the church higher than that of a baptized Christian.

The treatment of penance likewise repeats principles which Luther had developed in connection with the indulgence controversy.[17] Together with the key sacramental concept related to his theological breakthrough—the central place of the word of promise, received only by faith—Luther adds the perspective that the instituting words (from Matthew 16 and 18, John 20) were spoken to all Christians, not just to the apostles and their supposed successors. The hierarchy had taken all of the elements of repentance entirely captive, removing faith from contrition, demanding the enumeration of sins in confession, and prescribing works of satisfaction. Only in this way, under the control of the clergy, could sins be forgiven. Rejecting any theory of "reserved cases" administered by the pope and bishops only, Luther seeks to restore that word of absolution to all Christians in common. In faith they all have the freedom to speak it to one another and to accept it from one another, as God's own word. This again is a primary component of the common priesthood, as Luther is developing it. And as with the other two gospel sacraments which Christ has given to the whole church, their public administration must be about the exercise of ministry rather than the occasion for tyranny:

> For Christ has not ordained authorities or powers or lordships in his church, but ministries [*ministeria*], as we learn from the Apostle, who says: "This is how one should regard us, as ministers of Christ and stewards of the mysteries of God."[18]

In fact, for the development of the idea of common priesthood in *The Babylonian Captivity*, it is in rejecting the sacramental character of ordination that the elements of his argument in this writing are drawn together. It is no accident that this has a close connection to the mass, and it also speaks to his concern for the other sacraments as visible word, and the means of grace. It is the ministry of the church that has been taken captive, as much as the sacraments themselves. For Luther, the legitimate clerical office must be about practicing a true understanding of the word and faith, viewed from the standpoint of Christ and the gospel.

The authenticity of the three true sacraments rests in their biblical institution by Christ, and his word of promise gives them substance and meaning. For ordination, there is no authenticating word. It has been introduced into the church, says Luther, and while it may have legitimacy as a rite for appointing church officers, it cannot be claimed as a sacrament. This principle is now fundamental to Luther's ecclesiology, and it relates to his gospel breakthrough: "It is the promises of God that make the church, and not the church that makes the promise of God."[19] On exegetical grounds, he rejects the argument that a sacrament of orders was instituted at the last supper, and suggests that the commission of Christ to preach and baptise (Matthew 28:18) would have a stronger claim. But none of the fathers of the church claim ordination for a sacrament, says Luther. It has been introduced to elevate the clergy over the laity, "to the incredible injury of the grace of baptism and to the confusion of our fellowship in the gospel."[20] So this false sacrament represents one of the root causes for the decay of the church: "Christian kinship [*fraternitas Christiana*] has perished, here shepherds [*pastores*] have been turned into wolves, servants into tyrants, clergy into worse than worldlings."[21]

Now Luther deploys the concept of the common priesthood, as his response to the church's spiritual captivity. Once again, he argues that those currently named priests are to be ministers, only ruling in the church by "common consent." We are taught in 1 Peter 2:9 that "we are all priests," and 1 Corinthians 4:1 sets out Paul's own view of the New Testament ministry "as servants of Christ and stewards of the mysteries of God." Luther is identifying the New Testament priesthood in order to more clearly define the nature and role of the clerical office.[22] He continues in this section with an extended plea for the clergy to stick to their proper tasks, the preaching of the gospel and administering the sacraments according to their institution. In fact, all Christians as priests have that same "power" (*potestatem*) regarding the word; but publicly that can only be used "by the consent of the community or by the call of a superior." The discussion of what this power means for the common priesthood is not pursued by Luther here. The full extent of their liberty from ecclesiastical tyranny and captivity will be revealed in later writings, beginning with *The Freedom of a Christian*.[23]

It is important to emphasize that together with the polemical nature of these two writings, and their attack on the oppression and captivity of the church, Luther is arguing throughout for his positive insight into the nature of God's promise and faith to be given its proper place in the church. Indeed, it is for the sake of that insight that the reforms are necessary, and only reform grounded in the word, and unlocking faith's freedom, will achieve a God-pleasing result. It is in this context—both the negative attack, and the positive program—that a vital part is the recognition of spiritual equality among Christians, who are to be priests one for the other, and for the good of the whole community. One's standing before God is not a matter of position or status, but is ours only through salvation's gift freely given, received, and then shared.[24]

The Freedom of a Christian

The centrality of the word and faith is seen no more clearly than in this work, produced in November 1520.[25] Christians, Luther memorably writes, are free Lords (kings), and servants of one another (priests). In faith, they are "subject to none." Yet in love, they are "subject to all."[26] The freedom of faith is celebrated, and rests securely in Christ's word and work. There is no other office (*amt, officium*) for Christ, and in the church, than that of the word. Luther reprises the argument from *The Babylonian Captivity* that the clergy are to be ministers of that word, using again the text from 1 Corinthians 4:1.

From Christ's promise flows everything that benefits those who believe in him, and it is the source for their marriage of faith. This relationship makes them, like him, spiritual kings and priests. And that is also the basis for the reciprocal side to the paradox, the Christ-like person bound in love to serve the neighbor. The role of a true priesthood, based on 1 Peter 2:9, could not be any more prominent than it is in Luther's argument here. As Christ's fellow priests, "we may boldly come into the presence of God in the spirit of faith and cry 'Abba, Father!' pray for one another, and do all things which we see done and foreshadowed in the outer and visible works of priests."[27] In keeping with the theme of the treatise, the focus is on a priesthood arising from the relationship with Christ. The sacramental connections, prominent in the other works from 1520, do not figure here. With the privilege of mutual prayer, there is also that of teaching the word, but any further exploration of what the "works of priests" involve does not occur at this time.

Also in contrast to the other treatises, this writing largely lacks polemic and proposes no reforms, except implicitly in its understanding of the centrality of the word, with personal faith and the ethical life that flows from it replacing medieval spiritual practices. However, *The Freedom of a Christian* is still firmly located in the reformational context, being dedicated to Pope Leo X, and written at the urging of the papal envoy, Karl Miltitz. And the accompanying letter, addressed to the pope, in reality concedes little or no ground to those whom Luther sees as his theological opponents. But the treatise represents, perhaps, a final attempt for Luther to mitigate, and then avoid the fallout from his pending excommunication.[28] In that way it can be distinguished from the other two treatises.

For that reason, it is possible to question the commonly held assertion that Luther's promotion of the common priesthood at this time is chiefly the product of his opposition to the Roman church, its hierarchy and its ordained priesthood.[29] The presentation here in *The Freedom of a Christian* lends weight to the argument of this book, that the common priesthood can be legitimately located within the overall development of Luther's ecclesiology, his Christology, and thus also his understanding of faith and salvation. It had roots in his biblical studies predating the reformational conflict, as was argued above. These close connections with the main themes of his theology give reason to take a broader view of the significance of this concept, and provide an answer to the question why it endured in his teaching and preaching beyond the early 1520s.

Brief Summary

The three treatises are properly considered together as they introduce Luther's reformational program, even while there remain clear differences between them. In turn, they lay before separate audiences the necessity of reform, confronting each group with the challenge to restore the gospel to its rightful place in the lives of God's people. First, in *To the Christian Nobility*, the ruling classes of the German States are called to exercise leadership in keeping with their status as baptized Christians and fill the void left by the ecclesiastical authorities. Then, in *The Babylonian Captivity*, the hierarchy are themselves challenged to return the church to its biblical foundations, recovering its true priesthood, and reestablishing a sacramental ministry based on Christ's word of promise, rather than the tyranny of human tradition. Thirdly, *The Freedom of a Christian*, a work addressed to the pope as leader of the church, invites all believers without distinction to rediscover the power of the gospel to bring true freedom into the life of faith and love, transformed by the priestly service of God and the neighbor. Thus, the common priesthood runs as a uniting thread through these works, linking each target group, and charging each to consider their response to God's word on the basis of their shared baptismal faith, and their participation in the church as members of the one body of Christ, *the communion of saints* who together possess all that Christ has done.

SEVEN FURTHER WITNESSES TO THE COMMON PRIESTHOOD, 1520–1523

In order to explore Luther's new teaching in its depth and its breadth, it is necessary to look beyond the three primary sources to discover how he derived and employed the common priesthood in other writings from the same period. Their initial context is therefore largely polemical, as Luther articulates his argument with Rome. However, it becomes clear that Christian priesthood was not a "stand-alone" doctrine but rather a closely woven strand in his teaching, showing how faith is active in the life of the believer, with wider implications for the worship and life of the church as a Christian community. This process of integration is seen, first in its historical development in seven particular writings, and then according to its biblical roots and application drawn together from Luther's entire theological enterprise.

On the Papacy in Rome

Already in June 1520, Luther had written this work, answering a response to his teaching in the Leipzig debate, published by the Leipzig Franciscan, Alveld.[30] Alveld presents the case for one true church, the Church of Rome, under its papal high priest. In return, Luther argues for Christ as high priest and head of the church. The essence of the true church is that its members are those who are Christians by faith. This is Christendom, spiritually defined, and rather than the externals which characterise the church in Rome, it is "faith which makes true priests and Christians in the soul."[31] This signals the ecclesiological grounding for his call for reform in the treatises *To the Christian Nobility*, and *The Babylonian Captivity*. Luther draws together his thoughts regarding the church as *communio sanctorum*, with his emphasis on the spiritual equality of believers, and their equal participation in Christ's benefits. It is here that he first presents unequivocally the common priesthood, responding initially to Alveld's claims of an Aaronic papal priesthood. The writing is clearly polemical, published in opposition to Rome's theology, but once again we should not ignore its relationship to the suprainstitutional view of the church prominent in Luther's teaching prior to the controversy.

A Treatise on the New Testament

Shortly before the *Babylonian Captivity*, and as its own "prelude," Luther had published this treatise on the sacrament of communion, late in July 1520. It shows how Luther was moving quickly beyond the relatively cautious sermons on the three sacraments, in 1519.[32] Informed by his discovery of the nature of the Gospel, he is able to approach them with fresh eyes, and ears. The title of the treatise displays clearly how the word of promise has become for Luther the chief thing in the mass: it is the New Testament. So the words of Christ need to be spoken out loud, for the sake of all those present. And this in turn confirms the true observance of the mass—it is to be received in faith, and by faith. It can no longer be seen as a good work, to be constantly repeated, and offered in this way to God as our sacrifice for sin. Luther rather presents Christ himself as both priest and sacrifice, who offers himself to the Father for us, and offers us with our prayers and praises, joining him with his sacrifice through faith. In this way, all believers are priests with Christ, receiving the spiritual blessings with the outward "tokens" (*zeichen*) and the testament of sin's promised forgiveness. So here Christian priesthood has three significant points of origination. It comes from unity with Christ's own priesthood; then by participation in the sacrament, offering the sacrifices of prayer and praise; and especially it comes from faith, which "alone is the true priestly office."[33]

Answer to the Hyperchristian, Hyperspiritual and Hyperlearned Book by Goat Emser in Leipzig— Including Some Thoughts Regarding His Companion, the Fool Murner

In this period, 1519–1521, we see Luther caught up in a constant literary cycle of attack, response, and counterattack, with a number of opponents. Much of this came to swirl around the two reform treatises, which themselves developed from unresolved matters in the Leipzig Debate with Eck, and the publishing of the bull of excommunication. It included a lengthy series of exchanges with the humanist Jerome Emser, which had begun even before the debate.[34] In March 1521, Luther's *Answer to the . . . Book by Goat Emser* covered significant ground on the authority of Scripture and the role of tradition.[35] Beyond the ongoing argument on papal primacy, they also debated in some depth the nature of priesthood and ministry. Not surprisingly, Luther rejected Emser's exegesis of 1 Peter 2:9 and his attempt to establish a New Testament basis for a twofold view of priesthood, one spiritual and one ecclesiastical. But Emser's argument forced Luther to dig more deeply into the concepts he had embraced in the reform writings of 1520, and especially their biblical witnesses.[36] It is in this work that Luther then refers to "the common priesthood [*die gemeine priesterschafft*]," which he has contrasted sharply with Emser's "churchly priests."[37] In his ironical *Retraction*, published later the same year, Luther repeats the argument for a single New Testament priesthood in response to Emser's proposal that Peter's words in 1 Peter 2:9 apply to both a lay priesthood and a "priestly one":

> In this passage St. Peter calls all Christians priests. I insisted on this and said that all Christians are priests and that Scripture calls those who are now called priests not priests or *sacerdotes* but *ministri, presbyteri, episcopi*, that is, "servants," "elders," and "guardians."[38]

Soon after this, Luther made the journey to Worms, to face a more serious, public examination, before Emperor Charles V.[39] The outcome of this appearance before the Diet drove him into hiding, his enforced exile in the Wartburg Castle. Theologically, this was a fruitful time for Luther, removed from the university and with space to respond more carefully to his opponents. From this period flowed his work on translating the Bible, providing prefaces to the New Testament and its books, and preparing the first postils as guides for evangelical preachers. It was a time of personal spiritual struggle, overlaid with concern for the progress of reform in Wittenberg, and beyond.[40] So he had both room and need for intense reflection on the themes that would advance the cause of reform more widely. Certainly, the next two years saw the publication of three works which lay out in greater detail first the basis, and then the implications of the common priesthood. They represent a definite advance on the brief statements of the 1520 works, and their deeper integration into his theological framework. In many ways these writings are significant developments in Luther's ecclesiology. They explore what it means to be a Christian believer, nourished within the fellowship of the church, and serving God through the everyday stuff of life in family, community, and society at-large.[41]

The Misuse of the Mass

In 1522 (January), Luther turned once more to the subject of the mass. That he does so, as part of an ongoing series of writings on this topic, shows the importance of its role at the heart of medieval church life, and the corresponding imperative Luther felt for its reform, in order to progress the cause of an evangelical community. In this instance, he is looking towards his own ecclesiastical communities in Wittenberg.

In the publication of *The Misuse of the Mass*, Luther has moved beyond any hope that there would be any reform in the church by its hierarchy, "from above."[42] He had for some time abandoned his priestly duty to celebrate private mass,[43] and now sets out what was needed to reform the public celebration. The basic issue is still that of sacrifice. In the lengthy second section of the treatise, Luther builds on what he presented in *The Babylonian Captivity*, that the reform of the mass is to focus on the primary importance of Christ's own promises, given in the institution of the sacrament. No human additions are to obscure or replace these words; he rejects false understandings around sacrifice, the cult of saints, and purgatory.[44]

As a precursor to this argument, in the first part he embarks on a lengthy examination of the true conception of the priesthood. According to the New Testament every Christian is a priest; and the priestly office is one of preaching, not of making sacrifice. This is embedded in Christ's own priesthood, as Luther has stated consistently across a range of writings. For the first time, Luther assembles his three witnesses for close examination, 1 Peter 2:1–5, Revelation 5:10, and Revelation 20:6, as well as the related text from Romans 12:1. From these he makes the case that in the New Testament there are only spiritual priests and sacrifices; in this light, both the Roman mass and its priests lack any real legitimacy.[45]

In the third part, Luther returns to the theme of the first, contrasting what he has previously presented regarding the priesthood of Christ and Christians, with that which has prevailed under the papacy. The external nature of the latter, bound by its dead laws and practices, is wholly opposed to the gospel priesthood, in which life and faith rule, with the fruits of the Spirit. He then sets out how current practices in reality lead to the violation of each of God's commandments, and again compares the priesthood "of Christ" with that "of the Pope" in the form of a short table. Finally, in a further exegetical study, he contrasts the synagogue with the church, arguing that "all true Christian believers are genuine priests in the Christian congregation, as the Levitical priests were in the synagogue."[46]

This lengthy work was first addressed in Latin to the Augustinians in Wittenberg as encouragement for their reform, and then more widely published in German. Its presentation of Christian priesthood clearly serves a polemical purpose, in opposition to Rome, but its character as teaching for an evangelical church is also clear, in the detailed biblical arguments supporting Luther's view of priesthood and ministry. Some sixteen years later, Luther still recalled the careful planning that lay behind this work, and that reflects its importance even over against the more widely recognized reform writings.[47]

The Exposition of First Peter

On return to Wittenberg, Luther gave priority to the task of reformation in the church community over his university duties, as well as the publication of his German New Testament.[48] Part of the task included the preaching of expository sermons on the Old and New Testaments, expounding his theology for a broad audience. By May 1522, he had begun a series on First Peter, which was then published later that year.[49]

These sermons provided fertile ground for integrating Luther's understanding of the Gospel, his view of the church, and the nature of faith and Christian service. Given the late medieval narrative—and the arguments of his opponents—which elevated Peter as the chief apostle and first pope, it is hardly surprising that Luther took the opportunity to present an alternative view of Peter based on his reading of the New Testament sources. Together with the Pauline letters, he regarded First Peter as one of the writings which most clearly taught the truth about Christ and the Christian faith. He also took opportunity to expound the relationship between the testaments, and the proper use of the concepts of law and gospel. These were important for the laity, as well as his students, if they were to learn to rightly handle ("judge") Scripture and its doctrines. Picking up on his argument with Emser, Luther further unpacks his view of priesthood in 1 Peter 2:9, and faith's union with Christ through the "living and abiding word" (1 Peter 1:23) was given due prominence. Noting the importance of this text for his teaching on the church and its priesthood, he says, "We have argued extensively that those who are called priests today are not priests in the sight of God. And we have substantiated that with what Peter says here."[50]

The formative themes of equality and participation are also very apparent; Christians "share all Christ's goods." In many ways, echoes of *The Freedom of a Christian* are heard, including the marriage imagery of bride and groom. And this, together with the language of baptism, and kinship ("brotherhood") with Christ and with one another, leads into descriptions of priesthood which highlight sacrifice, prayer, and preaching as the three offices (*ampt*) given to all.[51] That all priests will proclaim God's word is fundamental to Luther's understanding, drawn here from Peter's words that Christians are to "declare [God's] marvelous deeds."

The question is, how then to relate this to Luther's emerging teaching on the public ministry of the word? That teaching is already apparent, for example, when he discusses 1 Peter 5:2 on "tending the flock of Christ." Martin Brecht notes how at this time when Luther is so often expounding the common priesthood, he was also discussing with Spalatin the urgent need for pastors and preachers in electoral Saxony.[52] Brecht sees this in terms of a direct connection between priesthood and ministry for Luther, while acknowledging that Luther always qualified his statements with the proviso that no individual can seize the public office for themselves. Deriving the public ministry from the priesthood represents an oversimplification of Luther's position at the very least, and these sermons on First Peter need to be kept in view for the resolution of this question.[53]

That a Christian Assembly has the Right and Power to Judge All Teaching and to Call, Appoint, and Dismiss Teachers, Established and Proven by Scripture.

While the immediate context for the 1522 sermons on *First Peter* is Wittenberg itself, the impact of his reforms meant that Luther could not limit himself to local concerns. After Easter that year, he undertook a preaching tour of surrounding towns.[54] In the final two works highlighted in this section, Luther is seen responding to situations both within and beyond the boundaries of electoral Saxony.[55] And again, while they reveal the development of his view of the common priesthood, the question about the ministry of the church remains apparent. While each writing addresses particular circumstances, requiring careful consideration, they have become paradigmatic for an evaluation of Luther's early teaching.

In May 1523, Luther responded to a request from the Saxon town of Leisnig to provide them with theological validation for their decision to appoint reform-minded clergy, in defiance of their established patron.[56] It is a brief German work, but its lengthy title indicates its significance.[57] For this reason, its publication quickly provided a pattern for others to follow, in aspiration at least. At the same time, Luther worked with the leaders in Leisnig as they developed a program for the relief of the poor—this also became a model for other Saxon towns.[58]

But first Luther confirms the fundamental need for the preaching of the gospel. Preaching of the word is the sine qua non of Christian fellowship. Where the bishops will not fulfil their responsibilities in this regard, congregations have every right to call qualified preachers for themselves. The common priesthood is placed firmly within that communal setting, with mutual dependence on the word, and responsibility for it. This is because, on the basis of 1 Peter 2:9, all Christians are fellow priests with their brother, Christ. All are bound to speak his word, in cases of necessity. Publically, preaching is the duty of those called for that purpose. The situation described by Paul in 1 Corinthians 14 is Luther's source here. He then explores the possibilities for the ideal: bishops and congregations working together to ensure that this "highest office" is fulfilled.[59] His ecclesiological principle of the "shared possession" of Christ's gifts is clearly in view here, with the themes of community and participation that flow on to meet the neighbor's material needs as well.

Concerning the Ministry

More complex was the situation addressed by Luther in advising the Christians in Bohemia, followers of Jan Huss. They lived under an unsatisfactory arrangement whereby their priests were trained and ordained in Rome. At the urging of one of their clergy, Gallus Cahera, Luther wrote to the Senate in Prague, encouraging them to establish their own independent ministry. Luther's extensive advice was written in Latin and published late in 1523. It can be seen as a more comprehensive version of the advice sent to Leisnig.[60] The title, however, was rather more concise: *Concerning the Ministry*, or (more accurately reflecting both the Latin title, and the contents), "Concerning the Need for Appointing Ministers in the Church."[61] This is the most detailed early discussion of the common priesthood prepared by Luther, more thorough even than that in the *Misuse of the Mass*, or in *First Peter*.

Luther explored a number of solutions to the Bohemians' dilemma. He begins with *An Exhortation Against Receiving Papal Ordination*, reflecting on the spiritual damage caused by the current arrangements, which have deprived them of God's word. His initial response is perhaps the most radical. He suggests that it would be better to establish a network of house churches, separate from the false ministry and "teaching of impious men," even if this meant that the Eucharist could not be received at this time.[62] His advice is that the current practice involves a false ordination, producing illegitimate ministers. It lacks the consent of the people, and a call to the ministry of the word. Instead, maintaining the fiction of an "indelible character," the Roman bishops consecrate men only for the sacrifice of the mass, and to hear confession. Christ's sacrifice is thus trampled underfoot, and Christian consciences are destroyed. So the answer lies in separating from Rome, and establishing a true ministry in Bohemia itself. The first step towards this goal involves recognition of the nature of both priesthood and ministry, and the relationship between the two. Priesthood, says Luther, includes all of God's people, who are born again in baptism as sisters and brothers of Christ, our true high priest. Ministry involves those named as presbyters (elders) or ministers in the New Testament, through their call into the service of the word.[63] But there are no spiritual distinctions; all have received the same word of God.

In order to demonstrate this point, Luther embarks on the significant feature of this work, presenting seven offices, "common to all Christians" as priests. These flow out from the first and primary office, the ministry of the word. In turn, Luther validates the common possession of baptism, Eucharist, keys, sacrifice, prayer for others, and judging doctrine. As he has done in nearly every writing from 1520 onwards, he stresses that no one has the right to the public exercise of these offices, except by common consent. And once again, those who do so are best called ministers or servants of the gospel, not priests, to make it clear that "the authority and dignity [*iure et dignitate*] of the priesthood reside[s] in the community of believers."[64]

In this way Luther argues against a sacramental ordination that confers a unique priestly character on its recipients. This is the basis on which he urges the Christians in Bohemia to recover for themselves the right to choose and appoint their own ministers for their churches. Luther does not prescribe how this must happen. It could take place directly through the congregations, or by appointment from the secular authority, or even by an existing bishop. But his program for reform was eventually rejected by the Bohemians, and Cahera ended his days in exile.[65] However, the appearance of seven German editions of this work, in the year following its Latin publication, are an indication that its wider importance was quickly recognized, and it was seen as a paradigm for evangelical churches.[66] It shows how Luther himself saw no contradiction between his understanding of the priesthood, common to all and possessing all the gifts of Christ, and the call to public ministry in the church.

Evaluating the "Ten Sources" for the Common Priesthood (1520–1523)

In these writings that reveal Luther's early teaching on the common priesthood, three transitional phases can be discerned, each in turn representing a twofold focus that mirrors the evolution of Luther's concerns as the reformation debate—and its subsequent implementation—spread more widely.

First, there is his initial reform agenda, which arose out of the indulgence controversy, and quickly involved not just the authority of the papacy but also a distinction between the true church and the false. This agenda is apparent when Luther is calling out abuses in the established church, its compromised ministry, and its "misuse" of the sacraments. And it is also seen in its positive form as he uplifts the promise of the gospel, and argues for the true church as the equal community of believers, established on God's word alone. This is the context for the first appearances of Luther's teaching on the common priesthood. The first phase is largely represented by the three reform treatises of 1520, but also includes the other early writings against the papacy, and his new teaching on the sacraments.

A second transitional movement is evident in his responses to the opponents whose reaction to his publications was to defend the papacy, the church's priesthood, and its sacraments. On both sides, this was marked by the personal polemics with the name-calling and (all too often) the crude invective which was to characterise the theological debate for the rest of

Luther's life. The lengthy debate with Jerome Emser (*Answer to Emser's Book*) typifies this period. At the same time, Luther undertook genuine efforts to educate the people of the church on the central matters of faith, to lead them into Scripture and to assist them in reaching a healthy spirituality. This began already with publications in 1519, but intensified after his excommunication. Among these sources, it is represented by the expository sermons on First Peter and the treatise on the *Freedom of a Christian*. The teaching on the common priesthood played a prominent part in these efforts to defend and then to build up the church.

The third movement is a development and consolidation of the first two, when it becomes apparent that there were no quick or easy resolutions to the questions that Luther had raised. Ongoing issues around the old forms of worship were explored in more depth as, for example, in *The Misuse of the Mass*. Further efforts at the implementation of reform led to clarification of the doctrine of the church, including the relationship between the common priesthood and public ministry. The widely-published advice on the right to call ministers, sent to Christians in Leisnig and Bohemia, shows this taking place.

Throughout these writings, the common priesthood has for Luther both an individual aspect (personal relationship to Christ, based on justification by faith, and granting access to God), and also its communal aspects (corporate worship and prayer, teaching and preaching, mutual love and pastoral care); in each aspect, this priesthood is active in the spiritual realm of the word, and faith.

This means that in the early-Reformation context, Luther's teaching of the common priesthood was not an occasional response to abuses in the church but represented an underlying motivation for much of his reforming work. It figured in his biblical lectures; he argued for it in debates about the nature of the church, its sacraments, and its ministry, both in his polemics against Rome and also in the establishment of a reformational church; it was also taught (or presupposed) in his sermons, and other early writings including his translation of the Bible and the *Prefaces* provided to assist readers in their understanding of its teachings; and it can be clearly seen in the preparation of new German orders and hymns that facilitated lay participation in worship, and the early catechetical forms for their instruction in the faith.[67]

Therefore, from the foundations of the common priesthood, Luther implemented the teaching that the spiritual life of the church is a shared privilege and responsibility for all baptized Christians—laity and clergy alike—who are gathered as the one body of Christ, the communion of saints. Together, they participate in hearing and speaking the word of God in manifold ways, to build up the community and to further the mission of Christ's church. This priesthood reflects Luther's biblical ecclesiology with its themes of unity and community, equality and participation, and lies at the heart of the changes brought about wherever the reformation of the church took hold.

NOTES

1. *To the Christian Nobility of the German Nation Concerning the Reform of the Christian Estate*; *A Prelude on the Babylonian Captivity of the Church*; *The Freedom of a Christian*.

2. See Brecht, "The Reformatory Program," *Luther* 1:349–388.

3. Roper, *Martin Luther Renegade*, 156–168. She offers a balanced and comprehensive summary of the three treatises, from a historical perspective.

4. "We are all equal priests," LW 44:128 (WA 6:408), *To the Christian Nobility*; "We are all priests," LW 36:113 (WA 6:564), *The Babylonian Captivity*; "Not only are we the freest of kings, we are also priests forever," LW 31:355 (WA 7:57), *The Freedom of a Christian*. For an alternative (but parallel) approach to the development of Luther's teaching on the common priesthood, see Christine Helmer, "The Priesthood and Its Critics," in *The Medieval Luther* 247–267. This detailed study finds the roots of this teaching in Ockham's political theology and the struggle for the reform of the papacy and the power of its priesthood, seen in a close relationship to Luther's "discovery" of justification by faith and its application in the three reform treatises. See also Christine Helmer, "The Common Priesthood: Luther's Enduring Challenge," in *Remembering the Reformation: Martin Luther and Catholic Theology* (Minneapolis: Fortress Press, 2017), 211–233.

5. LW 44:123–217 (WA 6:404–469), *To the Christian Nobility*. See Brecht, *Luther* 1:369; Lohse, *Introduction*, 127–128; Scott Hendrix gives a good account of the treatise, including the reactions to its publication, *Martin Luther Visionary*, 89–95.

6. LW 44:127 (WA 6:407).

7. Ibid.

8. LW 44:137 (WA 6:413).

9. LW 44:135 (WA 6:412).

10. LW 44:137 (WA 6:413).

11. LW 36:11–126 (WA 6:497–573), *The Babylonian Captivity*.

12. LW 36:18 (WA 6:501). See Bayer, *Theology*, 57.

13. LW 36:19–57 (WA 6:502–526). Brecht, *Luther* 1: 382; Lohse, *Theology*, 135; Lohse, *Introduction*, 128–129.

14. LW 36:54 (WA 6:525) (translation altered).

15. LW 36:57–81 (WA 6:526–543).

16. LW 36:74–81 (WA 6:538–543). This is Luther's consistent attack on the introduction of traditions that degrade the essential teaching of the word and faith; here it is the monastic tradition that has led to a devaluing of baptism and the unique status it confers. For Luther this misuse of church tradition is a crucial point where the gospel is at stake.

17. LW 36:81–91 (WA 6:543–549)

18. LW 36:82 (WA 6:543), 1 Corinthians 4:1.

19. LW 36:107 (WA 6:560).
20. LW 36:112 (WA 6:563).
21. LW 36:112 (WA 6:564) (translation revised).
22. LW 36:112–113 (WA 6:564).
23. LW 36:117 (WA 6:567).
24. For Luther, the fundamental Christian character of the church—grounded in the equality of faith—overrides the arguments of teachers like Cajetan for the ordered, hierarchical structures of the Roman Catholic Church. Cajetan recognized this already in 1518 and saw that Luther's new approach to faith and the sacraments "would make a new church." See J. Wicks, *Cajetan Responds* (Catholic University of America Press, 1978), 43 and 55. It is also the point of difference for a modern Catholic ecclesiologist like Yves Congar whose proposal for the dual nature of the church found acceptance at the Second Vatican Council. Congar acknowledged the correctness of Cajetan's concerns in *Martin Luther, sa foi, sa réforme: études de théologie historique* (Paris: Éditions du Cerf, 1983), 74. Ecclesiology also determines the nature of reform: for Luther it is the word that reforms the church; for Congar the church itself must initiate the reform, see Yves Congar, *True and False Reform in the Church*, trans. Paul Philibert (Collegeville, MN: Liturgical Press, 2011). See also chapter 5 nn20,62.
25. LW 31:333–377 (WA 7:49–73), *The Freedom of a Christian*. For a recent study, reading the treatise from the perspective of Luther's own life, see Robert Kolb, *Luther's Treatise on Christian Freedom and Its Legacy* [Electronic Resource] (Lanham: Lexington Books/Fortress Academic, 2020).
26. LW 31:344 (WA 7:49).
27. LW 31:353 (WA 7:57).
28. Brecht, *Luther* 1:406–409; Bayer, *Theology*, 235–238; Lohse, *Introduction*, 129–130.
29. See (e.g.) Lohse, *Theology*, 290–291.
30. LW 39:49–104 (WA 6:285–324), *On the Papacy in Rome*. See Brecht, 1:343–346. Lohse, *Theology* 280, 283–284.
31. LW 39:68 (WA 6:296).
32. LW 35:79–111 (WA 6:353–378), *Treatise on the New Testament*. See Brecht, 1:380–381; Lohse, *Introduction*, 126.
33. LW 35:101 (WA 6:370).
34. Brecht, *Luther* 1:332–335, 337–339.
35. LW 39:143–228 (WA 7:621–688), *Answer to Emser's Book*. See Bornkamm, *Mid-Career*, 13–14; Brecht, *Luther* 1:378–379.
36. LW 39:151–56 (WA 7:628–32).
37. LW 39:157 (WA 7:633).
38. LW 39:229 (WA 8:247), *Dr Luther's Retraction of an Error forced upon him by the Most Highly Learned Priest of God, Sir Jerome Emser* (1521).
39. Brecht, *Luther* 1:448–464.
40. Brecht, *Luther* 2:1–6; Bornkamm, *Mid-Career*, 1–50.
41. Unfortunately, these writings receive little attention in many accounts of Luther's common priesthood.

42. LW 36:133–230 (WA 8:482–563), *The Misuse of the Mass*. At the same time, he relied on the secular authorities in Saxony for their support of the Reformation.

43. LW 48: 281 (WA BR 2:372), *Letter to Melanchthon*, 1 August 1521, from the Wartburg.

44. LW 36:162–198 (WA 8:506–537), *Concerning the Words of the Mass, which Prove that the Mass is not a Sacrifice.*

45. LW 36:139–155 (WA 8:487–500), *The Misuse of the Mass* (First Part).

46. LW 36:220 (WA 8:555), *The Misuse of the Mass*.

47. LW 54:326 (WA TR 4:189, n4188).

48. Bornkamm, *Luther in Mid-Career*, 229–230.

49. LW 30:3–145 (WA 12:259–399), *Exposition of First Peter*.

50. LW 30:52 (WA 12:306).

51. LW 30:52 (WA 12:307–308). Luther understands this priesthood to be both personal and communal, based on faith and also located within the community of the church. For the argument that Luther misunderstood 1 Peter 2:9, interpreting it personally rather than corporately, see John Hall Elliott, *The Elect and the Holy: An Exegetical Examination of 1 Peter 2:4–10 and the Phrase Basileion Hierateuma* (Leiden: E.J. Brill, 1966).

52. Brecht, *Luther* 2:68–69; WA Br 2:580, *Letter to Spalatin*, 26 July 1522.

53. Surprisingly, these sermons have been ignored in most discussions of the common priesthood.

54. Brecht, *Luther* 2:67. "Again and again, Luther expressly affirmed the priesthood of all believers." Althaus cites one of these sermons on Mark 7:31–6 (*Theology*, 314), but does not provide the context.

55. Brecht, *Luther* 2:69–70, 72–4.

56. Brecht, *Luther* 2:69–70; Bornkamm, *Luther in Mid-Career*, 126–127. For a detailed examination, see Gert Haendler, *Luther on Ministerial Office and Congregational Function*. Translated by Eric W. and Ruth C. Gritsch (Philadelphia: Fortress Press, 1981), 57–65. Haendler sees this writing as an example of Luther's implementation of the common priesthood.

57. LW 39:305–314 (WA 11:408–416).

58. Heinz Schilling explores how the teaching of the common priesthood went hand in hand with these social concerns, *Martin Luther Rebel*, 359–364. In the document establishing the "common chest" in Leisnig, the parish assembly "by virtue of our universal priesthood" asserts their responsibility for administering the local church estate, LW 39:178 (WA 12:[16–30], *Fraternal Agreement on the Common Chest of the Entire Assembly at Leisnig* (1523).

59. LW 39:314 (WA 11:416). The bishops, "lassen das hohist ampt des wortts."

60. Brecht, *Luther* 2:72–74; Bornkamm, *Mid Career*, 127–128. See also Jaroslav Pelikan, *Spirit versus Structure: Luther and the Institutions of the Church* (London: Collins, 1968), 32–49. Gert Haendler does not include this work (see n56 above), perhaps because it does not support his argument for Luther's promotion of congregational autonomy.

61. LW 40:7–44 (WA 12:169–196), *Concerning the Ministry*. Latin title: *De instituendis ministris ecclesiae ad senatum Pragensem Bohemiae.* A German translation by Paul Speratus was entitled *Wie man Kirchendiener wählen und einsetzen soll.*

62. LW 40:10 (WA 12:171–172).

63. LW 40:18 (WA 12:178).

64. LW 40:35 (WA 12:190).

65. Brecht, *Luther* 2:74; Bornkamm, *Luther in Mid-Career*, 128–129.

66. Details of these editions are given in WA 12:164–165.

67. David Daniel reflects some of this intense activity on Luther's part in relation to the common priesthood in his account of the "third phase of Luther's ecclesiological development" from 1521–1526, "Luther on the Church," OHMLT, 340–343.

Chapter 4

The Biblical Data for the Common Priesthood

If you would interpret well and confidently, set Christ before you, for he is the one to whom it all applies, every bit of it.

—Martin Luther, *Prefaces to the Old Testament*

An examination of the biblical foundations for Luther's teaching could well begin with a survey of his use of the New Testament texts as the formal basis for the common priesthood, from 1 Peter 2:9 and Revelation 5:10 and 20:6. Alternatively, it would also be valid to examine these texts as adjuncts to the Pauline texts central to Luther's ecclesiology, and how together they shaped his view of Christian priesthood. However, the texts that first of all speak of Christ's own priesthood enjoyed some priority in Luther's reading of the biblical witness, and they are the formal source from which the broader concept of Christian priesthood flowed. He often used the unique status of Christ's priesthood to reject any other sacrificial priesthood in the church, and then as the foundation for the common priesthood, seen in its biblical context. From there he considers how that priesthood requires a Christian's reception of God's word, and the responses of prayer and sacrificial living. This in turn provides the context for its relationship to the church's public ministry. That progression provides the structure for what follows here. It becomes apparent how important these texts were for Luther's teaching, and how widely (and creatively) he used them during this period.[1]

CHRIST'S PRIESTHOOD (PSALM 110, HEBREWS)

For Luther, Christ's priesthood is first revealed in the Old Testament psalms, as one of the keys to their fulfilment in salvation history.[2] In the promised new

Israel, Christ is both king and high priest.³ For example, from the 1513–1515 lectures, Psalm 110 provided Luther with the typology of Melchizedek as priest, to be superseded by Christ who is high priest, and head of the church:

> The spiritual bread and wine is Christ Himself, the Head and the whole Church. Thus the apostle says, 1 Cor. 10:17: "We, being many, are one bread and one body." But Melchizedek could not offer this, but Christ alone offers this bread to God the Father forever. . . . So Christ is the eternal priest without beginning and without end.⁴

Then in keeping with Luther's theological breakthrough (or the journey towards it) that theme is broadened in his exposition of the book of *Hebrews* (1517). On Hebrews 5:1, it is presented in relation to faith and works, and in Christ's unique sin-offering he is the archetypical high priest in Aaron's mold, in contrast to the law-giver figure of Moses:

> If we have [Jesus as] High Priest, He is certainly for us and not against us, since "every high priest," even "one appointed and chosen from among men is appointed for men," as Ex. 28:38 states: "And Aaron shall take upon himself any guilt incurred in the holy offering which the people of Israel hallow." This definitely prefigured that Christ, the High Priest, would bear the sins of all who bring offerings, that is, who believe. For He not only shows sin, as Moses does; but He also bears sins and takes them away, as Aaron does.⁵

It is not surprising to find references to Christ as high priest in a commentary on Hebrews.⁶ And this identification of Christ—rather than the pope—as the fulfilment of Aaron's priesthood is also found in *On the Papacy in Rome* (1520), then in Luther's defence of the burning of the canon law.⁷ Another reference to Christ's priesthood occurs in *The Treatise on the New Testament* (1520).⁸ In all these writings the texts from Hebrews (and Psalm 110) are directly given, or implied, and the underlying importance of this role for Luther's ecclesiology is clear. Christ, as king and priest, rules—and serves—in the church.

While this connection of Christ's priesthood to the early formulation of the common priesthood is not so apparent in *To the Christian Nobility* or *The Babylonian Captivity* (both 1520), it lies at the very heart of *The Freedom of a Christian* (1520). Here, Christ's priesthood and kingship is central to Luther's portrayal of the nature of Christian life and freedom, and its essential integration into Christ's own life and work. Luther has grounded this in the person of Melchizedek (Hebrews 6,7), together with God's claim upon the first-born of Israel in Exodus 13:1. He writes,

That we may examine more profoundly that grace which our inner man has in Christ, we must realize that in the Old Testament God consecrated to himself all the first-born males. The birthright was highly prized for it involved a twofold honor, that of priesthood and that of kingship. The first-born brother was priest and lord over all the others and a type of Christ, the true and only first-born of God the Father and the Virgin Mary and true king and priest.[9]

Further exegetical background, employed in his polemic against the Roman priesthood, is apparent in *The Misuse of the Mass* (1522). Luther has concluded that there is no outward priesthood in the New Testament, except that of Christ, "who has sacrificed himself for us and all of us with him." He backs this up with references to I Peter 3:18 ("Christ died once for our sins"), and to Hebrews 10:14 ("a single offering").[10] This argument is developed further in *The Exposition of First Peter* (1522), which employs not only the bridal imagery of *The Freedom of a Christian*, but also has the internal evidence Luther needs to support his view of a Christian "spiritual priesthood" derived from Christ who "is High and Chief Priest anointed by God himself."[11] In *Concerning the Ministry* (1523), Luther returns to Psalm 110:4 and the perpetual "order of Melchizedek," to argue further that Christ's priesthood did not depend on outward rituals like the medieval ordination rites.[12]

In the *Prefaces to the Old Testament* (1523), Luther refers to *Hebrews* to explain his Christological hermeneutic of the Old Testament. In doing so, it is clear that the high priestly role figures strongly in Luther's approach to both Testaments:

> If you would interpret well and confidently, set Christ before you, for he is the man to whom it all applies, every bit of it. Make the high priest Aaron, then, to be nobody but Christ alone, as does the Epistle to the Hebrews [5:4–5], which is sufficient, all by itself, to interpret all the figures of Moses. Likewise, as the same epistle announces [Hebrews 9–10], it is certain that Christ himself is the sacrifice—indeed even the altar [Hebrews 13:10]—who sacrificed himself with his own blood. . . . He has gone in once for all through the curtain to God to make atonement for us [Hebrews 9:12]. Thus you should apply to Christ personally, and to no one else, all that is written about the high priest.[13]

Published in Luther's Bibles, this statement confirms the central place occupied by the priesthood in his Christology, and its importance for understanding both Testaments.[14] The rejection of papal claims as successors to the Aaronic priesthood is unstated, but clear: in Luther's theology of the church, only Christ occupies the high priest's throne.

Christian Priesthood (1 Peter 2:9, etc.)

Standing alongside of his use of the texts that speak of Christ as high priest, is Luther's early awareness that in the New Testament the title "priest" is then applied to all Christians. The primary text is 1 Peter 2:9, sometimes seen with Revelation 5:10 and 20:6. But taken overall, these latter two are only ever used as supporting texts. For Luther, the Latin of the Vulgate was often uppermost in his mind when he quoted Scripture. He then also worked with the Greek text, for his German translation(s).[15] Peter addresses his Christian readers as a "chosen race" (*genus electum*), a "royal priesthood" (*regale sacerdotium*), a "holy people" (*gens sancta*), a "people for his own possession" (*populus acquisitionis*).[16] In the original Greek, the central phrase is "a priestly kingdom" ($\beta\alpha\sigma\iota\lambda\epsilon\iota\text{ον}\ \iota\epsilon\rho\alpha\tau\epsilon\upsilon\mu\alpha\iota$);[17] As will be seen, Luther uses either wording, or a combination of phrases. Generally, his emphasis is on "priesthood," as he uses this text. He is well aware that these words are addressed collectively, to the "people" as a whole—his consistent use of the terms for Christian community make that clear. For him this also means that there can be no division in the church between "spiritual" priests and the rest (the laity) who are passive observers in the community's work of praise and proclamation. Personal faith makes each member of the "priestly people" spiritual, and they all share a level of responsibility for those God-given tasks as they participate in them.[18]

The verses from 1 Peter appear quite often in the early commentaries, when Luther is writing about Christ and his church. His exposition of Psalm 114:2 ("Judea was made his sanctuary") notes that Christ "is both priest and king. And we are his kingdom and priesthood," with references to 1 Peter 2:9 and Exodus 19:5–6.[19] Commenting on Psalm 109:8 (Vulgate 108:8, "his *episcopatum* let another take"), Luther says, "For all the faithful are priests and kings through Christ the Priest, according to Revelation 5:[10]."[20] 1 Peter 2:9 is then quoted in the *Lectures on Hebrews*, together with its precursor in Exodus 19. Luther is commenting on Hebrews 1:8, regarding God's throne, on which Christ sits as "King and Priest," ruling over his chosen people.[21] He uses it in the *Commentary on Galatians* (1519), where intercession for weaker brethren (Galatians 6:1–3) is a mark of the character of Christians, as "a priestly race, and a royal priesthood." The text is already so familiar for Luther that he can omit its source here.[22] Similarly, no direct reference is given in his comments on Psalm 2:10 (1519), "[t]oday, however, we all are priests."[23] The phrase *sumus omnes sacerdotes* will become a familiar expression of the common priesthood, and its first appearance here in Luther's published writings suggests that it is already well-established in his thought. He is arguing for the right of the laity to be taught in an open manner, able to question the teaching of their leaders.

In December 1519, he writes to Spalatin regarding his duties at court, "the apostle Peter convinces me very much, saying that we all are priests. John says the same in Revelation."[24] Peter and John are also the markers for a common priestly consecration in *To the Christian Nobility*. Luther quotes Revelation 5:9 verbatim, but is more free with the text of 1 Peter 2:9, perhaps for emphasis: "You are a royal priesthood and a priestly realm."[25] Similarly, in *The Babylonian Captivity*, when writing that "all of us that have been baptized are equally priests," he quotes 1 Peter 2 as "You are a chosen race, a royal priesthood, and a priestly royalty." He concludes, "Therefore we are all priests, as many of us as are Christians."[26] This free use of familiar, significant texts has already been noted above in regard to Luther's early use of the Pauline verses on the body of Christ.[27]

Likewise, in *The Freedom of a Christian*, "all who believe in Christ" are priests and kings, based on the same text which states, "You are a chosen race, God's own people, a royal priesthood, a priestly kingdom."[28] In the *Answer to Emser's Book* (1521), Luther emphasizes the common application of Peter's words: "'You are a royal priesthood and a priestly kingdom.' With this saying I proved that all Christians are priests, for Peter said it to all Christians, as the words clearly state and mention the people by name."[29] In Luther's devotional exposition of *The Magnificat* (1521), three key elements of the verse can be rearranged to illustrate the point he is making about God's gracious call of Israel, transformed by Christ's incarnation: "You are a holy nation, a chosen people, a royal priesthood."[30]

But the quotation can also be provided in its simpler form. In *Against the Spiritual Estate of the Pope and the Bishops* (1522), Luther quotes "St. Peter's saying, which he spoke to all Christians, "You are a royal priesthood."[31] Notably, it is only in a direct quotation like this that Luther uses the "royal priesthood," on its own (*das königliche Priestertum*).

In *The Misuse of the Mass* (1522), Luther presents the list of three witnesses to the New Testament priesthood, as he confidently repeats his attack on Rome's ecclesiological foundations. For the first, he introduces 1 Peter 2:5, adding "to be a holy priesthood and to offer spiritual sacrifices" to the standard text from verse 9. The second and third witnesses are the texts from Revelation 5 and 20. Luther has done his homework, and can claim, "apart from these passages this word 'priest' is not even mentioned by so much as a single letter in the whole New Testament."[32] But this priesthood is "common to all Christians."[33]

However, in the *Exposition of First Peter*, other Old Testament texts begin to be introduced, to provide the support for Luther's commentary on chapter 2. He writes, "Today everything is new and spiritual. Christ is the Priest, and we are all priests. Just as He sacrificed His body, so we, too, must sacrifice ourselves."[34] This common title, "priest," he says, is foreshadowed in God's election of Israel, quoting Deuteronomy 7:6 ("a people holy to the Lord") and Exodus 19:5–6 ("a kingdom of priests").[35] In *That a Christian Assembly . . . has the Right to Call*, Psalm 45:7 ("God has anointed you") is paired with 1 Peter 2:9, as support for the consecration of Christians as priests, who are "Christ's brethren."[36]

Most comprehensively, *Concerning the Ministry* (1523) begins by making the connection to baptism clear, speaking of a priest's spiritual birth, and echoing John 3:5–6 and Titus 3:5. A priest, Luther says, "was created, not ordained. He was born not indeed of flesh, but through a birth of the Spirit, by water and Spirit in the washing of regeneration Indeed, all Christians are priests, and all priests are Christians."[37] This is reinforced by references which emphasize for Luther Christian "oneness with Christ." Christ calls us "brethren" (Psalm 22:23), "fellows" (Psalm 45:8), and then in an outpouring of the familiar Pauline images, "one loaf, one cup, one body, members of his body, one flesh, bone of his bone, and we are told that we have all things in common with him." And then—to cap his argument—Luther brings into sight 1 Peter 2:9 and Revelation 5:10. "Such passages," he says, "I have sufficiently treated in other books."[38] This detailed exploration of priesthood in its ecclesiological setting indicates its importance for Luther, and speaks against this being an ad hoc treatment only reflecting the narrow circumstances of individual writings in the early reformational period.[39]

Aside from these key texts, during this period from 1520, Luther can also present Christian priesthood as a given. Sometimes this is in connection with another text, in other places with no apparent text at all. Arguing against the Roman priesthood in *On the Papacy in Rome*, Luther quotes Psalm 132:9 as foretelling the spiritual nature of our New Testament priesthood, in which "your priests will be clothed internally with grace."[40] In *The Treatise on the New Testament* (1520) he simply asserts that on the basis of Christ's priesthood, "each and all are, therefore, equally spiritual priests before God," presenting the sacrifice of faith in the Eucharist.[41] In a summary of Romans 12 in the *New Testament Prefaces* (1523), Luther says that Paul "teaches what true worship is, and makes all Christians priests."[42]

Luther does not consider this biblical designation of all Christians as priests to be the conferral of an honorary title, and he does not use it only in his polemic against Rome's priesthood. Rather, it reveals a personal connection to Christ and his work, and the deeper reality of the Christian community as its members share faith and life together as the body of Christ, and as the communion of saints.

The Word and the Priesthood (Isaiah 54:13 / John 6:45)

For Luther, the Old Testament priests were primarily teachers and preachers of God's word, alongside of their ritual duties in relation to worship, sacrifice and prayer. This may be a surprising emphasis, but it is his consistent understanding. In this way, the Aaronic priesthood prefigured the ministry of Christ, and of the church.[43] In the early lectures his criticism of the church of his day included the failure of priests and bishops as teachers and preachers, robbing the laity of participation in God's word.

A key text for Luther was Isaiah 54:13, not least because it was used by Jesus himself, "it is written . . . they shall all be taught by God" (John 6:45). Early on, he stressed that the word was spoken directly to each believer's heart, beyond the teaching of the priests. Later, in line with his breakthrough understanding, he emphasizes the sharing of the word in mutual Christian teaching, by the common priesthood. Later yet, he also gives priority to the public ministry of those called as preachers of God's word.

In the *First Lectures on the Psalms* (1513–1515), on Psalms 60 and 85, Luther uses John 6:45 to highlight God's "effective" speaking, without intermediary, conveying "internal, spiritual, and true things." Jeremiah 31:33 is also added here, "I will give my law into their hearts." Through Moses, and even the prophets, the word soon becomes veiled.[44] Writing on Psalm 119:97–104, Luther explores how "meditation on the Law of Christ" is far superior to the teaching of the priests and prophets, and in the church brings wisdom beyond those (including the popes), "who do not strive to progress towards the spirit."[45]

In 1517, Hebrews 8 prompts Luther to expound Christ's high priestly office in terms of its "more excellent ministry" and its "better covenant" (8:6). He explores Jeremiah 31:31–4, in verses 8–12:

> Therefore it happens in the New Testament that while the Word of life, grace, and salvation is proclaimed outside, the Holy Spirit teaches inside at the same time. Therefore Isaiah says (Is. 54:13): "All your sons shall be taught by the Lord." And in Jeremiah we read: "I will give My laws. . . . And they shall all know Me." Hence Christ refers to these two prophets when He says in John 6:45: "It is written in the prophets: 'They shall all be taught by God.' " . . . Thus we read in 1 John 2:27 that "His anointing will teach you all," and in John 14:26: "But the Counselor, the Holy Spirit . . . will teach you all things." Accordingly, this is how Scripture must be understood when it says that the laws are written in the minds and in the hearts.[46]

Significantly, in the 1519 commentary on Psalm 2, the first use of the phrase "we are all priests" is to make the point that the word is accessible to all Christians:

Today, however, we all are priests, and Is. 54:13 is now fulfilled: "All your sons shall be taught by the Lord," and Jer. 31:34: "No longer shall each man teach his neighbor and each his brother saying, 'Know the Lord'; for they shall all know Me, from the least of them to the greatest, says the Lord."[47]

Frequently in the early 1520s, Luther will repeat the same point, from the same text(s). In the *Freedom of a Christian*, Christ's teaching and prayer ("the two real functions of a priest"), are matched by our own, for "as priests we are worthy to appear before God to pray for others and to teach one another divine things."[48] A similar point is made in *The Misuse of the Mass*. Luther offers his own very free paraphrase of Hebrews 5:1, "Every priest is appointed in order that he might pray for the people and preach," and applies it to every Christian. Access to God in prayer is promised in Scripture (Romans 5:2, Isaiah 65:24). With this comes the privilege of being taught by God. Once again, the texts are Isaiah 54:13, Jeremiah 31:34, John 6:45, together with a new addition, Isaiah 11:9: "The earth is full of the knowledge of the Lord as with the water of the overflowing sea." With this host of witnesses, Luther is able to complete his circle: "Thus it follows that the priesthood in the New Testament is equally in all Christians."[49] In *That a Christian Assembly . . . has the Right to Call*, he uses John 6:45 to argue for the Christian's possession of the word, and anointing to the priesthood, backed up by Psalm 45:7 ("God has anointed you").[50]

A related aspect of the common priesthood in relation to the word is the right to make judgements in the area of faith, to test church teachings. In effect, Luther himself used this right as he questioned the practice of indulgences and the decisions of popes and councils, and then defended himself against charges of heresy. He then presents this as the "second wall" invented by the papacy that he seeks to break down in his address *To the Christian Nobility*. If all Christians have been "taught by God," as Christ says (John 6:45), then they have the right to speak and to question even those who occupy the highest places in the church.[51] Further, Paul's words about spiritual judgement (1 Corinthians 2:15) must be considered. Then, with 2 Corinthians 4:13 ("we all have one spirit of faith") in view, Luther can add in to this his now familiar summary of Christian fellowship: "Besides, if we are all priests, as was said above, and all have one faith, one gospel, one sacrament, why should we not also have the power to test and judge what is right or wrong in matters of faith?"[52] He takes a similar approach in *Against Henry, King of England* (1522), using the same texts, with the addition of Matthew 7:15 ("beware of false prophets"). Luther writes, "to examine and to judge concerning doctrine pertains to every single Christian . . . for Christ himself has established this right with invincible and varied statements."[53] More simply, the same point is made in *Concerning the Ministry* (1523): "Each is a most free judge of all who teach him, if he himself is inwardly taught of God, as John 6 says."[54]

Luther uses these texts as more than random "proofs" for his position. He is convinced that the church is revealed as the place where God's Spirit works through the word, to equip all of God's people for life together in his kingdom of grace. The priesthood is made up of all those who hear, speak—and discuss—God's word, individually and together. This is a fundamental Christian activity, part of what it means to be the church and to participate in its community. How this relates to the public preaching of the word is explored in the final section of this chapter, "Priesthood and Ministry."

Priesthood and Sacrifice (Romans 12:1, 1 Peter 2:5)

Luther's significant use of Romans 12:1 ("present your bodies as a living sacrifice") in the *Dictata super Psalterium* (1513–1516) was explored above.[55] His use of the language of mystical self-sacrifice and union with Christ was in keeping with his early stages of development. And as this theological exploration continued, he used the same and related texts during the time of his reformational discoveries, but now with the emphasis on self-offering as faith's response to Christ's unique sacrifice, rather than as a partner in his suffering. Because it is biblical, Luther still uses the language of priesthood and sacrifice, even as he moves away from a mystical understanding of faith, and strongly rejects the medieval idea of a sacrificial priesthood.[56] The nature of worship itself changed for Luther, being shaped by the priority given to the efficacious word and its refiguring of the sacraments of grace.

This change can already be seen in the *Lectures on Hebrews* (1517), where he writes on 5:7 that "calves, goats, and the other sacrifices—in addition to the fact that they signify tropologically the mortification of the flesh and the members on earth, as is taught in Rom. 12:1 and Col. 3:5—also prefigured offerings of prayers and praises."[57] The linking of the Romans and Colossians texts indicates that Luther is placing his emphasis on self-sacrifice here.

In the *Treatise on the New Testament* (1520), his connection of the "testament" (Christ's word of promise) and the faith of those who participate in the sacrament, helps him—at this stage, at least—to maintain a positive understanding of sacrifice in the mass. This faith "is the true priestly office" and rests in Christ who "is our priest, [who] offers himself for us without ceasing, and presents us and our prayer and praise, making all these acceptable."[58] This faith, Luther says,

> makes us all priests and priestesses. Through it, in connection with the sacrament, we offer ourselves, our need, prayer, praise, and thanksgiving in Christ

and through Christ; and thereby we offer Christ to God, that is, we move Christ and give him occasion to offer himself for us and to offer us with himself.[59]

The term, "acceptable sacrifices" reflects 1 Peter 2:5, and Romans 12:1 is in view here as well, but it is not until 1522 that Luther links these two texts overtly. In *The Misuse of the Mass*, he continues to make connections between Christ's primary priesthood, and ours, and between his sacrifice and ours. He writes, "Are not all Christians built like living stones on Christ, and so . . . they are priests who sacrifice not irrational animals, but themselves . . . when in the Spirit they put to death the deeds of the body?" Then further, "there is yet another sacrifice which is equally common to all, of which Psalm 51 speaks: 'The sacrifice of God is a broken spirit,' and Psalm 29: 'Offer to God a sacrifice of thanksgiving, which will honor me'." These spiritual sacrifices are an "office" which belong to all, quite separate from false offices of the "anointed and tonsured priesthood."[60]

Notably, in his conclusion to this writing, he uses Romans 12 for the linkage between Christ's unique priesthood and a Christian's daily sacrifice. Having once again rejected the ritual priesthood, which offers a propitiatory sacrifice in the mass, Luther insists that,

> Christ's sacrifice is a living sacrifice, his body being sacrificed once on the cross and our bodies being sacrificed daily, a living holy sacrifice, which is a rational service of God. His works and righteousness are the fruits of the Spirit (Galatians 5): faith, voluntary chastity, goodness, willing service to one's neighbor, etc.[61]

A similar conjunction of Romans 12:1 and 1 Peter 2:5 occurs in *Concerning the Ministry*, again with the careful language which shows the relationship between the one sacrifice of Christ, and that sacrifice in which all participate:

> [I]n the New Testament there is no sacrifice except the one which is common to all, namely the one described in Romans 12, where Paul teaches us to present our bodies as a sacrifice, just as Christ sacrificed his body for us on the cross. In this sacrifice he includes the offering of praise and thanksgiving. Peter likewise commands in I Peter 2 that we offer spiritual sacrifices acceptable to God through Jesus Christ, that is, ourselves, not gold or animals.[62]

Yet again, his mainstream use of these texts, and the concepts of Christian priesthood, is shown by their inclusion in the *Prefaces to the Old Testament* (1523) as well as the *Prefaces to the New Testament* (1522), which appeared in German Bibles during Luther's lifetime, and beyond. Introducing the Old Testament, he connects Christ to the high priest, Aaron, and states that only Christ's sacrifice removes "true sin." He continues, "The high priest's sons, however, who are engaged in the daily sacrifice, you should interpret to mean ourselves." These are our spiritual sacrifices, offered by faith:

> This is the interpretation that St. Paul makes in Romans 12 when he teaches that we are to offer our bodies to God as a living, holy, and acceptable sacrifice. This is what we do (as has been said) by the constant exercise of the gospel both in preaching and in believing.[63]

The summary of chapter 12 in the *Preface to Romans* has already been noted in the previous section. Similarly, in the *Preface to First Peter* Luther says, "[i]n chapter 2 he teaches them to know Christ as the Head and the Cornerstone, and like true priests to sacrifice themselves to God as Christ sacrificed himself."[64] *Hebrews*, he writes, "discusses Christ's priesthood masterfully and profoundly on the basis of the Scriptures."[65] Many generations of Luther's readers were directed to the themes of priesthood through these *Prefaces*.

Priesthood and Ministry (Texts from 1 Corinthians 12, 14, etc.)

In 1520, Luther's arguments for understanding Christian priesthood on the basis of 1 Peter 2:9 and other texts denied the medieval priesthood its claimed spiritual status in the church. He opposed a sacramental view of ordination, its conferral of an "indelible character," and the claims regarding its unique powers regarding the sacrifice of the mass, and the other sacraments. Even before this time, Luther had argued that the chief responsibility of the clergy and the bishops lay in proclaiming the word of God, and this becomes the overwhelming focus of his vision for a church that needed to be reformed in keeping with that same word.[66] And if word and priesthood were intimately connected, that task could not be reserved for the clergy alone. What scriptural evidence did Luther employ to pursue these arguments?

Luther had already claimed that the key elements of the sacrament of penance, confession and absolution, were not the exclusive property of the clergy, but could be exercised by any Christian. He insisted that the key texts of Matthew 16:19 and 18:18 were addressed "to all Christendom, and to each [Christian] in particular."[67] This is Luther's view that the church is a community in which its spiritual possessions are held in common. When he opposes the false status of the established priesthood, the texts which affirm "one body in Christ" (1 Corinthians 12:12, etc.) are now seen in close relationship to those which have convinced him that there is one, common Christian priesthood (1 Peter 2:9 etc.). These same texts speak to a shared responsibility for the work of the church, by which we serve one another. In *To the Christian Nobility*, he writes:

> All Christians are truly of the spiritual estate, and there is no difference among them except that of office. Paul says in 1 Corinthians 12 that we are all one body, yet every member has its own work by which it serves the others. This is because we all have one baptism, one gospel, one faith, and are all Christians alike; for baptism, gospel, and faith alone make us spiritual and a Christian people.[68]

In ordination, says Luther, the bishop acts only on behalf of the whole community, who—when the need arises—have the right to elect their own clergy. For, "no one dare take upon himself what is common to all without the authority and consent of the community." In cases of necessity, "anyone can baptize and give absolution." He concludes, "this would not be possible if we were not all priests."[69] It is interesting that, at this point, Luther sees no need to add any supporting texts, beyond those already given regarding the common status of believers (Ephesians 4), their gifts (Romans 12), and their priesthood (1 Peter 2). But later that year, when Luther is looking more closely at issues around priesthood and ordination in *The Babylonian Captivity*, he introduces 1 Corinthians 4:1, "as we learn from the Apostle, who says: 'This is how one should regard us, as ministers of Christ and stewards of the mysteries of God'."[70]

The elevation of the idea of clerical "ministry" is entirely consistent with his earlier thinking; in later Lutheran usage it becomes the formal designation of their office as public ministers. Here, because he is writing on the use of the sacraments, he emphasises how Christ himself has instituted these as ministries of service in the church. Mark 16:16 is the foundation for the ministry of baptism, Matthew 16:19 and 18:18 for absolution, and 1 Corinthians 11:24–5 for the Lord's Supper. The important point is that it is the word and faith that are operative in the sacraments, not priestly power.[71] This leads to a conclusion in line with the statements from *To the Christian Nobility*. Because "we are all equally priests . . . no one may make use of this power except by the consent of the community or by the call of a superior."[72] The same point is made in *The Freedom of a Christian*, where Luther again states that "although we are all equally priests, we cannot all publicly minister and teach. We ought not do so even if we could. Paul writes accordingly in 1 Corinthians 4, 'This is how one should regard us, as servants of Christ and stewards of the mysteries of God'."[73] In this way Luther distinguishes between the priesthood's common possession of Christ's gifts for the church, and their public use by those designated as its ministers and servants. All of Luther's references for the public ministry highlight its servant nature, rather than its divine institution, at this time.[74]

The texts used to support this approach can vary. In 1521, in *The Defense of All Articles*, it is Ephesians 4[:4–8] that teaches that the sacraments are to be held in common in the church. The pope has no more power than any other priest or Christian with regards to Baptism, the Lord's Supper, or Absolution.[75] He also presents "still stronger reasons" from 1 Corinthians 10:17. For Luther, Paul's narration that "we all partake of one bread and one cup," precludes any separation between clergy and laity in the one body of Christ, and in their common participation in the sacraments.[76]

Writing his *Answer to the . . . Book by Goat Emser*, also in 1521, Luther presents a whole raft of texts in support of his contention that there is but one spiritual priesthood in the church. In contrast to 1 Peter 2:9, the texts are among those which name the clergy as ministers, overseers (bishops), servants, and presbyters—but not priests. In 2 Timothy 2:24, says Luther, Paul "calls Timothy a servant of God in the special sense of preaching and spiritually leading the people." The message is the same in 2 Corinthians 11:23, in 1 Corinthians 4:1, and even in Christ's parable of the stewards in Matthew 24.[77]

A discussion of the derivation of "priest" from "presbyteros" leads Luther back into 1 Peter 5, and he relates "bishop" (episcopus) to "a guardian or watchman on the tower."[78] Luther expands his theme of priests and elders, quoting Acts 20 and Paul's farewell to the elders in Ephesus, to make his point regarding the equivalence of priests and bishops in the early church.[79] He quotes Titus 1 to support this view, and to reject the present day ordering of the church, which has developed according to "men's laws and regulations."[80] Rather, says Luther by way of a summary,

> Since in every Christian town they were all equally spiritual priests, one of them—the oldest or rather the most learned and most godly—was elected to be their servant, official, caretaker, and guardian in regard to the gospel and the sacraments, just as a mayor in a city is elected from among the common mass of all citizens.[81]

The Misuse of the Mass has been noted as Luther's most comprehensive rebuttal of the Roman sacrificial priesthood, presenting Christian priesthood on the basis of the "three witnesses" from 1 Peter and Revelation. He also opposes Rome's view of the preaching office, again because it is limited to the clergy alone. Quoting 2 Corinthians 3:6, he says, "I will show from the beginning with incontrovertible Scripture that the only true, genuine office of preaching, like priesthood and sacrifice, is common to all Christians." Paul's words, regarding "able ministers of the new testament" were, Luther claims, "spoke[n] to all Christians." Luther then acknowledges that in practice, not all can speak. For the first time (it seems), he quotes 1 Corinthians 14:40, that "all things should be done decently and in order." The need for this "command," he says, proves that all have the right to speak.[82]

Luther then deals with the objections to his teaching of the common right, including Paul's injunction in 1 Corinthians 14:34, that women should keep silence in the church. Attempting to maintain his principle of spiritual equality, Luther proposes that not all people are fit for the public task. In 2 Timothy 2:2, Paul instructs Timothy to appoint those "who will be able to teach and instruct others." The preacher needs the proper gifts for speaking, says Luther. Paul is saying that it is more fitting for a man to preach in the congregation, and he has the necessary skills. However, Luther is not able to ignore 1 Corinthians 11:5, where Paul also instructs the women to pray and prophesy: "Therefore order, discipline, and respect demand that women keep silent when men speak; but if no man were to preach, then it would be necessary for the women to preach." He then repeats: there is only one, biblical, office of preaching, and it is common to all Christians.[83]

Luther repeats these arguments in his *Exposition of First Peter*, commenting on 1 Peter 2:5. The "spiritual sacrifices" include the preaching of the Gospel. All are included because all are priests. Luther supports the "no distinctions" argument here with Galatians 3:28. He writes, "all may proclaim God's word, except that, as St. Paul teaches in 1 Corinthians 14:34, women should not speak in the congregation." But the rule is not absolute: "If, however, only women were present and no men, as in nunneries, then one of the women might be authorized to preach."[84] Continuing in the same chapter, Luther highlights again the responsibility for all Christians to "declare the wonderful deeds" of God. This, says Peter, "is the chief function of a priest." The text of 1 Peter 2:9 is sufficient for Luther here; he needs no further references.[85]

In *That a Christian Assembly . . . has the Right to Call*, we see how Luther's thinking is continuing to develop in relation to priesthood and ministry, as the Reformation progresses in Wittenberg and beyond. He still uses, for example, John 6:45 and 1 Peter 2:5–9 for the common priesthood, and "possession" of the word of God, but adds further texts which speak of the Christian's duty to "confess, to teach, and to spread his word." These include 2 Corinthians 4:13 and Psalm 116:10 ("I came to believe, therefore I speak"), and Psalm 51:13 ("I will teach the ungodly your ways"). Luther places the Christian in two situations.[86] Where there are no Christians, no further call is needed to speak God's word, other than the duty of mutual love. His examples are Stephen (Acts 6–7) and Philip (Acts 8).[87]

Within the Christian community, a different order applies. Arguing from Paul's description of the assembly in 1 Corinthians 14:26–33, Luther suggests that a Christian "should not draw attention to himself." Rather, he should wait for the invitation to speak—except where there is a lack of teachers. Then, one can come forward, "provided he does it in a decent and becoming manner" (1 Corinthians 14:40).[88]

This line of development is also apparent in *Concerning the Ministry*, from the same year. Here, writing against Rome's control of the appointment of clergy, Luther once again urges that the "common rights" of all Christians must be acknowledged. They cannot be excluded from the offices that are proper to the exercise of ministry in the church. The words which establish the various ministries in the church were spoken to all Christians, and Luther examines these at some length.[89] 1 Corinthians 14:26 reflects a situation in which a number of people are able to contribute to public worship. But, Luther insists, this cannot be a recipe for chaos, and Paul's teaching on order in the church (1 Corinthians 14:40), has priority for him. He says,

> It is one thing to exercise a right publicly; another to use it in time of need [*in necessitate*]. Publicly one may not exercise a right without consent of the whole body or of the church. In time of need it may be used as each one deems best.[90]

The church situation revealed in 1 Corinthians resonated strongly with Luther. He quotes 4:1 again for stewardship and service as the key characteristics of ministry. In their "time of necessity," he encourages the Bohemians to look to their own spiritual needs, on the basis of Paul's teaching in chapter 14, and also quotes 2 Timothy 2:2 as sanction for the local election of teachers for the church. This appointment to the ministry of the word is the key to the life of the church, and its ministries (1 Corinthians 12). In relation to preaching the gospel, even administering baptism is a "secondary office," as John 4:2 and 1 Corinthians 1:17 show.[91]

Luther's early view of priesthood and ministry is driven by his engagement with the biblical text, and its application to his experience of the church's life and work. In the first stage(s) of the Reformation, his "recovery" of a common priesthood includes the conviction that all Christians have a stake in the church's ministry. The church is a community of faith in which every spiritual "possession" (including the word itself) is held in common, and it should be ordered to reflect that imperative (Ephesians 4, 1 Corinthians 14). He rejects clerical domination of the word and sacraments, through penitential practices, excommunication (the "keys"), and the sacrifice of the mass. In the New Testament, he finds no authorization for this hierarchical priesthood and denies its basis in later church tradition; rather, under Christ's headship, leadership in the church is fulfilled only by serving God's people as God's "stewards," or ministers. But in practice this meant establishing orderly means for appointing pastors and preachers and in time this became more and more controlled by the civil authorities.[92]

Summarizing the Foundational Biblical Texts for Church and Priesthood

Luther teaching on the New Testament priesthood and the church developed from his engagement with the particular texts explored here and in chapter 2. These texts were used by Luther both individually and together to teach that the church is the communion of saints and its priesthood is common to all. His engagement with the "church" texts precedes his application of the texts for the common priesthood, but as the latter develops, both are being used in this close conjunction that dynamically links both concepts. In Luther's thinking the intersection of these texts is not haphazard or random, but it is fundamental both to the nature of the church and of its Christian people.

In keeping with his early Christological hermeneutic, Luther gives first place to Christ's priesthood, from biblical prophecy, in the New Testament, and in the church (Psalm 110, Hebrews *variously*). Because of their unity with Christ by faith and their incorporation into Christ's body, all Christians are priests. They are Christ's sisters and brothers, his family, (even) his children. This spiritual status is conferred by their baptismal consecration, and confirmed by their communion with fellow-believers (1 Peter 2; Galatians 3; Ephesians 4). In Christ, by faith, their lives are an act of self-offering (sacrifice); before God they pray for one another, and they worship in God's presence (Romans 12:1–8, 1 Peter 2:4–5).

Together with sacrifice, worship, and prayer, the primary work of the priests is to receive God's word and to proclaim it. All Christians have been "taught by God" (Isaiah 54:13//John 6:45). Every Christian has the right to judgement in matters of faith (1 Corinthians 2:15). Understood together with Luther's exposition and use of 1 Peter 2:9, it means that these priestly tasks are personal to each Christian, and are also the responsibility of the whole community working together.

Applying these New Testament texts as a significant challenge to the hierarchical nature of the medieval church, Luther limits the power and status of the clergy, and teaches that in the true church, all Christians "possess" as Christ's gifts God's word and the sacraments (Ephesians 4:4–6). He emphasises call and appointment to a public *ministry* of the word, as a service by and for the church (1 Corinthians 4:1). He also places a significant boundary around the common priesthood: all Christians are priests, but not all are called or appointed to be pastors (1 Corinthians 14, especially 14:40). How this radical (biblical) understanding of church, priesthood and ministry was then implemented—or constrained—amidst the ecclesiastical, social and political realities of sixteenth-century Germany is explored in the following chapters.

NOTES

1. This presentation on the basis of the common priesthood's biblical themes offers an alternative to those that follow a broadly systematic approach to Luther's teaching.
2. See Bornkamm, *Old Testament*, 104–109.
3. For a full study of Christ as King and Priest, see Karin Bornkamm, *Christus: König Und Priester: Das Amt Christi Bei Luther Im Verhältnis Zur Vor-Und Nachgeschichte*, Beiträge Zur Historischen Theologie, 106 (Tübingen: Mohr Siebeck, 1998). In her conclusions (301–303), Bornkamm summarizes how Luther used the twofold office of Christ—which is "communicated" to Christians through the word and faith—to express the unresolved tension of the Christian life in relation to God and the world, *simul justus et peccator*. Her concern is that separating Christ's "kingship" from his "priesthood" weakens that important insight. A question arises from passages examined here in this book as to whether Luther invariably portrays Christ as both king and priest; generally it seems to be the biblical context that determines whether he emphasizes one over the other, but obviously my focus has been on passages that emphasize "priesthood."
4. LW 11:369 (WA 4:234–235), *Dictata*, Psalm 110.
5. LW 29:168 (WA 57/3:165–166), *Hebrews* (5:1).
6. See, for example, LW 29:117 (WA 57/3:107). Here it is coupled with references to 1 Peter 2:9 and Exodus 19:5–6, "you shall be for me a priestly kingdom."
7. LW 39:80 (WA 6:305), *On the Papacy in Rome*; LW 31:389 (WA 7:171), *Why the Books of the Pope . . . were Burned by Dr. Martin Luther* (1520); see also LW 31:279–280 (WA 2:19), *Proceedings at Augsburg* (1518).
8. LW 35:100 (WA 6:369), *Treatise on the New Testament*.
9. LW 31:353 (WA 7:56), *The Freedom of a Christian*.
10. LW 36:138 (WA 8:486), *The Misuse of the Mass*.
11. LW 30:53–54 (WA 12:307–308), *Exposition of First Peter*.
12. LW 40:19 (WA 12:178–179), *Concerning the Ministry*.
13. LW 35:248 (WA DB 8:29–30), *Prefaces to the Old Testament*.
14. For the importance of these prefaces, see Maurice Schild, "Luther's Bible Prefaces and their Contemporary Significance" in *Luther@500 and Beyond*, 167–187.
15. Christopher Burger, "Luther's thought took shape in the translation of Scripture and Hymns," in OHMLT, 481–485. See also Lohse, *Introduction*, 112–119, discussing aspects of Luther's work of Bible translation.
16. 1 Peter 2:9, (Vulgate).
17. 1 Peter 2:9, (Greek text).
18. David Yeago rightly emphasises the corporate nature of the church in Luther's ecclesiology as a corrective to individualistic interpretations, but thereby loses Luther's undoubted focus on personal faith's "possession" of Christ's gifts to the church. David S. Yeago, "'A Christian, Holy People' Martin Luther on Salvation and the Church," *Modern Theology* 13, no. 1 (January 1997): 100–120.
19. LW 11:393 (WA 4:260), *Dictata* (Ps.114:2).
20. LW 11:356 (WA 4:224). Luther interprets Psalm 109 broadly, in the context of synagogue and church.

21. LW 29:117 (WA 57/3:107). *Hebrews*. "All the earth is mine, and you shall be to me a priestly kingdom, a holy nation" (Exodus 19:5–6).
22. LW 27:394 (WA 2:606) *Galatians* (1519).
23. LW 14:341 (WA 5:68), *Works on the First Twenty–Two Psalms* (1519–1521), Psalm 2.
24. WA Br 1:595, *Letter to Spalatin*. For an English translation, see Heinrich Boehmer, *Road to Reformation,* trans. John W. Doberstein and Theodore G. Tappert (Philadelphia: Muhlenberg Press, 1946), 301.
25. LW 44:127 (WA 6:407), *To the Christian Nobility*.
26. LW 36:113 (WA 6:56), *The Babylonian Captivity*.
27. See chapter 2 for the ecclesiological themes and the texts underpinning them.
28. LW 31:354 (WA 7:56–57), *The Freedom of a Christian*.
29. LW 39:152 (WA 7:628), *Answer to Emser*; see also LW 39:229 (WA 8:247), *Doctor Luther's Retraction* (1521).
30. LW 21:350 (WA 7:540), *The Magnificat.*
31. LW 39:279 (WA 10/2:140), *Against the Spiritual Estate of the Pope*.
32. LW 36:139 (WA 8:487–488), *Misuse of the Mass*.
33. LW 36:140 (WA 8:488).
34. LW 30:54 (WA 12:308), *Exposition of First Peter*.
35. LW 30:62 (WA 12:316).
36. LW 39:309 (WA 11:411–412), *The Right to Call*.
37. LW 40:19 (WA 12:178), *Concerning the Ministry*.
38. LW 40:20–1 (WA 12:179–180).
39. As suggested by Bernhard Lohse, *Theology*, 289–291, and implicit in Wengert's presentation.
40. LW 39:78–9 (WA 6:303), *On the Papacy in Rome*.
41. LW 35:100–1 (WA 6:370), *Treatise on the New Testament*.
42. LW 35:378 (WA DB 7:25), *Prefaces to the New Testament*.
43. See also LW 10:82 (WA 3:81), Psalm 8:2, where Aaron the priest is Moses' "mouth," i.e., a preacher (Exodus 4:16).
44. LW 10:293 (WA 3:347), *Dictata* (Psalm 60); LW 11:161 (WA 4:10), *Dictata* (Psalm 85).
45. LW 11:481 (WA 4:353), *Psalm 119*.
46. LW 29:198 (WA 57/3:198), *Hebrews* (8:8–12). Isaiah 54:13 is also quoted when Luther comments on Hebrews 6:8 (LW 29:183, WA 57/3:183).
47. LW 14:341 (WA 5:68), *Works on the First Twenty–Two Psalms* (1519–1521), Psalm 2.
48. LW 31:354 (WA 7:56), *The Freedom of a Christian*.
49. LW 36:139 (WA 8:486–487), *The Misuse of the Mass* (translation altered). John 6:45 is also quoted at LW 36:150 (WA 8:497).
50. LW 39:309 (WA 11:411), *The Right to Call*.
51. LW 44:134 (WA 6:411), *To the Christian Nobility*, and also 1 Cor.14:30 on order in the assembly.
52. LW 44:135 (WA 6:412), also citing 1 Corinthians 2:15 ("The spiritual person judges all things").

53. LW 61:55 (WA 10/2:217), *Against Henry the Eighth, King of England*.
54. LW 40:32 (WA 12:188), *Concerning the Ministry*.
55. See chapter 1 at nn68–72. Examples of Luther's use of Romans 12:1 from Psalms 50, 66, 81, and 84 are given.
56. For the most comprehensive study of Luther on sacrifice, see Carl Fredrik Wisloff, *The Gift of Communion: Luther's Controversy with Rome on Eucharistic Sacrifice*, trans. Joseph M. Shaw (Minneapolis: Augsburg, 1964), 73–97.
57. LW 29:175 (WA 57/3:174), *Hebrews* (5:7).
58. LW 35:100 (WA 6:369), *Treatise on the New Testament*.
59. LW 35:102 (WA 6:371). In *The Babylonian Captivity* (LW 36:83, WA 6:544), faith is "called forth" by Christ's words of institution to bring certainty to those who receive the sacrament that they have the forgiveness of sins.
60. LW 36:145–146 (WA 8:492–493), *Misuse of the Mass*.
61. LW 36:201 (WA 8:539).
62. LW 40:28–29 (WA 12:185), *Concerning the Ministry*.
63. LW 35:247 (WA DB 8:29–30), *Prefaces to the New Testament*.
64. LW 35:390 (WA DB 7:299).
65. LW 35:395 (WA DB 7:345).
66. See also LW 36:113 (WA 6:564), *The Babylonian Captivity*, where Luther argues that those who do not preach are no priests and, quoting Malachi 2:7, that ordination is a rite "by which the church chooses its preachers."
67. LW 35:22 (WA 2:722–23), *The Sacrament of Penance* (1519); see also LW 51:59 (WA 2:248), *A Sermon on the Festival of St. Peter and St. Paul by Doctor Martin Luther* (1519), on Matthew 16:13–19.
68. LW 44:127 (WA 6:407) *To the Christian Nobility*. He also adds texts from Romans 12 and 1 Peter 2.
69. LW 44:128 (WA 6:407).
70. LW 36:82 (WA 6:543), *The Babylonian Captivity*.
71. LW 36:82–3 (WA 6:543–544).
72. LW 36:116 (WA 6:566).
73. LW 31:356 (WA 7:58), *The Freedom of a Christian*.
74. E.g., LW 36:113 (WA 6:564), *The Babylonian Captivity*, positions in the church are "nothing but a ministry" (1 Corinthians 4:1).
75. LW 32:51–52 (WA 7:381–382), *Defence of All Articles*. Luther argues from Ephesians 4:5 that there is one baptism administered in the church, of equal benefit.
76. LW 32:57 (WA 7:391).
77. LW 39:154 (WA 7:630), *Answer to Emser's Book*.
78. LW 39:154 (WA 7:630).
79. LW 39:155 (WA 7:631).
80. LW 39:155 (WA 7:631).
81. LW 39:155–156 (WA 7:631). Luther conducts a similar discussion of "ministry" in LW 30:132–133 (WA 12:387), *Exposition of First Peter*. In WA 10/2:220–221, *Against Henry VIII, King of England*, Luther quotes Acts 6 (the election of the deacons), as an example of the people's common consent. For the proper designation(s) for the clergy, see also LW 40:35 (WA 12:190), *Concerning the Ministry*.

82. LW 36:148–149 (WA 8:495), *Misuse of the Mass*.

83. LW 36:151–152 (WA 8:497).

84. LW 30:54–55 (WA 12:308–309), *Exposition of First Peter*. See further references to women preachers in, for example, chapter 5, nn72–74.

85. LW 30:64–65 (WA 12:318–319).

86. LW 39:309–310 (WA 11:411–412), *The Right to Call*.

87. LW 39:310 (WA 11:412)

88. LW 39:310–311 (WA 11:412–413).

89. LW 40:21 (WA 12:180), *Concerning the Ministry*. This begins with the "first office . . . the ministry of the word," and the right (*ius*) and the command for all Christians to declare God's wonderful deeds given to them as royal priests in 1 Peter 2:9. Using the appropriate texts this is repeated for all seven offices.

90. LW 40:34 (WA 12:189) (translation altered). LW translates "*necessitate*" as emergency; for translating the German equivalent, "*not*," see chapter 6 (*On the Councils*) at n66, and also chapter 8 (*Sermons on John 20:19–31*), especially at n91.

91. LW 40:35–36 (WA 12:190–191).

92. See Schilling, *Martin Luther Rebel*, 357–364, for his discussion of how these reformatory changes were implemented in practice, including the developments in Leisnig and other Saxon towns. By the end of the decade the program of parish visitations was introduced under the direction of Elector John of Saxony, and Luther was producing his catechisms as handbooks for the teaching and preaching of the Christian faith.

Chapter 5

Luther's Ecclesiology and the Challenge of Reform, from 1524

Fathers and mothers are "family bishops" and in their homes they serve as we do, partners in the church's ministry.

—Martin Luther, *Sermon on the First Commandment*

This pivotal chapter introduces Luther's later ecclesiology in the context of reform from 1524–1525, and foreshadows the ways in which the common priesthood persisted as an essential component of his teaching (chapters 6 to 8). Necessarily, it has to consider his silence on this teaching in writings such as his catechisms, where it could be expected to feature strongly; it also takes account of the "negative evidence," the writings where Luther so emphasises the need for an evangelical preaching office that he can appear to discount what he had previously written about the common priesthood.

Despite these factors, Luther's creative synthesis of key biblical texts continued to support his teaching on the church, and the definitive texts for the common priesthood will be seen to underpin the discussion of that topic. The themes of unity, communion, and equality are apparent whenever Luther discusses the nature and purpose of the church, and—notwithstanding the difficulties caused by unauthorised preachers—Luther did not set aside an understanding of ministry that is true to his original vision for a participatory Christian community shaped by the word and faith, at the same time as it accommodates the emerging reality of a church led publicly by its pastors and preachers.[1]

THE CHURCH IN LUTHER'S CATECHETICAL AND CONFESSIONAL WRITINGS

In its essential core, Luther's ecclesiology did not change after the first stage of the Reformation. It continued to reveal his commitment to the church's inner spiritual identity, and his aims for its outward, ordered reality as well.[2] From the early expressions of the church as the people of God, gathered by the word, it did not change, essentially, despite the organisational needs of the emerging German churches, or because of the dangers posed by Rome's hold on hierarchical power, or in response to the teachings of other reformers. As Luther met these challenges he continued to define the church in terms of community in Christ at the same time as he worked to provide a solid foundation for the church's public ministry.[3]

The Catechisms

By 1528, it had become apparent that Luther's prayer books and published sermons needed to be augmented by a formal catechism which, together with sermonic studies, could be used for teaching and preaching.[4] For his teaching on the church, Luther continued to focus on the creedal statement, "I believe in the holy Christian church, the communion of saints." *The Small Catechism* emphasises its meaning for the individual, called by the Gospel and gathered by the Spirit, into the community where forgiveness reigns.[5] *The Large Catechism* emphasises the unity of that spiritual community, lifting the eyes of the faithful to a place above and beyond the everyday conflicts which afflicted the life of the organised church. In doing so, it also brought strongly back into view the themes that had shaped Luther's primary ecclesiological concerns:

> I believe that there is on earth a little holy flock or community (*ein heiliges heufflein und Gemeine*) of pure saints under one head, Christ. It is called together by the Holy Spirit in one faith, mind, and understanding. It possesses a variety of gifts, yet is united in love without sect or schism. Of this community I also am a part and member, a participant and co-partner in all the blessings it possesses. I was brought to it by the Holy Spirit and incorporated into it through the fact that I have heard and still hear God's Word, which is the first step in entering it.[6]

The work of the Spirit, unifying the community in faith and love, and giving equal participation in the gifts held in common, is central here. It is closely allied to the imperative for God's word to be heard and believed. Behind these words in the *Catechism* lies the influence of the key texts from 1 Corinthians, Romans, Galatians, and Ephesians, but Luther has now fully integrated them and does not quote them explicitly. His language in the catechetical writings clearly shows the persistence and interdependence of the four themes of unity and community, equality and participation.

In the first three parts of the *Large Catechism*, Luther includes surprisingly few biblical quotations, in comparison with most of his earlier writings.[7] Neither does he overtly discuss the common priesthood in relation to the church or its public ministry, although his approach to the nature of the community is entirely consistent with those themes. His presentation centres on the sanctifying work of the Spirit, and God's word, preached, believed, and lived. The catechism is itself at the forefront of Luther's reform agenda, that all Christians should know the basics of the faith, be able to apply the word of God in their daily lives, and to engage with the teaching of pastors who have themselves been called into the public office that requires them to learn and to teach that same word.[8]

The "Great Confession"

In the third part of Luther's *Confession concerning Christ's Supper*, also from 1528, the image of the church as the "bride of Christ" appears alongside of the terms expressive of the gathered community.[9] Again, there are no direct citations from Scripture. The focus is on Christ as head of the body, with "the bishops or priests" in subsidiary positions as the community's servants, or friends:

> Next, I believe that there is one holy Christian Church on earth, that is, the community [*die gemeine*] or number [*zahl*] or assembly [*versamlunge*] of all Christians in all the world, the one bride of Christ, and his spiritual body of which he is the only head. The bishops or priests are not her heads or lords or bridegrooms, but servants [*diener*], friends, and—as the word "bishop" implies—superintendents, guardians, or stewards.[10]

In the first parts of this *Confession*, Luther had continued to wrestle with exegetical issues around the presence of Christ in the Eucharist, in opposition to Zwingli and his fellow Swiss reformers.[11] The *Confession* was written at a time when Luther was still recovering from major health problems. "Part Three" is a summary of his teaching, beginning with the Apostles' Creed, and represents a kind of theological last will and testament. Bornkamm calls this "the most important and beautiful statement of its kind we have of him." Brecht states, "we can see very precisely in it what was the centre of the Christian faith for Luther."[12]

That this emphasis on the community of the church persisted in Luther's teaching is seen in a 1535 sermon on "The Great Supper" (Luke 14:16–17), where once again he challenges the separation of clergy and laity and condemns distinctions being made between Christians. Using the key texts with their rich imagery of unity in Christ, Luther makes a connection between the equal participation of Christians in the sacramental life of the church and their lives of mutual love and common care for one another.[13] He says,

> It should be in Christendom just like a bond, which binds the Christians most intimately together. They are just like one bread or one cake, not only because they together have one God, one Word, one Baptism, one Sacrament, one hope, and all the grace and benefits of Christ in common without any distinction, but also in their whole external life they are one body, since each member is to assist, serve, help, aid, sympathise, etc., with the other.[14]

The Smalcald Articles

Then, in the context of the ongoing struggle for ecclesiastical legitimacy by the German Lutheran territories, and in anticipation of the long-awaited General Council of the church, Luther produced the statement of faith that became known as the Smalcald Articles (1537).[15] Specifically, these articles present Luther's position on matters of controversy with the Roman church—revisiting issues such as penance, the mass, and the papacy—but also providing the overall framework for evangelical teaching in relation to the central article of God's promise of salvation in Christ, received by faith. As always in these situations, Luther's polemical edge is apparent in most articles, but his statement on the church characterised as God's flock is remarkable in its simple clarity. The emphasis is on the word, and faith, shared even by its youngest participants; these are the spiritual heart of the church, the basis for its holiness:

> [B]ecause, praise God, a seven-year-old child knows what the church is: holy believers and "the little sheep who hear the voice of their shepherd" [cf. John 10:3]. This is why children pray in this way, "I believe in one holy Christian church." This holiness does not consist of surplices, tonsures, long albs, or other ceremonies of theirs that they have invented over and above the Holy Scriptures. Its holiness exists in the Word of God and true faith.[16]

Luther's vision for the church is also apparent in his article on the papacy.[17] Not surprisingly, he maintains his rejection of the papal claims to rule the church "by divine right" and rehearses the arguments that had convinced him of its anti-Christian character. By his own standards the invective is mild. But (perhaps in view of the proposed council), he also offers his proposal for the church's governance, having rejected the need for the papal office in its present form, as well as its right to rule. Luther acknowledges that a democratically elected pope was an unlikely scenario, from any standpoint. He therefore returns to his core understanding and offers a biblical alternative for the church's rule in keeping with his ecclesiological principles:

> Therefore the church cannot be better ruled and preserved than if we all live under one head, Christ, and all the bishops—equal according to the office (although they may be unequal in their gifts)—keep diligently together in unity of teaching, faith, sacraments, prayers, and works of love, etc.[18]

While this is entirely speculative on Luther's part, it does show that he has thought through his opposition to the papacy and can still envisage the church ordered in a way that preserves its historical dimensions at the same time as it embraces a theologically coherent program for the reform of a corrupt and deficient hierarchy. The "marks" by which the church is recognised are clearly visible here, as the signs of unity that the bishops' office shares with the whole church. There are also echoes of the Pauline synthesis of texts, Luther's New Testament ecclesiology. Most certainly he is not seeking here to tear apart the church, but to build it up.

These summaries of Luther's later teaching on the church illustrate the consistency of teaching and the freedom of expression which characterises his ecclesiology. They show the best of Luther as a communicator and teacher, able to rise above the rhetoric of conflict that so easily surrounded this topic, to produce statements which combine theological depth and biblical fidelity, offering a lucid summary of what it meant to be *the community of saints* at that time.[19] They are written to counter the Roman concept of the church as a hierarchical institution, with its spirituality that stressed the performance of meritorious acts of devotion; at the same time, they also challenge the radical reformers who emphasised the religious experience of believers, and downplayed the necessity of the external word.

The common priesthood does not figure overtly in these summaries, but their contents are entirely consistent with the themes of Luther's teaching when he deals with church and priesthood together in other writings. Alongside the importance of the word is the equal status of those who stand together as Christians, under that word—including children. It is from this core understanding that Luther's inclusive descriptions of the church's community present its ministry in terms which leave in the background (or unidentified) those who publicly serve in that office. The work of the word is presented objectively because the church is the creation of God's Spirit and of the word itself, with Christ as head of his body, the church. Luther's presentation, therefore, counters papal claims to lordship over the church and the elevated spiritual status of its clergy, offering, instead, positive statements about the life of the whole Christian community in a context where the focus is on building that community rather than on the destructive forces which threaten to overwhelm it. Luther's later emphasis on the need for the public office(s) has not brought about a revision of his ecclesiology; indeed, to do so here would contradict his consistent understanding of the essential character of the church and its members.[20]

LUTHER'S REFORMS AS EXPRESSIONS OF THE COMMON PRIESTHOOD

That vital connection between the church's faith and its life was seen as Luther introduced specific reforms to benefit and build up the Christian community, by worship and education. The reforms stood alongside the establishment of the public ministry as a preaching office, and were supported by it. This can be seen as a practical outcome of Luther's teaching on the common priesthood, through which he worked to support and promote the full participation of the people of God in the life of the church. It is, however, necessary to note that Luther himself did not characterise this work as the implementation of the common priesthood in the church. More fundamentally, he describes it in the most basic terms of Christian identity, that "all who wish to be Christians in fact as well as name, both young and old, may be well trained in [the parts of the catechism] and familiar with them."[21]

While this work had begun in the early Reformation period, it came to fruition in the later years of the 1520s, and continued throughout Luther's career.[22] In these writings Luther seeks to engage the entire Christian community in the essential work of the church.[23] They include the publication of German translations of the Bible, with explanatory prefaces to each book, and marginal notes to the text;[24] collections of sermons to provide model expositions of the Gospel message;[25] prayer books and catechisms to build a culture of personal spirituality, and enable a unified approach to Christian education in the home and the school, alongside the church;[26] and the all-important work of the reform of worship, including the introduction of congregational liturgy and song, enabled the meaningful participation of all Christians in the church's worship and its sacramental life.[27]

In all of this, a Christian's responsibility for their own spiritual life—their priesthood—was still to be promoted, to stand alongside the church's ordained ministry rather than to supplant it. At this level of essential Christian teaching, Luther made no distinctions between laity and clergy, between levels of spiritual need, or achievement. The word is all; faith is all; and so is the ministry of mutual encouragement. But when Luther raised the possibility of a "truly evangelical [worship] order" for those who were serious about the gospel and their Christian faith, clearly the people were not ready.

It represents a moment of hard reality for Luther in regard to their common priesthood: "for we Germans are a rough, rude, and reckless people, with whom it is hard to do anything, except in cases of dire need."[28]

So Luther's high aims were not easily achieved, and progress in this work was hindered by the realities of the lack of education and the indifference of many to religion and faith other than through ritual observances. These natural boundaries to practical reform often frustrated Luther, and this may well be the reason why he never proposed a more thorough or formal program of church renewal with a more prominent role for the common priesthood.[29] However, as the *Catechisms* make clear, Luther saw teaching the Christian faith in the home as a particular duty for parents, one by which they fulfilled a role as "pastors and bishops" to their own families and households.[30] The significance that Luther gives here to the role of parents as part of the church's essential ministry of the word is seen by the way he aligns it with the "predigtamt." It was here in the home and family, therefore, that the "horizons" inherent in Luther's teaching were now to be found.[31]

EDUCATION, SCHOOLS, AND THE PUBLIC MINISTRY

The need for publicly funded schools was a necessary concern for Luther, related to the reformational needs highlighted in the previous section. In 1524, he had written *To the Councilmen of all Cities in Germany That They Establish and Maintain Christian Schools*.[32] In August 1530, he published *A Sermon on Keeping Children in School*, to encourage parents and to ensure that, with the abolition of the monasteries, education for service in the church and state should continue.[33] A key element was that Latin and the biblical languages should continue to be taught, so that the study and teaching of Scripture should not be compromised. Luther also argued that women should be equipped for the raising of children.[34]

However, already in 1524, some people were distorting Luther's teaching on the common priesthood, saying, "If the spiritual estate is no longer to be of any account, we can just as well let education go and not bother our heads about it."[35] But that was opposite to his intention, and he labours the point at some length. Without educated pastors, teachers, and parents the work of reformation would fall to the ground, and he expressed frustration at the slow progress being made. This lack of pastors—and the reluctance of the people to accept their own need for growth in Christian faith and understanding—means that Luther promotes education as God's work, and upholds the importance of the public ministry, and the need to support it. This involved a broad perspective on that work, backed by Scripture. In 1530 he writes,

> The spiritual estate [*Der geistliche stand*] has been established and instituted by God, not with gold or silver but with the precious blood and bitter death of his only Son, our Lord Jesus Christ [this is not the spiritual estate of the celibate clergy]. . . . The estate I am thinking of is rather one which has the office of preaching and the service of the word and sacraments and which imparts the Spirit and salvation, blessings that cannot be attained by any amount of pomp and pageantry. It includes the work of pastors, teachers, preachers, lectors, priests (those called chaplains), sacristans, schoolteachers, and whatever other work belongs to these offices [*solchen emptern*] and persons. This estate the Scriptures highly exalt and praise.[36]

Luther maintains an inclusive view of the church here, even while emphasising the particular need for preachers and other church workers in their offices. The use of the term "spiritual estate" is notable and could represent a shift in his thinking—or at least an accommodation to an established expression—beyond that of the Reformation treatises.[37] He uses no particular biblical text here, or theological argumentation, to support God's institution of this "estate."[38] But this corporate spiritual activity is still tied to the word and faith, and depends on Christ's work, who promises in John 14:12, "He who believes in me will also do the works that I do; and greater works than these will he do." To this Luther adds,

> If the single believer can accomplish these things working independently with individuals, how much more will the preacher accomplish working publicly with the whole company of people? It is not the individual, though, that does it. It is their office, ordained by God for this purpose. That is what does it—that and the word of God which is taught. The preacher is only the instrument through which it is accomplished.[39]

Luther's energetic argument for the education of the clergy, for their vital office and service, adds a significant dimension to his earlier statements regarding the equality of all Christians, and their participation in the work of God's word. It is important to consider the context of his words, and the rhetoric which advances a cause in which he passionately believes, and to which he has dedicated his life. While Luther certainly prioritises public ministry over the cause of the common priesthood at this time, a careful reading reveals that Luther has not moved beyond his core convictions. The "single believer" already serves the ministry of the word, broadly understood, in addition to the essential work of those called to a public office. There is both a community emphasis and individual participation in the tasks of ministry being considered here. While there is—over all—a unitary "service of the word and sacraments," its work is fulfilled by numerous "offices and persons," which includes the offices of pastors and preachers, and also requires parents and teachers who will prepare their children for this kind of service.[40]

THE NEED FOR REFORM AND RESPONDING TO THE RADICAL CHALLENGE

As Luther continued the work of reform and tackled the needs of the emerging evangelical congregations, two related issues came to the fore. To respond to those who challenged the reformational teachings, he emphasised more strongly the church's dependence on the word and the need to supply parishes with pastors. Even before the mid-1520s, he focused on the essential role of those called to the preaching office, those whose ministry is the public face of the gospel in the life of the church. But events surrounding the Peasants' War (1524–1525) reinforced for Luther the need for this emphasis, as did his ongoing debates with those who promoted a more radical approach to the work of reformation.[41] And then, in connection with the gathering at Augsburg in 1530, he returned to the defense of evangelical teaching in the face of continuing opposition from Rome, and the imperial authority of Charles V. This defense included his understanding of the common priesthood. Here, when writing against unauthorised preachers, the teaching on the common priesthood does not figure universally, but its background in his understanding of spiritual equality and participation is still apparent in much of what he writes.

In terms of his ecclesiology, in relation to the radical reformers, Luther's concern is to maintain order in the church, responding to what amounts to an "emergency situation" by upholding the need for a properly called public preaching office (*predigtamt*) and good order in the church (1 Corinthians 14:40). Addressing Rome, his concern continues to be for the nature of the church itself, to defend an inclusive, biblical view of the church as the people of God and the body of Christ among whom the gifts of God are freely shared, over against the authority and status claimed for those ordained to an exclusive "spiritual estate."

Luther's Response to the Twelve Articles of the Peasants

The Twelve Articles of the Peasants (1525) claim the "right to call pastors" and freedom from serfdom and tithes, under the gospel.[42] In his initial reply (*The Admonition to Peace*[43]), Luther concedes the justice of many of the peasants' demands, but only if these matters proceed on a truly Christian basis.[44] He admonishes the princes for fostering the circumstances in which these grievances have come to the fore.[45] But responding to the peasants' text, Luther has a number of concerns. He notes that their use of Scripture is often of doubtful relevance: Luther does not dispute the need for preachers, but 1 Timothy 3, for example, teaches about the public ministry, not about a general right to call.[46] Further, says Luther, appointments have to follow orderly procedures, which include the financial realities of a particular situation. The peasants' tithes cannot legitimately be withheld for this purpose.[47] More seriously, their demand for social equality is a misuse of the gospel, which only teaches spiritual freedom.[48]

Neither the Twelve Articles themselves, nor Luther's response, mention his teaching on the common priesthood, even though it certainly lies in the background to this situation.[49] In Luther's less restrained follow-up writing, *Against the Robbing and Murderous Hordes of Peasants* (1525),[50] he takes the peasants to task again for false arguments on Christian freedom. According to Luther they have misunderstood the first chapters of Genesis, and also the teachings of Jesus and Paul on baptism and submission to earthly authorities: "for baptism does not make us free in body and property, but in soul; and the gospel does not make goods common."[51] In this catastrophic situation, Luther was forced to clarify and even reframe his teaching in its social setting, even though he risks losing the support of many through so doing. Part of that reframing involved placing boundaries on the application of the rights of the common priesthood.

Luther's commitment to an ordered ministry of both pastors and congregations is now seen consistently in the writings of this period and beyond.[52] The *Instructions for the Visitors* (1528) has this as its specific concern,[53] and his *Confession Concerning Christ's Supper* of 1528 reflects Luther's view of God-ordained structures in society, the "holy orders" of ministry (church), marriage, and government. Together, they exist under "the common order of Christian love."[54]

Lectures on Paul's Letter to Titus

This lecture series, delivered in late 1527, shows how Luther was now teaching his students in Wittenberg about the biblical underpinnings for the church order that was being introduced into the Saxon territories.[55] Martin Brecht illustrates the situation at this time with an account of the problems caused by the apocalyptic preaching of Melchior Hoffman, a lay preacher who had received some training from Luther and Melanchthon, but then travelled widely preaching wherever he could.[56] In the lectures, Luther repeats his original formula ("though all are priests, not all are pastors") and still presents the basis for the common priesthood from 1 Peter 2:5–9, and from Isaiah 54:13 ("they shall all be taught by the Lord"). The office of priests is to "teach, pray, and to sacrifice." But he repeats, while "all have a priesthood . . . not all have the priestly function." Luther uses Paul's instructions to Titus to describe the orderly appointment of elders and bishops, and how they supervised the preaching of the word and the spiritual life of the congregations. But, says Luther, "this apostolic type of episcopacy has long since been done away with," and he describes the New Testament form for ordination, with the laying on of hands by the gathered elders themselves.[57] Early the next year (1528), Luther followed up with similar lectures on the First Letter to Timothy, as the work of congregational reorganization continued and preparations were made for the parish visitations.[58]

Psalm 82: "The Christian Prince"

In his exposition of Psalm 82, probably completed in April 1530 before leaving Wittenberg for Augsburg, Luther addressed the rulers regarding their obligation to act against those who usurped the preaching office for themselves.[59] The secular and spiritual estates may be distinct spheres, but both exist under God's ordinance, and share a mutual responsibility. In an emergency, the government (as "gods," Psalm 82:1,6) had the command to protect society from false teachers and to provide for the support of the public ministry.[60] In addition, the psalm also teaches the duty to care for the needy and to maintain peace (verses 3,4).[61] He also maintains a positive view of a world in which human life can flourish, if those who seek its harm are restrained. He writes, '[s]uch communities are God's work, which He daily creates, supports, and increases, so that they can sit at home and beget children and educate them." This kind of statement goes some way to counter an evaluation of Luther as a spiritual pessimist, who regards humanity as lost in sin and incapable of worthwhile achievements on any level.[62]

As an example of the "darkness" that invades ordered society (Psalm 82:5), Luther notes how both Müntzer and Karlstadt had neither the call nor the command to "sneak and creep into other . . . parishes." The apostles had this general call, from Christ himself (Mark 16:15), but now, directed by texts such as 1 Peter 5:3 and Titus 1:5, every bishop or pastor has their own allotted "part." Luther makes a connection here to the Greek, *klerous*, from which the term clergy is derived. This rule, he says, also includes preaching without consent to the people of a "papistic or heretical pastor."[63] Then, Luther offers some clarification on the common priesthood. It cannot be used to pre-empt the pastoral office, in these parish situations:

> It does not help their case to say that all Christians are priests [*Priester*]. It is true that all Christians are priests, but not all are pastors [*Pfarrer*]. For to be a pastor one must be not only a Christian and a priest but must have an office [*ampt*] and

a field of work [*kirchspiel*] committed to them. This call and command make pastors and preachers [*Prediger*]. A burgher or layperson may be learned; but this does not make them a lecturer [*Doctor*] and entitled to teach publicly in the schools or to assume such offices, unless they are called to it.[64]

Two points can be made here. First, Luther uses ostensibly secular offices as a comparison to clarify the role of pastor and preacher. In everyday terms, the pastoral office reflects the ordering that pertains in society at-large. Any office requires individual competence, and a "call," that is, appointment to its particular duties. Luther does not quote Scripture here for the "call and command," and neither does he pursue broader issues of vocation or calling. Nor does he in this case further elevate the office of preaching, although that could perhaps be implied from his presentation. Elsewhere, it is the "highest office."[65] But, secondly, Luther's words here ground this office in the church: it is for those who are already "Christian[s] and priest[s]." Even when (as here) Luther needs to promote the office, he does not forget to emphasise what is shared by all in the church, their spiritual identity and competence. The implicit formula ("all are priests"—"but not all are pastors") represents his consistent teaching from the beginning of the Reformation, and he continues to apply it here.[66]

Infiltrating and Clandestine Preachers

This "emergency" did not disappear, and Luther addresses it yet more vigorously in *Infiltrating and Clandestine Preachers* (1532).[67] He argues that a call or commission is required to hold a public office, in this case the office of the ministry, and in its absence those who claim the right to speak should be enjoined to silence.[68] Here Luther revisits 1 Corinthians 14:29–33, which just a few years earlier he had interpreted as allowing wide freedoms to speak in the Christian assembly.[69] Paul refers, he now says, to "the prophets, who are to teach, not [to] the people, who are to listen."[70] Interlopers (*die Schleicher*) cannot be allowed to steal the preacher's office, and neither can any layperson who "wants to, get up in church and preach." 1 Corinthians 14:40 ("let all things be done decently and in order") provides the governing principle here.[71]

As an example, Luther acknowledges the ministry of women prophets in the Old Testament (e.g., Deborah) and Philip's daughters in the New Testament (Acts 21:9).[72] His point is that here also a call from God must have been involved, else their work would not have been blessed. In other places, Luther cited the apostolic injunctions for women to be silent (1 Cor. 14:34; 1 Timothy 2:12);[73] here he adds them almost as an aside, while still affirming women's right to participate in worship, and to minister to one another with the Scriptures.[74] Likewise, in this work the role of the laity (*Leien*) in the congregation (*Gemeine*) is firmly delineated from that of the preachers (*Predigers*), once more using his revised interpretation of 1 Corinthians 14 (:4,12,16) to make that distinction.[75] In line with this, there is no reference here to the common priesthood, not even with the caveat that "not all are pastors."

If *Infiltrating and Clandestine Preachers* and Psalm 82 represented the final word from Luther's teaching on church and ministry, the conclusion would be that an irreversible change had taken place in the course of the ten years from his early Reformation treatises. The ideals of the common priesthood—still present in the *Lectures on Titus*—recede from view in these works, as Luther wrestles with an emergency that might be said to be of his own making, the confusion and disruption caused by those who claimed the right of their own inner conviction as a call to speak God's word to any church gathering. However, *Infiltrating and Clandestine Preachers* addresses the specifics of a particular situation and it does not stand alone as the definitive word of Luther on this topic even at this time. Once again it can be noted that Luther does not discuss these challenges in terms of his understanding of the church, in marked contrast to his approach when debating his Catholic opponents and as will be seen in a work such as *The Private Mass and the Consecration of Priests* (1532).[76] It is these additional factors that Hans-Martin Barth and others appear to ignore when he writes that Luther effectively abandoned the common priesthood in these writings, effectively a missed opportunity for the reformation.[77]

The Common Priesthood in a Time of Reform

In this transitional period, Luther worked to embed the insight that God's word is at the very heart of the life of the church, teaching that the commission to teach and preach is given by Christ himself and mediated in various ways through the community of believers—including now the important opportunities for teaching in the home and family, and the reform of worship and the publication of the German Bible. These are practical manifestations of the common priesthood, even when not named as such. The concepts of "office" and "call" are important for Luther, as he considers the need for the education and orderly appointment of pastors, preachers, teachers (and others) to the church's public ministry. The ways in which this is done can vary from place to place. This process can also be seen in the outcomes of disputes with colleagues like Karlstadt, the peasants and other "spiritual" reformers, leading to the writing of, for example, *Infiltrating Preachers*, and the exposition of Psalm 82 in 1530. These works reflect the "emergency situation" to be countered by upholding the need for a credible and viable public ministry for the church, rather than the more thoroughgoing ecclesiology of the disputes with Rome over the nature of the church itself.

But Luther's developing ecclesiology is confirmed in other more measured writings as well his polemical works. *The Large Catechism* and *The Smalcald Articles* teach that with Christ as its head the church is a spiritual communion, a community of word and faith that is not tied to specific persons, a time or a place, or to any institutional form. Rather than a destructive oversimplification of the church's essential structures, Luther's reforms of worship and education have become the way in which his biblical insights into the true nature of the church allow it to be rebuilt on the foundations of the word and faith. However, the social and political circumstances of the times in which Luther lived and worked as a reforming theologian imposed their own restrictions upon the outcomes of his work and the extent of his reforms. Social and religious upheaval, together with a base-level lack of education and literacy were factors that meant that his vision for the common priesthood was constrained within the boundaries of these realities.

Considering all the circumstances, it is perhaps remarkable that while Luther reinforces the boundaries around appointment to the public ministry of called preachers and omits discussion of the common priesthood in several key writings, he did not abandon the teaching at this time. It is also true that he does not present a full theological rationale for the public office of the ministry in, for example, his catechisms or confessional writings; it is simply assumed as a "given" in the ordered life of the church. And it is worth noting that Luther allowed collections of his works to be published in these later years, and these always included the writings in which his teaching on priesthood and ministry had earlier been presented.[78] And—as will be shown—in these years Luther continued to lecture, to produce new writings and to preach sermons in which the message of the common priesthood of all Christians sounded clearly alongside of the necessity for a public ministry. For Luther, "the word" was the only God-given vehicle for building and preserving the church, and the choices he and his colleagues made in establishing the preaching ministry reflect that conviction.

NOTES

1. See Lohse, *Theology*, 291: "In later years Luther spoke less often and in less pronounced fashion of the universal priesthood." David Daniel says that in "phase four" from 1526–1530 events "moved Luther to prioritise good order, and regularise appointment to ministry" (OHMLT, 343–344). While Luther's arguments for the ordered preaching office suggest movement back towards an institutional view of the church, initially (at least) this was his reaction to challenges to "good order" in

the church from unauthorised preachers. As with the lack of evangelical bishops, this crisis of ministry represented an "emergency situation." That is the context for the persistence of the common priesthood alongside a necessary emphasis on the church's public offices (*predigtamt; pfarramt*). The full picture is revealed in chapters 6 to 8.

2. Dorothea Wendebourg notes that Luther consistently states that the church "is the communion of those who hear the gospel and believe in it" (OHE 219). Bernhard Lohse also summarises Luther's ecclesiology in terms of "the unconditional preeminence of the Word and the definition of the church as the fellowship of those who hear it" (*Theology*, 278). This is also the theme of Heinrich Bornkamm's great essay entitled "What is the church?" written in the aftermath of the Second World War, in *Luther's World of Thought*, trans. Eric W. and Ruth C. Gritsch (St Louis: Concordia, 1958), 134–155.

3. Daniel (see n1) concludes by stating that is Luther's understanding of the church's "Christological nature and kerygmatic task" (OHMLT 347). This is correct, because Luther's Christology is the basis for the church's unity and communion, its commission to preach the gospel, and the equality of its members as well.

4. In his preface to the *Small Catechism* (1528) Luther reflects on the ignorance of "ordinary person[s]" and pastors who were "completely unskilled and incompetent teachers" (BOC 347). These are the social realities that led Luther to prioritise the establishment of a competent preaching ministry to safeguard the progress of the Reformation.

5. BOC 355–356, *Small Catechism*.

6. BOC 437–438, *Large Catechism*.

7. No discussion of this has been found in the literature, but it appears to be the case in many of Luther's later writings.

8. See the exhortatory preface to *The Large Catechism* (BOC 379–383) where Luther urges pastors and preachers—now freed from less profitable spiritual duties—to take seriously their need and responsibility to learn and teach the basics of the Christian faith presented in the catechisms.

9. See chapter 1, on Luther's early use of relational imagery in his descriptions of the church (*The Church as the People of God and the Body of Christ*).

10. LW 37:367 (WA 26:506). Luther's *Confession* of 1528 and other articles of faith produced by the Wittenberg theologians in 1529 (e.g., *The Schwabach Articles*, 1529) were forerunners of *The Augsburg Confession*, composed by Melanchthon. Luther's influence is seen throughout, including its statement that the church is "the assembly of believers among whom the Gospel is preached in its purity and the holy sacraments are administered according to the Gospel" (BOC 42, article seven). For the background documents, see Robert Kolb and James Arne Nestigen, eds., *Sources and Contexts for the Book of Concord* (Minneapolis: Augsburg, 2001).

11. See Brecht, *Luther* 2, 293–339; Bornkamm, *Luther in Mid-Career*, 501–551.

12. Bornkamm, *Mid-Career*, 549–551; Brecht, *Luther* 2:320–322.

13. Compare the sermon on *The Blessed Sacrament* (1519), chapter 2 at nn21–23.

14. *Sermon on Luke 14:16–17*; first version in WA 41:281 (1535); revisions in LW 78:82 (WA 22:19), Cruciger's edition of the *Church Postil*, 1544.

15. See BOC 295–296 for a brief introduction to the *Smalcald Articles*; also Brecht, *Luther* 3:178–185.

16. BOC 324–325.

17. BOC 307–309 (*Smalcald Articles*, part two, article four).

18. BOC 308. For these statements on evangelical church order examined in a modern context, and as an encouraging example of "receptive ecumenism," see *The Petrine Ministry in a New Situation* (Adelaide: Lutheran-Roman Catholic Dialogue in Australia, 2016), 31–33. For a study of the role of bishops, see *The Ministry of Oversight* (Adelaide: Lutheran-Roman Catholic Dialogue in Australia, 2007). See also *Pastor and Priest* (Adelaide: Australian Lutheran-Roman Catholic Dialogue, 1990). As a current member of the Lutheran dialogue team, I was involved in the preparation of the reports on Petrine Ministry and Oversight.

19. For other summaries of Luther's word-focused ecclesiology, in addition to nn1–3 above, see Veli-Matti Kärkkäinen, *An Introduction to Ecclesiology,* Second edition, 43–46; Cheryl Peterson, *Who is the Church?* 38–41.

20. In response to the criticism that Luther's reforms were a destructive oversimplification of the church's divinely instituted character, Luther's confession of the church as "the community of saints" grounded in the word and faith stands as the evidence for the coherence and viability of his ecclesiological vision—and as the basis on which those reforms were implemented. An added dimension is, for example, his vision for the church and its bishops in the *Smalcald Articles*, which offers an alternative to the papacy with a biblical basis and historical integrity. For a Roman Catholic perspective, see Yves Congar in chapter 3 n24, and below n62.

21. BOC 383–384, *The Large Catechism* (preface). This included the ability to judge teaching, "a task traditionally only assigned to hierarchical church structures." Mary Jane Haemig, "Catechisms" (DLLT, 130–131). Also Haemig, "Recovery Not Rejection: Luther's Appropriation of the Catechism," *Concordia Journal* 43, no. 1–2 (2017): 43–58.

22. Brecht, *Luther* 2:273–280. Lyndal Roper characterises this as Luther's work of "consolidation." She says that Luther had "tacitly abandoned the project of reforming *the* Church. Instead he began to create a church of his own." *Martin Luther Renegade*, 343–344. She sees this happening either side of the Diet of Augsburg (1530), together with Luther's vexed relationships with other reformers. Heinz Schilling provides further social and political perspectives on this activity, *Martin Luther Rebel*, 364–384.

23. See, e.g., the way in which Luther's *Baptismal Booklet* (1526) encourages participation in the rite and earnest prayer for the spiritual well-being of children presented for baptism. He concludes, "For baptism is our only comfort and the doorway to all of God's possessions and to the communion of all the saints," BOC 371–373.

24. Bornkamm, *Luther in Mid–Career*, 79–87; Brecht, *Luther* 2:46–56 and *Luther* 3:95–107.

25. See Brecht, *Luther* 3:251 for the later publication of Luther's sermons; also chapter 8, *The Church Postil*.

26. Carter Lindberg, "Piety, Prayer, and Worship in Luther's View of Daily Life," OHMLT, 414–426. Lindberg gives publishing statistics for prayer books; Mary Jane Haemig, "The Influence of the Genres of Exegetical Instruction, Preaching, and

Catechesis on Luther," OHMLT, 458: "The catechism . . . introduced laity to the Bible, and it provided laity with what they needed to exercise the priestly task." See also Brecht, *Luther* 2:273–280.

27. Bornkamm, *Mid-Career*, 475: Luther's reform of the mass was "an end to silencing the people in favour of the priest and choir." See Brecht, *Luther* 2: 129–135 (German Hymns) and 251–259 (Shaping the Worship Service). Scott Hendrix weaves the importance of music for Luther into the attempts to spread the reformation beyond Wittenberg and its immediate surrounds, including writing the catechisms and the church visitation program. *Martin Luther Visionary*, 191–202.

28. LW 53:63 (WA 19:75), *The German Mass*, 1526. See Brecht, *Luther* 2:255.

29. For Luther's ongoing frustrations with the Wittenberg congregation, see Brecht, *Luther* 2:288–292, 433–439, *Luther* 3:11–17, 249–262.

30. "Every father of a family is a bishop in his house and the wife a bishopess . . . in your homes help us to carry on the ministry [*das predigtampt treiben*] as we do in church" LW 51:137 (WA 30/1:58), *Sermon on the First Commandment*, 1528). See further comments in chapter 8, *Sermons on John 14–16* at nn56–57.

31. See Timothy J. Wengert, *Martin Luther's Catechisms: Forming the Faith* (Minneapolis: Fortress Press, 2009), 16–20; John T. Pless, *Luther's Small Catechism: A Manual for Discipleship* (Saint Louis: Concordia Publishing House, 2019), 1–16. See also the references below, at n54. However, neither Wengert nor Pless explore the "ministerial" implications and connections for educating Christians. Pless includes a worthy account of the "royal priesthood" in relation to the use of the catechism in daily life, 171–195. However, he states that Luther "removed sacrifice from the sanctuary and relocated it the world" (181), which ignores Luther's strong identification of sacrifice with the work of the word in worship, through the "sacrifice of praise and confession" (see chapter 7, *Minor Prophets* at nn20–23 (*Malachi*), 28–30 (*Zechariah*) and especially *Isaiah 40–66* at nn37 and 43). Pless also places the priesthood so firmly under the oversight and teaching authority of "the Pastoral Office" (185) that there seems to be little room here for an educated laity's involvement in the ministry of the word, as Luther's reforms envisaged in potential at least (see also the previous note on the home setting).

32. LW 45:339–378 (WA 15:9–53) *To the Councilors . . . That They Establish Christian Schools*. See Brecht, *Luther* 2:139–141.

33. LW 46:207–258 (WA 30/2:517–88), *On Keeping Children in School*. See Brecht, *Luther* 2:381–382. This work was reprinted in 1541 with a new preface. See also Thomas Kothmann, "Luther as Educator: His Vision of Teaching and Learning and Its Significance Today," in *Luther @500 and Beyond*, 221–250.

34. See Karant-Nunn and Wiesner-Hanks eds., *Luther on Women*, 9–10. Luther argued for women's access to education to equip them for household management and the training of children, despite his sharing common opinions that devalued women's intellectual abilities. Hans-Martin Barth explores the ambiguous nature of Luther's views, *Martin Luther*, 290–291.

35. LW 45:349 (WA 15:29), *To the Councilors*.

36. LW 46:219–220 (WA 30/2:526–528), *On Keeping Children in School*.

37. LW 44:127 (WA 6:407), *The Babylonian Captivity*, "All Christians are truly of the spiritual estate [*geistlichs stands*]."

38. For Luther's view of the three estates—the "holy orders" of church, family, and society—see, for example, *The Great Confession*, at n54 below.

39. LW 46:224 (WA 30/2:534), *On Keeping Children in School* (translation modified).

40. Note that *On the Councils and the Church* refers to the church's "offices" [*empter*] rather than a single office, (LW 41:154, WA 50:632).

41. For extended analysis of this complex period, see Bornkamm, *Mid-Career*, 355–399; Brecht, *Luther* 2,172–194.

42. English text: LW 46:8–16, *The Twelve Articles*. German text of *Zwölf Artikel der Bauernschaft* accessed 15 April 2021, Stadtarchiv Memmingen: https://stadtarchiv.memmingen.de/quellen/vor-1552/12-artikel-1525.html.

43. LW 46:17–43 (WA 18:291–334).

44. LW 46:17–19 (WA 18:291–293).

45. LW 46:19–23 (WA 18:293–299).

46. LW 46:37–38 (WA 18:325), on the peasants' *First Article*.

47. LW 46:38 (WA 18:325–326), *Second Article*.

48. LW 46:39 (WA 18:326–327).

49. *That a Christian Congregation . . . Has the Right to Call* (1523) can be seen as a basis for the peasants' demand for the right to appoint pastors (see chapter 3, "Seven Further Witnesses").

50. LW 46:49–55 (WA 18:357–361), *Against the Robbing and Murderous Hordes*.

51. LW 46:51 (WA 18:358–359).

52. See n1 for more on the "ordering" of the church.

53. See the preface, LW 40:269–273 (WA 26:195–201), *Instructions for the Visitors*; also Bornkamm, *Mid-Career*, 481–500. Heinz Schilling (*Martin Luther*, 364–370) describes the negotiations for the visitation in some detail, questioning why Luther chose to "invest so completely in the secular authorities . . . why did he not favor an episcopal constitution, why would have given the Saxon church far greater independence"? The answer presumably lies in the political realities of the day, and perhaps also in the personal support Luther had received from those same rulers.

54. LW 37:364–365 (WA 26:504–505), Luther's "Great Confession" (1528). See Brecht 2321. In *The Large Catechism* (1529), Luther writes of "fathers by blood, fathers of a household, and fathers of the nation . . . also spiritual fathers" (BOC 408). For an attempt to make this the basis for Luther's teaching on public ministry, see David Jay Webber, *Spiritual Fathers*, second edition (Phoenix: Klotsche-Little Publishing, 2015).

55. LW 29:3–90 (WA 25:6–69), *Lectures on Titus* (1527). Unpublished during Luther's lifetime, these lectures were delivered during an outbreak of plague in Wittenberg and his own increasing health problems (Brecht 2210).

56. Brecht 2315–317. Hoffman's prophecies supported a radical Anabaptist agenda, and were still current well into the 1530s, Lyndal Roper *Martin Luther Renegade*, 348–349.

57. LW 29:15–16 (WA 25:16–17) *Lectures on Titus*.

58. Brecht 2248–249. Scott Hendrix weaves together an account of these years and their many challenges for Luther, his colleagues and their families, around a description of the implementation of the parish visitation program, *Martin Luther Visionary*, 173–190.

59. LW 13:39–72 (WA 31/1:189–218) Psalm 82 (1530). See Brecht, *Luther* 2:344. For other expositions of the psalms by Luther during this period, see chapter 7 below, *The Psalms Revisited*.

60. LW 13:44 (WA 31/1:192).

61. LW 13:58 (WA 31/1:205). Luther connects "Ritter" (Knight) with "retten" (to rescue).

62. LW 13:47 (WA 31/1:194). The Catholic reformer, Yves Congar, wrote that Luther's pessimistic view of human nature and society negatively influenced his principle of interpretation, and his view of life in the church, *Martin Luther, Sa Foi, Sa Reforme*, 67–68 and 75. See also n20 above, and chapter 3 n24. For a balanced assessment of Congar's view of Luther, see Joseph Famerée, "Yves Congar, lecteur de Luther," *En 500 Après Martin Luther. Reception et conflits d'interpretation (1517–2017)*, ed. Stéphane-Marie Morgain (Turnhout: Brepols Publishers, 2018), 189–201.

63. LW 13:64 (WA 31/1:210–211).

64. LW 13:65 (WA 31/1:211), (translation modified).

65. See, for example, LW 46:221 (WA 30/2:529), *Keeping Children in School*.

66. See, for example, LW 36:117 (WA 6:564), *The Babylonian Captivity*.

67. LW 40:379–394 (WA 30/3:510–527), *Infiltrating Preachers*.

68. LW 40:386 (WA 30/3:521).

69. See *Concerning the Ministry* (1523), where Luther uses this passage as part of his argument that all Christians have the responsibility to see that the "highest office"—the ministry of the word—is fulfilled in the church, LW 40:22–23 (WA 12:181); LW 40:32–33 (WA 12:188); LW 40:37–38 (WA 12:191–192).

70. LW 40:388 (WA 30/3:522), *Infiltrating Preachers*.

71. Luther here deals with 1 Corinthians 14 at some length, concluding that what was applicable in apostolic times was no longer appropriate in his own context, LW 40:388–393 (WA 30/3:522–527) *Infiltrating Preachers*. For 1 Corinthians 14:40 see LW 40:390 (WA 30/3:524,1–9).

72. LW 40:390 (WA 30/3:524).

73. For Luther's conflicted views on women preachers in the church, see, for example, chapter 4 (at nn83,84), *Misuse of the Mass* and *Exposition of First Peter*; chapter 6 (at nn66–68), *On the Councils and the Church*.

74. LW 40:390–391 (WA 30/3:524). Luther also notes that Joel 2:28–29 had foretold the ministry of women.

75. LW 40:391 (WA 30/3:524).

76. Cheryl Peterson provides this helpful summary: "In his later years Luther does not abandon th[e] concept of the church as a spiritual community, even as he finds himself increasingly defending order and structure against the spiritualists' attacks" (DLLT, 146–147).

77. Barth, *Martin Luther*, 301–302.

78. For example, the first volume of Luther's collected German writings published in 1539 (Brecht, *Luther* 3:142) began with the *Exposition of First Peter* (1522), with its detailed treatment of 1 Peter 2:9, "you are a royal priesthood" (etc.). The collected Latin writings (1545–1546) include all the early reformational treatises, and *Concerning the Ministry* (1523) with its advocacy of the common priesthood standing alongside of the public ministry. For Luther's *Prefaces* to these collected works see LW 34:283–288 (WA 50:657–661), *German Writings* and LW 34:327–338 (WA 54:179–187), *Latin Writings*.

Chapter 6

The Response to Rome: Next Instalment

> *We have been born of this bridegroom* [Christ] *and bride* [the church] *through holy baptism and thus have become true clerics in Christendom in a hereditary manner, sanctified by his blood and consecrated by his Holy Spirit.*
>
> —Martin Luther, *The Private Mass and The Consecration of Priests*

In relation to the radical reformers, Luther's concern was to prevent disruption to worship and teaching in the local churches under his care, responding to what he experienced as an emergency situation for those churches. This confirmed the establishment of an authorised public preaching office, with its biblical basis in Paul's call for good order (1 Corinthians 14:40). But addressing Rome—and the ongoing disputes of the original Reformation conflict—his concern was for the nature of the church itself, to defend an inclusive, biblical view of the church as the people of God and the body of Christ among whom the gifts of God are freely shared, over against the authority and status claimed for those ordained to an exclusive "spiritual estate." The imperial diet at Augsburg in 1530 showed that this debate would not be easily won, and that the vision for Rome's reform remained a fond hope rather than an emerging reality. The seven works in this chapter were written to address that situation, as Luther vigorously defends evangelical teaching at the same time as he continues his attack on Rome's errors. It is here that the common priesthood continues to play an important role, albeit one that is not recognised to any degree by the majority of Luther's interpreters.

EXHORTATION TO ALL CLERGY ASSEMBLED AT AUGSBURG

In May 1530, Luther, who had been excluded from the gathering at Augsburg from political necessity and for his own safety, nevertheless presented his own reform agenda in an *Exhortation to All Clergy Assembled at Augsburg*.[1] The exhortation is addressed to "all clergy" (*die ganze Geistlichkeit*), but he writes primarily to the Catholic bishops at the diet. He sees the need for an agreed settlement for the benefit of the church in order to resist the rise of the fanatics. The need for reform had been acknowledged by many on the side of Rome. But the central topics of confession, absolution, and the ban (excommunication) had not been addressed, and neither had disputes over clerical marriage and the mass. These abuses skew the public ministry of the church into a completely false direction. As with private masses, the gift of God is turned into a commodity to be bought and sold or, at best, to be earned and achieved. Luther defends himself against the charge of innovation, responding that current practices represent the real innovations, introduced into the church contrary to God's word. For the ecclesiastical authorities, money predominates. So Luther has a radical solution: he offers to take over spiritual matters—preaching the Gospel—from the bishops, leaving them free to continue as secular princes! "We will perform the duties of your office; we will support ourselves without cost to you; we will help you remain as you are."[2]

He concludes the *Exhortation* with two lists: the first, "topics with which it is necessary to deal in the true Christian church"; the second, "the things which have been practiced and are custom in the pretended church." The first list of thirty–two topics begins with "Law, Gospel, Sin, Grace," and includes "Baptism, Mass, Church, Keys, Bishops, Preaching Office."[3] The second list begins with "Indulgences" and "Sacrificial Masses," and then offers nearly a hundred other ways by which the teaching of the faith has been obscured with human traditions, in Luther's view. The "Sacrament of priesthood" (*Priesterschafft*) is listed early on; then, after numerous examples of fringe practices and traditions, he gives up after "St Blasius' lights."[4] Brecht notes that the *Exhortation* bypasses detailed questions about church order, and the political concerns around reform; as usual, Luther's concern is for the cause of the gospel.[5] When Luther includes bishops and preachers in his list of essentials, he does so from the understanding that these offices are there to ensure that the faith is being taught, and the sacraments are rightly administered. Beyond this, ecclesiastical structures are almost never a primary concern in his teaching on the church. This is despite his inevitable involvement in such matters on a day-to-day basis, as his letters testify.[6]

The Keys

Luther's treatise on *The Keys* was written in the weeks following the presentation of the *Augsburg Confession* (June 1530).[7] It is not clear whether it was written as a response to the diet, but he continues to focus on the fundamental issues facing the church. Rome's hierarchy continues to promote an illegitimate use of power over the means of salvation, through the control exercised by the higher clergy, the pope and the bishops alike. Claiming that "Peter" alone has the keys leads to a series of abuses, which include the sale of indulgences, interference in the secular realm, and the establishment of an exclusive papal teaching office. This confuses and corrupts the true, spiritual use of the keys, which is directed solely towards the forgiveness of sins, and the ministry of the whole church.

With this analysis in *The Keys*, Luther continues his assault on the Roman church, begun in *The Babylonian Captivity*.[8] In this matter, Luther consistently denied the power of the clergy and released Christians from falsely-imposed limitations for one reason only: because they involve the office or work of the Gospel, the keys are "a power or command given by God through Christ *to all of Christendom* [*Christenheit*] for the retaining and remitting of peoples' sins."[9] The commands to "bind and loose" given in Matthew 16:19 and 18:18 entail a responsibility for the ministry of the word entrusted to the whole church, and thus to laity and clergy alike. Illustrating how the abuse of the keys is symptomatic of a misuse of power—and the double-standards—in regard to all the sacraments, Luther's language echoes the basis for the common priesthood. He writes, "A Christian is not allowed to touch a consecrated chalice, although he be baptized and redeemed, consecrated, and sanctified through the blood of Christ."[10] "Consecrated" (*geweihet*) is the normal term for the ordination of a priest. So baptised Christians are indeed permitted to "touch" the keys, says Luther, to receive the promise of forgiveness without clerically-imposed limitations and to share it freely with one another.

Admonition Concerning the Sacrament of the Body and Blood of Our Lord

The teaching on the common priesthood is also very apparent in the *Admonition Concerning the Sacrament* (September 1530), also written from Coburg.[11] Arguing against the chief use of the mass by the clergy alone, Luther writes as advocate for the whole Christian community. Revisiting the debate over participation in the sacrament, he presents the arguments for the laity's reception of both bread and wine, and against private masses. His own experience in Wittenberg has shown him that the old attitudes still persisted.[12] So the dispute over a true view of sacrifice, and the need for full participation in a sacrament of communion, remain vital concerns for Luther here, which he must continue to address. Of special interest is the way in which he places the lord's supper in the context of baptism, preaching, and worship. He begins with the statement that the preaching office has not been instituted (*stiften*) to produce lazy preachers, or reluctant Christians.[13] Therefore, "Whoever is not willingly and gladly a Christian or does not go to the sacrament in that frame of mind let him remain far away from it and go his own way."[14] The sacramental acts of remembrance, praise, and confession of Christ are closely related to the act of preaching—which necessarily includes the act of hearing—and are intimately connected to the priestly worship of the community in which all participate, as they are able. This is the true worship, stripped of the trappings of meritorious ritual. Luther says,

> If I cannot or must not preach, I still want to listen; whoever listens also assists in thanking and honoring God, since, where there are no listeners, there can be no preacher. If I cannot listen, I nevertheless want to be among the listeners; at least I want to be present there, with my body and its members, where God is praised and glorified. Even if I could do no more, I still desire to receive the sacrament for this reason, that by such reception I might confess and bear witness that I also am one who would praise and thank God, and therefore desire to receive the sacrament to the glory of God. Such reception shall be my remembrance with which I think of and thank him for his grace shown me in Christ.[15]

This shows us how Luther has thought through the full implications of the priestly possession of God's word, as it draws all of God's people into a mutual ministry of speaking and hearing, of praising and confessing. His earlier statements which had emphasised the equality of Christians as priests are now carefully delineated, perhaps assisted by his study of the first testament prophets.[16] While upholding the necessity of the public preaching office, Luther affirms its essential connection to the priestly work of the word, which is common to all:

> Simultaneously, [a Christian] carries out the highest office of a true priest in a twofold way: By thanking, praising, and glorifying God he performs the most beautiful sacrifice, the supreme worship of God, and the most glorious work, namely, a thank offering. With his confession before men he does as much as if he preached and taught people to believe in Christ. Thereby he assists in augmenting and preserving Christianity, in confirming the gospel and the sacrament, in converting sinners and in assaulting the devil's kingdom. In short, he assists in whatever the teaching of the word accomplishes in the world and participates in the same work. But who can relate what great benefit results here?[17]

Luther then introduces a new line of thought, to highlight the inequality between the traditional priesthood and ordinary Christians. Making a sacrifice of the sacrament limits its use to the priests alone, while the laity has to make do with only half of the "plain sacrament," as they are denied the cup. "However," says Luther, "Christ gave and left behind for all his Christians alike, one baptism, sacrament, and gospel, and did not want to have a distinction made between persons."[18] This synthesis of the key Pauline texts emphasises that the Eucharistic celebration should be shared by all. Luther states, "I will not tolerate the 'superpriest' in this common and universal sacrament."[19]

Luther's focus in the first half of the *Admonition* is on the sacrament as communion, including the Christian responsibility to benefit the neighbour by joining the worship of the community. There is an emphasis on "remembrance" as the faithful proclamation of Christ's blessings, shared by all. In the catechisms, and the writings against Zwingli et al., Luther had concentrated on the real presence, and the importance of the forgiveness of sins as the chief sacramental gift. The personal benefits of the sacrament are the subject of the second half of the *Admonition*,[20] and, taken as a whole, "the treatise is a moving testimony to Luther's deep appreciation of the Lord's Supper as Christ's gift of his body and blood to his people."[21] It also demonstrates Luther's continuing appreciation of the church as the communion of saints, and his determination to embrace a vision of the church ruled by the Gospel and its fruits of faith and love, a rule entirely removed from the burdens of ecclesiastical law.

This writing is an important addition to a consideration of Luther's teaching on the common priesthood, and the church. It presents a complex understanding of the integration of the work of priests and preachers within the church's ministry of the word. It features in none of the accounts of Luther's teaching noted in the introduction, but confirms—yet again—how significant examples of Luther's use of this teaching are to be found in his later period.

The Private Mass and the Consecration of Priests

The importance of these issues for Luther means that he had not yet finished with his attack on Rome's distorted view of priesthood and sacrifice, or his exploration of the meaning of the sacrament for the whole community's participation.[22] This is shown in the 1533 publication of the *Private Mass and the Consecration of Priests*.[23] This work, which stands in close relationship with the *Admonition*, was produced over the course of three drafts, with Luther shifting his main focus from priestly consecration to the mass itself. A period of illness had delayed its completion. The heart of Luther's argument is that the church has been robbed of the true sacrament by the proliferation of priests consecrated to celebrate private masses, from which substantial income was derived. Imagining his own past culpability as a priest, through the literary device of a disputation with the devil, Luther questions whether a rite so far removed from the purposes of its original institution can validly offer the sacramental gifts of Christ's body and blood.[24] Even a public communion in which the laity receives only the bread and not the cup is closer to the intention of God's word than a "sacrificial" private mass.

In the course of this discussion, Luther examines again the entire sacramental ministry, providing an insight into his conviction that wherever and however the word is at work, the church will survive. He gives thanks that despite the abuses and superstition, the church and its ministry had been preserved in public worship, through baptism, the vernacular reading of the Gospel, the forgiveness of sins and absolution, and the reception of the sacrament of the altar, at least at Easter. Parish ministry also remains, the preaching office along with the comfort offered by the care of souls. The use of the Lord's Prayer, the Creed, and the psalms continues, and even the singing of "good hymns and canticles" have aided the survival of the true church, and of the Christian faith itself.[25] All this had only happened by the power of Christ, despite the failure of the bishops to fulfil their proper ministry.[26] This is a version of Luther's list of the marks or signs of the church that makes it clear that his conception of a spiritual fellowship is grounded in the realities of the life and worship of the faithful community. Where these things are, there the Spirit preserves the "holy place" (*heilige stete [stätte]*), even in what appears to be a place of sacrilege, a place where the word is silenced and its ministry abused.[27]

Luther's intention was to examine each of these "marks," to demonstrate in detail how their use had been degraded by the work of pope and bishops. In effect, this was the activity of the antichrist, and the devil.[28] He covers the mass and baptism at some length, and particularly ordination ("chrism," *weihe*), then regretting that the length of the treatise left no room for a discussion of the keys (forgiveness) and prayer.[29]

First, Luther repeats his reasons for attacking the private mass and the consecration of priests whose sole task is its celebration, and the effective subordination of the sacrament of the altar. This is to the great detriment of the laity, whose faith is thereby endangered, and misdirected.[30] The next section, on baptism, is where Luther fulfils his original intention, exploring how opposing this abuse of priestly consecration stood as a prime objective for the reform of the church. As on other occasions, his criticism has both negative and positive elements, to remove what is corrupt and hinders the Gospel, and so to restore the essential practices of Christian ministry according to their original purposes.

Baptism, he writes, has been dishonoured in the church, being replaced by penitential practices and other "higher works." Some have even said that baptism is for original sin only, with works of satisfaction needed to remove actual sin.[31] Among these higher works is entry into the religious life. So consecration—here usually connected to the practice of chrism (*cresem*), anointing with oil—is being used to "produce clerics in the holy church, that is, a far, far higher and holier estate than baptism bestows." Yet baptism is the true washing and anointing, by the blood of Christ and the Spirit's chrism, given for eternal life—not to celebrate private masses. But the clergy are being elevated in name and by their external appearance, and especially by "the spiritual mark [*das geistliche malzeichen*] in the soul, which no ordinary Christian [*kein gemeiner Christ*] is supposed to have except the consecrated priest alone."[32]

Luther insists that what is being called consecration properly involves "a call or a conferring of the office of the ministry [*Pfarrampt*] or of the office of preaching [*Predigtampt*]."[33] He cites the laying on of hands as the apostolic practice, with the use of chrism added later by "the dear fathers."[34] Luther does not explore the meaning of ordination any further here; he is consistent in emphasising the centrality of the call to office. Rather, he repeats in some detail his case for the abolition of distinctions in the spiritual estate, between clergy and laity. He emphasises the term "cleric," to intensify the contrast with current practices. Like true priests, clerics are born, not made. The priesthood is the hereditary right of all Christians, as the children of him who is "the true cleric and high priest." We are also the children of our mother (the church), who is the high priest's bride, "herself a priest and a bishop [*eine Priesterin oder Bisschoffin*]." As previously, Luther's authorities here are Psalm 110:4 and 1 Peter 2:9, together with Christ's own sacrifice on the cross, effective in our baptism.[35] He then states,

> We have been born of this bridegroom and bride through holy baptism and thus have become true clerics [*rechten Pfaffen*] in Christendom in a hereditary manner, sanctified by his blood and consecrated by his Holy Spirit.[36]

Only this priesthood is able to offer the true spiritual sacrifices, such as those mandated in Romans 12. Further, we are Christ's brethren, as well as his children (Psalm 22:22, Matthew 12:50), "So we are not only true clerics and priests according to our right as children but also according to our right as brothers."[37] In case we thought he had abandoned them, Luther has here assembled the whole array of his texts in support of the common priesthood. This New Testament view of priesthood, based on our baptism, needs to be upheld in the church, says Luther, to counter the damage being done by the private mass. It was no accident, but the work of the Spirit that originally prevented the name of priest (*sacerdos*) which belongs to all Christians being applied exclusively to those appointed to offices in the church. To "priest" he adds "cleric" (*clericus*) to emphasise how only baptism can consecrate or anoint Christians for service in the church, and that there is no higher spiritual status than that of Christian. Rather, as Luther consistently taught,

> [N]one of us is born as apostle, preacher, teacher, pastor through baptism, but we are all born simply as priests and clerics. Afterward, some are taken from the ranks of such born clerics [*gebornen Pfaffen*] and called or elected to these offices which they are to discharge on behalf of all of us.[38]

In other writings in this period Luther emphasised the divine institution of the public ministry, and its importance.[39] Here he is able to use, without any contradiction, the language of equality among Christians that expresses entry into that ministry by means of call or election. But that is not at issue here. Luther is writing against a Roman view of the priesthood and the church, and their corruption of the Eucharist and baptism; he is not opposing the radical preachers, those who "elect" themselves. In a similar vein he deals with the Roman abuses of preaching (and its office), returning again to attack at some length false views of consecration to the priesthood, and the ways in which baptism and the mass have been corrupted.[40] All of it would have been ruined, if not for the presence of Christ and his word, the only effective power in the sacraments. In the midst of all that has been lost, the church remains:

> However, where God's word is pure and certain, there everything else must be: God's kingdom, Christ's kingdom, the Holy Spirit, baptism, the sacrament, the office of the ministry [*Pfarrampt*], the office of preaching [*Predigampt*], faith, love, the cross, life and salvation, and everything the church should have, as Christ says: "We will come to him and make our home with him" [John 14:23]; "And lo, I am with you always, to the close of the age" [Matt. 28:20].[41]

This is Luther's textual synthesis on the church from Ephesians 4 and 1 Corinthians 12 (etc.) remarkably expanded and shaped beyond its previous boundaries, to include the church's ministry with its offices and the marks of its consecrated life as well, all bound together by the promise of Christ's presence. This leads (after some further digression) to Luther's account of a "true mass," as celebrated in the evangelical churches, and he moves beyond polemics into a statement that reveals his vision of the church, according to its essential configuration and practice, and grounded in the reality which unites body and spirit in sacramental action:

> For, God be praised, in our churches we can show a Christian a true Christian mass according to the ordinance and institution of Christ, as well as according to the true intention of Christ and the church. There our pastor, bishop, or minister in the pastoral office [*diener in Pfarrampt*], rightly and honorably and publicly

called, having been previously consecrated, anointed, and born in baptism as a priest of Christ, without regard to the private chrism, goes before the altar. Publicly and plainly he sings what Christ has ordained and instituted in the Lord's Supper.[42]

Then, the bread and the wine are distributed and received by all present, who are fully participating in all aspects of this sacred meal, with the pastor who is "the mouth for us all":

Particularly we who want to receive the sacrament kneel beside, behind, and around him, man, woman, young, old, master, servant, wife, maid, parents, and children, even as God brings us together there, *all of us true, holy priests, sanctified by Christ's blood, anointed and consecrated in baptism by the Holy Spirit*. On the basis of this our inborn, hereditary priestly honour and attire we are present, have, as Revelation [5] pictures it, our golden crowns on our heads, harps and golden censers in our hands;[43] and we let our pastor say what Christ has ordained, not for himself as though it were for his person, but *he is the mouth for all of us* and *we all speak the words with him from the heart and in faith*, directed to the Lamb of God who is present for us and among us, and who according to his ordinance nourishes us with his body and blood. This is our mass, and it is the true mass which is not lacking among us.[44]

This is a highly significant statement by Luther, encapsulating the essence of his teaching on the church, its priesthood and its ministry within a description of the celebration of the lord's supper. This may be the only time that Luther uses the Revelation text as the sole identifier for the common priesthood. But the context of worship, and the heavenly vision of the *communion of saints*, gathered around the "Lamb who was slain," make its use here to describe the reality of that spiritual communion—hidden and yet revealed—especially appropriate, and powerful. It is a prime example of how Luther's ecclesiology is grounded in the actual life and experience of the Christian community, and how—while steadfastly refusing to identify any other basis for the church than the word and faith—his teaching does not abandon it (or its participants) to the realms of spiritual make believe.

Returning to the matter of appointment to the church's ministry, Luther emphasises the importance of preaching the Gospel. He writes, in words which echo the *Augsburg Confession*, "Where the gospel is rightly and purely preached, there a holy Christian church must be."[45] This church ("we," says Luther) possesses (*haben*) what is important and necessary, namely "God's word, Christ, the Spirit, faith, prayer, baptism, the sacrament, the keys, the office of the ministry [*Ampt*], etc." It ("we") must "also possess . . . the power and right to call some persons to the office of the ministry [*zum ampt beruffen*]."[46] This repeated use of "we" confirms that Luther is working with his inclusive, participatory view of the church here, against any suggestion that these appointments are the exclusive domain of the Roman hierarchy. "What kind of church would this be," asks Luther, without this fundamental "right to call" those who will serve God's people with word and sacrament?[47] Christ's promised presence with his people in Matthew 18:19–20 ("Where two or three are gathered in my name") is at stake here, as it is in the commission to preach to the nations in Matthew 28:16–20. Christ here seems to have forgotten about the chrism used in papal consecrations, says Luther! Paul's practice of ordination is also based simply on the command to preach, and the assent of the assembly (2 Timothy 2:2).[48] Behind Luther's polemic against Rome, the fundamental question is always, "who—and what—is the church?" The answer begins and ends with the "ordinary Christians," those who have been baptised and who are to be served with God's gifts, as well as those who serve them. This inclusive view of church and ministry is usually to the fore, whenever Luther discusses these fundamental issues.[49]

On the Councils and the Church

In the late 1530s Luther produced what was to be his final major theological treatise, *On the Councils and the Church*, also in anticipation of the proposed Council.[50] Its third part has a confessional character, and contains Luther's most extensive treatment of the marks of the church.[51] In this comprehensive study he explores his familiar description of the church as the gathered people of God, using "Christendom" (*Christenheit*) as his summary expression of that reality. For Luther, this emphasises the fundamental unity of the church in its broader context, perhaps as an alternative to "catholic."[52] While Luther never loses sight of the full presence of the church in the gathered, local congregation, neither does he ever ignore the worldwide dimensions of the confession of "one church." Both comprise and reflect the same reality. He writes,

> [S]etting aside various writings and analyses of the word "church," we shall this time confine ourselves simply to the Children's Creed, which says, "I believe in one holy Christian church, the communion of saints." Here the creed clearly indicates what the church is, namely, a communion of saints, that is, a crowd [*hauffe*], assembly of people who are Christians and holy, which is called a Christian holy assembly, or church.[53]

And then concludes:

Thus the "holy Christian church" is synonymous with a Christian and holy people or, as one is also wont to express it, with "holy Christendom," or "whole Christendom." The Old Testament uses the term "God's people."[54]

Luther emphasises that the word "church" (*ecclesia*) simply means an assembly. What makes the Christian assembly unique is what happens when these people gather, and who they become, as God's people. Through faith in Christ, the Sanctifier, the Holy Spirit, makes them a holy people, the *communion of saints*.[55] After this introduction, he continues with an exposition of his major thesis, that the church as the people of God is known by their "possession" of the source of its holiness, the word of God.[56] The word accomplishes everything in the church, including driving out the "devils" of error. This was Luther's chief conclusion in his evaluation of the church councils in the first parts of the treatise; now he includes those he regards as the present day enemies of the word.[57]

From late medieval piety, Luther draws on the imagery of the holy relic (*Heiligtum*) to explain the significance of God's word for the confession of the church as the *Holy Christian* people, *the communion of saints*. "The word is holy," he writes, "and sanctifies everything it touches . . . the Holy Spirit himself administers it and anoints or sanctifies the Christian church with it, rather than with the pope's chrism." This latter phrase is a reference to consecration to the priesthood; in this way, Luther includes the common priesthood as an essential component of his ecclesiology, without needing to explain its significance further.[58] The meaning is clear: the holy Christian people are all those anointed as priests and saints by the holy word of God, "administered" by the Spirit.

Rather than reliance on relics of doubtful provenance, offered as pay-to-view salvation, Luther points to the ways in which God's grace is freely distributed among God's people. With the word of Christ at the centre, the other "marks" are clustered around, each of the seven in its own way an active sign that here the holy people are present, with God at work among them. "God's word cannot be without God's people," says Luther, "and conversely, God's people cannot be without God's word."[59]

Hierarchical appropriation of the sacraments is rejected, just as firmly as it was in *The Babylonian Captivity*.[60] Thus, "the holy sacrament of baptism" and "the holy sacrament of the altar" clearly proclaim the presence of God and God's people, even where all the traditional paraphernalia of public religion are nowhere to be seen. This latter point is especially true for the celebration of the lord's supper. All that matters is the word, and faith:

> [T]he question of whether you are male or female, young or old, need not be argued—just as little as it matters in baptism and the preached word. It is

enough that you are consecrated and anointed with the sublime and holy chrism of God, with the word of God, with baptism, and also this sacrament; then you are anointed highly and gloriously enough and sufficiently vested with priestly garments.[61]

This is a clear statement of the common priesthood, and the essential involvement of all Christians with the spiritual purposes for which the word and the sacraments are given and received. This is what it means to be a "Christian holy people." It grounds Luther's understanding of the church in a known reality: one that is at one and the same time "spiritual" (based on the word and faith) and is also open to lived experience. This is true, even if the presence of the Christian holy people—the church—is only to be perceived by faith. It represents a corporate, bodily understanding of the work of the word at the same time as it maintains the necessity for the faith of the individual. For Luther, without the word—and faith—there is no church.[62]

Luther continues by discussing the role of each of the other marks or signs. The "office of the keys" both publicly and privately enacts the work of forgiveness in the church, restoring sinners, and excluding the unrepentant.[63]

The fifth mark, the public ministry, is considered in relationship to the first four. Luther's sequencing and wording here is important: he does not designate this as a "holy ministry" in its own right. The public sign is not the clergy in and of themselves, but rather the sign is that *the church* "consecrates or calls ministers, or has offices that it is to administer."[64] The clerics ("bishops, pastors, or preachers") administer "the holy possessions" on behalf of the church, "the holy Christian people," because they (the possessions) "have been instituted by Christ." Luther quotes Ephesians 4:8, a text he uses to confirm that the public ministry has a divine origin, but then adds his familiar argument, that in the community one person must necessarily act on behalf of the many.[65] Once more, the two aspects of ministry are juxtaposed, without apparent contradiction.

Luther also notes the exclusion of women, children, and "incompetent people" from this public office, allowing for emergencies (*not*).[66] Both Scripture and nature reinforce this rule; these people "cannot and shall not occupy positions of sovereignty." However, they rightfully share, in God's word and sacraments, and are also "true, holy Christians."[67] Luther's arguments from the natural order, and allowing for cases of "necessity," suggest that even here he is not making an absolute judgement on this matter.[68]

Service in public ministry is not an end in itself, as the orientation of Luther's statements makes clear.[69] This is also reinforced by its placement after the other signs, and in facilitation of them. His larger concern for the spiritual health of God's people remain apparent, whenever the gifts of God in Christ are received. If this is God's business, then the focus must be on the gift itself, and on its true giver, not on the person who places it in your hand. Then, as with all gifts, its lasting value is only realised when it is received and used.

> For all of it is given, not to the person who has the office, but to the one who is to receive it through this office, except that they can receive it together with you if they so desire. Let them be what they will. Because they are in office and are tolerated by the assembly, you put up with them too. Their person will make God's word and sacraments neither worse nor better for you.[70]

Luther digresses here for several paragraphs, pursuing the argument with Rome over fitness for office, particularly in relation to the marriage of priests. Finally, he returns to the "precious holy possessions whereby everything is sanctified." In the sixth place, he says, there is public prayer and praise of God. Typically, he singles out the Lord's Prayer, and the psalms, together with the Creed and the Ten Commandments. The Spirit works through these, and thereby "sanctifies the holy people of Christ." These are the common possession of all Christians, to be freely used. Their use is not limited, and is not under the control of the church's hierarchy.[71]

The seventh sign revealing the holy Christian people draws Luther back into his original thought, that of *das Heiligtum*, here "the holy possession of the sacred cross."[72] But this is no "relic" in the sense of an item to be venerated, but rather the existential reality for all those who follow Christ in faith through suffering and the cross in all the circumstances of everyday life. It is, in fact, at the heart of what Luther proposes in this treatise, that the true church is not to be recognised by all the trappings of wealth, honour, and elaborate ritual—or even momentous doctrinal pronouncements—but in humble yet sacred gifts, and even in rejection and loss for the sake of the gospel.[73] This is what it means, to be a Christian people.

At this point, Luther's theology of the church is of a piece with his theology of the cross. It is also a key point in relation to the "hiddenness" (or "invisibility") of the church. As well as emphasising the role of faith, Luther is comparing the high social profile of the church and its hierarchy in Luther's day, with its wealth, ostentation, magnificent buildings and grand ceremonial, over against the reality of true Christian community as he proposes it, almost lost from sight (as it were) amidst the stuff of everyday life, and the unheralded nature of parish sermons and village baptisms.

In a similar vein, he suggests that the entire Christian life, namely the works of love enjoined in the second table of the Decalogue, could also be considered a sign of God's people. These are also the work of the Spirit in us, for our sanctification. However, he draws back from this, noting the uncertainty of relying on behaviour which can be matched by non-Christians, and that Christians themselves often fail to fulfil! The primary possessions, however, are the "reliable" signs, because their character depends on God's command and promise, not on human performance.[74] To avoid confusion, Luther suggests that they should not be called sacraments but the "seven principal parts of Christian sanctification or the seven holy possessions [of God's holy people]."[75]

This work represents Luther's mature conclusions on the church, and it confirms the remarkable consistency in his thinking over the course of more than twenty years of a tumultuous career. Even given the tension between his initial rejection of an exclusively clerical church, and the later demands of a reform agenda, with its need to manifest in practice his theological convictions, Luther maintained this basic understanding of the word at work among God's "holy Christian people." In this way, he was able to articulate a living connection between what is known only to faith, how that faith experiences God's word at work in the church and in the world, and then goes to work for God, and the neighbour.

Against Hans Wurst

Two years after Luther wrote *On the Councils and the Church*, with its comprehensive exploration of the church's seven "holy possessions," he proposes yet another version of these marks in the polemical writing *Against Hans Wurst* (1541), to demonstrate the Lutherans' identification with "the true ancient church [*die rechte alte Kirche*]."[76] They are not innovators, or heretics. Luther argues this in the most edifying section of this work, which is otherwise an unpleasant invective against Duke Henry of Brunswick, who had previously attacked Luther's elector, John Frederick.

In contrast to *On the Councils* and its "marks" (*zeichen*), Luther simply describes the presence of the ancient church among the Lutherans on the basis of its possessions, the things that the church "has" (*haben*) by Christ's institution and apostolic practice. The list begins with baptism, which Luther here places as the "first and most important sacrament," the foundation of the church: "First, nobody can deny that we, as well as the papists, have received holy baptism and because of that are called Christians."[77] It then continues with the sacrament of the altar, and "the true and ancient keys" correctly used, to bind and loose sins.[78] The fourth point joins "the preaching office and the word of God, that we teach and preach diligently."[79]

For these four possessions, instituted by Christ, Luther uses the familiar texts to identify the church by the word and its sacraments. For baptism, it is Ephesians 4:5 ("one baptism"). For the sacrament of the altar, he quotes 1 Corinthians 11[10:17], that we are united in the one church in "one body and one loaf." The keys are used "in accordance with Christ's institution"

(Matthew 16:19, John 20:23). God's word is taught and preached "just as Christ commanded," with Luther's wording reflecting Matthew 28:19–20 or Mark 16:15.

Six additional possessions (or spiritual activities) are given, to reinforce the argument that the Lutherans teach and practice in accordance with the true ancient church. They "hold, believe, sing, and confess the Apostles' Creed. . . . They have the same Lord's Prayer . . . and sing the same psalms. . . . They teach honour for the temporal powers . . . and pray for them." Also, they praise and honour marriage as a "divine, blessed, and well-pleasing ordinance of God's creation." Like the ancient church, they experience persecution and suffering, also "like the Lord Christ himself on the cross." In response (the tenth "possession"), they do not seek revenge, but "endure, admonish, and pray for others."[80]

Luther concludes, "Thus we have proved that we are the true, ancient church, one body and one communion of saints [*eine gemeine des Heiligen*] with the holy, universal, Christian church."[81] He challenges the papists to do likewise, and then revisits his list (with numerous additions) to prove that they "are the new false church . . . Satan's whore and synagogue." This unfortunate polemic is always close to the surface when Luther is writing at this time, and stands side-by-side with his more positive phrases which present the nature of the church as God's creature, and the participation of ordinary Christians within its fellowship. So he writes:

> The church is a high, deep, hidden thing which one may neither perceive nor see, but must grasp only by faith, through baptism, sacrament, and word. Human doctrine, ceremonies, tonsures, long robes, mitres, and all the pomp of popery only lead far away from it into hell—still less are they signs of the church [*die Kirchen anzeigen*]. Naked children, men, women, farmers, citizens who possess no tonsures, mitres, or priestly vestments [*Messegewand*] also belong to the church.[82]

This statement can be added to the other summaries of Luther's teaching on the church in this chapter, and like them it reflects the synthesis of Pauline texts ("one church, one faith, etc.") that underpins his understanding, and this in its turn is organically related to the broad sweep of his biblical ecclesiology. Therefore, once again it is the priority of the word and faith, active among God's people in the everyday essentials of the church's ministry and its common sacramental life of prayer, worship and service, that commands his attention here, and ours.

Against the Roman Papacy

Preparations for the council continued, at the same time as imperial negotiations continued to seek for a religious settlement between Lutherans (evangelicals) and Catholics in Germany. In order to keep control of this process, in August 1544 Pope Paul III wrote demanding that the emperor should act swiftly to extirpate the heretics in his lands.[83] Luther responded late in 1544, unleashing the full force of his invective *Against the Roman Papacy, an Institution of the Devil*.[84] The work is indefensibly crude and harsh, even allowing for Luther's age and ill health. However, as with other writings against his opponents both to the left and the right, it is still possible to strip away his invective and discern the lineaments of a more positive theology beneath the antipapal bile.

When these necessary corrections are made, there emerges another powerful restatement of his ecclesiology, affirming the unity of the church, with its core business of word, sacraments, and prayer, and its equal possession of all the gifts of "faith and Spirit." These are the infallible signs by which the presence of the church is known throughout the world. And, as we have seen throughout this period, Luther does not often directly quote the foundational biblical texts (Ephesians 4, etc.) but here they are, once more clearly visible in what he writes:

> We know that in Christendom it has been so arranged that all churches are equal, and there is only one single church of Christ in the world, as we pray, "I believe in one holy, Christian church." The reason is this: wherever there is a church, anywhere in the whole world, it still has no other gospel and Scripture, no other baptism and communion, no other faith and Spirit, no other Christ and God, no other Lord's Prayer and prayer, no other hope and eternal life than we have here in our church in Wittenberg. And their bishops are equal to our bishops, pastors, or preachers; none is lord or servant of the other; they all have the same mind and heart; and everything belonging to the church is equal [*alles gleich*].[85]

Even though expressions of faith, and the use of faith's gifts in the service of the church, may necessarily vary, they do not determine its underlying spiritual reality. In essence, the church is comprised of all Christians, each one of equal standing before God and able to participate in its ministry.[86] Therefore—in regard to the claims of the papacy—"of course no one on earth has the right to judge or condemn the pope—except only everyone who is baptised, or still in possession of human reason, and all God's creatures."[87] Early in his career, commenting on the psalms, Luther had written of those who are "spiritual" (*spirituales homines*), who alone had the power to discern (*iudicant*) in their inmost being the very word of God. The significant text was 1 Corinthians 2:15.[88] Now, much later, it is the baptised child who stands in that place of judgement, and the text is not quoted:

> For when a person is baptised, they, or the godparents [*Paten*] in their stead, must first swear that they renounce the devil and all his works and all his nature. Now the nature and works of the pope are nothing but the devil's works and nature, as has been amply proved. That is why every baptised child is not only a judge over the pope, but also over his god, the devil.[89]

Whether or not in practice Luther ever afforded children—including the representative "seven-year old" of the *Smalcald Articles*—the right to judge *his* teaching, probably misses the point.[90] His position on the church's ministry remained consistent within the evolving reformational landscape from 1520 until 1546: neither priestly, nor even papal consecration confers a unique spiritual authority in matters of God's word. For Christians, only the Holy Spirit's anointing gives that power, bestowed through the word itself at work in our baptism. However the ministry may be ordered or configured, according to the needs and circumstances of God's people, its foundations in the spiritual realities of the word and faith can neither be avoided or ignored.

Luther's Later Ecclesiology, and the Status of the Common Priesthood

In these later years as he continued to argue the case for the reform of the church, and to defend it against attacks both perceived and actual, Luther's writings as teacher and pastor maintained a view of church, ministry and priesthood derived from his biblical understanding. While he is less prolific in quoting the biblical texts that support his arguments in this period, its Pauline basis is still clearly visible and is repeated in his varied summary formulations and by his presentation of the church's marks or "possessions" characterising its ministry, worship, and life of service, all of which resonate with Christ's own presence in the church. In this way the *key texts* earlier identified in relation to his teaching on the church and the common priesthood continued to ground, shape and contextualize the life and teachings of the emerging evangelical communities.

Whether "priesthood" is explicitly named or not, this is the spiritual reality held in common by all Christians: they are God's people who by faith receive all the fruits of Christ's life and service (his "office"), and are those who participate as equal members in the unity of his body, the communion of saints. This means that Christology (and justification by faith) remains the foundation for Luther's later view of the church, consistent with the way in which he employs the themes of priesthood and kingship. Christ is head of the church, ruling through his word. This is especially seen in relation to the ongoing dispute with the Roman church in the writings on *The Keys*, *The Private Mass,* and *Against the Papacy in Rome*. And just as he continued to teach from the psalms, especially that Christ is revealed to be king and high priest, the teaching persists that through baptism and by faith all of Christ's people share and participate in the blessings of his reign and priesthood (*The Admonition concerning the Sacrament*).

At the same time, both the social constraints and the theological debate leads Luther to teach with more clarity that even though it is primarily the community of faith and thus a spiritual entity, this church is not "invisible," but can be recognised by the public enactment of the gifts of God through which it lives (*The Private Mass, On the Councils*). Preeminently, this is the proclamation of the word itself, and participation in the sacraments (*Admonition concerning the Sacrament*). This is the church's essential ministry. But the church is also known by the resultant expressions of faith: genuine Christian piety, prayer, worship, and even in the lived experience of the cross in the lives of believers (*On the Councils, Against Hans Wurst*). It is these clarifications which mark the development of Luther's teaching on church and priesthood, from the earlier to this later period. Even so, throughout this period Luther's use of his "key texts" remained remarkably consistent, even in their adaptation to meet the changing reformational and social context.

Likewise, to maintain the life of faith, the church needs leaders (bishops, pastors, "guardians") who continue the public ministry of Christ and the apostles, called into this office of service from among their fellow Christians. They "rule" by serving God's people with God's word (*The Exhortation to All Clergy*). This same church also requires faithful people, who actively participate in hearing, receiving and then sharing the word and sacraments, praying the Lord's Prayer and the psalms (*Admonition concerning the Sacrament*). These twin aspects of reform are memorably summarised in *The Private Mass*: the pastor "is the mouth for us all," and those who celebrate mass with him as "true, holy priests" are "speak[ing] the words with him from the heart and in faith." This shared participation of people and pastor is at the heart of Luther's enduring vision for the church's worship and for its ongoing life and mission as well.[91]

NOTES

1. LW 34:3–61 (WA 30/2:268–356), *Exhortation to All Clergy*. See Brecht, *Luther* 2:385–6; Bornkamm, *Mid-career* 669–673; for other views of events at Augsburg, see Roper, *Martin Luther Renegade*, 321–342, and Schilling, *Martin Luther Rebel*, 384–390.

2. LW 34:51 (WA 30/2:343).

3. LW 34:52–3 (WA 30/2:345–346).

4. LW 34:54–8 (WA 30/2:347–351). St Blasius was the patron saint of sufferers with throat problems.

5. Brecht, *Luther* 2:386–387.

6. See Brecht's account of Luther's involvement in local disputes, *Luther* 2:439–447.

7. LW 40:321–377 (WA 30/2:465–507), *The Keys*. Brecht, *Luther* 2:400–401, and Brecht *Luther* 3:74.

8. LW 36:81–91 (WA 6:543–549), *The Babylonian* Captivity. Rome's "captivity" of the sacrament of penance (see chapter 3).

9. LW 40:366 (WA 30/2:498), *The Keys* (emphasis added, translation modified). See also chapter 8, for the Easter *Sermons on John 20:19–29*.

10. LW 40:369 (WA 30/2:500).

11. LW 38:91–137 (WA 30/2:595–626), *The Admonition Concerning the Sacrament*.

12. For the circumstances of this writing and reactions to it, see Brecht, *Luther* 2:382–3.

13. Althaus, *Theology,* 324n2, gives this as a reference to the divine institution of the ministry. LW 38:100 (WA 30/2:598), *The Admonition*: "We know that teaching and admonishing are based on God's word, office and divine mandate [*befehl*], and we also know, as Isaiah 55 says, that they cannot be without fruit."

14. LW 38:101 (WA 30/2:598).

15. LW 38:109 (WA 30/2:604).

16. See chapter 7.

17. LW 38:111 (WA 30/2:606) (translation has not been modified for this longer quotation, but—despite the pronouns—"Christian" is always to be understood as a term that is not gender-specific).

18. LW 38:120 (WA 30/2:612).

19. LW 38:122 (WA 30/2:614). "Superpriest" = *der Sonderling*. LW sometimes translates this "eccentric" or "individualist"; here it refers to the priests who destroy community by setting themselves apart and reserving the full sacrament for themselves. See, for example, LW 69:109 (WA 28:188).

20. LW 38:124–137 (WA 30/2:615–626).

21. Martin E. Lehmann (translator) in his introduction to the *Admonition Concerning the Sacrament of the Body and Blood of Our Lord* (LW 38:95).

22. In the *Babylonian Captivity* (1520), Luther had claimed that the survival of the papacy depended on the "fiction" of sacramental ordination and its *character indelibelis* (LW 36:116, WA 6:567).

23. LW 38:139–214 (WA 38:195–256), *The Private Mass and The Consecration of Priests*. Brecht, *Luther* 3:42,74–78,193.

24. LW 38:149–156 (WA 38:197–204).

25. LW 38:177–178 (WA 38:221).

26. LW 38:178–179 (WA 38:222–223).

27. Compare *On the Councils*, below, where the word and its sacraments comprise the "holy things."

28. The references to the devil's activity in the Roman church persist throughout the whole work. Its value as an exposition of the sacrament and its priesthood remains, despite the unfortunate polemic.

29. LW 38:210–211 (WA 38:250 and 252), *The Private Mass.*

30. LW 38:180–183 (WA 38:224–225).

31. LW 38:183–184 (WA 38:226).

32. LW 38:185 (WA 38:227–228).

33. LW 38:186 (WA 38:228).

34. LW 38:186 (WA 38:228).

35. LW 38:187 (WA 38: 229).

36. LW 38:187 (WA 38:229).

37. LW 38:187–188 (WA 38:230).

38. LW 38:188 (WA 38:230).

39. See, for example, LW 46:219 (WA 30/2:527), *Keeping Children in School* (1530).

40. LW 38: 188–208 (WA 38:231–247), *The Private Mass.*

41. LW 38:196 (WA 38:237). Compare (once again) this list with the "holy possessions" in *On the Councils and the Church*, and with Luther's synthesis of the Pauline texts for the church (see chapter 2).

42. LW 38:208 (WA 38:247)

43. Probably Revelation 5:6–14, the vision of heavenly worship.

44. LW 38:208–9 (WA 38:247) (emphases added, translation modified).

45. LW 38:211 (WA 38:252) (compare BOC 42, *Augsburg Confession*).

46. LW 38:212 (WA 38:252–253).

47. LW 38:212 (WA 38:253).

48. LW 38:212–213 (WA 38:253–254).

49. See Dorothea Wendebourg's useful discussion of the "two dimensions" that persist in Luther's view of the church, the outward dimension where distinctions between persons pertain, and the hidden dimension where all people—as believers—"are equal" (OHE, 221–222). It is only in worship—Luther's description of the "true mass"—that this equality becomes truly "visible," as the community united in Christ participates in receiving God's gifts, offering together their confession of faith and praise of God.

50. LW 41:9–178 (WA 50:509–653), *On the Councils and the Church*. See Brecht, *Luther* 3:193–198. He titles this as Luther's "Final Position" on the church.

51. LW 41:143–178 (WA 50:624–653). See Lathrop and Wengert, *Christian Assembly*, 17–36, and 81–112. Wengert argues for Luther's innovative use of this concept ("das Zeichen") throughout his career. See also chapter 1 (at n56); chapter 2 (at n29); and above nn27,41.

52. BOC 325n165 explains that from the fifteenth-century German versions of the *Apostles' Creed* read "Christian" rather than "Catholic" church. Luther followed that usage.

53. LW 41:143 (WA 50:624), *On the Councils*. Luther defines the church . . .

54. LW 41:144 (WA 50:624–625). . . . as God's people.

55. LW 41:144–145 (WA 50:625). It is the "communion of saints."

56. LW 41:148 (WA 50:628). It possesses God's word.
57. LW 41:150–151 (WA 50:630). Opposition to the word.
58. LW 41:149 (WA 50:629). The church, consecrated by the Holy Spirit.
59. LW 41:150 (WA 50:629–630). The word is essential.
60. E.g., "The sacrament does not belong to the priests, but to all people," LW 36:27 (WA 6:507), *The Babylonian Captivity* (translation altered).
61. LW 41:152 (WA 50:631), *On the Councils*. See chapter 7 *Isaiah 40–66* (at nn60); *Psalm 110* (at nn100,115, 119); *Genesis 37* (n170); and chapter 8, *Galatians 3:27* (n12) for other references to "priestly garments."
62. See Bornkamm, *Luther's World of Thought*, 135–137.
63. LW 41:153 (WA 50:631–632) *On the Councils*. Luther refers to both "public" and "private" absolution, given in a range of situations (see above for *The Keys* and chapter 8 for Luther's *Sermons on John 20:19–29*).
64. LW 41:154 (WA 50:632). Also LW 41:164 (WA 50:641), "the [offices] cannot be without the church." Contrast Timothy Wengert's understanding, which reverses Luther's order and gives priority to the office in the church, *Priesthood, Pastors, Bishops*, 27–28; a similar approach is taken in Carl E. Braaten and Robert Jenson, eds., *Marks of the Body of Christ* (Grand Rapids: Eerdmans Publishing, 1999), 123–136. This approach compromises the identity of the church as "the Christian holy people" and appears to go hand in hand with the need to subordinate the common priesthood to the public office. Compare Oswald Bayer's broader perspective of the church's "other offices" in Luther's teaching, *Theology*, 277. Bayer—like Hans-Martin Barth and other German theologians—seems more comfortable with the co-existence of the common priesthood and public ministry in the church.
65. LW 41:154 (WA 50:632–633), *On the Councils*.
66. Translating *not[h]* as "necessity" or "need," rather than "emergency," shifts Luther's meaning here. See also chapter 4 at n90 (*Concerning the Ministry*) and the discussion in chapter 8 at n91 (*Sermons on John 20:19–31*).
67. LW 41:154–155 (WA 50:633), *On the Councils*.
68. Already in the early 1520s Luther explored these arguments (LW 36:151–152 (WA 8:424–425), *The Misuse of the Mass*; LW 30:55 (WA 12:309), *Exposition of 1 Peter*), and struggled to reconcile the equal spiritual rights afforded by the common priesthood and the biblical examples of women leaders, with Paul's injunctions and his own socially conditioned prejudices regarding women's natural limitations. See, e.g., *Infiltrating Preachers*, chapter 5 nn73–74. For further examples, see Susan C. Karant-Nunn and Merry E. Wiesner-Hanks, eds., *Luther on Women*, 58–87. See also Charlotte Methuen, "In her soul, a woman is not different from a man": How Scholastic Was Luther's View of Women?" in *Remembering the Reformation: Martin Luther and Catholic Theology* (Minneapolis: Fortress Press, 2017), 75–97.
69. See also, for example, LW 73:320 (WA 39/2:182), *Disputation on the Church* (1542). Luther states, "It is true that the church is bound to the ministry [*ministerium*]: to the Gospel, but not to the ministers [*ministros*]." This reinforces the point that Luther remained consistent in not granting the clergy unique spiritual status within the church.
70. LW 41:156 (WA 50:634), *On the Councils* (translation modified).

71. LW 41:164 (WA 50:641).
72. LW 41:164 (WA 50:641–642).
73. LW 41:164–5 (WA 50:641–642).
74. LW 41:166–167 (WA 50:643).
75. LW 41:166 (WA 50:643) (translation modified).
76. LW 41:179–256 (WA 51:469–572), *Against Hans Wurst*. The discussion of these "marks" begins at LW 41:193–194 (WA 51:477). See Brecht, *Luther* 3:219–222; Hendrix, *Martin Luther*, 267–269, leading to a reflection on "true and false" religion.
77. LW 41:194 (WA 51:479).
78. LW 41:195 (WA 51:480) ("The Sacrament"); LW 41:195 (WA 51:480–481) (The Keys).
79. LW 41:196 (WA 51:481).
80. These are presented in six short sequential paragraphs, LW 41:196–198 (WA 482–485).
81. LW 41:199 (WA 51:487).
82. LW 41:211 (WA 51:507–508).
83. Brecht, *Luther* 3:357–359.
84. LW 41:257–376 (WA 54:206–299), *Against the Roman Papacy*. Brecht, *Luther* 3:359–365.
85. LW 41:358 (WA 54:284).
86. LW 41:358 (WA 54:284).
87. LW 41:359 (WA 54:285).
88. WA 3:179 (Gloss on Psalm 32:7, not in LW). See Hendrix, *Ecclesia in Via*, 163–164.
89. LW 41:359 (WA 54:285), *Against the Roman Papacy*. See Brecht, 3:360–361.
90. BOC 325, *The Smalcald Articles*.
91. For an account of how Luther maintained an optimistic view of the church, see Scott Hendrix, "The Kingdom of Promise: Disappointment and Hope in Luther's Later Ecclesiology," Luther Congress, Copenhagen, 2002.

Chapter 7

The Common Priesthood in Luther's Old Testament Writings, 1524–1546

For these two, preaching and prayer, are the principal affairs of the church. They are our sacrifice and service, which belong properly to God and by which we are made priests.

—Martin Luther, *On Psalm 45*

The interrelatedness of Luther's writings—expository, doctrinal, polemical, and devotional—is demonstrated in these lectures and sermons, and shows the broad reach of his work as a biblical theologian. Within this theological synthesis, he continued to employ the themes of Christian priesthood because it was a biblical teaching that was embedded in his understanding of Christian piety, worship, and life. Detailed study and exposition of the first testament expanded the horizons of Luther's theology by confirming its deep roots in salvation history, and by contrasting the spiritual dynamics of both covenants. Luther read these ancient texts with all of his prejudices and presuppositions on display at the same time as the word spoke to him, informing and shaping his own theological development. As Luther expounded his reformational theology in relation to these texts, there was significant discussion of the work of priesthood in relation to preaching and worship, sacrifice and prayer. The turbulent contexts of church and society into which Luther wrote also played their part, as explained in the preceding chapters.

The view that Luther had earlier conceived and then laid aside "the priesthood of believers" after 1523 means that much of this later material has received only limited attention in studies of the common priesthood.[1] However, this chapter confirms the persistence of this teaching in his work on the prophets, Psalms and Genesis. Luther continued to use the key texts which underpinned the early development of his teaching, so that within the theological framework of the word of promise and justification by faith the themes of the common priesthood were aligned with his understanding of the church as the people of God, the communion of saints in which all participate.

THE PROPHETS

Lectures on Deuteronomy (Published 1525)

In early 1523, Luther began lecturing on Deuteronomy to "a small gathering of close associates," and prepared his notes for publication in Latin.[2] In his letter of dedication, he urges that Moses should be seen as "the father and fountain of all the prophets and sacred books."[3] Bornkamm suggests Luther used these lectures to sharpen his spiritual application of law and gospel in both Old and New Testaments, in contrast to teachers like Karlstadt and Müntzer for whom God's word was about regulating human behaviour. For Luther, the essence of the commandments—the command and promise, summarised in the words, "I am the Lord your God"—are universal in their application and their meaning for faith becomes clear in the light of Christ's fulfilment.[4] While these lectures do not contain many references to the common priesthood, it serves to link the fulfilment of God's word from the Old Testament to the New.

Luther applied the laws on worship and sacrifice in Deuteronomy 12 to the mystical sacrifice of "the common and spiritual priesthood" in Romans 12:1.[5] A related discussion of where worship rightly happens (Deuteronomy 17:8) reveals that for Christians, the "one common place" for worship is Christ himself, as accessible in Spirit and in truth to the maid and the farmer as he is to the pope himself. This includes spiritual discernment. Luther says, "[f]or faith is the property of all [*omnium enim est fides*], and 'he that is spiritual judges all things' (1 Cor. 2:15)."[6] He explains, "[h]ow much more should the priests of the faith and the Gospel [*Sacerdotes fidei et Euangelii*] define and teach everything, not by their own spirit but by the sure Word of God! And this neither the pope nor the councils have ever done."[7] A similar point is made about the right to judge the teaching of a "lawful prophet," which Luther upholds on the basis of Matthew 7:15 ("Beware of false prophets"). Luther had not abandoned this "right to judge," even though its use by the radical groups was becoming a cause of conflict. However, already here he emphasises the government's sole right to enact sanctions against false prophets.[8] The principle of "judgement" had not changed for Luther, but its application was aligned with his view of the sociopolitical realities.

A key passage was Deuteronomy 18:15, "The Lord will raise up for you a prophet like me." Here, Moses' word of law is contrasted with the future role of prophecy, when Christ comes. Then the word will make alive and console, rather than kill and terrify. For Luther, this requires its full operation in the lives of God's people, where the prophets foretell "another future covenant, word, and priesthood." This confirms the promise of a new covenant in Jeremiah 31:31–2, and of Christ's own priesthood in Psalm 110:4.[9]

In all situations—both "old" and "new"—Luther teaches that the servant of God's word is not to be despised but should be supported because they speak for God.[10] This focus on the word and those who speak it means that these lectures connect quite seamlessly to Luther's subsequent treatment of the prophetic writings, as Bornkamm says.[11]

Lectures on the Minor Prophets (1524–1527)[12]

Luther saw that God's word challenged Israel's response to their calling as God's people, with their possession of land, temple, priesthood, and sacrifice. For Luther, the prophets' words of judgement on the cultic priesthood and its defective sacrifices were mirrored in the flawed practices of the medieval church. Examples of apostasy abound, as the prophets condemned a reliance on human works rather than trust in God's mercy. Bound to the law of Moses, the priests had failed to proclaim God's word and to offer the true sacrifices of praise, the only appropriate response to God's word of promise. In the mouths of the prophets, that promise now included a new priesthood that drew all people into God's word and worship.

Luther makes this point in the lectures on Joel (1524), where the prophecy of the outpouring of the Spirit confirmed that "all will be teachers and priests of God." He writes,

> There will not be some order—as there was in that old people—of those who alone had the power of priestly function [*officium*]. Instead, the Holy Spirit will be poured out on all flesh. All will be teachers and priests of God.[13]

He does not explore how this takes place, or (at this point) the relevance of Joel's words to the roles of women and men in the church but his comments lead into a discussion of the priesthood and the sharing of God's Word, including the parallel text from Isaiah 54:13 (and John 6:45) that "all will be taught by God."[14]

Luther sharpens his focus on this teaching activity when commenting on Hosea, the story of Israel's unfaithfulness and its failed priesthood.[15] In chapter 14, the repentant people finally pray for forgiveness, and then in response to God's word of grace they are to offer "the fruit of our lips."[16] Luther understood "lips" to refer to preaching, and then to the related act of praise.[17] So, writing on Micah 6:6–8 and its powerful theme of "loving mercy," Luther says,

> Faith is the beginning of justification, as all Scripture reveals. Being justified by faith, we neither can nor should offer anything to God other than the sacrifice of praise; that is, that we bear witness with our preaching of the grace we have received, that we magnify God, that we preach His glory, and do this preaching through the Gospel. These are the "fruits of our lips."[18]

As the prophet teaches, this "fruit" also includes the good of the neighbour, when the blessing of salvation is shared.[19] The contrast between Old and New Testaments is even stronger in Luther's comments on Zephaniah 3:10, on the worship of those to be drawn to Jerusalem from all nations:

> Whatever is to come will be new—a new way to pray, a new method of making sacrifice, and a new people. . . . After all, the Law forbids one to sacrifice and pray in any way except in the designated fashion and in a definite place, the temple at Jerusalem. But Christians daily offer spiritual sacrifices to God, as Paul says in Romans 12:1, "Offer your bodies as a living sacrifice, holy, etc.."[20]

In his comments on Malachi, Luther relates this to the sacrifice of the Gospel by which preachers "offer" their hearers to God (Romans 15:16), and (again) to the teaching of justification by faith.[21] Writing on Malachi 1:11, he says,

> Word and prayer . . . are the two sacrifices of Christians. Prayer takes place along with thanksgiving and praise. The sacrifice of Christians is clean, because they themselves are without fault, because they have been washed by the blood of Christ, etc.[22]

This means that "the sons of Levi" (Malachi 3:3) will be purified by God's word and a new priesthood will be established in Christ's "totally sacerdotal" kingdom (*totum sacerdotale*), where there are no spiritual distinctions for "[e]veryone in this kingdom is Christ's brother. Through Christ, each can come to God and pray and teach."[23]

In the lectures on Zechariah, published in Latin in 1526 followed by a German version edited by Luther himself in 1527, he again compared the old priesthood and the new, developing the ideas expressed in the previous lectures.[24] The vision of Zechariah 3 reveals God's gracious dealings with the troubled high priest, Joshua, promising the future true priest who will take away sin: "[t]hus later there will be further need for no other day, no other priesthood, no other sacrifice."[25] The prophet's visions, like the seven-branched lampstand in chapter 4, represents for Luther unity among the preachers and teachers of God's people, and corresponds to the gifts of the one Spirit in the New Testament. The connection is reinforced by the use of his "key texts" here.[26]

Zechariah's final sacrificial image is a vision of the future church which Luther interprets according to his ecclesiology, using the themes of unity with Christ and the equality of God's people. In 14:20–21 the prophet foresees a time of universal salvation in Jerusalem, when all vessels will be sacred, and all who come will offer pure worship to the Lord. The Gentiles will join the people of God, and there will be an end to spiritual divisions among them, between priesthood and laity, rich and poor: "In sum: All, both great and small, both high and lowly stations, are to be subject to Christ."[27] Moreover, all share in Christ's holiness:

> [I]n the New Testament all Christians that worship God shall be sacred, consecrated, and fit for the priestly office, so that henceforth there will be no difference between the consecrated and the unconsecrated, because they all have been consecrated with the Spirit of Christ.[28]

This reference to baptismal consecration is followed by the familiar conclusion, and the text that Luther consistently uses in this period: "[t]hey are 'all priests,'" even though not all are "in the office and service"; but that sacrifice and service is now open to all, for "all are taught by the Lord (Isaiah 54:13)."[29] This fits with Luther's purpose in publishing the German commentary, "for those who like to read the Scriptures at home and wish to be strengthened in their faith."[30]

These are occasional and brief explanations of the common priesthood, within Luther's exposition of the Old Testament, with little direct reference to his ecclesiology. However, they sit alongside of a growing emphasis on the preaching office, and show how Luther now applied his insights about church and priesthood, and continued to make use of his key texts, particularly Romans 12:1 in relation to sacrifice, and Isaiah 54:13 for the inclusive teaching of God's word. The priesthood and its sacrifices represented a significant concern for the prophets, and Luther drew them into his own priorities to establish a firm link between worship and preaching. He made connections between the spiritual lives of God's people, ancient and modern, and emphasised the unity of all, in Christ. In this context, the common priesthood meant more than the establishment of a new church order in opposition to Rome: once again, it showed how the faithful promises of God were to be nurtured in a community of equal participants.

Lectures on Isaiah 40–66

After the Minor Prophets, Luther began an extensive series of lectures on Isaiah from 1528 to 1530.[31] He recognised that chapters 40–66 represented a change in Isaiah's prophecy, and it is in these chapters that the themes of priesthood occur. Both Brecht and Bornkamm comment on the significance of this series, that as "one of Luther's great lectures," it is "powerful and often too little esteemed."[32]

The theme of Christian equality is a constant in Luther's writing and its application to the activities of Christian discipleship is everywhere present, dependent upon God's word. By now, these points often require no further explication. This is the case with his teaching that all Christians are priests, and all participate in the proclamation of God's word (1 Peter 2:9), just as all have first received and heard that word. At the same time, the caution that not all should claim that right to speak publicly is emphasised by Luther because of growing disruption and disorder within the Christian community. It is all the more noteworthy that he continues to affirm the common priesthood in these lectures, while he clarifies the boundaries for its application. Echoes are heard of his favoured verse on order in the church, 1 Corinthians 14:40.[33]

His treatment of Isaiah 40 follows this pattern of acknowledging the horizons of Christian ministry at the same time as its limits are confirmed. The text celebrates the proclamation of the Gospel, and Luther recognises that all are involved ("every valley") in announcing the "good tidings." There can be no spiritual distinctions here, as there were among the monks.[34] But, he continues, "[e]very Christian is also an evangelist, who should teach another and publish the glory and praise of God. But the order [*ordo*] must be preserved intact so that we do not teach in a confused manner." Luther says, "I would, however, rather hear him who has been sent, and I will hear him, than preach myself, unless I were sent myself."[35]

Christian sacrifice as praise of God is here also, as it was in the previous lectures. And, significantly, the work of preaching not only evokes the response of praise, but is itself praise offered to God. It is a priestly act, a song of praise. Therefore, from God's standpoint, our worship is a unity, involving the whole community. Commenting on Isaiah 42:10, Luther says,

> The point at issue here is the worship of the New Testament. It is nothing else than song, praise, and thanksgiving. This is a unique song. God does not care for our sacrifices and works. He is satisfied with the sacrifice of praise. Bring God the sacrifices of righteousness and praise and of Psalm 110:3: "Your people will offer themselves willingly."[36] . . . To sing, therefore, is to praise, to give thanks, to preach, to do kindly deeds, to extol, to magnify. The preachers of Christ sing, and their hearers respond with thanksgiving. This is the song and evangelical worship [*cultus Euangelii*]. I, therefore, am a priest when I deal

with the Gospel. A worldly priest is characterized by an offering of works. This passage, too, marks the end of all specified places. For the new song knows no place or person.[37]

Luther is not only contrasting the traditional priesthood with those who are preachers, the clergy. This is a "new song," and it requires a new priesthood in which all believers share. He continues, "All those inhabitants of the earth, including the *islands*, such as Cyprus, Pontus, and Crete, must be priests of the universal [*generalis*] article of faith in Christ."[38]

He makes much of the identification of God with his people in this commentary, and of their equal participation in his blessings, and his work. An important text is Isaiah 43:2, *I have called you by name, you are mine*.[39] This means that "Christian" is a common noun which belong to all believers, those formed and made by God. He writes,

> A Christian is already one with Christ [*unus cum Christo*] and already has participation in him. . . . So the Christian in his entire being [*tota creatura*] becomes a participant with God. . . . So we are altogether Christ's, since Christ has called us, and all our works are not our own but Christ's.[40]

These clear statements, and others like them, are important to keep in view when considering whether Luther in his later emphasis on the preaching office teaches that only ordained ministers act or speak *in persona Christi*.[41] Here it is apparent that the focus is on the whole people of God, as the bearers of Christ's word to the world. Commenting on Isaiah 43:21, he compares the old people with the new:

> I have given them the whole New Testament with its own form of worship [*ritu*], and I have abolished the Old Testament, so that the people might declare My name. This people was formed and created by Me . . . this is My people, formed by Me, together with their office, kingdom, and priesthood [*officium et regnum et sacerdocium*].[42]

For Luther, the priestly "declaration of praise" here in Isaiah 43 is a significant summary of Christian worship, which is always centred on God's word of promise and the corresponding primacy of faith over works. It means

> to teach and to preach and to praise God, at the same time rejecting everything else. These are the sacrifices and whole burnt offerings that reject all our own offerings before God. To declare the praises of Christ is the priesthood and kingdom of the Christians. In the act of praising we become priests and kings [*sacerdotes et reges*]. . . . This is the greatest sacrifice, not our own offerings.[43]

By preaching the word, pastors build people up and bring them to "the eternal High Priest, who should kill all sins of the whole world." This is Christ's activity, his business, when as "God the Forgiver" [*deus deletorens*] he sweeps away sins "like cloud and mist" (Isaiah 44:22).[44]

Other descriptive titles in these chapters of Isaiah which Luther applies to Christ include that of "my servant" (49:3), and "covenant to the people" (49:8). And having been applied to Christ, the title of servant now belongs to the church and its ministry. Through the public offices, Christ works with the word. And this public service [*publicam funccionem*] includes, for example, fathers and mothers serving their families and households.[45] The covenant is the means by which God and the people are reconciled, for "[t]his office of Christ has been transferred [*translatum est*] to the church. Let no one think that Christ is dead. Rather, the ministers function in his office."[46] But Luther is still careful to emphasise that the operation of the word is not limited to a spiritual elite. Commenting on Isaiah 49:9, *they shall feed along the ways*, he says, "Here, however, the word sets forth pasture for every estate [*in omni statu*], and for all circumstances and people. The woman, the servant, the girl can hear the word of God at home, on the hills, and in the woods."[47] Within the reach of the gospel, all walks of life are equal before God and its ministry operates effectively on many levels.

Isaiah 54:13, quoted by Jesus himself (John 6:45), is one of Luther's key texts: "All your children will be taught by the Lord."[48] Here, after the struggles with Karlstadt and Muentzer, and the Peasants' War, he devotes a lengthy paragraph to its proper application. It does not teach the immediate work of God's Spirit, as Luther himself had once suggested.[49] Christians are the offspring of "mother church [who] bears her children through the word," who feeds and supports her own.[50] Both word and Spirit are necessary:

> The word is from the mother, the Spirit from the Father. The voice gathers us [*congregat nos*] into the church, and the Spirit unites us [*nos copulat*] with God. Thus a child of the church hears the word and is a disciple of God.[51]

This is a striking trinitarian expression of Luther's theology of the word. It both complements and contrasts Luther's brief explanation of the third article of the Creed in his *Small Catechism*, written around the same time: "The Holy Spirit has called me through the gospel."[52] In the *Large Catechism*, he describes the church as the mother "who begets and bears every Christian through the word of God."[53] In both cases, the agency for God's activity is the church, which fully possesses and ministers God's word.

Isaiah's "servant song" was important for Jesus' own self-understanding (Luke 4:18–19, "The Spirit of the Lord is upon me"), and Luther notes that Jesus was anointed as messiah, king, and priest [*ad Messiam, regem, sacerdotem unctum*].⁵⁴ Christ thus comes as "servant, messenger, apostle" [*Minister, nuncius, Apostolus*], entrusted with the office of the word [*officium verbi*], and bringing good news to the poor.⁵⁵ It is the breadth of the messianic work that is all-important to Luther; the titles reflect his understanding of Isaiah's text. Nowhere does Luther seek to constrain or systematise these offices within a formula such as "prophet, priest, and king."⁵⁶ Observing that those who receive this message then join in the servant's work and office, the sacrifices of praise and confession (61:3–4), Luther says,

> These are the two tasks of the Christians [*officia Christianorum*], to glorify God and to convert others. He who converts an ungodly man brings the best sacrifice, not offering an ox but a living sacrifice [*viventem hostiam*]. This is the sum of the prophets, to attribute to the Christian these two sacrifices: to praise God and to convert sinners, instead of all the endless ceremonies of the Law.⁵⁷

Isaiah 61:6 ("You will be called priests of the Lord") develops this thought for Luther, placing "ministers of our God" in parallel with "priests of the Lord" and Luther also connects the two, within what appears here as a broad understanding of the "public office" [*publico officio*]. The teachers "will be priests," but that title "must not be applied to a particular person in the New Testament." It belongs to all those who restore God's people, who "build up" and "convert." As previously (Isaiah 43:21, above), their sacrifice unites teaching and praise: "Such a one is a priest [*Hic est sacerdos*]."⁵⁸ This is reinforced by his comments on verse 10, the image of the bridegroom and his bride "clothed with the garments of salvation." Luther says this refers to "Christ and to the church" [*ad Christum et ad Ecclesiam*], and concludes that "all of us who believe are by faith [*per fidem*] bridegrooms and priests, something the world does not see but faith accepts."⁵⁹

The reference to spiritual clothing is one of the biblical triggers for Luther to reintroduce the priesthood into his discussion, especially when he can relate it to the special priestly robes. He often commented negatively on the robes worn by those who occupied the spiritual estate in his own day, when seen as a mark of their separation from the laity. For Luther, by faith all Christians wear the special garments, and here, at least, the boundaries between clergy and laity are readily dismissed.⁶⁰ What matters is that the word is shared, and the church is built up to the praise of God.

In the final chapter of Isaiah, Luther reflects on the prophet's rejection of established piety and worship, all elite religion including that of the temple and its priests. Once, all of it appeared to have God's enduring promise, but now it must give way to faithful acceptance of the ultimate word of promise, namely Christ himself who "walks like a layperson." The same applies today, says Luther, and the central teachings of faith and justification involve rejection of the theology and practice of the Roman church:

> So here the temple, the sacrifice, and the whole worship are rejected. In the same way the priesthood, monasticism, and every kind of hypocrisy are rejected today. Christ walks like a layperson [*incedit sicut laicus*], he teaches faith alone and repudiates all self-righteousness like tow,[61] and chooses what the hypocrites fear. Today we see by experience that he is rejecting the highest worship associated with the mass and the cowl.[62]

The penultimate verses (Isaiah 66:20–23) present a vision of the gathered nations, and a new priesthood, and so Luther gathers together his thoughts on the priesthood, scattered throughout this lengthy commentary. The preachers offer the nations to Christ, serving as "sacrificing priests [*sacrificulus*]" (Romans 15:16),[63] and thereby God also repeals the sacrifices and priesthood of Moses and the Levites, to establish "a new order of priests."[64] Today, like the Levites, "all teachers are priests," but this is no longer bound to a particular tribe; in fact, says Luther, "[w]e are all priests" [*omnes sumus sacerdotes*]. Sacrifice is the priest's office, and today that is done through "prayer [*oracionem*], mediation [*mediacionem*], and worship [*invocacionem*]." Like the new heavens (verse 22), "Christ and all who believe in Him will be priests forever. Here that new priesthood begins, and it will last forever."[65]

The christological importance of Isaiah 40–66 adds significance to Luther's treatment of the common priesthood here. As with the Minor Prophets, it fits naturally with the themes of worship and how Luther embeds that in his concern for teaching the word. Exposing the inadequacy of a religion based on sacrificial ritual and the ceremonies of the law further connects it to justification by faith. While the New Testament ministry with its preaching of the word is Luther's primary focus, this office is not seen in isolation but stands alongside the responsibility for the Gospel given to all who follow Christ. This is because the primary office, the ministry and the priesthood all belong to the servant Christ himself. Within these themes of equality and participation there remains the promise of an enduring reality: "We are all priests."

THE PSALMS REVISITED (1530–1539)

One of Luther's ongoing projects was a revision of his translation of the psalms, along with other Old Testament books.[66] In 1528, this included a new preface in which he presents the psalter in glowing terms as "a little Bible," encompassing the promise of Christ's salvation and providing a "book of examples of all Christendom or all saints."[67] Luther endeavours to share with his readers the deep significance that these spiritual songs and prayers continued to hold for his own journey of faith, and for his theology as well. His personal faith was rooted in the community of faith, the communion of saints, and Luther urges Christians to speak and to sing in their company.[68] He concludes,

> In a word, if you would see the holy Christian Church painted in living color and shape, comprehended in one little picture, then take up the psalter. There you have a fine, bright, pure mirror that will show you what Christendom is. Indeed you will find in it also yourself and the true *gnothi seauton* ["know yourself"], as well as God himself and all creatures.[69]

Martin Brecht explains the significance of the psalter for Luther, detained at Castle Coburg in 1530, and when his father died.[70] Brecht says, "It is not by chance that during the following years he returned again and again to the psalms in his literary activity, his lectures, and his work within the circle of his own home."[71] This fresh activity also shows Luther's theological development from his earlier work on the psalms before 1520. The ecclesiological themes of community and participation persist, and while Luther emphasises the prime importance of the preaching of the word, neither does he leave unspoken the themes of the common priesthood when the text of the psalms calls them forth.

Psalm 118 and Psalm 117

Written in the second half of June 1530, during the days leading up to the presentation of the *Augsburg Confession*, Luther's interpretation of Psalm 118 represents a personal confession of praise, with the confidence of faith in God's protection in the face of many enemies.[72] In the celebratory verses that lead to the psalm's concluding words of praise, Luther takes up the theme of the Lord's new day (v.24), as a prophecy of the Gospel.[73] All God's people are now able to fully participate in the priestly worship of God's house and join the procession to the altar (v.27). He writes, "There is no longer any difference between the Levites and the people. Everyone who believes may approach the altar, a privilege not granted in the Law."[74] The branches symbolise that people should "adorn, praise, beautify, and exalt the name of God with joyful, fresh, green, and beautiful preaching and singing."[75] The old animal sacrifices have ended, to be replaced by this sacrifice of praise and thanksgiving: "Now everything that formerly was outwardly performed by the Levites is done by thanks and praise, preaching and teaching."[76] As he did with the prophets, Luther now consistently identifies sacrificial worship with the ministry of the Gospel, characterised as the community's praise and confession of God.

In the same vein, he comments on Psalm 117, while still at Coburg during first part of August 1530. The difficult negotiations continued between the parties in Augsburg, and in his many letters Luther's frustrations became apparent. But his confidence remains that God's will would triumph, despite appearances to the contrary.[77] It leads him to combine this brief psalm's universal accents of praise with the specifics of evangelical teaching. Praise of a merciful God (v.2) must preclude the false spirituality of religious orders who elevate themselves above ordinary Christians, because "[t]he estate of the Christian [*Christenstand*] should cover all things in heaven and earth, for it is the estate [*stand*] of Christ himself and of God's own work."[78]

This also reveals the true nature of Christian worship as a priestly offering of praise and proclamation that is appropriately summarised by 1 Peter 2:9:

> First we must recognize in our hearts and believe that we receive everything from Him and that He is our God. Then out with it, and freely and openly confess this before the world—preach, praise, glorify, and give thanks! This is the real and only worship of God, the true office of the priest [*das rechte priesterlich ampt*], and the finest, most acceptable offering—as St. Peter says: "You are a royal priesthood, that you may declare the wonderful deeds of Him who called you out of darkness into His marvelous light."[79]

In his exposition, Luther also takes opportunity to recall his basic argument against medieval teaching on sacrifice, and states that making offerings in terms of "giving to God" is not acceptable. His witnesses here are Psalm 51, the offering of a "broken spirit," and the rejected offerings of Malachi 1:10–11. Rather, "This is the offering of thanks, when by preaching and confession in all the world the name of the Lord is magnified and glorified. To make His name great is the fine, pure offering of which the psalmist is speaking here."[80] Yet again, the proclamation of God's word, and faith's response of praise, stand in close relationship to one another. This is the priestly work of the community, and also of the individual believer. In Luther's ecclesiology, each aspect draws on the other, and are diminished when they are separated. These conjunctions—word and faith, the community and the individual—now figure prominently whenever Luther brings to the fore the themes of worship and priesthood.

Commentaries on Psalms 2, 45, and 51

Luther lectured on Psalms 2, 45, and 51, in the course of eight months in 1532. Later, they were prepared for publication by Veit Dietrich on the basis of notes by Georg Rörer.[81] While they do not provide substantial material on the common priesthood, they do indicate how Luther applied the psalms for students preparing for public ministry, including their teaching on sacrifice and worship.

For Luther, the significance of Psalm 2 is its teaching on Christ's incarnation. It reveals his spiritual kingship, and his office as "a priest who teaches the church."[82] In his introduction to this psalm, and perhaps for the whole series, Luther comments to his students on the lowly status of teachers and theologians. But this is only so before the world; in reality, theologians and preachers are dealing with the knowledge of God and people's salvation. Thus, "[they] also offer to God in heaven Himself the most pleasant sacrifice and [are] truly called the priest[s] of the All–highest."[83] He contrast this activity with the false worship of the mass and its "sacrifice":

> [T]he true worship has now been restored, that is, the preaching of the Word of God, by which God is truly made known and honored. Therefore I, too, as one of the great number of priests of God, wish to take up and explain the Second Psalm. I do this not only to teach you and learn for myself, but also thereby to bring to God a pleasing sacrifice.[84]

By referring to the "great number of priests," he makes it clear that this activity is taking place within the community of the church. Luther's understanding places God's word at the heart of Christian sacrifice; however it is "offered" in accordance with an individual's appointed task, office, or calling. Here, there is a particular relationship to the word. Setting the agenda for their study of the psalms, and in the context of the theological training of pastors and teachers for the church, he says,

> Let us, then, unite our studies and labours—you by hearing, I by teaching. And so, as our calling requires, we shall perform this service to God which He everywhere demands of us, so that by this discussion of the Word of God, faith will be confirmed in us and the glory of God will be increased. This is a sacrifice pleasing and acceptable to God.[85]

This union of teaching and hearing has a significance outside the lecture hall, to the pulpit and beyond. As in his interpretation of Psalms 117 and 118 above and in many other places, it is the way Luther now consistently presents the involvement of all Christians as priests in the office of the word. It is what makes their whole lives "spiritual," whatever their calling. In his comments on this psalm, he frequently notes how Karlstadt and Zwingli have made the Christian life a matter of externals by stepping apart from the word.[86] Christ himself, however, exemplifies what it means to fulfil a

God-given calling, and Luther urges his students to "embrace him . . . as a priest and a teacher."[87]

In the same lecture series (1532), Luther says that Psalm 51 is "about the chief parts of our religion, about repentance, sin, grace, and justification, as well as about the worship we ought to render God."[88] He recalls its historic use in the church as a penitential psalm, and—unsurprisingly—at length unpacks its significance for evangelical teaching. In connection with verse 7, Luther notes Christ's sole sacrifice for sin,[89] but it is in the final division (verses 15–19) that he explores this in some detail. As the psalm moves from personal experience to corporate worship, Luther says, "The prophet is not dealing here with a private conversation between God and the sinner, but with the whole church [*de tota Ecclesia*], the ministry and the ministers and the whole people of God [*toto populo Dei*]."[90] And this priesthood offers not animal sacrifices, "but humble and contrite hearts."[91]

But the most telling comparison for Luther is between the pope's sacrifice of the mass, performed "in a pomp worthy of kings," and the sacrifice of

> one sinner who says, "God, be merciful to me," like that publican in Luke 18:13. He is a real pope and a real priest [*verus Papa et verus sacerdos*], pleasing to God, because he offers to God a most acceptable sacrifice, a heart that is contrite and yet trusts in His mercy.[92]

Here, the common priesthood is located at the very heart of the teaching of justification by faith, and thus displays its deep relevance also for ecclesiology, together with Luther's theology of worship. It is striking to note that in the year before these lectures on the psalms, Luther had completed his second series on Galatians, what Martin Brecht calls the "high point in Luther's work as a teacher."[93] While Luther may not systematise his theology, its organic unity is often clearly visible, and this is integral to any presentation of his thought.

These theological connections also appear in his treatment of Psalm 45, which he introduces for his students as a royal wedding psalm. For Luther, this portrays the spiritual marriage between Christ and those who belong to him through faith, recalling the striking imagery of *The Freedom of a Christian* (1521).[94] He interprets the psalm according to the theme of kingship, and introduces no messianic link with Christ's priesthood. Christ the king is head of the church, and having overcome sin is the saviour of his people.[95]

However, the themes of the common priesthood are also present in Luther's exposition. The language of the psalm draws him into the use of allegory in verse 9, invoking images of crowns and harps from Revelation (Rev. 4:4, 5:8, 14:2), as well as incense (Rev. 8:3–4). Luther sees here the hidden reality of faith, which exalts the humble as daughters of the king.[96] The harps are the voice of God, and incense is prayer: "For these two, preaching and prayer, are the principal affairs of the church. They are our sacrifice and service, which belong properly to God and by which we are made priests [*sacerdotes efficimus*]."[97] But, says Luther, the allegory is not altogether necessary, because in fact many noble women—king's daughters—have been strong in the spirit and faith.[98]

This understanding of faith is prominent as Luther interprets v.11 ("adore the king"): it "is a remarkable verse, and I therefore commend it to you."[99] It teaches the worship of God, believers bowing down to adore the King. Once again, faith in Christ is the key, not the ceremonies of the monks or Turks. In this way the royal wedding robes now serve as priestly garments, as those who accept God's word in faith join in the worship of the king:

> [L]aying hold of this King and believing He is the Son of God, who suffered for us and rose again; moreover, acknowledging Him in reverence, accepting His Word, believing, and doing everything through faith in Him, to His glory, so that everything may take place, as Paul says, "in the name of Jesus" (Colossians 3:17). In this way we are all priests [*Sic omnes sumus sacerdotes*], clothed and adorned with the same holiness of Christ, whom we receive through faith, much more beautiful than all righteousness of the Old Covenant and the papacy.[100]

Through these three psalms Luther instructs his students and encourages them to learn Hebrew so that they can study the Old Testament for themselves, and then accurately preach its message.[101] He shares with them the comfort and encouragement that he has found in the psalms, and presents their fulfilment in Christ's new covenant. That includes a new way of worship, based on faith, and thus they are to teach a new, universal priesthood as well: now, "we are all priests."

Sermons on Psalm 110, "Concerning the Kingdom of Christ"

Dating from 1535, and published in 1539, this exposition is a major contribution to the investigation of Luther's later teaching on the common priesthood.[102] Heinrich Bornkamm suggests that Luther "elevated Psalm 110 above the others," along with Psalm 2.[103] It originated in a series of eight sermons preached in Wittenberg during May and June 1535. As with other sermons and lectures, the finished publication was the work of Caspar Cruciger, on the basis of notes by Georg Rörer.[104] Luther often commended Cruciger for his work as a theologian and editor who excelled in making his thoughts accessible to a wider public in an accurate form.[105]

For Luther, this psalm is preeminently a messianic prophecy revealing Christ's reign as king and his service as high priest. This interpretation assumes that its original composition, with the imagery employed, are all directed towards this prophetic teaching. Luther is, of course, aware that in Matthew 22:43–5 Jesus applies its opening verse to himself, "The Lord said to my Lord."[106] This means that he can move freely from the time of King David to the work of Christ, and to the institution of the New Testament church. The themes of ministry and priesthood are directly addressed and provide significant insights as to their relationship in his mature ecclesiology.

In verse 2, the "sceptre sent forth from Zion" is Christ's institution of the public ministry. It begins with his own work of preaching, and is then furthered "by his messengers, the apostles and their successors, and to be continued until the Last Day."[107] This is the way Christ now rules on earth, and by which his kingdom is established:

> This will be done only through the oral Word or the preaching office [*predigt ampt*], sounding forth among the people about this King and thus entering their hearts so that He may be known and accepted.[108]

This becomes Luther's test for authentic Christian teaching, to be applied to the papal church on the one hand, and the enthusiasts on the other. It must conform to the apostolic teaching, which began in Jerusalem (Luke 24:47–8). He writes, "Hence this is the touchstone by which all doctrine is to be judged. One must take care and see whether it is the same doctrine that was published in Zion through the apostles."[109] It is not surprising to Luther that there is conflict and opposition to God's word; it is confirmed for him by verse 2(b), that the Lord "rules in the midst of [his] foes."[110] Luther notes that this public proclamation was instituted by Christ, who commands the witness and ministry of the apostles. This is the historical grounding for Luther's insistence that the public, ordained office is a ministry of the word, a preaching office. This order, from Christ to the apostles and then to their successors, is Luther's understanding of "tradition": the preservation of the gospel as it is passed on from one generation to the next.[111] How the public ministry is located within the church becomes clear as he proceeds with his interpretation of the psalm.

The psalm implies a transition, for Luther, from those who were God's people, to those who now become the people of God. This continues, even after Christ has come. Luther looks back to the time of David, and then to his own day, as he writes, "God will accept no people, no priesthood, no worship, no life at all except that which belongs to this King. Later in the psalm we read of the new priesthood, God's new servants and liturgy [*neuen Gottes dienem und Gottes dienst*]."[112]

These new people are those who willingly offer themselves and appear before God in "holy array" (Psalm 110:3). They are the people of faith, distinct from the old Levitical priesthood, but no less beautifully dressed (Exodus 28): "By this expression [the psalmist] makes priests out of all the people of this King, that is, his believing Christians [*Seine gleubige Christen*]."[113] There is no greater honour, says Luther, than to serve as a priest, and to be close to God.[114] For Christians, the priestly garments ("array") are the Spirit's gifts for the ministry of the church (Ephesians 4:11–12), and Luther here cements the connection he often makes between priesthood and ministry. The gifts are those given "to Christendom to advance the knowledge and the praise of God, which is carried out pre-eminently by the ministry of preaching the Gospel [*das Predig ampt des Euangelii*]."[115] But this is also ministry in its broadest configuration, to bring people to the knowledge of God, and which includes the public confession of faith with its proclamation:

> This is the reason why we are God's servants and are called priests [*heissen Priester*]. Whatever we do, our teaching and our life ought to shine like a beacon of light to the greater knowledge, honour, and praise of God, as Christ also says (Matt. 5:16).[116]

1 Peter 2:9 also figures here, and so the "holy array" or "adornment" signifies the praise and honouring of God, preaching and confessing the Gospel, and giving thanks for God's grace. This is all for the extension of God's kingdom, and only Christians can do this, "for they are the true and holy priests [*rechte, heilige Priester*] before God."[117] These priests are altogether different to those in Levitical or Roman orders, says Luther, as is their "ordination" performed by the High Priest Jesus Christ and his Holy Spirit.[118] The ostentatious outward trappings no longer apply, whatever useful teaching purpose they may have originally signified:

> But Christians who have the word of God, as, thank God, we do, who believe it, preach it, and confess it, also have the right adornment. They have the right mitres on their heads, mitres adorned with verses and illustrations from the Scriptures instead of with precious pearls. Thereby they can instruct and comfort people [*unterrichten, trösten*]. They wear a cross of real gold or pearls on the tips of their mitres because they are people ready to suffer everything for the sake of confessing Christ, who is the Lord and the glory of our heads (1 Corinthians 11:3). They are clothed with an alb of pure white linen, that is, with a good conscience, a pure life, and good works.[119]

As he does in many other places, Luther translates the psalm in accordance with his overall understanding of its message, within the context of his theology. "Ordination" to the new priesthood is by baptism. So, in verse 3(b), the difficult Hebrew reading "the dew of your youth" is rendered by Luther as "your children will be born to you like the dew of the morning."[120] The nature of the church, he says, reflects this heavenly birth, the unfathomable working of the Spirit like the wind, as Jesus teaches Nicodemus (John 3:6). Luther says,

> You can see the water of baptism as you can see the dew, and you can hear the external or spoken Word as you can hear the wind; but you cannot see or hear or understand the Spirit, or what He accomplishes thereby: that a human being is cleansed in Baptism and becomes a saint in the hands of the priest, so that from a child of hell he is changed into a child of God.[121]

He is following the sequence of the psalm, and at verse 4 introduces the priesthood of Christ, which would usually precede discussion of the common priesthood. David has announced that Christ is King and Lord; now he makes him "priest and pope [*Priester und Babst*]," as the necessary mediator between God and his people. Both offices have been assigned to Christ: "He is to be the everlasting King and Priest."[122] This is David's surprising innovation, says Luther, and he discusses at length how this supplanted the Levitical priesthood instituted under Moses, with a new order to be inaugurated with the reign of the coming Messiah.[123]

Luther then explores the story of Melchizedek, also at some length, arguing from Genesis 14 and Hebrews 7 that this new priesthood is instituted to share God's blessing with all God's people. The papal claim that it prefigures the private sacrifice of the mass is here rejected by Luther, as in previous writings.[124] Rather, he says, Scripture teaches that "the priestly office consists of three parts: to teach or preach God's Word, to sacrifice, and to pray [*Predigen, Opffern und Beten*]."[125]

Drawing his discussion of verse 4 to a close, Luther introduces what becomes an excursus on Christian priesthood and ministry. In the New Testament, Christ alone is High Priest, but he has bestowed the title of priest on us also, "so that we who believe in him are also priests [*auch wir Christen Priester sind*], just as we are called Christians after him."[126] The offices in the church—bishop, pastor, preacher—do not confer this priesthood. They are neither priests, nor Christians, by virtue of their office. Rather, "every baptized Christian [*iglich getauffter Christen*] is a priest already, not by appointment or ordination from the pope or any other man, but because Christ Himself has begotten him as a priest and has given birth to him in Baptism."[127] They are children of the Priest, offspring of a spiritual birth, sharing the same status as their father. Luther reinforces baptism's conferral of the name of priest, repeating the argument that he employed in earlier works, for example in *Concerning the Ministry*.[128] In extravagant fashion he draws together the familiar texts from Ephesians 4 and Galatians 3 as well, teaching the fundamental unity that exists in the communion of saints and used here to confirm the common priesthood, just as they were in earlier writings:

> Every baptized Christian is, and ought to be, called a priest, just as much as St. Peter or St. Paul. St. Peter was a priest because he believed in Christ. I am a priest for the same reason. Thus we all, as I have said before, have become priest's children through Baptism. Therefore it should be understood that the name "priest" ought to be the common possession of believers just as much as the name "Christian" or "child of God." We all have one Baptism in common, one Gospel, one kind of grace, one kind of inheritance of the kingdom of heaven, one Holy Spirit, one God the Father, and one Lord Jesus Christ (Ephesians 4:4–6). We are all one in Him, as he says in John 17:22 and as St. Paul says in Galatians 3:28: "You are all one in Christ Jesus."[129]

He then returns to the matter of offices in the church. The distinction is drawn between the priestly office, common to all, and the ministerial offices, to which people are chosen and appointed. Luther draws a comparison with civic offices, which are conferred on those who are already citizens. Likewise, suitably qualified people are set apart to work in the church. Luther suggests, as he has before, that this is indicated by the New Testament term "presbyter." He says that its literal meaning, "elder," designates someone qualified by experience to exercise a leadership role. Likewise, "bishop" means "overseer."[130]

Luther then introduces a significant new expression: the office does "make a difference between Christians [*machet einen unterschied zwischen im und andern Christen*]."[131] It does not change a person's spiritual status—that is irrevocably given, in baptism—but within the ordering of the church, as in society at-large, there needs to be those who are appointed to positions of leadership. He writes, "Out of the multitude of Christians some must be selected who shall lead the others by virtue of the special gifts and aptitude which God gives them for the office." Significantly, Luther bases this on Ephesians 4:11–12, verses from the same source just used to confirm the common priesthood. It teaches that the one body of Christ needs the gift of leaders to build up the community: apostles, prophets, evangelists, pastors, and teachers.[132] Luther then adds his often-repeated caution, that "not all of us can preach, teach, and rule." The office-bearers are chosen as servants "of all the others, who are priests." If and when that service ends, the office "is conveyed to someone else, and they become a Christian like any other [*ein iglicher gemeiner Christen*]."[133]

"This is the way," Luther says, "to distinguish between the office of preaching [*das Predigt ampt*], or the ministry [*Dienst*], and the general priesthood of all baptized Christians [*dem gemeinen priesterstand aller getauffter Christen*]."[134] He then poses the all-important question, "Wherein does this priesthood of Christians consist, and what are their priestly works?" The answer is, as before, "teaching, sacrificing, and praying."[135] But these, he insists, are above all the work of Christ himself, the only High Priest. Only as he shares his work with us do we "possess" this priesthood. It is his teaching which saves us; his sacrifice which reconciles us to God; and he alone can make intercession for us, and bring our prayers into God's presence. He then spells out the implications of each of these priestly activities.

By Christ's own priestly office which is ours through baptism and faith, "each one, according to his calling and position [*beruff und stand*], obtains the right and the power [*recht und macht*] of teaching and confessing before others this word which we have obtained from him."[136] Once again, although not everyone has the public office,

> [E]very Christian has the right and the duty to teach, instruct, admonish, comfort, and rebuke his neighbour with the Word of God at every opportunity and whenever necessary. For example, father and mother should do this for their children and household; a brother, neighbour, citizen, or peasant for the other. Certainly one Christian may instruct and admonish another ignorant or weak Christian concerning the Ten Commandments, the Creed, or the Lord's Prayer. And whoever receives such instruction is also under obligation to accept it as God's Word and publicly to confess it.[137]

This Christian responsibility for the neighbour's welfare—including parents for children—involves serving them with the word. It is therefore a task of the ministry entrusted to the church, one in which all must share. The called public ministry differs in terms of its particular context, responsibilities, and its broader reach; in this way it fulfils Christ's specific institution. It is a distinct, public exercise of ministry, but it is neither separate nor unique. This is an important statement of Luther's teaching here, and emphasises why the work of teaching the laity is so important, and reveals the strong connections between the common priesthood and the catechetical emphasis in his reforming work.[138]

Again, the priestly duty to sacrifice requires specific parameters. It is not a sacrifice for sins, to effect atonement or reconciliation, either for oneself or for others. That remains Christ's work alone. Rather, "[t]he sacrifices of Christians exist for the purpose of honouring and glorifying God." Romans 12:1 ("present your bodies") applies here, and involves the Christian experience of the cross and suffering.[139] Especially when it means suffering loss for the sake of confessing Christ, this is to God's glory, and serves as a good example, as did the Christian martyrs. Not only bishops and preachers, but also women and children are included: "[a]ll these have been true priests and priestesses, for they sacrificed their bodies." Luther uses the example of St Agnes. But, in different ways, this sacrifice of praise is common to all Christians.[140]

The third task of the priest, Christian prayer, "accompanies such sacrifices," through the mediation of Christ alone.[141] Everything has its source in him, including the right to appear before God in prayer. Thus, only as a Christian, anointed by Christ, can one do this, and that includes teaching and sacrifice as well. Not all who claim the authority to teach in the church do so as Christians, but

> If, for example, a young child who is baptized prays the Ten Commandments, the Creed, and the Lord's Prayer each morning or evening at the table, it is a true prayer; and God hears him. Such a child prays as a Christian and a priest, born in Baptism and ordained by Christ.[142]

These are the priestly works of all Christians. But "the communal [*gemeine*] office of public teaching" is also necessary.[143] Luther uses the arguments for "good order" here, without quoting 1 Corinthians 14:40. Those selected and ordained to preach and teach have a responsibility for the sacraments; that cannot be a matter for each household. It "belong[s] to the public office [*ein gemein, offentlich Ampt*] which is performed in behalf of all those who are priests, that is, Christians."[144]

In relation to verses 6 and 7, Luther explores opposition to Christ's kingship, and his priesthood, by the earthly authorities. The psalm's comfort here is for Christians who hold onto the eschatological hope of the king's final triumph over his enemies. In keeping with this, the final verse is a prophecy of a messiah who will share his people's suffering and cross, and in this way bring redemption to all who believe in him. Christ "is an eternal Priest, who makes us all into priests, although we see neither church nor altar nor the rite of ordination."[145] Luther concludes his exposition with a reminder that the psalm portrays a spiritual kingdom. Psalm 110 "is the very core and quintessence of the whole Scripture. No other psalm prophesies as abundantly and completely about Christ."[146]

In summary, for Luther this most significant psalm celebrates the messianic mission and ministry of Christ, sent into the world as king and priest bearing the word of God. It is the clearest explanation we have of how he views the close relationship of priesthood and ministry: distinguished, but not separated in Cruciger's careful editorial work. In this psalm, Christ's own proclamation becomes the mission and ministry of the church, to the praise of God. To that end, all Christians receive Christ's priesthood, to which they are ordained by the Spirit in the waters of baptism. Each one participates in the priestly work of teaching, sacrifice, and prayer, according to their various callings. For this Christian community, and from within it, Christ has instituted the preaching office and the sacramental ministry of those who are chosen for public service from among their fellow priests.

THE FINAL LECTURES

Lectures on Genesis (June 1535–November 1545)

In Martin Brecht's judgement, the lectures on Genesis "are unquestionably monumental documents of Luther's mature theology, and they also reflect his participation in the developments, problems, and conflicts of the last decade of his life." In spite of its diverse and contested transmission, "the bulk of this commentary, with its amazing richness of features and allusions, undoubtedly does come from Luther, and his spirit is evident in it."[147]

For Luther, the activity of God's word from the very beginning meant that all those who heard its commands, and believed its promises, were already "the church." They worshipped and sacrificed not just in anticipation of a future blessing, but as those who were engaged with a present reality.[148] In their life of faith the true church lay hidden, already in conflict with the outward religion of the false church. In Luther's narrative this struggle was as real for the patriarchs as it was for him in his own day.

Selecting a few examples, it can be shown how Luther revisits his previous work on priesthood and ministry in these lectures, and how he illustrates those concepts from the lives of these spiritual ancestors. Despite the rather obvious ways in which he invests Genesis with all the challenges and presuppositions of the sixteenth century, his clear endeavour is to uncover a common heritage of faith in the prototypical salvation history of God's people.

In Adam and Eve, the institution of the church preceded that of the family, and the state.[149] They "perform the office of priests [*Sacerdotum officio*]"[150] and their sacrifices were offerings of prayer and praise, signs of grace always connected to the word.[151] Abel's acceptable sacrifice marks him as the true priest; Cain as the false.[152] This leads to the discussion of the true and false churches that Luther pursues in these lectures, and the persecution of the former by the latter.[153] The conflict between Jacob and Esau also follows this pattern.[154]

With Noah (the "supreme pontiff and priest"[155]), the two duties of the priesthood are clearly seen. He turns to God, in prayer for himself and for others. He turns from God, to bring the word of repentance to his family and neighbours.[156] So both Adam and Noah are public ministers, and this is the usual way for God's word to be communicated in this world.

His broad view of that ministry means that ordinarily this is "through parents and the teachers of the church."[157] Exceptionally, there is revelation, "by an angel, or by the Holy Spirit himself." But Luther's concern is to uphold the validity of the ministry of the word, from the very beginning: "The word of God is truly the word even when it is uttered by a human being." So he suggests that God's message to Cain, for example, had been mediated through the voice of his father, Adam.[158] Commenting on Genesis 8, Luther suggests that the priestly office was handed on to Noah through "the right of primogeniture" and God's command to Noah contains his call both as a priest and as a prophet.[159]

Thus, also Abraham—who, says Luther, first heard God's call through the patriarch Shem—assumes the priestly duties of teaching, prayer, and sacrifice.[160] In this way, Abraham was obedient to God; he did not follow a self-chosen path, apart from the external word. In words that provide significant context for this commentary's heavy emphasis on the public office, Luther tells his students,

> You must have the same conviction about the general call, when you are called to the ministry of teaching [*ad ministerium docendi*]: you should consider the voice of the community [*Respublica*] as the voice of God, and obey.[161]

In the same way, Abraham's companions are not simply his household, "but the true and holy church, in which Abraham was the high priest."[162] In the activity of building an altar (Genesis 12:7), Luther says, "those who gather there hear the Word of God, pray, give thanks to God, praise God, and carry out those forms of worship which He has commanded."[163] Apart from the word and the worshippers' priestly service all else is idolatry, as for example is seen in the sacrifice of the mass, says Luther.[164]

In the royal figure of Melchizedek (Genesis 14:18–20), Luther finds validation that Christ's priesthood is of a different order than that of the Levites, and will supersede it. This is confirmed for Luther by references to Hebrews 7, and Psalm 110, and he argues against the interpretation that Melchizedek's offering of bread and wine prefigures the sacrificial priesthood of Rome. Melchizedek is a priest of God's word, who preaches and prays, as he brings Abraham his blessing.[165] Luther also makes reference to the tradition that Melchizedek is to be identified with the patriarch Shem, and therefore represents continuity within the narrative of Genesis rather than a mysterious intervention.[166]

Abraham's married status is significant for Luther in his consideration of the patriarch as priest. Applying the church's tradition, Luther says, Abraham is "a plain layman." There can be nothing "spiritual" about him, by medieval standards. But drawing support from Hebrews 11:8–10, Luther uses the yardstick of faith to assert the significance before God of "ordinary deeds." Abraham is one who "everywhere sustained himself with the divine promises."[167] Using this example of Abraham, Luther affirms that the word and faith have always been essential to the true biblical priesthood:

> We declare that those are true priests who believe the word of God, offer the sacrifice of praise and of the cross, and do not walk about in long garments but walk about in the gifts and jewels of the Holy Spirit: faith, patience in death, and the expectation of another and better life.[168]

In the same way, Jacob was appointed king and priest, not with pomp and ritual, but "mortified through faith," and with only a bag and staff, "is driven into exile." From this scattered seed comes Christ, "the eternal king and priest."[169] At the same time as Luther draws deep comfort and encouragement for the church from the patriarchs' faith in the midst of many trials, he also seems to find their nomadic existence appealing, and more than once draws a link between their tents and his own concept of the church, transcending institutional boundaries:

> Abraham had in his tent a house of God and a church, just as today any godly and pious head of a household instructs his children and domestics in godliness. Therefore such a house is actually a school and church, and the head of the household is a bishop and priest in his house. Thus the tents in which Jacob dwelt were sacred, and there he sought first the kingdom of God (Matt. 6:33).[170]

In summarising the ecclesiology of these lectures on Genesis, Heinrich Bornkamm has indicated how close Luther remained to his original insight into the nature of the church: "The church was to him never anything else but the hidden community of saints, the people of God living from the word of God."[171] In these lectures, the priesthood is always presented in its relationship to the word, in accordance with Luther's long-standing interpretation. And public ministry is significant here, at least in part because he is lecturing to students who will become pastors and preachers. It is also important for Luther to show that the patriarchs' priesthood is superior to the ritual service of the Levites, and in this way prefigures that of Christ himself, and of the church. These men, with their wives, minister as high priests for their extended families, as those among whom the word was proclaimed and believed, and by whom God was worshipped.[172] They have nothing in common with a consecrated, hierarchical priesthood.

Luther's treatment of the common priesthood in Genesis occurs largely by anticipation and implication, within his casting of the patriarchs as the forerunners and high-priestly heralds of the true church. The themes of equality and participation are certainly present, along with his understanding that the church is a community gathered around the word, before it is an institution. However, in presenting the patriarchal life of faith amidst struggles and temptations he was also portraying his own participation in the church's life in the world with its many setbacks and trials: as such, this reflects Luther's own "patriarchal" experiences in Wittenberg, in his personal life and in his own household as well as among his colleagues and co-workers. It was here that faith in the church as the communion of saints continued to be tested and shaped.[173]

Summarizing Luther's First Testament Ecclesiology

This chapter is an important addition to this study of Luther's common priesthood, exploring these dimensions of public and private worship especially in the *Lectures on Isaiah* and the published sermon series on Psalm 110. As well as their particular biblical content they add significant later perspectives to this teaching, showing its persistent presence throughout his exegetical and expository work well beyond the initial stages of the Reformation. However, as a body of work on the First Testament, or as individual publications, these commentaries and sermons have been largely bypassed or ignored in discussions of this subject.

The connections that Luther makes between God's covenant with Israel and the New Covenant in Christ means that this is a rich source for his teaching on the prophetic preaching of the word, the worship, sacrifices and prayers of God's people. The true nature of priesthood is seen in relation to God's word (*Deuteronomy, Minor Prophets*). It is perhaps surprisingly that the primary task of the priest is to proclaim the word, and to teach one's fellows, but for Luther these are the true sacrifices of praise and confession. This happens publicly in worship and teaching, and on a more personal level (reflecting Luther's own spiritual practice) it is most often seen in the direct address to God, the spiritual struggles and meditations of The Psalms. In his final lectures, Luther presents this preaching and worship as the high-priestly actions of the patriarchs, especially in their own households (*Lectures on Genesis*). This priestly activity will all be bound together in its fulfillment by Christ's own kingly priesthood, remarkably prefigured by the appearance of the character of Melchizedek in Genesis 14 and recalled in Psalm 110.

The Genesis lectures also present, prototypically and yet contemporaneously, the conflict between the true church and the false, originating within the sacrificial activity of the priesthood. For Luther, the true priestly offerings are the response to God's gracious action, rather than an attempt to satisfy the requirements an angry deity (see also Psalm 117). This reformational teaching had also been explored in the work of the prophets, who were sent to reject a reliance on the ceremonial requirements of the Mosaic covenant (*Minor*

Prophets, Isaiah). In the earlier lectures, the failure of the cultic priesthood (the Levites) to honour God's purposes, and their complicity in the failure of Israel to live as God's people, is countered by the prophets' denunciation, and their announcement of the promised messianic new day. Luther draws strong parallels with his own church and its need for reform. The proper, priestly (sacrificial) response is therefore praise and confession. Celebrating God's goodness involves the proclamation of God's saving mercy (*Isaiah*), with a close connection to justification by faith; this also reveals the true dimensions of sacrifice. Another aspect of the true priestly office is the responsibility to pray for the community, in all of its needs. Luther repeatedly highlights the Lord's Prayer as he again makes connections to his own, Christian context.

These reforms of spiritual life (both the old and the new) require a new worship, and a new priesthood, in which all of God's people play their part. The themes of unity, equality, and participation are apparent here in the prophets' proclamation, but persist especially in the psalms, which express the faith of the individual in its community setting. Accordingly, the true priesthood of Melchizedek is realised by its fulfillment in Christ, who in his own person brings to fruition all of God's promises, including the relationship of faith implicit in the designation of Israel (old and new) as a "nation of priests."

In their wider context, these writings often reflect the turbulent situation of church and society in the late 1520s and the 1530s. They also show how Luther maintained his teaching on the common priesthood during these years, even when it was absent from the other writings discussed in chapter 5. Most particularly, the *Sermons on Psalm 110* provide a comprehensive account of Luther's own answer to the "problem" of the relationship of priesthood to the church's public office that places them alongside of one another in a mutually beneficial relationship, to the advantage of both expressions of the church's ministry. There is no disjunction between the priesthood shared by all God's people, and the church's mandate to appoint those who will publicly proclaim God's word. Together both priesthood and ministry speak and act as Christ's voice in the world.

Luther also used the familiar ecclesiological texts that had underpinned the early development of his teaching, so that within the theological framework of the word of promise and justification by faith the themes of the common priesthood were aligned with his understanding of the church as the people of God, the communion of saints in which all participate. While they do not occur with great frequency in these writings he uses the texts as biblical foundations—connecting the old religion and the new—to explore and explain the full dimensions of the worship and service of all Christians in the life and community of the church. This further confirms the integrity of his approach to the church, its ministry and its priesthood within the wider biblical context.

NOTES

1. See chapter 5, n1 for Bernhard Lohse's judgement that the universal priesthood decreased in importance for Luther. Very few studies of the "priesthood of believers" include these later writings. For an exception that includes some of this material, see the introduction n14, for Thomas Winger's article, "We Are All Priests." His conclusion is that the priesthood plays only a minor role in Luther's ecclesiology after the early reformational period. He does not explore the many connections Luther makes between teaching, preaching, worship, the sacrifice of praise and the confession of God's name, all of which unites Christians as those who hear and speak God's word.

2. LW 9:ix–x; Bornkamm, *Luther in Mid-Career*, 242.
3. LW 9:6 (WA 14:499), *Lectures on Deuteronomy*.
4. Bornkamm, *Luther in Mid-Career*, 242–244.
5. LW 9:124 (WA 14:645).
6. LW 9:169 (WA 14:670).
7. LW 9:168 (WA 14:670). See the previous chapter for the development of these thoughts in relation to his later works, *On the Councils and the Church* (1539) and *Against the Roman Papacy* (1545).
8. LW 9:129 (WA 14:647). See chapter 5, "Responding to the Radical Challenge."
9. LW 9:182 (WA 14:680).
10. LW 9:140–141 (WA 14:653).
11. Bornkamm, *Luther in Mid-Career*, 244–247.
12. See the introductions to LW 18–20, *Minor Prophets*, for lecture and publication dates, and other details on the provenance of these commentaries.
13. LW 18:108–109 (WA 13:111), *Lectures on Joel*.
14. For Luther's comments on women as preachers, see also *Psalm 45* (n98); chapter 4 (nn83,84); chapter 5, *Infiltrating Preachers* (n73–74); and chapter 6, *On the Councils and the Church* (nn66–68).
15. For the corruption of the priesthood, see LW 18:33–34 (WA 13:29–30), *Lectures on Hosea* (6:8–9).
16. LW 18:74 (WA 13:65).
17. Is the sacrifice of praise in Hosea 14:2 represented by sacrificial "bulls" or "fruit"? Following Hebrews 13:15, Luther suggests that Psalm 51:15 (and 19) is a possible source of confusion and he chooses the Septuagint's reading of "fruit of our lips" to reinforce the New Testament connection between sacrifice and the word.
18. LW 18:261 (WA 13:333), *Lectures on Micah*, (6:6–8).
19. Ibid.
20. LW 18:357 (WA 13:504), *Lectures on Zephaniah*, (3:10).
21. LW 18:396 (WA 13:681) *Lectures on Malachi*.
22. LW 18:397 (WA 13:682).
23. LW 18:411 (WA 13:695).

24. For Luther's interpretation of the Old Testament, including his use of allegory, see above chapter 1, *Christ, and the Word* (nn13–15 and 27–30). Still unsurpassed on this topic is Bornkamm, *Old Testament*, 89–96. In his preface to this commentary on Zechariah, Luther comments on "frivolous" allegories used by freelance preachers to display their cleverness, rather than to promote the message of faith, LW 20:157 (WA 23:487).

25. LW 20:41 (WA 13:583), *Lectures on Zechariah*. Luther points to Hebrews 7 here, Christ prefigured by Melchizedek.

26. LW 20:45 (WA 13:588). Luther cites Romans 12:6; 1 Corinthians 12:4; Ephesians 4:7.

27. LW 20:345–46 (WA 23:663).

28. LW 20:346 (WA 23:663).

29. Ibid.

30. LW 20:157 (WA 23:487);

31. Bornkamm, *Mid-Career*, 575–580; Brecht *Luther* 2:249. Bornkamm dates the first lectures on Isaiah from 1527. Incomplete versions of the lectures were published in Wittenberg in 1532 and 1534. The text used in LW 17 (WA 31/2:261–585) is from lecture transcriptions discovered in the twentieth century.

32. Brecht, *Luther* 2:249; Bornkamm, *Mid-Career*, 580.

33. See, for example, LW 17:127 (WA 31/2:360), *Lectures on Isaiah* (45:9), that righteousness "springs up" in the church.

34. LW 17:9 (WA 31/2: 266–267).

35. LW 17:13 (WA 31/2:270). This recalls Christ's words from John 20:21.

36. Translation altered: Luther uses his own Latin version of the problematic Hebrew text.

37. LW 17:72 (WA 31/2:317), Isaiah 42:10 "do not fear . . . I am with you."

38. Ibid.

39. LW 17:85 (WA 31/2:328).

40. LW 17:90 (WA 31/2:332).

41. See chapter 8, *Sermons on John 20:19–29*, on absolution pronounced in Christ's name by laity and clergy alike.

42. LW 17:97 (WA 31/2:338), Isaiah 43.

43. Ibid. See also LW 17:324 (WA 31/2:511), "[the] sacrifice of praise . . . is the preaching of the gospel."

44. LW 17:116–17 (WA 31/2:352–353).

45. LW 17:172 (WA 31/2:395). See chapter 5, for parents as "pastors and bishops" (nn30–31), and also chapter 8, *Sermons on John 14–16* (nn56–57).

46. LW 17:178 (WA 31/2:400).

47. LW 17:181 (WA 31/2:402) (translation altered).

48. See chapter 4 above, *The Word and The Priesthood*.

49. For the interpretation of Isaiah 54:13, see chapter 1, *Christ, and the Word* (at nn22–25, and at n89). See once again *The Word and the Priesthood* in chapter 4. See also Luther's *Sermons on John 6* (1530), where his interpretation of John 6:45 stresses the importance of the external word, received by faith as the "divine word" which the Father speaks to our hearts, using the voice of the preacher (LW 23:97, WA 23:148).

50. LW 17:243 (WA 31/2:449–450).
51. LW 17:243 (WA 31/2:7–9) (translation altered).
52. BOC 355–356, *The Small Catechism.*
53. BOC 436, *The Large Catechism.* See chapter 5 above, *The Catechisms.*
54. LW 17:330 (WA 31/2:515,15–17).
55. LW 17:330 (WA 31/2:515,23–27).

56. This shows Luther the biblical theologian in contrast to, for example, John Calvin, for whom the systematic approach was best satisfied by the [traditional] formula. See also chapter 4, *Christ's Priesthood* (n3), for Karin Bornkamm's study of Luther on Christ as "King and Priest." Bornkamm says that Luther subsumes the office of "prophet" within the other two, confirming what he says about the office of the priest in relation to the word.

57. LW 17:336 (WA 31/2:521).
58. LW 17:337 (WA 31/2:521).
59. LW 17:342 (WA 31/2:525).

60. See similar remarks on "priestly robes" in Psalms 45 (n100) and 110 (n115, 119) below, with Genesis 37:3 for Joseph's robe (n170), and also "putting on" Christ in Galatians 3:7, chapter 8 n12.

61. "Tow" = flax, an image for destructive self-reliance (see Isaiah 1:31).

62. LW 17:402 (WA 31/2:574) (translation altered).
63. LW 17:414 (WA 31/2:584). See above on Malachi 1:11 (at n22).
64. LW 17:414–15 (WA 31/2:584).
65. LW 17:415 (WA 31/2:584).

66. See Brecht, *Luther* 3:95–113 for an account of Luther's work "completing the translation of the Bible," from 1525 onwards.

67. LW 35:254 (WA DB 10/1:99–100), *Preface to the Psalter.*
68. LW 35:256 (WA DB 10/1:103).
69. LW 35:256 (WA DB 10/1:104) (translation modified).

70. Brecht, *Luther* 2, 372–380. For example, "he took his psalter, withdrew into his bedroom," 378.

71. Brecht, *Luther* 2, 380.

72. Brecht, *Luther* 2:391–393. He notes the title for Psalm 118's publication, *The Beautiful Confitemini.*

73. LW 14:99–101 (WA 31/1:173–75) Psalm 118.
74. LW 14:104 (WA 31/1:180).
75. Ibid.
76. Ibid.
77. Brecht *Luther* 2:401–402.
78. LW 14:22 (WA 31/1:240), Psalm 117 (translation altered).
79. LW 14:32–33 (WA 31/1:251).
80. LW 14:33 (WA 31/1:252).

81. LW 12:vii–ix. Psalms 2, 45, 51. There is some dispute over the exact dating of this series.

82. LW 12:6 (WA 40/2:196), Psalm 2.
83. LW 12:4 (WA 40/2:194).

84. Ibid.
85. LW 12:5 (WA 40/2:195).
86. LW 12:42 (WA 40/2:243–244).
87. LW 12:43 (WA 40/2:245).
88. LW 12:303 (WA 40/2:315), Psalm 51.
89. LW 12:360 (WA 40/2:399).
90. LW 12:393 (WA 40/2:446).
91. LW 12:403 (WA 40/2:457–458)
92. LW 12:406 (WA 40/2:462).
93. Brecht, *Luther 2*, 452. Commenting on the early verses of Galatians 3 in 1530–1531, Luther moves from Christ's crucifixion and his work as high priest (Galatians 3:1), to Abraham's "supreme sacrifice" of faith, which justified him. See LW 26:226 (WA 40/1:360) on Galatians 3:6.
94. See chapter 3 above, *From Captivity to Freedom*.
95. See n56, Karin Bornkamm's study, *Christus: König Und Priester*.
96. LW 12:258 (WA 40/2:554), Psalm 45.
97. Ibid.
98. LW 12:258–9 (WA 40/2:554). Women, for Luther, are the "weaker sex." But he often argues against himself on the basis of examples from the Bible, and history. Here he adds that Mary Magdalene was stronger in spirit than Peter. For more of Luther's statements on Mary Magdalene, see Karant-Nunn and Wiesner-Hanks, *Luther on Women*, 82–87. Compare also n14, and, for example, chapter 6, *On the Councils and the Church* (nn66–68).
99. LW 12:289 (WA 40/2:595).
100. Ibid. For "priestly robes," see n60 (etc.).
101. LW 12:199 (WA 40/2:474–475), Psalm 45 (superscription).
102. LW 13:225–348 (WA 41:79–239), Psalm 110. Luther treated this psalm often, notably in 1518 (WA 1: 689–710; WA 9:180–202). See also chapter 1, "The church as the people of God" in the *Dictata*.
103. Bornkamm, H., *Luther and the Old Testament*, 106–107.
104. A publication summary for Psalm 110 is given in LW 13:xii.
105. From 1528, Cruciger was preacher at the Castle Church in Wittenberg, and a member of the theological faculty, assisting Luther with his translation of the Bible (LW 49:104 n12) and also as his editor (see chapter 8, *The Church Postil* (n3), and *Sermons on John 14–16* (n49). Scott Hendrix relates that after his early death in 1548 (aged forty-four), Cruciger was memorialized as Luther's "much beloved son" (*Martin Luther*, 237). For more bibliographical details, see "Cruciger, Casper, Sr." in DLLT, 180–181.
106. LW 13:232 (WA 41:85), Psalm 110.
107. LW 13:265 (WA 41:123).
108. LW 13:266 (WA 41:124) (translation altered).
109. LW 13:271 (WA 41:130).
110. LW 13:274 (WA 41:133).

The Common Priesthood in Luther's Old Testament Writings, 1524–1546

111. For the way in which Luther subordinated Tradition to Scripture, see *Scripture and Tradition*, Lutherans and Catholics in Dialogue, 9 (Minneapolis: Augsburg, 1994), 27–28.

112. LW 13:286 (WA 41:145) (translation altered).

113. LW 13:294 (WA 41:153).

114. Ibid.

115. LW 13:295 (WA 41:154) (translation altered).

116. LW 13:295 (WA 41:154).

117. LW 13:295 (WA 41:154).

118. LW 13:295 (WA 41:155).

119. LW 13:296 (WA 41:156–57). For the priestly robes, see also Psalm 45 n100 above, and c.f. Isaiah 40–66 at n60.

120. LW 13:297 (WA 41:158).

121. LW 13:303 (WA 41:166). For Christians being "born" by baptism as priests, not being "made" by ordination, see *Concerning the Ministry*, WA 12:178; LW 40:19.

122. LW 13:304 (WA 41:167–168).

123. LW 13:304–313 (WA 41:167–179).

124. LW 13:313–314 (WA 41:179–182). For Melchizedek and Christ, see chapter 4, *Christ's Priesthood*, and *Genesis* at nn165–166 below.

125. LW 13:315 (WA 41:183). It is in this later period that Luther uses this threefold designation for priesthood; each of the elements (preaching, sacrifice, and prayer) occurs earlier, but they are not presented together in this way (see chapter 4, *Christian Priesthood*).

126. LW 13:329 (WA 41:203).

127. LW 13:329 (WA 41:205).

128. See chapter 4, a priest's spiritual birth in *Christian Priesthood* (at n37).

129. LW 13:330–331 (WA 41:207). See chapter 1 (e.g., at n53 and n104) for the early uses of these Pauline texts before 1520, and then in, for example, *Concerning the Ministry*, LW 40:20 (WA 12:179), chapter 4 nn38–39.

130. LW 13:331 (WA 41:207–208).

131. LW 13:332 (WA 41:209).

132. Ibid.

133. LW 13:332 (WA 41:210) (translation altered). In *The Babylonian Captivity* Luther opposes the theory that an "indelible character" is conferred on the ordained priesthood, stating that priests can be deposed from their office, LW 36:117 (WA 6:567).

134. Ibid.

135. Ibid.

136. LW 12:333 (WA 41:210–211).

137. LW 13:333 (WA 41:211).

138. Often that connection is left unspoken, or implied: see the discussion in chapter 5 on the importance of the reforms that presuppose and support the concept of the common priesthood.

139. LW 13:333 (WA 41:211).

140. LW 13:333–34 (WA 41:211–212).

141. LW 13:334 (WA 41:212).
142. LW 13:334 (WA 41:213).
143. Ibid.
144. LW 13:334 (WA 41:214). LW translates *von wegen Gemeine* as "by the authority of the congregation." In the context, the translation "for the sake of the congregation" makes more sense.
145. LW 13:348 (WA 41:237).
146. LW 13:348 (WA 41:238).
147. Brecht 3:136. Heinrich Bornkamm notes that Luther repeatedly engaged with Genesis, in 1519–1521, 1523–1524, and then in 1535–1545 (*Mid-Career*, 236). The published commentary originates from lost notes by Rörer and Cruciger, edited and published by Veit Dietrich from 1544 onwards. In the introduction to LW 1 Jaroslav Pelikan examines the evidence questioning Luther's authorship and concludes, "The hands are sometimes the hands of the editors, but the voice is nevertheless the voice of Luther" (see LW 1:xii, and subsequent introductions to LW 2–8).
148. See Brecht 3:137–138, and especially Bornkamm, *Luther and the Old Testament*, 207–218. Bernhard Lohse, however, makes no references to these lectures or their publications in either his *Theology* of Luther or his *Introduction* to Luther's life and work. The other biographies also tend to focus on the problems facing Luther after 1530, rather than his theological output (see also n173).
149. LW 1:103–104 (WA 42:79), *Lectures on Genesis 1–5* (Adam and Eve).
150. LW 1:247 (WA 42:183).
151. LW 1:248 (WA 42:184).
152. LW 1:251 (WA 42:186), Cain and Abel.
153. LW 1:252–255 (WA 42:187–189).
154. Brecht 3,138 (Jacob and Esau).
155. LW 2:13 (WA 42:271), *Lectures on Genesis 6–14* (Noah).
156. LW 2:19 (WA 42:275).
157. LW 2:83 (WA 42:321), on Genesis 7:1.
158. LW 1:262 (WA 42:194), on Genesis 4:6, Adam as God's voice.
159. LW 2:114 (WA 42:342–343), Noah as priest and prophet.
160. LW 2:249 (WA 42:439), Abraham.
161. LW 2:272 (WA 42:456), the call to ministry.
162. LW 2:280 (WA 42:462), Abraham as High Priest.
163. LW 2:284 (WA 42:465).
164. LW 2:284 (WA 42:465).
165. LW 2:384 (WA 42:537). See also LW 2:393 (WA 42:545). Melchizedek does not represent the Levitical priesthood. Bornkamm comments that for Luther "the Jewish cultic community was not the prototype of the Christian church," and "Luther never thought institutionally, from one cultic association to another, but always from divine action, from the word also effective in the sign, and from the faith resulting from it," *Old Testament*, 216 and 218.
166. LW 2:381–382 (WA 42:535–536). However, this renders problematic the account of Melchizedek in Hebrews 7:3, "without genealogy."

167. LW 3:317–318 (WA 43:103) *Lectures on Genesis 15–20* (20:1), Abraham's journey south, away from Sodom.

168. LW 4:122 (WA 43:223), *Lectures on Genesis 21–25* (22:11), Abraham's sacrifice of Isaac.

169. LW 5:184 (WA 43:555) *Lectures on Genesis 26–30* (27:46), Jacob's exile from his parents' home.

170. LW 4:384 (WA 43:412), *Lectures on Genesis 21–25*. Luther later suggests that the special garment bestowed on Joseph by his father Jacob in Genesis 37:3 was a (white!) priestly robe, and therefore a source of considerable antagonism with his older brothers (LW 6:323–324 (WA 44:241), *Lectures on Genesis 31–37*). For more on priestly robes, see above (nn60,115,119), and also chapter 8 below on Galatians 3 (at n12).

171. Bornkamm, *Old Testament,* 217. Any discussion of the "hidden" church also needs to take account of Luther's presentation of the church's "marks" in, for example, *On the Councils and the Church.*

172. For Luther's positive view of the wives of the patriarchs, see Karant-Nunn and Wiesner-Hanks, *Luther on Women*, 58–60. For his other statements on women, see above n14 and, for example, chapter 6, *On the Councils and the Church* (nn66–8), etc.

173. See Brecht's later accounts in *Luther* 3,1–23 (1532–1536) and 3:229–265 (1537–1546). Roper includes much detail on Luther's personal trials in his final years (*Martin Luther Renegade*, 363–379); Schilling relates Luther's remote involvement with events outside of Wittenberg and Saxony in this later period (*Martin Luther Rebel*, 405–449). Hendrix, at least, manages to weave something of Luther's ongoing theological work into his final chapters, including a brief mention of the *Genesis* lectures (*Martin Luther Visionary*, 254–255).

Chapter 8

The Common Priesthood in Luther's New Testament Preaching, 1522–1546

Christ says: "If you remain in Me, I will consecrate you to be holy priests—priests of My Father."

—Martin Luther, *Sermons on John 14–16*

In this selection of Luther's New Testament sermons the teaching that "we are all priests" is examined in Luther's preaching in the pulpits of Wittenberg and beyond, as the culmination of this study of the common priesthood. In fact, this is the natural setting for the message that there is no spiritual elite in Christ's church, as the preacher encourages all of God's people to join in proclaiming Christ as High Priest and King and to participate together in the worship and life of the Christian community. Luther's sermons spoke directly to the cause of the word and faith in the life of the church and its people. They were not lectures, although here they are presented in their edited, published form. Christian teaching was a major aspect of their content as he expounded the biblical texts; their aim was not primarily polemical, although Luther rarely missed an opportunity to point out the errors of his opponents from both sides of the reformational divide. Above all for Luther, preaching "is God's very own audible address to all who hear it, just as surely as if Christ himself had spoken it."[1]

Here, three groups of sermons present the different ways in which Luther preached the themes of church and priesthood, often expounding his key texts as he did so. First, a group of sermonic studies from the *Church Postil* show one of the chief ways in which Luther's core teachings (including the common priesthood) were disseminated to a wide audience of clergy and laity throughout the German lands over the course of many years. This is followed by sermons on John 14–16 and 17, preached in Wittenberg and published in the late 1530s as expositions of Christ's high-priestly discourse in the "upper room." The third group is a series of eleven sermons on John 20:19–29 revealing the continuity and development of Luther's teaching on confession and absolution ("the keys") within an eighteen-year timeframe. Finally, a remarkable sermon from late in Luther's life shows how he used the themes of the common priesthood to draw together his congregation at the dedication of the Castle Church in Torgau, encouraging them to join him in consecrating the new place of worship through the word and prayer.

LUTHER'S "CHURCH POSTIL" (1522–1525 & 1540–1544)

The influence and significance of Luther's postils has been noted, in connection with his reforming program from its beginnings.[2] These collections of sermonic studies underwent expansion and revision, from their origins at the Wartburg and throughout the rest of his career. In part, this was because versions were printed without Luther's approval. Finally, Luther himself corrected and published an authorized version of the *Church Postil* in 1540. The first half, from Advent to Easter, represents Luther's own revisions; the second half became the work of his trusted editor, Caspar Cruciger, who published a further revision in 1544.[3] In these postils, the readers would have encountered Luther's teachings on Christian equality, participation in Christ and priesthood. Where they appear, these themes are set within the framework of word and faith, grace and law. As he explores each text, other themes are apparent, relating to Christology and ecclesiology. It is not suggested that a thematic program was followed in these sermons, that were based on the church lectionary. Rather, one hears Luther at work as preacher and pastor, as he expounds biblical texts including those which led to his earlier theological breakthrough, and its later development. As in 1522–1525, so also in 1540–1544 his teaching was offered for diverse audiences of lay people and less-educated clergy.

Sermons for St Stephen's Day and the New Year

This expository process can be seen within the sequence of sermons included for the post-Christmas period and for the Epiphany season, in the first half of the postil. The sermon for St Stephen's Day, otherwise located within the celebration of Christmas, is on the accounts of Stephen's preaching in Jerusalem and his subsequent stoning for blasphemy against the temple (Acts 6:8–14 and 7:54–60).[4] Focusing on the content of Stephen's sermon (omitted from the appointed reading), Luther argues that "faith alone builds the house of God." Building churches, says Luther, does not earn God's favor as a work of pious devotion; rather, it is to provide places for prayer, hearing God's word and receiving the sacraments. The "true and proper churches" rest in the souls of those who follow Christ. But—perhaps with the building of St Peter's in Rome in mind—he points to the abuses of his own day, stating that "it would be good . . . to overturn at once all the churches in the world, and to preach, pray, baptize, and fulfill all Christian duties in ordinary houses or out in the open."[5] Rather than endowing churches, the real works of faith and love involve care for one's neighbor in need.[6]

Consequently Luther holds up Stephen as an example of faith, a Christian whose love for God's word led him to oppose the false piety of the Jewish religious authorities. In the same way, "each Christian . . . is obliged to rebuke the pope."[7] Stephen, he says, "was a plain, insignificant man, not a priest or consecrated."[8] His story is thus an example of the circumstances under which "the [layperson] can also preach," as Stephen does in the everyday course of his office as a "steward" (deacon). Under the papacy he would have been burned as a heretic, "since he was not a priest or a cleric." These titles, says Luther, are given to all Christians in the Scriptures, but the papists "have grasped [the titles] to themselves, and call the others 'the laity,' just as they call themselves 'the church,' as if the laity were outside of the church."[9] But Stephen, Luther notes, followed the order that Paul would subsequently lay down in 1 Corinthians 14, only preaching when the apostles were not present to do so. That Luther allows this description and account of Stephen as an self-appointed preacher to remain unedited in the later editions of the *Church Postil*, provides a further perspective to his comments on unauthorized preaching in a work like *Infiltrating Preachers*. It seems that context and the gospel purposes of "church order" remain decisive for Luther, rather than its rigid application. "Order" is also set aside here for the spiritual claims of the common priesthood. However, neither early nor late does he extend this sermon to explore how he envisaged the contemporary application of Stephen's example.

For the New Year, Luther offers two sermons on the traditional texts, for the circumcision and naming of the infant Jesus, within the Christmas season. The first, on Galatians 3:23–29, is another exposition of faith and works.[10] This is a significant sermon, on one of Luther's key texts. Variously, it pictures two children: one enslaved, under law, the other living in the freedom of God's grace. So Luther presents the gospel, as he has embraced it, from a Pauline perspective. The key is faith, which in baptism connects us to Christ. This spiritual union involves reception of Christ, and not merely imitation. This is further conveyed by the imagery of being clothed with Christ (Galatians 3:27). The beautiful clothing of Christ's blessings reminds Luther of Jacob's colorful robe—the gift for a favored child—and then also of Aaron's costly robes, which adorn the high priestly service of God.[11] And more than this: in the divine exchange, Christ takes the soiled clothing of our sin, and in his suffering and death "refines the children of Levi" (Malachi 3:3), so that we are clothed with his own holiness.[12] These priestly images apply to all, without distinction. For Galatians 3:28, Luther emphasizes that "all are of equal value" and any external differences of our bodily lives cannot preempt faith in regards to spiritual matters, our standing before God.[13] At length, he explains that the priest, monk, or nun has no advantage over the lay person in matters of salvation. Only faith is of value: "before God there is neither layperson nor priest, man nor woman, each is like the other in faith."[14]

Luther's teaching undercuts the basic assumptions of medieval religious life. The elevation of an evangelical lifestyle, over that of the religious orders and the traditional priesthood, remained relevant in 1540, although Luther reduced the argument to its essentials.[15] This sermon is a popular version of the teaching proposed in the reformational treatises. It contends for spiritual equality among Christians, and that remained vitally relevant for the later period. Based on God's word of promise and justification by faith, Luther radically reenvisioned participation in church and society for all those who read and hear his words. Despite his insistence that the gospel did not overthrow the social order and that a distinction between spiritual and worldly realities must remain in force for the Christian, changes such as the removal of the religious orders from the life of the church brought about a profound shift in the landscape of everyday life in sixteenth-century Europe.[16]

The Gospel sermon for New Year expounds Luke 2:21, "after eight days it was time for his circumcision, and he was named Jesus."[17] Luther emphasizes circumcision as a sign of the covenant with Abraham. Christ submits to it to signify the removal of sin by God's grace, in the same way as he later submits to baptism. As Christ is Lord over sin and death, so are all who are baptized in his name. This blessing is received by faith, and so the naming of Jesus is likewise shared with those who believe:

> [A]s Christ gives us all that is his, so he also gives to us his name. Therefore all of us are called Christians from him, all God's children from him, Jesus from him, Saviour from him, and whatever is his name, that also is ours.[18]

This is Luther's argument that the simple name of "Christian" represents the highest spiritual status, signifying that we belong to Christ, and in faith receive all that is his. Following on from the message of equality in Galatians 3, it prepares the ground for those texts which then reveal a shared kingship, and a common priesthood received from Christ himself. The proximity to the teaching of, for example, *The Freedom of a Christian* is apparent here.[19] Once more, "priesthood" served to apply the themes of salvation and faith which continued to occupy the central place in Luther's public teaching, together with faith's constant partner, "love." It therefore conveyed a radical understanding of the interrelatedness inherent in Christian life and community—the themes of unity and participation.

Sermons for Epiphany

"Participation in Christ" is one of themes for the sermons for "The Day of the Three Holy Kings," Epiphany. The first text is Isaiah 60:1–6, an "exhortation to faith." Using the themes of light and darkness, it explores what it means to live under the Gospel, or the Law.[20] The light is Christ, who said "I am the light of the world," and in whom the nations are gathered as God's people.[21] Luther suggests that a spiritual reading of verse 6 is therefore appropriate; it is not a direct prophecy of the wise men (kings). Christians share the blessings they have received, the "possessions" given to the church. The text says that "they shall proclaim the name of the Lord" and this is what the followers of Christ do. For us, "the true and proper Christian work is that we confess our sin and shame, and preach only God's work and grace in us." Proclamation [*Verkündigen*] of God's name is the work of "true Christians," who glory in Christ's light, not their own.[22]

The Epiphany themes also underpin his extensive treatment of Matthew 2:1–12.[23] Isaiah's nations, represented by the heathen "kings," are drawn to Christ, first by the light of a star, and then by the light of prophecy. Those who are the great and the mighty hear only a terrifying message; the Gospel's consolation is for those who are "humble and despised."[24] Herod represents the corrupt powers of both church and state, all those rulers who place themselves above the word and will of God. To faith, Herod is quickly abandoned, because Christ is revealed as king, priest, and redeemer by the Magi's gifts. In this overlong presentation, the gospel can be hard to find as Luther exposes the failures of the Roman church, in great and lurid detail.[25] Although two substantial polemical sections were omitted in 1540, the reader must still persist through many pages to arrive at the positive heart of his message.[26] Finally, with the Magi, and led by the star of God's word, "they come into the house." Luther says this house is

> the Christian church, the assembly of all believers on earth [*die vorsamlung aller glewbigen auff erden*], in which alone you can find Christ and his mother; for in the Christian church alone are those who, pregnant and fruitful by the Holy Spirit, bring forth in a Christian way [*Christlich geberen*] and lead a Christian life. Everything that is outside of this house, however beautiful it may glitter, however reasonable it may be, has neither Christ nor his mother.[27]

This shows how Luther can use his ecclesiology to enhance the interpretation of a text in creative and unexpected ways. Then, in keeping with his method in the early postil sermons, Luther now presented a spiritual understanding of the text, beyond its simple meaning as an historical account.[28] Thus, the "house" becomes the church, and the Magi's offerings express the hidden reality of Christ's human nature, which conceals his divine origin and working.[29] In this spiritual use, the offering of gold confesses that Christ is king, the frankincense reveals his priesthood, and myrrh foretells his death and burial. These three then signify the Christian's sacrifice of praise and thanksgiving, which is a confession of faith in Christ as King, Priest, and Redeemer. All three work together here, says Luther, as they do in the key text, Psalm 110:

> Scripture always mentions the kingdom first, then the priesthood, then his dying, as Psalm 110 also does . . . one might also say, he will taste the myrrh, therefore he will become a Priest, therefore he will also be a King—so that one follows from the other, one is the cause of the other, and they follow one upon the other.[30]

Christ's priesthood encompasses his intercession and mediation with God, and brings the gift of a clear conscience to those who believe in him. It means that trust in Christ is able to defend us against sin and God's wrath; bearing our sin, Christ offers himself to God. Implicit here is faith's own priestly self-offering, through acceptance of Christ's sacrifice, and that is the theme treated in the next sermons, based on Romans 12, another major text. The sermons model the movement from Christ's birth in us, and our participation in him by faith, to our sharing in the work of his priesthood. Once again, the statement of the common priesthood is in terms of Luther's core teaching, the work of Christ. The church as the people of God is also close at hand, as the setting in which faith is taught, nurtured, and expressed. All this means that it is not adequate to describe this "priesthood" as an evangelical slogan or metaphor, paraded for use solely as an anti-Roman rallying cry.

Sermons on Romans 12:1–21 (The Sundays after Epiphany)

Its publication delayed by the pressure of events, the *Lent Postil* first appeared in 1525, and was eventually incorporated into the *Church Postil* of 1540 and 1544. Luther characterizes his earlier work in the *Wartburg Postil* as dealing with faith, love, and hope, which comprise the Christian life. Following those sermons, which remain a point of reference, he will now show how "all divine doctrine contains nothing but Jesus Christ."[31]

He begins the *Postil* with Romans 12:1–3(6), the Epistle for the First Sunday after the Epiphany. Alongside of 1 Peter 2:5, these are key verses for teaching on Christian sacrifice, the offering of self. With 1 Peter 2:9, these verses form for Luther the basis for the common priesthood, in concert with other supporting texts.

Luther compares this text with Paul's words in Galatians 5:24, Ephesians 4:22, Colossians 3:5, which speak of "crucifying the flesh" and "putting to death your members."[32] The language of sacrifice draws a Christian into the high and holy work of priesthood, but, paradoxically, it does so from a position of weakness and humility. It is a sacrifice of one's self. Luther contrasts those with the outward status as against those bearing the spiritual gift. The first priesthood belonged to an elite group; the second "is common to all Christians [*aller Christen gemeyn*]." One required ritual anointing, but the other can be given only by the Holy Spirit. One is a human ordinance, apart from the word; the other exists only to "preach and extol God's grace and God's glory." The one "leaves the body with its desires unsacrificed," while the other "mortifies and sacrifices the body with its desires." One receives offerings of worldly goods, the other lets them go, and accepts only the reverse of honor and wealth. One claims the corrupt power to "sacrifice Christ," the other "lets it be enough that Christ was sacrificed once, and sacrifices itself with him and in him in one and the same sacrifice."[33] This is all summarized in words which resonate strongly with Luther's other early writings on Christian priesthood:

> As little as Christ became a priest by being smeared with oil and tonsured, so little is the second priesthood given to anyone by smearing or shaving. Yet Christ is a priest with all his Christians [*dennoch ist Christus priester mit allen seinen Christen*]. "You are a priest forever after the order of Melchizedek" (Psalm 110). This second priesthood does not let itself be made or appointed [*nicht machen odder ordenen*]. Here no one is made a priest; they must be born a priest [*er mus priester geboren sein*], and bring it with them as an inheritance from their birth. I mean, of course, the new birth of water and the Spirit; in that way all Christians become priests, children and co-heirs of the Most High Priest, Christ.[34]

The human title of priest is a prized possession, says Luther, but its true, sacrificial work is not so readily accepted. Christ's own priesthood teaches this lesson, and is the example for those who have accepted the salvation he offers. "It is costly work, to be endured not to benefit ourselves but to serve our neighbor, and to praise and honor God, just as Christ sacrificed his body."[35] These are the spiritual sacrifices spoken of in 1 Peter 2:5, and while Paul calls this "offering your bodies," there is no contradiction. When you put aside your own selfish desires, whatever is motivated by the Spirit, apart from the rewards of the law or the fear of hell, is spiritual.[36] Luther claims "even eating and drinking are spiritual works if they happen through the Spirit." On the other hand, even the soul's deepest secrets can be "works of the flesh."[37] He then considers 1 Peter 2:9, which adds a further dimension:

> Here Peter touches on the preaching office [*das predig ampt*], which is the true sacrificial office, of which the psalmist says, "Whoever offers thanksgiving is the one who praises me" (Psalm 50[:23]). God's grace is extolled through preaching, and that is called offering up praise and thanks, as also St Paul boasts that he sanctifies or offers up the Gospel (Romans 15[:16]). We are not here speaking about that sacrifice,[38] though it can be considered a part of that spiritual sacrifice in the congregation, as follows afterward. Whoever offers up their body to God also offers up their tongue and mouth to preach, confess, and extol God's grace.[39]

While making a strong connection between proclamation and priesthood, Luther does not pursue sacrifice, preaching, and public praise further here, as interrelated aspects of the priestly office, common to all.[40] He sticks with his text, and now works through it verse-by-verse. Paul, he notes, uses the exhortations of the Gospel, the appeal to God's mercy, rather than the threats of the law. This is the only way to produce the joyful response which enables sacrificial living. In contrast to the old offerings, to "present our bodies" is the unique New Testament sacrifice, which brings life to the sacrifice, not death; it is holy, when God works in us.[41] God's acceptance of this sacrifice far outweighs any human standard of value or worth (Romans 12:2). And the "reasonable worship" does not focus on externals, but is grounded in the lives of those who offer themselves in God's service, together with Christ.[42] Verse 3 ("do not think of yourself more highly than you ought") prompts Luther to introduce the themes of equality and humility, which, he says, are common to all of Paul's letters. There is no room for pride among Christians, in contrast to those who imagine themselves to occupy meritorious spiritual orders. But even though faith may be unequal among Christians, its "possession" is not. "In faith," Luther writes, we "all have the same possession—Christ."[43] This sets the stage for the exposition of the remaining verses of Romans 12, Paul's teaching on the body of Christ, appointed for the second and third Sundays after Epiphany.[44]

This means that Luther's treatment of the common priesthood and its sacrificial self-offering, can be seen in these sermons in its closest relationship to Paul's ecclesiology with its themes of communion and participation. This is in addition to its place as an expression of what it means to be united with Christ, by faith. After noting the connection to the earlier verses, Luther says that Paul:

draws the differing gifts in the differing members to the one common body [*einem gemeinem leibe*] which we are in Christ. This is a very clear illustration, which he often cites (such as in 1 Corinthians 12; Ephesians 4). It beautifully teaches that all Christians should be equal and satisfied with one common faith [*einigen gemeinen glauben*] . . . not as if someone were godly, saved, or better before God through [their gifts] than another.[45]

This postil on Romans 12:1–3, taken together with those which precede it, and the following two which extend the passage to verse 21, represent vital links in the chain of transmission of Luther's core teaching from 1520 to 1540, and beyond. At the later date, he found no reason to change what he had earlier published as his interpretation and application of this passage. Together with the other sermons considered here, it also illustrates his sustained use of the same foundational texts that underpinned his earlier teaching.[46]

In its essentials, Luther's understanding of those key texts has not changed in this later period, but his use of them is thoroughly integrated within his teaching. "We are all priests" was never a casual slogan, directed only at Rome's failings and asserting the equality of all Christians. Criticism of Rome is often apparent, but in the postil it is not the dominant theme of Luther's teaching. Rather, the proper understanding of priesthood rests close to the heart of Luther's spirituality and his ecclesiology. Together and individually, pastors and people are priests in Christ's church. This priesthood's derivation from Christ's office as priest and king and its dependence on God's word shows how it stands alongside of the work of the preaching office, and participates in it without subverting it. In this way, it is an integral feature of the life of faith and love lived *sub cruce*, a life which clings to Christ alone, its worship grounded in the word and enabled by the Spirit.

SERMONS ON JOHN 14–16, AND 17

Luther often expressed his admiration for the Gospel of John, and valued it for its profound exposition of Christ's own message.[47] Over the years, he preached a series of sermons on John 16–20 (1528–1529), 6–8 (1530–1532), 14–16 (1533–1534), and 1–4 (1537–1540) when he substituted for Bugenhagen during the latter's absences from the town church.[48] The sermons on the early chapters of John were not published during Luther's lifetime, but Casper Cruciger had published the sermons on John 17 in 1530 and then the series on chapters 14–16 in 1538–1539. Luther regarded this as among his best work.[49]

The upper room discourse in John's gospel, culminating in the high-priestly prayer of John 17, shows how Luther continued to integrate the themes of priesthood and ministry within these later sermons.[50] At a time when Luther repeatedly emphasized the ordered call to the public ministry as a divine ordinance, he did not lay aside his understanding that Christ bestowed the fullness of his ministry upon the whole church. Led by their called ministers, all Christians have responsibility to ensure that the word is heard. In John's Gospel this derives from the work of Christ himself who acts through his disciples, who are sent out to serve in their particular contexts and offices.

In the upper room, Christ commissions and consecrates all Christians to be his representatives, according to Luther. It is not just the apostles who receive this charge; although their primary responsibility is clear, as is that of those who would be called to public ministry. The word is spoken to all and is for all, and its transmission ("confession") is the responsibility of all who hear and receive it. Commenting on John 14:10 ("The words that I speak to you"), Luther says, "It is all from God, who condescends to enter the mouth of each Christian or preacher [*inn eines iglichen Christen oder predigers mund*]."[51] This is consistent with Luther's understanding of the common priesthood, even when it is not specifically named; at this point his chief emphasis is on the apostolic transmission of the word. Themes of equality and participation are behind the spiritual realities at work when Jesus addresses his disciples, preparing them for what must happen to him, and how they are to respond to these imminent events. In preaching this, Luther's concern is to bring his hearers into the dialogue between Christ and his disciples. When Jesus speaks of the "greater works" to be done by those who believe in him (14:12), there is no distinction being made between the apostles and the rest of Christendom:

> Every individual Christian [*Ein iglicher einzales Christ*] is one such as the Lord Christ Himself was on earth. Each one accomplishes great things. Each is able to govern the whole world in divine matters. Each can help and benefit everybody, and does the greatest works on earth. Each one is also regarded more highly by God than the entire world is.[52]

Because of this, the world is preserved for the sake of the Christians, and because of the work they perform for its benefit. Luther says, "In the first place, Christians have the Gospel, Baptism, and the Sacrament. . . . They are able to teach and instruct people in all walks of life and to help them live in a Christian and blessed way."[53] In the second place, there is prayer, through which both spiritual and temporal blessings come. And then,

> All this, Christ says, is to come to pass through the Christians, because they believe in Him and derive everything from Him as their Head. Yes, all this is to be done by each individual Christian, and Christ can say: "The works which I

do are done by every baptized Christian today." Consequently, the Christians are genuine helpers and saviors, yes, lords and gods of the world.[54]

This work involves both prayer and teaching, and a restless compulsion to share a "spirit of compassion and supplication" with one's neighbors (Zechariah 12:10). "With these and the following words," Luther says, "Christ also demonstrates what constitutes a Christian's true office and work [*ampt und werck*], and how necessary the exercise of this is in Christendom."[55]

In practice, this happens through the natural orders God has placed in his world. For Luther, these always include the church and the home, each with its own appointed servants. Speaking of the delusion of separating God from his work in the world (John 14:11), he says:

> Ask yourself if you delight wholeheartedly in what Christ proclaims and does for you through his Christians [*seine Christenheit*], such as preachers, father, mother, and other pious people. . . . He ordered and ordained all the offices and estates in Christendom for the purpose of filling the entire world with the works of God; and you ignore all this as though it were of no account. You think to yourself: "God dwells up in heaven among the angels and is occupied with other matters. How can a preacher or a father or a mother help me? If only I could hear and see God Himself!"[56]

This is in keeping with other places where Luther places parents alongside of preachers, as an example of those whose God-given task (*Amt*) involves the teaching of the gospel.[57] Yet always this identity as God's servants does not depend on human credentials, but it is the work of Christ himself, and the gift of the Spirit (John 14:15–31). Otherwise, the distinctions that apply in human society would still also pertain to the body of Christ. The church is always the communion of baptized saints, the fellowship of those justified by faith in Christ. And Luther grounds this spiritual reality very close to the actual places where his hearers live and work:

> This is our comfort and our trust, that with good reason we may glory and confidently say: "We are holy [*Wir sind heilig*]. We are members of a holy fraternity in Wittenberg, in Rome, in Jerusalem, and wherever holy Baptism and the Gospel are. And we do not regard one another otherwise than as saints of God. Even though we are still sinners and many failings always remain in our flesh and blood, He covers up our sins and impurities. Thus we are accounted entirely pure and holy before God, as long as we cling to Christ and His Baptism and rely on His blood."[58]

These thoughts are intensified as Luther moves onto John 15:5 ("Whoever abides in me"), and the Johannine parable of the vine and the branches.

Luther adds a favorite image from his ecclesiology (1 Corinthians 10:17) to describe the Christian community, and its work of love:

> Thus Christ and the Christians become one loaf and one body [*ein kuchen und ein Leib*], so that the Christian can bear good fruit—not Adam's or his own, but Christ's. For when a Christian baptizes, preaches, consoles, exhorts, works, and suffers, he does not do this as a man descended from Adam; it is Christ who does this in him. The lips and tongue with which he proclaims and confesses God's Word are not his; they are Christ's lips and tongue. The hands with which he toils and serves his neighbor are the hands and members of Christ, who, as he says here, is in him; and he is in Christ.[59]

This proclamation of unity in Christ has set the scene for Luther to introduce the themes of priesthood and sacrifice into his exposition, even though the text of John 15 does not directly require them. But by taking up the thought of the disciples producing "much fruit" (15:8), he explores the way in which this happens, to God's glory. It means that those who live as Christians are "priests and servants of God who offer holy and acceptable sacrifices to my Father without ceasing."[60] Christ himself in these words rejects any distinction between those considered to be "spiritual" (the clergy), and those who "worked on earth."[61]

Rather, Luther says, Christian sacrifice is twofold, in keeping with the dual nature of the life God desires. According to the first three commandments, "the highest and foremost service of God is to preach and hear God's Word, to administer the Sacraments, etc." But also the second table of the law is involved,

> to honor father and mother, to be patient, to live chastely and decently. For whoever lives such a life serves and honors the same God. Christ says: "If you remain in Me, I will consecrate you to be holy priests—priests of My Father."[62]

The connection to Christ is what makes this possible, and that drives the unitary nature of Christian ministry. Luther makes little distinction between the status of laity and clergy in these verses, because they all serve God equally, as they are called do.

For Luther, this account of true Christian spirituality also means that the Father can only reject those who bring their own status or holiness, their own self-devised sacrifices (like the mass) into God's presence. He directly ascribes Peter's words (and Paul's) to Christ himself: "But you," *says Christ*, "are a holy people, true priests consecrated to God (1 Peter 2:9); and your works are holy and acceptable sacrifices" [Romans 12:1]. This is the highest service, and the highest offering, because it follows Christ and does what he does.[63] Along with the reference to 1 Peter and the key verse from Romans

12, also Psalm 110 is quoted here by Luther, confirming that this is no casual introduction of the themes of priesthood into the discussion of the basic character of the Christian life. In what amounts to a classic summary statement of the common priesthood, highlighting its key biblical witnesses, he says,

> The apostle St. Paul enlarges on this in Romans 12:1–2 when he says that our perfect spiritual service [*Geistlicher Gottesdienst*] of God is really nothing else than to be this man's disciples and to become like him, those whose entire office and work is the pure worship of God and a holy sacrifice. Thus Psalm 110:4 declares: "You are a Priest forever"; he also makes us who abide in Him such priests.[64]

Apart from Christ, there is no true worship or priestly service (*priesterthum*) of God, there is only self-devised "priestcraft" (*pfafferei*), typified for Luther by the sacrifice of the mass.[65]

Later, (John 15:16), where Jesus returns to the subject of prayer, Luther indicates the acceptability of Christian prayer. As with the "Our Father," all Christians have the right to bring their prayers to God, in Jesus' name, and because of his promise:

> We have been ordained through him to the priestly office [*zu dem priesterlichen ampt geweihet*]. Hence we can and must step before God joyfully, as we bring both our own need [*not*] and that of others before him, assured by his promise that our prayers will be heard and that he will say yes and amen to them.[66]

Luther's ecclesiological core can still—at times—carry him beyond consideration of the harsh realities of the current church situation, and the polemics with which he engaged in this struggle.[67] Christ's promises are for all Christians who share the same word, the sacraments, the creed, and the Lord's Prayer. In this way, the "true church" includes all those—throughout the world—who are "gathered and united in Christ."[68] So, in keeping with Christ's words to his disciples, and anticipating his high priestly prayer in John 17, Luther returns to the theme of unity, introducing Pauline terms:

> He makes us equal to himself in all things; his prayer and ours must be one [*ein kuchen sein*], just as his body is ours and his members are ours. Thus St. Paul says in Ephesians. 5:30: "We are members of his body," of His flesh and bone.[69]

In this way, this sermonic exposition of John's Gospel is important for our understanding of how Luther continued to integrate and apply his view of the church and priesthood into his preaching. Once again, the biblical text itself drives his teaching, and leads him to consider more deeply the meaning of the Gospel for his own community of faith. In this, Luther's later teaching is entirely consistent with his early work, and while the content he presents carries the themes of John's Gospel that message can be seen to have a close relationship to Luther's Pauline ecclesiology. His inclusion of the common priesthood with material that teaches the apostolic foundations of the Christian community is an important development in his use of this concept.

Sermons on John 17

As noted, Luther had already preached a series of eight sermons on John 17, at the Town Church during August to October 1528. They were first published in 1530 by Caspar Cruciger, and Luther himself provided an introduction to a Latin version in 1538.[70] In the sermon, Luther identifies the significance of this chapter as Christ's high-priestly prayer:

> After a good sermon belongs a good prayer . . . [the Lord Christ] had to offer up a final supplication as well, both for [the disciples] and for all Christians, so that he might perfectly fulfil his office as our sole High Priest and leave nothing undone that might serve to strengthen and sustain them.[71]

This unique priestly office involves the self-offering on the cross, by which Christ sanctifies himself (John 17:19),[72] and then sanctifies his disciples. This means, says Luther, that the holiest life or estate on earth is not an earned holiness, but "none other than the common Christian estate [*die gemeine Christen stand*]."[73] The true saints, he says, are those who are not ashamed to pray for forgiveness: they must be "good strong sinners" [*gute starcke sunder sein*].[74] So Christ prays that all would believe, through the apostles' word (John 17:20), and that they would all share in his unity, with the Father (John 17:21). Christ's prayer means that a believer is "one body and loaf with all Christendom," and each participates and shares in the struggles and joys of the other. This "friendly exchange" includes "bearing faults" and sharing possessions.[75] This recalls Luther's early stress on Christian fellowship that is often missing in his later work.[76] But here the priority of the word is also firmly in view. Christendom, he says, is "a powerful lady [*gewalltige fraw*] and an empress in heaven and on earth . . . when she speaks a word."[77] In the fertile rhetoric of Luther's pulpit, Mother Church becomes Queen Christendom, and she proclaims the same word that first bestowed royal status on her and all her children.

These sermons on John 14–17 confirm how this Gospel was prominent in the development and later expressions of Luther's theology.[78] His Christological focus was abundantly clear, and this shaped his teaching on church and priesthood. There is an emphasis on Christian participation in Christ's priesthood, and its relationship to the teaching on word and faith. It also presents the themes of unity and communion within that same context. In this way, it shows how Luther sharpened his original insights on the common priesthood to reveal its connections to Christ's own teaching. He is able to use the Johannine presentation of Jesus' self-understanding, his incarnation and his relationship with the disciples, to portray the priesthood's primary connection to the work of Christ. The themes of the key texts are often apparent in his teaching, even when he is not quoting them directly.

THE OFFICE OF THE KEYS

Sermons on John 20:19–29 for the First Sunday after Easter

Luther's criticism of the late-medieval church's control of penitential practices was one of the first steps that led to the assertion of the priesthood of all Christians in relation to spiritual governance in the church.[79] The related insistence that all Christians have the authority to forgive sins, in the name of Christ, was a consistent feature of his early teaching on the common priesthood.[80] This right (*ius*) was asserted when Luther confronted the Roman claims regarding the unique sacramental power of its clergy, and its authority to enforce rules regarding spiritual practices and penalties.[81] His criticism of papal power in the secular realm, framed in terms of Peter's possession of the "keys," was also in view there.

In the revision of the *Large Catechism* (1529), Luther also added "A Brief Exhortation to Confession."[82] Having been set free from rules and coercion in regard to confession, Christians now needed encouragement to make responsible use of their freedom. Helpfully he explains that "the common confession of Christians" comes in three forms. We can confess our sins to God alone or (secondly) to our neighbor alone, and in accord with the Lord's Prayer this should happen whenever and wherever it is needed, throughout our lives: "[f]or this is the essence of a genuinely Christian life, to acknowledge that we are sinners and to pray for grace."[83] The third form of confession is "the secret confession that takes place privately before a single brother or sister . . . when some particular issue weighs on us or attacks us . . . by divine ordinance Christ himself has placed absolution in the mouths of his Christian community and commanded us to absolve one another from sins."[84] Although confession to the pastor is implicit in Luther's "Exhortation," his wording does not make that an absolute requirement: it is about one Christian sharing God's word with another. That is in keeping with his earlier statements about the keys, as an office which belongs to the common priesthood.[85]

To demonstrate how Luther preached on this third kind of confession, LW 69 presents eleven sermons from 1522–1540 based on the Easter text, John 20:19–23 ("Receive the Holy Spirit. . . . If you forgive the sins of any, they are forgiven").[86] From these sermons it is possible to determine whether Luther modified his teaching in later years, making lay absolution an exception only for "emergency situations" *in extremis*, and whether it is correct to characterise "the office of the keys" as the sole prerogative of the public ministry.[87]

In the first sermon Luther states that Jesus' words about imparting forgiveness mean that "this power [*gewalt*] is given to all Christians," although he makes it clear that Paul's requirement that "all things should be done according to order" must also apply here.[88] Then in 1523, he connects Christ's own mission to that of Christians sent into the world to share God's love. Luther says, "It is the office of everyone to instruct his neighbor, etc. And this power [*potestatem*] is given not to the clergy alone (though [here it is] spoken to the apostles) but to all believers."[89] It includes the power to forgive sins, "placed spiritually in every Christian's mouth."[90]

Taken together, this series of sermons shows how Luther's teaching continued to include this affirmation of lay participation in the church's sacramental ministry of absolution (the office of the keys), at the same time as he upheld its central place in the work of those called to that ministry. In the later sermons, especially when Luther is preaching against those who disrupt the public ministry of the church, or misusing its office, then lay participation tends to be more strongly limited to cases of "need":

> Christ gives the Holy Spirit to his whole church and Christendom—to the apostles and the apostles' successors, pastors, preachers, yes to every Christian in time of need (*in der Not*)—everything that pertains to the office, that they might preach, teach, comfort, forgive and retain sins: in sum that they might be sent just as the Father has sent him.[91]

Of particular relevance is a reference to the common priesthood in the last of these sermons, preached in Wittenberg on the Sunday after Easter, 1540, probably at an ordination service. It was published in 1541, and then a revised version was included in the edition of the *Church Postil* edited and published by Cruciger in its 1544 revision.[92]

In this sermon Luther teaches that the office of the keys refers only to spiritual "government" in the church on the basis of Jesus' word in Matthew 16:19 on the "keys of the kingdom" and the binding and loosing of sin. This means that forgiveness is freely given in Christ's name; it can have no conditions attached. Its purpose is to comfort the spiritually afflicted and is received only by faith so that questions of merit earned by religious observances play no part here. In the same way, the pronouncement of absolution is not a commodity to be bought and sold in the church. However, given the struggle to establish to an evangelical ministry, Luther takes the opportunity to urge financial support for the public ministry; the laborers are "worthy of their hire" (1 Timothy 5:17–18).[93]

Many times in the sermon, Luther strongly affirms the responsibility of the public ministry to provide the comfort of absolution for those with troubled consciences, and especially for those who are dying. When they do so, the pastor is to be heard, "not as a human being, but as God."[94] However, several times Luther also makes it clear that Christ's command and promise in this text applies not to the clergy alone, but to all Christians equally. And yet again, in cases of necessity (*die not*), where the pastor is not present, Christ's word retains its efficacy:

> I am not speaking only of those who are ministers but of all Christians. They are able, in case of need or peril of death, to lift up one another.[95]

This is because the same words are to be used either by the called pastor, or by a neighbor, a friend or brother (sister), when "We do nothing but say, "I remit your sins, not on my own behalf, but in the stead of Christ the Lord.""[96] Throughout these sermons, the words of absolution do not change according to who speaks them.[97] And—these being Easter sermons—Luther reminds his hearers that this absolution has the power of Christ's resurrection behind it.[98]

This understanding of absolution is confirmed in Luther's *Sermons on Matthew 18* (1537), where he says, "Thus it is just as valid, no matter who speaks the absolution to you. If it is God's word, then we should be certain that our sins are forgiven us."[99] A further statement about the efficacy of lay absolution occurs in a sermon on Matthew 3 from January 1544, where, if no preacher is there, "a boy or a woman" can speak the absolution to me, "because both are members of Christ and have his power [*habet potestatem*]."[100]

An important aspect of this final sermon in the series on John 20 is that Luther includes the common priesthood in his explication of Christ's comforting promise. Jesus commissions the disciples with the words, "As my Father has sent me, so I am sending you" (20:21). He then breathes the Spirit over the disciples, sharing with them with the responsibility to forgive sins, or retain them. At one point in this sermon, however, Luther focuses on the significance of these words of sending, at the same time making it clear that the commission is also given to all:

> Here Christ has consecrated us all and made us priests [*Christus hat uns alle geweihet und zu priestern gemacht*], from the priest to the lowest, where he says,

"As the Father sent me, so I send you." I come in the name of my Lord Jesus Christ. Do you hear? You should not tremble and shake ... be at peace, what you desire to have, I bring to you, freely, and pronounce you free and absolved from your sins in the name of the Father and of the Son, and of the Holy Spirit."[101]

After Luther's death, John 20:19–23 became an important text in some Lutheran rites for pastoral ordination. Robert Smith states that, by using this key text from the Roman rite,

the Wuerttemberg order [1547/1559] retained a closer affinity to its Roman predecessors ... explain[ing] the spiritual gift given in ordination and the centrality of the power to forgive sins as constitutive of the office of the ministry.[102]

But here, in this sermon from Easter 1540, Luther's use of Jesus' words shows that the responsibility to declare the forgiveness of sins is given to all Christians in common, even as the public role of the pastor is affirmed. Generally, Luther's interpretative rule is that Jesus' words to the disciples are intended for the whole church, even when he speaks to Peter (and/or the apostles) alone.[103] Whatever the case, this sermon confirms that Luther himself does not make a fundamental distinction between clerical and lay absolution, and here he does so with additional support from the foundations of the common priesthood.[104] The universal need for the comfort of absolution is what is critical here, together with Christ's promise.

This issue goes to the very heart of Luther's ecclesiology.[105] The life of the church is characterized by the Christ-like actions of a fellow-believer, a neighbour. At the highest level of God's word and faith, it is about the comfort of that word. The practice of mutual forgiveness is front and center of Luther's view of the Christian community, the communion of saints.[106] This remained true, even as he confirms the position of the called office of public ministry. Unlike a hierarchical priesthood, the church's true office fulfils its responsibilities for the benefit of all, as an essential and inclusive service of its ministry.

TORGAU CASTLE CHURCH CONSECRATION, 1544

Sermon on Luke 14

The Castle Church at Torgau in Saxony was the first church built and consecrated for use as an evangelical place of worship and preaching. The sermon that Luther preached was recorded by Rörer and prepared for publication by Cruciger. He also performed the rite of dedication, urging the congregation to join him in prayer. This inclusive act shows how Luther portrayed the pastor (bishop) and the congregation as priests working together in the worship of God. This celebration of God's word as a gathered community recalls Luther's account of evangelical mass in *The Private Mass and the Consecration of Priests* (1533).[107]

Luther preached on the Gospel for the day, Luke 14:1–11, Jesus' teaching about the Sabbath. There are relatively few polemics here; in this setting, Luther has no need to refute the errors of opponents from the schools of tradition or innovation. He begins with encouragement for participation with him in blessing and consecrating the new house of God in Christ's name, for the purposes of hearing the word and appropriate responses of prayer and praise. He urges that at the conclusion of the sermon, all should join with him in praying the Lord's Prayer as together they consecrate the new building to the glory of God.[108] After explaining how Christ himself had taught the Jewish people about true worship and the right use of God's temple, Luther says,

> But we, who are in the kingdom of our Lord Christ, are not thus bound to a tribe or place, so that we must adhere to one place alone and have only one race or one particular, separate kind of persons. Rather we are all priests [*wir sind alle Priester*], as is written in 1 Peter 2 [:9]; so that all of us should proclaim God's Word and works at every time and in every place, and persons from all ranks, races, and stations may be specially called to the ministry [*Predigtampt*], if they have the grace and the understanding of the Scriptures to teach others.[109]

For Christians, this priesthood means putting the third commandment into practice, for a true keeping of the Sabbath. It involves the active reception of God's word, to bring forth the fruits of faith and love, and to hold on to the confession of God's name, by prayer, praise, and thanksgiving. It also includes the identification of individuals suitable to be called to public ministry, which Luther encourages here on the basis of 1 Peter 2:9. In these later years, Luther always affirms the role of the preaching office in the church, and here he uses the text that teaches the responsibility of all Christians to "proclaim God's word." Further, he then presents the ordering of public ministry in terms similar to that he had reached some twenty years earlier:

> For when I preach, when we come together as a congregation, this is not my word or my doing; but is done for the sake of all of you and for the sake of the whole church. It is only that it is necessary that there be one who speaks and is the spokesman by the commission and consent [*aus befehl und verwilligung*] of the others, who, by reason of the fact that they listen to the preaching, all accept and confess the Word and thus also teach others. Thus, when a child is baptized, this is done not only by the pastor, but also the sponsors, who are witnesses, indeed, the whole church. For baptism, just like the Word and Christ himself, is the common possession of all Christians. So also they all pray and sing and give

thanks together; here there is nothing that one possesses or does for him alone; but what each one has also belongs to the other.[110]

Here, we are very close to the heart of Luther's integrated teaching on priesthood and ministry. The way he uses the example of baptism, alongside of 1 Peter 2:9, suggests the continuing influence of Ephesians 4, and its verses that unite the community's common possessions (4:4–6, "one Lord, one faith, one baptism"), with the call to the work of ministry (4:11–12, "He gave some to be apostles . . . pastors and teachers"), in order to bring about the goal of faith (4:13, "the fullness of Christ"). This is in keeping with how Luther often presents his mature understanding of the church and its ministry, without the need to parade the whole band of familiar references.[111] Luther is likely to have Ephesians 4:1–10 in mind because it was the text on which he preached later that afternoon. In the face of many threats to the peace of the church (the Turks, Rome, and other opponents) his second sermon affirmed the enduring promise of "one Lord, one faith, one baptism."[112]

Continuing the themes of priestly service, the morning sermon concluded by presenting an evangelical version of the traditional acts associated with the consecration of a worship place. Luther describes what takes place that day in terms of the common, priestly use of the word and prayer, proposing that the assembly was using the "holy water" that blesses and consecrates. Together, they have shared in the privilege of confessing God's word, and now as a Christian community they offer the rising smoke of their faithful prayers:

> And now that you, dear friends, have helped to sprinkle with the true holy water of God's word, take hold of the censer [*Reuchfas*] with me, that is, seize hold upon prayer, and let us call upon God and pray. First, for his holy church, that he may preserve his holy word among us and extend it everywhere. . . . And then also for all governments and public peace in German lands, that God may graciously preserve and strengthen the same. . . . And finally, also for our beloved government, the sovereign prince and the whole nobility and all ranks, high and low, rulers and subjects, that they may all honor God's word, give thanks to God for it, administer their offices well, be faithful and obedient, and show Christian love to their neighbors. For this is what God would have from us all, and this is the true incense [*das rechte Reuchwerck*] of Christians—to pray earnestly for all of these necessities [*not*]. Amen.[113]

This sermon stands as an eloquent confirmation that a full understanding of the common priesthood persisted in Luther's teaching and preaching until his final years. The church-blessing context is significant, with Luther himself leading in an act of worship which affirms the core purposes of the Christian community. Preaching on the text for the day, he makes a series of natural connections between the themes of priesthood, worship, and ministry for his hearers. These include the shared responsibility for the work of word and prayer in the church, and the awareness that "keeping the Sabbath" involves the sacrifice of praise, which then leads to acts of love and mercy (Luke 14:3). The new church building at Torgau, erected and dedicated for the preaching of the gospel, itself stood as the symbol and epitome of all that Luther sought for the priestly people of God. His purpose was that they would all enjoy "the common possessions of all Christians," rejoicing to share and participate in the gifts of word and faith not only as the church's foundation but encompassing its life and its worship as well.

The New Testament Sermons as a Summary of the Common Priesthood

This selection of sermons has illustrated from Luther's voluminous preaching output how the biblical insights that shaped his own convictions about the nature of the church and a Christian's rightful place within it, became the driving forces for the reform of that same church and the establishment of Christian communities founded on those same convictions.

While the sermons highlighted in this study represent only a small percentage of his recorded output, they serve to indicate the breadth and depth of his preaching, and show how the theology of church and priesthood was proclaimed throughout his ministry.[114] By means of published sermons including the *Church Postil*, his reach extended well beyond his familiar pulpits in Wittenberg and its neighboring Saxon towns, and beyond the limits of his lifetime as well.

The consistent, primary focus of Luther's preaching was on the word and faith, and in the midst of the rich variety of its biblical expression he continued to identify "the baptized Christian" as the chief recipient of God's grace and blessing. Those who hear the word should also respond with praise and confession of God's name, with faith and acts of love and mercy. Before God, and within the church as a spiritual community, there is no differentiation according to status (Galatians 3:28); the only imperative is that of service, ministry. These are recurrent themes throughout Luther's preaching, and they reveal the context for his understanding of Christian priesthood and the church. The fact that Luther's teaching *can* be preached and applied with clarity and spiritual depth is a significant consideration when it is otherwise evaluated as lacking a theological system or complex thought.

In these sermons, the common priesthood conveyed the reality of the baptized believer in their personal relationship to God, their union with Christ, their equal possession of God's gifts and the equality of faith under the gospel (*Sermons on John 14–16*). In opposition to religious individualism (including the monastic orders), true priesthood expressed the sacrificial lives of Christians within a sacramental, serving community (*Sermon on Romans 12*, etc.), and their unity in Christ. Luther maintained his rejection of a hierarchical priesthood, along with its unique consecrated status and aspects such as the work of sacrifice in the mass. This is because the teaching of the common priesthood was always dependent on Luther's major reformational insights regarding the word and faith and the primacy of Christ's work and its trinitarian focus; it did not preempt or supplant them and remained subordinate to them.

As in his lectures, and his published theology, Luther frequently highlights here Christ's own office as priest and king as the source for the priesthood of Christians (Psalm 110), and their royal identity as members of Christ's kingdom (1 Peter 2:9). The work ("office") and mission of Christ is being fulfilled in the ministry of the church, through the service of all Christians, and especially for the "later Luther" through those called to the public preaching office. This was the reality for church life in sixteenth-century Europe. But his understanding that Christ's words are addressed to all Christians in common is matched to the continuing assertion that "we are all priests." This means that Christ's comforting words of forgiveness and absolution, at the very heart of the church's ministry, can—and should—be spoken by any Christian to another as the voice of Christ in their time of need (*Sermons for the First Sunday after Easter*). Once again this does not downgrade the regular ministry of the ordained clergy, but upholds and broadens its reach and effectiveness at every level of Christian community.

NOTES

1. Fred W. Meuser, "Luther as Preacher of the Word of God," CCML, 137.

2. Brecht, *Luther* 2:15–18, places the creation of the postils within the context of Luther's reforming work, and highlights their importance. Heinz Schilling includes a description of the postils in a wider account of Luther's enduring significance for the German peoples, *Martin Luther*, 221–225. For the significance of the 1540/44 *Church Postil*, see the evaluation in LW 75: xxiv–vi.

3. The full history is summarized in LW 75:xiii–xxiv, *Church Postil I*, concluding with an account of Cruciger's important editorial work. For a further discussion of Luther as preacher and the later revision and publication of the postils, see Brecht, *Luther* 3:249–253.

4. LW 75:317–329 (WA 10/1.1:248–270), *Church Postil I: Sermon on Acts 6:8–15, 7:54–60*.

5. LW 75:320 (WA 10/1.1:253–254).

6. LW 75:322 (WA 10/1.1:257).

7. LW 75:324 (WA 10/1.1:261).

8. Ibid.

9. LW 75:325–326 (WA 10/1.1:263–264).

10. LW 76:3–38 (WA 10/1.1:449–503), *Church Postil II: Sermon on Galatians 3:23–29*.

11. LW 76:20–1 (WA 10/1.1:475–77).

12. LW 76:21–2 (WA 10/1.1:477–78). From chapter 7, see Isaiah 61:6 (n60), Psalm 45 (n100), and Psalm 110 (nn 115,119) for the clothing imagery in an Old Testament context, as well as Joseph's robe, Genesis 37:3 (n170).

13. LW 76:22–23 (WA 10/1.1:478–480).

14. LW 76:28 (WA 10/1.1:487–488).

15. E.g., at LW 76:30 (WA 10/1.1:491), (n79). This paragraph on "lay or clergy" is omitted in the later edition.

16. Steven Ozment, *Age of Reform* (New Haven: Yale, 1980). See, for example, 260–289 (and 381–396) for the changes brought about by clerical marriage. Carter Lindberg, "Luther's Struggle with Social-Ethical Issues" CCML, 165–178, argues persuasively that marriage and other social welfare issues were "rooted in his theology and his ethics." See also Heinz Schilling's wide-ranging discussion of Luther's approach to economic and social issues, *Martin Luther Rebel*, 434–449. For a more vigorous argument for Luther's impact upon society, based on a selective reading of some of the sources examined in chapter 3, see Nathan Montover, *Luther's Revolution: The Political Dimensions of Martin Luther's Universal Priesthood* (Havertown: Casemate Publishers, 2012).

17. LW 76:39–47 (WA 10/1.1:504–519), *Sermon for New Year, Luke 2:21*.

18. LW 76:47 (WA 10/1.1:519).

19. See chapter three, *From Captivity to Freedom*, and chapter 4, *Christian Priesthood*.

20. LW 76:48–70 (WA 10/1.1:519–555), *Sermon for Epiphany, Isaiah 60:1–6*.

21. LW 76:50 (WA 10/1.1:523–524).

22. LW 76:69–70 (WA 10/1.1:555). Linking the praise of God with the confession of sins and gospel proclamation is characteristic of Luther's holistic view of the ministry of the word; both early and late (see chapter 4 above, *The Word and the Priesthood*, and chapter 7, especially *Psalm 51*).

23. LW 76:71–180 (WA 10/1.1:555–728), *Sermon for Epiphany: Matthew 2:1–12*; see also LW 52:159–286.

24. LW 76:71 (WA 10/1.1:557).

25. See LW 75:xxv, *Church Postil I*, on Luther's "digressions."

26. LW 76:138–161 (WA 10/1.1:634–667), *Matthew 2:1–12*: "Appendix I, *On 2 Timothy 3:1–9*." LW 76:162–180 (WA 10/1.1:681–709), "Appendix II, *On Clerical Vows*." The first is a wide-ranging attack on the corruption of the papacy; the second, a more pointed analysis of religious practices. A summary was retained as a sub-section of the 1540 postil, entitled *True and False Worship* (LW 76:121–126, WA 10/1.1:674–680). Both of the longer expositions were later included in volume 4 of the Wittenberg edition of Luther's German Works (1551).

27. LW 76:128 (WA 10/1.1:711–712), *Sermon on Matthew 2:1–12*.

28. See, for example, chapter 7 above, *Minor Prophets* (at n24) for comments and further references for Luther's hermeneutic in relation to his limited use of allegory in the service of the Gospel.

29. Compare LW 76:104 (WA 10/1.1:614) where Luther suggests that the worship offered by the Magi took the form of the homage due to a human king.

30. LW 76:133 (WA 10/1.1:721).

31. LW 76:181 (WA 17/2:5). See Brecht 2:16 for the circumstances which delayed publication.

32. LW 76:181 (WA 17/2:5–6), *Sermon on Romans 12:1–5*.

33. LW 76:182 (WA 17/2:6).

34. LW 76:182 (WA 17/2:6). Compare the baptismal connections made in *Concerning the Ministry* (chapter 3) and in the *Sermons on Psalm 110* (chapter 7).

35. LW 76:182–3 (WA 17/2:7).

36. LW 76:183 (WA 17/2:7).

37. LW 76:183–184 (WA 17/2:8).

38. That is, this text (Romans 12) it is not about public preaching—although that is part of this sacrificial dynamic.

39. LW 76:184 (WA 17/2:8). Note carefully: "Preaching" for Luther is not only about the formal public proclamation of God's word. Proclaiming the word happens in many ways, in many places—but they are all interconnected in the lives of God's people (people and pastors, all saints and priests together), and all occasions serve the word's same purposes.

40. Therefore, see chapter 7 for preaching as praise and sacrifice in the psalms and the prophets.

41. LW 76:185–87 (WA 17/2:9–12).

42. LW 76:187–89 (WA 17/2:12).

43. LW 76:190–91 (WA 17/2:14–15).

44. LW 76:209–237 (250) (WA 17/2:32–60,71–72). *Sermon(s) on Romans 12:6–16, 12:17–21*.

45. LW 76:209–210 (WA 17/2:33).

46. Luther's last sermon in Wittenberg (17 January 1546) was on Romans 12:3, "the measure of faith" (LW 51:371–380, WA 51:123–134).

47. In his introduction to LW 24 (*Sermons on the Gospel of John*) Jaroslav Pelikan says "[o]f all the books in the New Testament, Luther seems to have prized the Gospel according to St. John most highly. And within this Gospel his favorite portion was the closing discourse of Jesus, set down in chapters 14, 15, and 16" (LW 24:ix).

48. See Brecht, *Luther* 2:285, 433; also the introductions in LW 69:xv–xxii, *Sermons on John 17–20*, updating the information given in LW 24.

49. See LW 24:x for Luther's comment, "This is the best book I have ever written. Of course, I did not write it; Cruciger did." For further details see LW 69:8, *Sermons on John 17–20*.

50. For their integrated presentation of the common priesthood, these sermons stand alongside other works from the 1530s such as *The Private Mass* and *Psalm 110*.

51. LW 24:66 (WA 45:521) *Sermons on John 14*.

52. LW 24:78 (WA 45:532) (translation altered). Compare Luther's similar use of John 14:12 in *Keeping Children at School* (1530), where the specific emphasis is on the public ministry (chapter 5). Here the identification of every Christian's work with Christ's own ministry is especially powerful.

53. LW 24:79 (WA 45:532–533), *Sermons on John 14*.

54. LW 24:82 (WA 45: 535). Luther uses similar language in his lectures on 1 John in 1527, that having been anointed to be a priest (1 John 2:27), a Christian who "teaches the word of God, is like God in the world" (LW 30:261, WA 20:687–688.

55. LW 24:87 (WA 45:540) (translation altered).

56. LW 24:68 (WA 45:522–523).

57. See e.g., Luther's final sermon in Eisleben (15 February 1546), where he encourages his listeners to celebrate their access to God's word, hidden from the wise and powerful: "You hear [it] at home in your house, father and mother and children sing and speak of it, the preacher speaks of it in the parish church," LW 51:390 (WA 51:193), on Matthew 11:25–30. For the ministry in home and family as a reform initiative, see chapter 5 at nn30–1 and 54; also chapter 7 at n45.

58. LW 24:171 (WA 45:617).

59. LW 24:226 (WA 45:667–668), *Sermons on John 15*. See chapter 2 above, *Christian Community and Unity in Christ*, for the earlier uses of this text.

60. LW 24:242 (WA 45:682).

61. LW 24:242 (WA 45:682).

62. Ibid. This kind of life, says Luther, is "the precious service of God."

63. LW 24:243 (WA 45:682–683) (emphasis added).

64. LW 24:243 (WA 45:683).

65. LW 45:243–244 (WA 45:683).

66. LW 24:264 (WA 45:702) (translation modified).

67. LW 24:264–298 (WA 45:703–733). John 15:18–27 leads Luther to discuss the persecution suffered by the evangelicals, the inescapable reality for all those who follow Christ and preach his cross.

68. LW 24:309–310 (WA 46:11), *Sermons on John 16*. There are those who are the church in name only, and those who cling to the church's "essence," salvation by faith in Christ alone. See also LW 24:304 (WA 46:6), where Luther "concedes . . . that the papacy has God's word and the office of the apostles [*Apostel ampt*], and that we have received Holy Scripture, Baptism, the Sacrament, and the pulpit from them."

69. LW 24:407 (WA 46:98) (translation modified).

70. These details are provided in LW 69:3–9, *Sermons on John 17–20*.

71. LW 69:15 (WA 28:73).

72. LW 69:98–99 (WA 28:174–175). In Rörer's notes, Luther uses the Latin "pontifex" for priest here.

73. LW 69:100 (WA 28:176).

74. LW 69:101 (WA 28:177).

75. LW 69:104 (WA 28:182).

76. See chapter 2 above, especially on *The Blessed Sacrament of the Holy and True Body of Christ and the Brotherhoods* (1519) at nn18–23; also chapter 5 (sermon on the "Great Supper") at nn13–14.

77. LW 69:105 (WA 28:182–183).

78. Jaroslav Pelikan explains that Luther preferred the Gospel of John "because it concentrated upon the discourses of the Lord rather than his miracles" (*Luther the Expositor*, 60 and also 36n47).

79. For this issue in the *Ninety-five Theses* (1517) and the *Sacrament of Penance* (1519), see chapter 2, *Equality in the Body and Participation in the Gospel*.

80. See, for example, *Concerning the Ministry* (1523) LW 40:26–27 (WA 12:183–185), the "fourth office . . . belong[s] to the whole church and to each of its members." Also *The Keys* (1530) LW 40:366 (WA 30/2:498). To these sources can be added the sermon *On Confession and the Sacrament* (1524), included in the *Church Postil* (LW 76:433–449, WA 15:481–505). The gospel, Luther says, "should unceasingly sound and ring in the mouths of all Christians," LW 76:436 (WA 15:486).

81. Jonathan Trigg, "Luther on Baptism and Penance," OHMLT, 317–320.

82. BOC 476–480, *Large Catechism*.

83. BOC 477, 8–9

84. BOC 477, 13–17.

85. References in nn79–81 above.

86. See LW 69:313–326, *Sermons on John 20:19–31* for the introduction to this study, and then LW 69:327–436 for the eleven sermons on this text, drawn from various WA sources.

87. See n102, Ralph Smith's statement that "the power to forgive sins [is] constitutive of the office of the ministry." Effectively, then, only the ordained clergy have that "power." Werner Elert considers the differing approaches of Luther and Melanchthon to this question, tracing the process whereby Christ's command to forgive (and retain) sins became bound up with clergy seen as moral arbiters. *The Structure of Lutheranism*, 352–367.

88. LW 69:330 (WA 10/3:9), *John 20:19–31* (1522).

89. LW 69:336–337 (WA 11:96), *John 20:19–31* (1523).

90. LW 69:337 (WA 11:97).

91. LW 69:358 (WA 28:470), *John 20:19–31* (1529). See also LW 69:354 (WA 34/1:327) (1531); LW 69:412,416 (WA 41:543,546) (1536). As has been previously noted, whether *Not* is translated "emergency," "necessity," or "need" is of some significance here (see also chapter 4 at n90 [*Concerning the Ministry*], and also chapter 6 at n66 [*On the Councils*]). To limit it to deathbed crises (the final "emergency") does not do justice to the range of situations described by Luther, or his intentions for the church's ministry.

92. LW 69:424–436 (WA 49:135–142). This gives the original text from 1541; see also LW 77:126–153 (WA 21:289–297) for the text in the *Church Postil* (1544).

93. LW 69:434–435 (WA 49:141). Financial support for the clergy is often a recurrent theme when Luther is urging due respect for the public ministry.

94. LW 69:434 (WA 49:140) (translation modified).

95. LW 69:431 (WA 49:139). Other statements in this same sermon that include (or imply) lay participation in the ministry of comfort are: LW 69:431 (WA 49:139); LW 69:432 (WA 49:139); LW 69:434 (WA 49:141); LW 69:435 (WA 49:141) ("through

ministers, *etc.*"); LW 69:435 (WA 49:141–142) ("God who comes in my neighbor"); LW 69:436 (WA 49:142) ("Christ commanded his apostles and everyone to preach").

96. LW 69:430 (WA 49:138).

97. An earlier sermon from 1536 expresses this very clearly: "Go to the pastor; in case of need, tell your neighbor to recite the absolution in the name of Christ. Then you have the word; when they do it, Christ has done it" (LW 69:416, WA 41:546).

98. LW 69:436 (WA 49:142); see also LW 69:416 (WA 41:546) (1536).

99. LW 67:414 (WA 47:303), *Sermon on Matthew 18* (1537).

100. LW 58:75 (WA 49:312), *Sermon on Matthew 3* (1544).

101. LW 69:434 (WA 49:141). From the same source see also the sermon in the *Church Postil*, LW 77:141.

102. Ralph Smith, *Luther, Ministry, and Ordination Rites in the Early Reformation Church* (New York: Lang, 1966), 217. John 20:19–23 is commonly used in present-day Lutheran ordination rites in keeping with Melanchthon's use of the text in CA 28 on *The Power of the Bishops* (BOC 93). See also Martin Krarup, *Ordination in Wittenberg,* (Tübingen: Mohr Siebeck, 2007).

103. See, for example, LW 67:275 (WA 38:617), *Annotations on Matthew 1–18.* Luther writes that Christ's promise to Peter (Matthew 16:17–18) is spoken to all, just as Peter speaks on behalf of us all.

104. This is not explicit in the previous sermons on this text, but nothing in them excludes this understanding which is consistent with Luther's teaching on the "keys" (see n80 above).

105. For Luther, the promises of the Gospel will always override the legal framework of tradition and structure of the institutional church.

106. "This is the greatest thing about the community for Luther . . . [that] God's word . . . is close to me in every brother," Althaus, *Theology*, 317–318; also Bayer, *Theology*, 276–278, quoting from Luther's later sermon on Matthew 18 (n99).

107. LW 38:208–209 (WA 38:247) *The Private Mass*. See chapter 6 above.

108. LW 51:333 (WA 49:588) *Sermon for Torgau Church Consecration* (1544), Luke 14. Scott Hendrix provides some excellent details regarding the construction of the church, and Luther's message to his diverse congregation, who "all are made equal by faith." *Martin Luther*, 278–280.

109. LW 51:335 (WA 49:590–591).

110. LW 51:343 (WA 49:600).

111. For example, he follows a similar pattern in a postil sermon for the Fifth Sunday after Trinity on 1 Peter 3, LW 78:188–189 (WA 22:57–58).

112. WA 49:615–620, *Sermon on Ephesians 4:1–10* (Torgau, 1544); also in the morning sermon on Luke 14, Luther refers to the text for the afternoon and its message of "one body" (etc.) to contrast the equality of faith with the necessity for social distinctions. Preaching to a congregation drawn from the electoral court, his vision did not rise above the conventions of his day, (LW 51:351, WA 49:610).

113. LW 51:353–354 (WA 49: 613–614) (translation modified).

114. Of course this selection barely scratches the surface of Luther's recorded preaching. Over 2,000 sermons and 412 postil sermons are listed in Kurt Aland, *Hilfsbuch zum Lutherstudien,* fourth edition (Bielefeld: Luther-Verlag, 1996).

Chapter 9

Summary Conclusions

MARTIN LUTHER'S COMMON PRIESTHOOD: ITS BOUNDARIES AND HORIZONS

The Common Priesthood: What Does This Mean?

The lineaments of Luther's teaching have been traced and explored across some thirty-three years of his career as teacher of Biblical theology at the University of Wittenberg, his preaching in the town's pulpit and his authorship of many books, treatises, commentaries, and occasional works: polemical, exhortatory, confessional, devotional, liturgical and catechetical. Its early basis in a range of biblical texts and their continuing relationship to Luther's Pauline ecclesiology has been shown and further explored in his later writing and preaching. The task of these final conclusions is to make sense of these diverse findings and then to draw them together into a coherent and unified portrayal of the common priesthood, demonstrating its meaning and its purpose in Luther's thought and within his ecclesiology. Keeping in view the questions raised for this study in the introduction, its status as Luther's consistent teaching will be summarized in terms of its persistence, pervasiveness and theological integrity. In my judgement, while the ways in which Luther applied and presented the common priesthood were adapted and developed according to the changing context(s) he was addressing, the teaching itself did not substantially change. This contextual development will be addressed from the perspective of the question "Who are the priests?" together with an account of its biblical footprint—the sources and texts that first formed, shaped and then maintained this teaching in his thinking and writing. The penultimate step will be to consider ("discern") the particular results of this investigation that run counter to a conventional view of the "priesthood of all believers" and also offer a further response to the critical voices that discount the importance of this teaching for Luther studies. Finally, my own account of Luther's common priesthood and its wide horizons will urge its relevance for today's Christian community as Christians serve God together, as Christ's people in God's world.

THE STATUS OF THE COMMON PRIESTHOOD

Its Persistence

Even before 1520, Luther taught that *all* Christians are priests on the basis of 1 Peter 2:9, the royal priesthood that Christ shares with all those who believe in him. By faith they stand in an equal spiritual relationship with God, as God's baptised people who are "all one in Christ Jesus" within the community of the church (Gal. 3:26–29). This priesthood affirms the participation of all Christians in the "offices" of the word, and the spiritual value of their lives of sacrifice and of prayer. The persistence of this teaching is confirmed by its presence in a number of works from the length and breadth of Luther's career, and not just in the three Reformation treatises of 1520 (*To the Christian Nobility, The Babylonian Captivity, The Freedom of a Christian*). The following contain the most substantial accounts of the common priesthood: *The Misuse of the Mass* (1522), *The Exposition of 1 Peter* (1522), *Concerning the Ministry* (1523), *The Private Mass and the Consecration of Priests* (1533), *Sermons on Psalm 110* (1535), *Sermons on John 14–16* (1537), and *The Sermon at the Dedication of Torgau Castle Church* (1544). Even if there were no other evidence, these published works establish beyond any question the continuation of this teaching in Luther's theology. Many other significant references to the common priesthood are to be found throughout Luther's writings and in his sermons. These occur, for example, in *Answer to the Book by Emser* (1521), *That a Christian Assembly . . . has The Right . . . To Judge All Teaching and to Call* (1523), *Sermon on Romans 12:1–5* (1525), *Lectures on the Minor Prophets* (1524–1527), *Lectures on Isaiah 40–66* (1527), *On the Councils and the Church* (1539), *Lectures on Genesis* (1538–1545), and *The Church Postil* (1540/45).[1] Their accumulated witness also serves to confirm that the common priesthood was embedded in his understanding of the church and was for Luther an important way in which he continued to describe the full biblical dimensions of Christian life and worship.

Its Pervasiveness

The importance of this teaching is similarly confirmed by its pervasive presence across the full compass of Luther's works, and not only in writings for a particular situation or audience. Taken up and developed in connection with his conflict with Rome about the nature of the church, its ministry and its sacraments (*On the Papacy in Rome, Treatise on the New Testament, To the Christian Nobility*), Luther upheld his teaching of the common priesthood not only to reject the exclusive claims of the ordained, hierarchical priesthood and their control of the church's sacramental ministry (*The Babylonian Captivity, The Private Mass, On the Councils and the Church*), but also to present a holistic view of the Christian life and of the church and its ministry (*The Freedom of a Christian, The Exposition of First Peter, Concerning the Ministry, Sermons on Psalm 110*). It represented the underlying motivation for much of his reforming work and his concern for the participation of all Christians in the life and faith of the church. This is seen in his translation of the Bible and the inclusion of *Prefaces* introducing each book, the preparation of new German orders and hymns that facilitated lay involvement in worship, and the catechisms for their instruction in the faith. Neither is its importance diminished by the weight Luther necessarily attached to the preaching office as the public expression of the church's ministry (*Keeping Children in School, Psalm 82*). Particularly in *The Church Postil* (as revised in 1540–1544) and his published biblical expositions, Luther continued to include the common priesthood as a substantial statement of life and service as a baptised Christian together with fellow believers in the community of the church (*Sermons on Psalm 110, Sermons on John 14–16, Lectures on Genesis*).

Despite the boundaries imposed upon Luther's teaching by conflicts with Rome and with radical preachers, and the lack of education among the church's laity and the other constraints inherent in the society in which he worked, Luther's biblical and creedal understanding of the church as the priestly people of God and the communion of saints is evident across the full range of his written and preached theology.

Its Integrity

The integrity of this teaching is demonstrated by its consistent presentation across the works noted above, and by its close connections to the major elements of Luther's theology: his ecclesiology, Christology, and the teaching on justification by faith. This relationship to his primary insights regarding the word and faith means that even in works that do not directly name or discuss the common priesthood, its teaching is not negated by its absence from the discussions of those chief teachings. For example, the common priesthood is not always named when Luther examines the "office of the keys," the forgiveness of sins by Christ's command. But—based on the texts in which he interprets Christ's words as being addressed to all Christians (e.g., Matthew 18:18, "whatever you loose on earth"; John 20:23 "if you forgive")—Luther affirms the right and authority of any Christian to speak God's liberating word and to forgive sins in Christ's name, sister to sister, sister to brother. His discussion of this as a ministry of the word is entirely in keeping with how he elsewhere teaches about the nature of Christ's priesthood, and ours. The application of the common priesthood's themes can often seen to be underlying Luther's discussions of worship and the church's sacramental ministry, as well as ordination and church order. The extensive use of terms such as "offering" and "sacrifice" is one indication that this is taking place.

Luther used a variety of formulations and emphases to articulate this teaching and to explore its meaning. In its most direct form he used the phrase "we are all priests," adding in a number of places that this priesthood is conferred by the anointing or consecration that takes place in baptism (*Address to the Christian Nobility, Concerning the Ministry, The Private Mass*). It is an expression of the spiritual equality that exists among Christians, and of the freedom they all enjoy in Christ derived from faith and their common possession of God's word and the blessings it brings (*The Babylonian Captivity, The Freedom of a Christian, Exposition of First Peter*). In the same vein, it has a close connection to the doctrine of justification by faith, each believer's personal reception of salvation in Christ. In communal terms, this is membership in the body of Christ and participation in the communion of saints. Priesthood itself is dependent on unity with Christ, the true High Priest: "We are all priests with Christ" (*The Misuse of the Mass*; see also *The Treatise on the New Testament, The Freedom of a Christian*, et al.). Therefore, its only "sacrifice" is the proclamation of Christ and his work, and the resultant spiritual works of faith and love (*The Private Mass*). Sacrificial Christian living (the life of faith), prayer and preaching are the three priestly offices, shared by all (*Exposition of 1 Peter*). The three offices become seven (closely related to the "marks" of the church) in *Concerning the Ministry*. In *On the Councils and the Church*, these become the "holy possessions" of the church, "the holy Christian people." The unifying thread continued to be the word as the critical element in Luther's reformational breakthrough. It is "possessed" in common by all Christians as priests—who together can "judge" its teaching—and this means that public preaching is the duty of those chosen by the consent of the priestly community to be its ministers (*Sermons on Psalm 110, Sermon at Torgau*). The integrity of the priesthood thus rests in the continuing dynamic of Luther's teaching: from Christ, to the word, to its embodiment in faith and then in the faithful community. In the commentaries on The Minor Prophets and Isaiah, and on Psalms 2, 45 and 51, the teaching of the word is explored in its wider relationship to the worship of God's people, the community's sacrifices of prayer and praise.

The common priesthood's persistent, pervasive presence in Luther's thought, together with its theological integrity, means that it was not merely an expedient teaching for his quarrel with Rome, quickly abandoned when it was taken up by other more radical reformers or when Luther himself prioritized the preaching office. Its use as an anticlerical slogan or as a platitude about Christian spiritual autonomy bears little relation to Luther's original teaching. Neither is its teaching adequately expressed when it is reduced to a general proposition in the debate over the rights of the congregation *versus* the authority and status of the church's public ministry. Rather, the common priesthood is a significant teaching with deep scriptural roots that was integral to Luther's understanding of the church and of the character of Christian faith, worship and life.

THE CONTEXTUAL DEVELOPMENT OF THE COMMON PRIESTHOOD

Who are the Priests?

To approach this question, it is instructive to consider the people and groups to whom Luther addressed the challenge to realise their true priestly status, with the words "*we* are all priests." And when its historical sequence is followed, the question becomes a window into the development of Luther's teaching from a theological perspective as well as its wider impact in early modern society.

Among the earliest references to the common priesthood by Luther (1519) is his application of it in regard to the situation of his friend Spalatin, who while an ordained priest was serving as an [advisor] in the court of Frederick the Wise. Luther reminds him, almost in passing, that his priestly status did not differentiate him from other counsellors for as Peter and John teach "we are all priests." It is Spalatin's service (his ministry) that sets him apart.[2] This indicates how, before the break with Rome (and prior to the writing of the "reformation treatises"), Luther could use the teaching in entirely nonpolemical manner, without any need for explanation beyond its biblical references. Similarly, two years later he urges that Melanchthon as a lay teacher of the Bible should be able to preach in Wittenberg because "he is truly a priest" although not ordained.[3] This use in relation to individual situations indicates that Luther had already reached an understanding of priesthood—consonant also with his ecclesiology—that could be then applied to the reformational situation and the dispute with Rome, rather than being a new teaching that first arose out of that situation.

This is further illustrated by its use in those three reformation treatises, discussed in chapter 3. In *The Address to the Christian Nobility*, Luther urges the whole group of German leaders to take up responsibility for the reform of the church in a time of emergency, which they can rightly do because they are Christians and priests along with all the baptised. Again, this is presented as the application of an existing teaching, not as a novelty being introduced into the church. What is "new" is the way that Luther applies his ecclesiology and its teaching of the common priesthood, expanding its reach from the spiritual realm to the political and social, and breaking down the boundaries that allowed the clerical hierarchy to claim an exclusive right to order the affairs of the church.

Similarly, in *The Babylonian Captivity* Luther addresses the clergy themselves, challenging their hold over the church and its sacraments. The new teachings, he argues, are the barriers placed around the sacraments by a self-appointed band of clerics, robbing the laity of what should be possessed equally by all Christians. He emphasises that "the priesthood is properly nothing but the ministry of the word" and teaches that public ministry requires the consent of the whole church ("congregation"), or a superior's call. This is sometimes seen as a later development in Luther's teaching, but it is already in place here and is used to remind the clergy of the conditions under which they serve and who they could be as "true priests."

The reformation treatise that describes in greater detail the reach of the common priesthood itself is *The Freedom of a Christian*. It is addressed to the pope, perhaps ironically and by implication as the representative of *all* Christians! While it may represent Luther's final attempt to reconcile with Rome, it also shows how far his understanding of the church has come in its presentation of the life of faith entirely removed from any external works of piety. In this form, the common priesthood is rooted in the individual Christian life that shares the word and prayer, as spiritual works accessible to all people as the gifts of the Christ who is Lord of the church and its great high priest. As a work of Christian spirituality, grounded in the word, it reflects the theological agenda for the careful program of reform that Luther was introducing into the church.

This reform of spirituality also marks a division between Luther and other reformers and their understanding of the needs of the church and the nature of Christian priesthood. Luther parts company with his colleague Andreas Karlstadt, at least in part because of Karlstadt's piecemeal attempts to drive forward the cause of reform in the areas of worship and church order. Likewise, Luther largely rejected the peasants' demands in 1525 for wholesale reforms because they represented a misapplication of his teaching of spiritual equality to the situation in society at-large. It could be argued here (with Hans-Martin Barth and Bernhard Lohse) that Luther thereby missed the opportunity to apply the full implications of his insights into the common priesthood to promote the cause of radical reform. Luther himself defended his cautious approach, at least in part because of his social conservatism but also because he believed that the word itself set the agenda for change, first by changing the hearts and minds of those who heard the word and accepted it in faith. It is also true that like many at the time he regarded social upheaval as a great evil contrary to the will of God, and he supported draconian measures to prevent it. And yet he had urged the nobility to take over the work of reforming the church, and his active rejection of the monastic life, clerical celibacy and the sacrificial priesthood brought about major and very visible changes in the socioreligious landscape of late medieval Europe.

Within the existing structures, Luther urged the need for reform by those who had the authority to implement it. Therefore, he encouraged the established leaders of congregations and town councils, using the teaching of the common priesthood to justify their appointment of preachers and ministers sympathetic to the message of the gospel (*The Right to Judge Teaching and to Call*, *Concerning the Ministry*). These changes, where implemented, began the shift from the spiritual domination of a hierarchical Catholic Church over the lives of ordinary people, to the emergence of local church communities governed by their rulers and civic leaders and pastors—creating, in time, a new Protestant church that also held sway over the lives of its members on almost every level. This also includes the long period when the civil authorities functioned as de facto "emergency bishops" for the German churches. Why and how far the initial positive changes left behind the ideals of Luther's common priesthood in subsequent years involves a complex historical judgement, beyond the reach of this study. But in the church today, free from many of the social and political constraints of Luther's day, we can embrace his teaching as a prophetic voice and seek its fulfillment in our own time of reformation and change.

Closer to home, and more effectively, Luther also encouraged parents and employers to take responsibility for the spiritual development of those under their care. He referred to them as "priests and bishops" in their own families and businesses, and provided the catechisms together with the German Bible and other teaching material to facilitate Christian education at a domestic level. That, too, is a result of Luther's teaching of the common priesthood applied within the social and domestic settings, and together with the changes in church government it transformed every day life in early modern Europe over the next decades and centuries (see chapter 5).

In *The Exposition of First Peter* (1523), Luther had expressed the hope that "this word 'priest' were used as commonly as the term 'Christian' is applied to us all." That did not happen, probably because of the entrenched everyday usage of "priest" and "priesthood" to represent the ordained clergy. Luther himself at times reverted to that familiar use. That reality could be the reason for the common priesthood's absence from the *Catechisms* and, for example, the *Order for Baptism*, to avoid confusion. It becomes all the more significant, therefore, that Luther does continue to address his hearers—his students or church congregations—as "priests" in order to make the connection between the biblical teaching and their lives as Christian people. Even while he stressed the importance of the called preaching office (*Keeping Children in School*, 1530; *Infiltrating and Clandestine Preachers*, 1532), Luther still argued that from a spiritual perspective the common priesthood transformed the role of the laity in worship from passive bystanders to active participants in the essential life of the church, uniting them in divine service with their pastors and teachers (*Lectures on the Minor Prophets*, *The Private Mass and the Consecration of Priests*, *Sermons on Psalm 110*).

Notably, almost at the end of his own long ministry, this is the way that he addressed the church community in Torgau (1544)—doubtless gathered from a broad spectrum of society and including senior clergy, nobles, as well as their servants and other townspeople—and urged them to regard themselves as priests together with him in the work of the word, in prayer and in the dedication of a new place of worship, with all that it represented for the mature stages of his reform program at that time. This is part of what Martin Brecht has characterised as Luther's concern for "the preservation of the church."[4]

The title of "priest" applied to all Christians from every walk of life was not only a corrective to the ecclesial thinking that placed a sacramentally-ordained clergy in a special category over against the laity. Luther also taught that the establishment of a reformed church led by its public ministers was not the exclusive task of a new ecclesiastical hierarchy, a separate and self-perpetuating "holy office." For Luther, a true reform means that all Christians, each according to their calling and station in life, share responsibility for the work—the office—of the word. Variously and together they are engaged in hearing and speaking the word, learning and teaching it, judging and discerning its meaning and application, receiving and celebrating the sacraments, praying, forgiving, confessing, praising, encouraging, suffering, consoling and believing. In all of these ways, in the community of the church, at home, or with neighbours in the marketplace, each Christian shares in the "possession" of the word in the fellowship of Christ's body. Where these things are happening and are embraced, the church's priestly work continues among God's people, all those who are rightly named "priests" (*Sermons on Psalm 110*).

Its Biblical Footprint within Luther's Ecclesiology

Luther's early use of the texts for the church's priesthood and its ministry was summarized in some detail in chapters 2 and 4, showing that Luther was not using a random assortment of texts but one that reflected his careful reading of the biblical witness and its assimilation into his theology. Beginning with

Christ's own priesthood, Luther saw that this is taught not only throughout the Letter to the Hebrews but is also prefigured in Psalm 110 and Genesis 14 (the Melchizedek account), showing that "Christ as king and priest rules and serves in the church." From here it is a simple step by way of 1 Peter 2:5–9 to Christian priesthood, not just as an honorary title but as the deeper reality of life in the church. The text's call to "declare [God's] praises" leads Luther to emphasize priesthood's work of proclamation. This is for all Christians, because Isaiah 54:13 (taken up by Jesus in John 6:45) reinforces the priestly status of all believers, who as people united to Christ by faith "shall all be taught by God." As has been noted earlier, Luther's hermeneutic consistently proposes that Christ's recorded words to his first disciples and apostles (including Peter) are intended to be applied to all Christians without distinction. Here, this intersection of priesthood and ministry with equality among Christians also produces Luther's rejection of the medieval understanding of priestly sacrifice. He achieves this by invoking Romans 12:1 and 1 Peter 2:5 to teach that the true spiritual sacrifices stand in opposition to the sacrifice of the mass and its hierarchical priesthood. Rather than an exclusive priesthood, the church's clerical office is a ministry that is open to all and serves God's people with the word. Early on, Luther found 1 Corinthians 14 and its account of shared ministry instructive here; later, it was its call for "order" in the church that he stressed.

While Luther's later lectures and other writings generally lack the prolific scriptural citations of, for example, the *First Lectures on the Psalms*, Luther continued to use the "priesthood" texts, especially in relation to Christ's own priesthood, the sacrifices of self-giving and praise (Romans 12), and the work of the word (*Lectures on the Minor Prophets, Sermons on Isaiah 40–66*). The texts on church and ministry continue to appear more widely in his work on the New Testament but are also prominent in the *Sermons on Psalm 110* and in *The Private Mass and the Consecration of Priests*.

Allowing for some variations, in the years after 1525 Luther's application of the key texts for church and priesthood is still seen across a range of publications. These include Ephesians 4:1–12; Galatians 3:26–29; 1 Corinthians 10:17, 12:12–13 (etc.); 1 Peter 2:5,9; Romans 12:1–8; and Psalm 110. They function as contextual markers and reference points for his theological expositions, and they are also are expounded in their own right. Their use can be characterised as demonstrating theological enrichment rather than exegetical development. Having established the nature of the church and the common spiritual status of all Christians, Luther further explores the implications of concepts like sacrifice and offering for the worship of believers and their daily lives, finding supporting texts in his exegetical work on the *Minor Prophets* and his *Sermon on Isaiah* (e.g. Joel 2:28–29, Malachi 1:11, Isaiah 42:10). In an extended form, the *Sermons on the Gospel of John* show how

Luther fully integrates this mature understanding of priesthood within John's rich exposition of the relationship between Christ and those who through faith belong to him.

However, some texts are less prominent and are used in a restricted way in this later period, as Luther counters the influence of those he regards as unauthorised preachers. For example, this applies to Isaiah 54:13 with John 6:45 ("they shall all be taught by God"), which he had regularly used to support the idea of a common priesthood. Now, preaching on John 6 he uses this text to uphold the need for the church's teaching ministry as the vehicle for an individual encounter with the word of God. He begins to employ Isaiah 55:10–11 ("my word shall not return to me empty") as a more favored text. His source for "ordering ministry" (1 Corinthians 14), from which Luther drew extensively in earlier years to explore the dimensions of congregational worship, is now rarely cited, except more conservatively to limit rather than encourage active participation in public preaching. Even 1 Corinthians 14:40 ("Let all things be done decently and in order") is used more sparingly. It seems that Luther now relies on his own authority for what had become the established practices in the evangelical churches, reflected in documents such as the *Visitation Articles* (1528), rather than needing to draw on biblical examples to promote order in worship and church affairs. However, in the *Lectures on Genesis* Luther does consider the patriarchal stories to be a biblical basis for the role of parents as teachers and preachers within their own households. Similarly, it is the stories of other prominent biblical women (and some medieval saints!) that encourage Luther to think more broadly about the possibilities for the ministry of women.[5]

But most notable for its persistence is the way in which Luther continued to incorporate into his writing the texts for the church as a sacramental community united by Christ in faith and love, presenting free-form versions of them as an evocative shorthand for his characteristic theology. Commenting on Psalm 122:1 before 1515 he had already written,

> But if we are citizens of this city, behold, there is one bread, one cup, one faith, one Lord, and all things are one for us. But Christ is all things in us.[6]

In *Concerning the Ministry* (1523), the themes of Christ's priesthood are intimately connected to those of communion and participation from Paul's letters:

> Wherefore we are priests, as he is Priest, sons as he is Son, kings as he is King. . . . And many similar expressions indicate our oneness with Christ—one loaf, one cup, one body, members of his body, one flesh, bone of his bone, and we are told we have all things in common with him.[7]

Maintaining this emphasis when preaching on Luke 14:16–17 in 1535, Luther says:

> [Christians] are just like one bread or one cake, not only because they together have one God, one Word, one Baptism, one Sacrament, one hope, and all the grace and benefits of Christ in common without any distinction, but also in their whole external life they are one body, since each member is to assist, serve, help, aid, sympathise, etc., with the other.[8]

And then in 1544, in his final writing against the papacy, he states:

> Wherever there is a church, anywhere in the whole world, it still has no other gospel and Scripture, no other baptism and communion, no other faith and Spirit, no other Christ and God, no other Lord's Prayer and prayer, no other hope and eternal life than we have here in our church in Wittenberg.[9]

With remarkable freedom and theological creativity Luther integrated into his writing and preaching the key texts in forms that emphasise the church's unity and community, and the equality and participation of all its people. The sources for this textual synthesis include Ephesians 4 ("there is one body and one Spirit, just as you were called to the one hope of your calling, one Lord, one faith, one baptism"), the familiar phrases from 1 Corinthians 10 ("because there is one bread, we who are many are one body, for we all partake of the one bread") and also from Galatians 3 ("all of you are one in Christ Jesus"). These—with all their kindred texts—reveal the enduring biblical foundations for his understanding of the church, and the basis of its common priesthood as well.

DISCERNING THE COMMON PRIESTHOOD

In order to confirm the significance of Luther's teaching, it is helpful to underline the points where it parts company with a simple understanding of the "priesthood of all believers" and becomes the more nuanced and complex teaching that is the "common priesthood." In doing so, I can highlight several aspects that are particular to Luther and in some cases reflect unexpected or even surprising dimensions of this teaching.

The common priesthood did not suddenly appear in Luther's reformation agenda as a "new discovery" in 1520, and neither did it disappear because it became an inconvenient truth in his arguments with the more radical reformers. In this study I have found that his awareness of this teaching is already present in his early lectures, and was developing as an aspect of his ecclesiology even before his breakthrough understanding of justification by faith. It has been possible to clearly demonstrate its persistence across a wide range of his writings, from early to late, as has its integration within a clear biblical framework provided by his consistent use of a whole series of texts for church and priesthood.

In contrast to the received view, I have also concluded that the three widely-quoted "reformation treatises" are not the only or even the best sources for the study of the common priesthood, however important they may be as seminal documents in their own right. To show its full integration into his ecclesiology and its connection to his theological core, it is necessary to include content from the other works listed in these conclusions. To cite three examples: *The Misuse of the Mass* is an extensive examination of the meaning of Christ's priesthood and the Christian priesthood derived from it; *Concerning the Ministry* considers in some detail the word as priesthood's primary office, and the other related offices necessary for the life of the church; and *The Sermons on Psalm 110* offer a later exposition of Luther's teaching that shows the necessity for Christians to be involved in the church's ministry and worship, and (once again) includes important material on the significance of Christ as High Priest. These later sermons do so from the perspective of the same biblical texts for church and priesthood that Luther had used in 1520 and earlier.

This broad approach is needed because, for Luther, priesthood—even in its first testament guise—is indeed an office of the word, bearing responsibility for the teaching of God's people. This is certainly true for Christians; those who hear the word must also speak it to one another, and then proclaim it publicly when called to do so. Priesthood in this understanding is not primarily an activity focused on sacrifice and prayer, although these are by no means absent from the way in which the word works in the life of the believer. Prayer, praise and self-offering become more prominent when Luther later explores the meaning that priesthood has in connection with the worship life of the church community. But once again this begins with the word and faith, which then naturally include the responses of prayer and praise, and also encompasses the lives of believers who work out priesthood's sacrifice of self in the service of others. As has been shown, the dimension of priestly worship represents a fuller expression of Luther's teaching that was now seen in his lectures on the prophets, absent from but not precluded by, for example, a work such as *The Babylonian Captivity of the Church*. Again, this must take account of his insistence that "we are *all* priests" with the insight that this priestly activity is by no means for the clergy alone. All are engaged in the ministry of the word. In worship, Luther teaches that this includes those who listen as much as those who speak. This suggests an ongoing dialogue, one that results in learning and growth and forms, I think, the setting for the contentious business of "judging" the teaching of the word. Luther's underlying concern here appears to be spiritual discernment and defence: Christians uncovering together the word's positive teaching as well as protecting the community from false teaching (Luther quotes Jesus' saying in Matthew 7:15, "beware of false prophets" and first of all applied it to the papacy). My conclusion is that he did not teach what some protestants have called "the right of private judgement," not in the form that represents an individualism separate from the community of faith.

For all of these reasons it is critical to see how Luther sets the priorities (always in first place is the word, then faith and community, and then worship and ministry), before approaching the question of the contested relationship between the common priesthood and the church's public ministry. Taking this approach, it is apparent that there is no conflict here for Luther. He sees that the public ministry exists because any community of faith necessarily chooses suitable leaders, those who are able to guide, teach and encourage others in the use of God's gifts, the word and the visible promises of God's blessing. And he knows that this ministry exists because Christ called chosen disciples into an apostolic ministry, and through the church Christ still calls people from within that same community to serve it with God's gifts and to be its voice, and his. But this service of the word is a common responsibility and task because we *all* are priests, people and pastors alike; and so there can be no separation between the divine call and the community's authorisation, not unless one aspect is elevated above the other. This approach also pushes Luther to account for the public role that women have been called to play in relation to the word. Despite the social and biblical constraints that he raises (and sometimes desperately clings to), in the end he knows that this work of Christ and the Spirit cannot be denied, regardless of gender.

The concept of "need" or necessity (German: "Not") also features here in Luther's thinking. Often, this has been presented in terms of "emergency situations," crisis events like the baptism of a newborn child in imminent danger of death. But from a wide reading it is clear that Luther uses this concept more broadly than this, to cover any spiritual need where the called pastor is not at hand (or cannot, or should not be present). In situations where fellow Christians need the comforting reassurance of God's word (or its instruction, admonition, or warning), any Christian can speak that word with the same authority that the called pastor does (see chapter 8, the sermons on *John 20*). In fact, Luther is well aware that spiritual needs are constant and universal, reaching far beyond the boundaries of any system of church order.

This relates to yet another aspect of Luther's account of the common priesthood seen throughout his writings from early to late, that there is no opposition between its personal application and its corporate manifestations, not least because Christians serve as Christ their high priest did. They are priests not for themselves, but for others. The church exists as a community of faith, and for faith. All who serve (not least its public ministers) do so from within the community and not apart from it, or over against it—even though they do so on the basis of their personal faith and calling.

These multiple dimensions of priesthood represent the application of the ecclesiological themes that have been employed throughout this study, in which the fullness of Luther's teaching emerges as an expression of his primary understanding that the church is the communion of saints. In unity with Christ and with one another, the church is the community of those who through faith possess the common status of God's children, enjoying an equal participation in God's blessings. It confirms that through this priesthood all Christians embody Christ in the church and in the world. They do so by hearing and speaking the word, and they are engaged together in discerning its teaching; celebrating its sacraments; pronouncing forgiveness; praying for others; and reaching out to them in sacrificial service. An inclusive, participatory nature of the church and its ministry is at the heart of Luther's teaching, persisting and prevailing even when the necessities of reform lead him to prioritise the ordering of the church and to place boundaries on the public expressions of its priesthood. But even here he is able to find room for its broader dimensions, looking to the home and the family as a church-complementary setting for the work of the word, and never denying the basic priestly ministry of all Christians in the "mutual conversation and consolation" of those who are sisters and brothers in Christ.

It should not be a surprise (but perhaps it is?) that all of this confirms that our priestly identity is best revealed in worship, at the beating heart of the life of the Christian community. Simply, to be a priest means to be intimately involved in this core business (our ministry), to participate in it, and on some level to be responsible for it. In the course of this study, this aspect of Luther's teaching has become most apparent in his later writings and that is perhaps why it has gone missing from many accounts of the common priesthood.

Thus, Luther's concept of the church is dynamic and purposed, reflecting the Triune God's own nature, will, and mission (*The Catechisms*). As the body of Christ, the church is a holy, priestly people, called and sent to share God's living voice. Through the work of the Spirit, the church is indeed *the communion of saints*, bearing the means of grace. Together, clergy and laity comprise the church's common priesthood, those who in their baptism are consecrated for Christ's service in the church and in the homes of God's people, and in the wider reaches of human society as well.

It is this understanding of the church as the New Testament people of God and the body of Christ that remains determinative for Luther's teaching on the common priesthood, and on public ministry as well. Luther's application of these concepts is contextual, and can vary according to the situation and its particular needs, its emergencies and exigencies, while the underlying ecclesiology remains constant. For example (once again), when he writes and comments on the role of women in the church, his ecclesiological core constantly pushes against his own limited vision and social conservatism, forcing him to acknowledge his own teaching that in the realm of faith and the Spirit, there are no boundaries! And even when writing a polemical work, Luther has at least one eye on the continuing needs of his colleagues and congregations, encouraging them to hold on to the positive aspects and implications of his basic teachings as the strongest form of defence against the innovations that had corrupted and devalued the authentic life of the church.

My conclusion is that while the common priesthood per se may not be a fundamental doctrine of the Christian faith, its proximity to and its coherence with those core beliefs, and its value as a particular expression of biblical teaching, meant that it had earned its continuing presence in Luther's thinking and in his published writing as well. Luther's ecclesiology *is* one of his central teachings and the common priesthood should not be omitted from its explication. It stands alongside his understanding of the church's public office as a complementary partner in its ministry of the word, each dependent on the other and only taking priority when "necessity" (or the biblical text) dictates otherwise. To force Luther's teaching to say more—or less—than this is to rob the church of the resources it needs to fulfill its mission as it continues to work and to pray in keeping with Christ's own prayer, "Your will be done, your kingdom come."

THE CONTEMPORARY HORIZONS OF LUTHER'S TEACHING

To repeat: Luther insisted that *all* Christians are priests. But, as in his day, the term "priest" is problematic for us because in everyday usage it still represents a member of the clergy, a person distinguished from the laity by their presumed spiritual status. Most Christians would draw back from describing themselves as priests, just as they would hesitate to accept the designation of "saint," no matter how often its New Testament meaning might be explained to them. However, both concepts carry too much biblical weight to be abandoned without the attempt to incorporate them into a deeper awareness of the church and of a Christian's rightful standing within its fellowship. The terms can certainly be prominent in our teaching, even if we are reluctant to use them as a form of public identification.

As Luther taught it, the term "priest" represents an important part of our spiritual identity as Christians. It means that by faith each of us stands in an equal spiritual relationship with God, sharing the same status with one another within the community of the church and with access to all the blessings and privileges of God's children, sisters and brothers in unity with Christ (Galatians 3:26–29). We can also recognise that beyond the boundaries inherent in the situation in which Luther lived and worked, with his own prejudices and failings, and the limitations that the church itself has at times imposed upon Luther's teaching, there are clear markers ("horizons") in his teaching that point towards the application of the common priesthood in the life of the church today. Not least this is because the church-constitutive texts that spoke so clearly to Luther as he considered the crisis of his own time and place are often the same texts that are now being used to cut through the centuries of division between Christians to uncover our identity and essential unity in Christ. From that place we also discover the meaning and purpose of the contemporary church in all its manifold contexts. These same texts can also promote the continuing examination of appropriate forms for leadership in the Christian community, and the critique of its persistent traditions of hierarchy and clericalism. Without this renewed awareness of the full dimensions of Luther's teaching, reaching into the heart of our understanding of who the church is and what it is for, our more practical reforms lack the credibility and viability to be effective agents of the church's true life and mission.

In working with Luther to apply his teaching, those biblical foundations need to be acknowledged and embraced. Luther taught that the common priesthood is founded on Christ's own messianic office as eternal king and priest (Psalm 110:4, Hebrews 7). Baptized into Christ and united with him by faith, Christians are consecrated into Christ's priestly service (Ephesians 4, Galatians 3, 1 Peter 2:1–10). With no exceptions, the title "Christian" conveys the highest spiritual status in the church and this needs to be more clearly expressed in the ways that the church speaks to itself, and presents itself to the world. Perhaps we could begin by eliminating the use of questionable honorifics such as "Reverend" and its elaborations? The simple descriptors "Pastor" and "Bishop" should be sufficient acknowledgement of their important role for most clergy. I am, of course, writing from within the egalitarian Australian social context where those who insist on "titles" are regarded with amused suspicion.

But for all of us the common priesthood sits at the interface of the church's inner, spiritual reality and its outward, public ordering as an expression of the life of Christ in the church. In and of itself, the status of this priesthood remains hidden, just as the word and faith themselves work largely unseen in the lives of individual Christians, and in the Christian community (Ephesians 4:1–6). Its presence is perceived, as is the life of the church, by the marks of the church (the word, its sacraments, its ministry); in its practices of worship and prayer; and by the fruits of faith (sacrificial love, humility, patience, etc.). To adopt Luther's view of priesthood means to recognize that it has two interrelated aspects: individual Christian identity and communal Christian character. Respectively, and together, they answer the questions, what does it mean to be a Christian and what does it mean to be the church?

As a priest, each individual Christian stands in a direct relationship with God, through faith in Christ ("justification by faith"). Through the ministry of God's word and by the work of the Spirit, all Christians hear God's voice (John 6:45), and receive all of God's promises in Christ, and are called into God's family (Galatians 3:26–29). In faith, they respond to God with prayer and praise. With Christ's own authority, they tell of God's love in word and deed (John 20:21–23). Through Christ, they offer the "living sacrifice," the life of faith manifested in love and service (Romans 12:1–8).

As priests together, the Christian community displays its essential character when it gathers to worship God (1 Peter 2:4–9). Together, Christians participate as equal priests in the church's ministry of word and sacraments, hearing and speaking God's word, receiving and sharing as their common possessions the gifts of God's grace (Ephesians 4, 1 Corinthians 14). This means that they offer each other the comforting promise of forgiveness in the name of Christ ("the office of the keys," Matthew 16:18–19, 18:18–19). Together, they enact and celebrate the eucharistic presence of Christ in communion with him and with one another. Children are baptised and nurtured in the family and in the church. Christians pray and work for one another, for God's world, and for all its people. They teach and encourage one another with God's word. In all of these ways, Christians share a common responsibility to maintain the apostolic ministry of the church, reflecting its character as the body of Christ (1 Corinthians 12:1–13).

Both aspects require pastors who will not only teach that message, but are also able to model its working through their own service in a congregational setting. While pastors are recognised and called as people with God-given gifts for the public ministries of preaching, teaching, and the sacraments of grace (Ephesians 4:11–16), that never means that lay people are merely bystanders, spectators in the church and the passive recipients of this ministry. They affirm, support, and work together with those who have been entrusted with the public offices of the word, and their pastors should offer the same encouragement in return. For the church's ministry has a broader context and greater needs than can be adequately fulfilled by the most gifted of individuals, or even by the most "professional" team of clergy. Luther's teaching means that people and pastors—as priests together—are called to a mutual engagement in the worship and life of the Christian community so as to nurture and share all the gifts of God, to the glory of God and the welfare of Christ's kingdom (Romans 12:1–8, 1 Corinthians 12:1–13, Ephesians 4:1–13, 1 Peter 2:1–10). What Christ offers and promises to one, is given to all for the benefit of all.[10]

Here the great ecclesiological themes of unity and communion, equality and participation, also challenge us to strive for their contemporary application, lest the church's witness be fatally compromised by the exclusion of particular groups and minorities from the fulness of the community and active participation in its life of faith and love and service, even beyond the traditional divide between laity and clergy. When the community gathers for its essential task of worship it should be clear who we are and what we stand for. Even in communities that are (for whatever reason) less diverse, the people we pray for, the language we use and the causes we support will all reveal (or betray) our identity as the communion of saints.

Another challenge, explored above, is the Christian's "right to judge" in matters of faith ("those who are spiritual discern all things," 1 Corinthians 2:15). It has been a fraught and controversial aspect of Luther's teaching, and its implications presented a challenge that he struggled with himself and probably never adequately resolved.[11] But in an age of universal and lifelong education, and gifted with every resource that our technology can provide, there is no excuse for churches to act as if pastors are the only theological experts able to discern and determine the meaning and application of the message of Christ in the life of the church and its people. Here there should be no boundaries, only horizons. Without a theological enterprise shared at all levels of Christian experience, or when sermons and other teaching remain hollow messages aimed at unresponding pews, the church denies itself the promised blessing spoken through the prophet and taken up by Jesus himself: "They shall all be taught by God" (Isaiah 54:13//John 6:45). Here we should be able to move beyond the limitations and fears that held back Luther and his colleagues from encouraging the ministry of the word to be freely enacted throughout the church community.[12]

I am convinced that Luther's prophetic vision for the common priesthood approaches its fulfillment when any church encourages the active cooperation of laity and clergy in positions of leadership to develop and expand its mission and ministry, doing so from a sound theological understanding that articulates the fulness of God's plan for the church. For Christian communities today, such cooperation does not subvert the position of the church's called public ministry but rather mobilises its God-given resources at the service of the gospel in the world. When appropriately gifted lay people are identified, trained, chosen and appointed from within the congregation to participate alongside pastors in the worship, teaching, and caring ministries of the church, they can do so in order to strengthen and enhance those ministries and are not supplanting or limiting the role of the pastor. This also applies to the exercise of the church's ministry in its broadest reaches, through the everyday lives and the manifold callings of Christian people whoever and wherever they may be. All of this begins to fulfil the potential inherent in the nature of the church and its gathered people as the communion of saints, and it benefits the church by releasing pastors and other professionals for more effective and targeted ministry and by helping and encouraging all Christians to discover what it means for their lives of faith, worship and service, that as God's people "we are all priests." Of course, this will happen more effectively when seminaries and synods, together with theologians and bishops, work together to study, teach, equip, resource, encourage and implement an inclusive vision for their church communities that truly represents these ecclesiological insights.

All of these dimensions—expanding and uniting within the personal and communal spaces—are integral to the realisation of Luther's teaching that the church is God's holy people, gathered in worship around the word and the sacraments and then placed in God's world to proclaim God's love in Christ to all people. This is the church's enduring vision, the bright horizon illuminated by the living sacrifice of its great High Priest, namely, that *together* God's people work to fulfil the promise and the challenge of 1 Peter 2:9, that "you are a chosen people, a royal priesthood, a holy nation, God's special possession, that you may declare the praises of him who called you out of darkness into his wonderful light." United with Christ in his "office of the word," they are the communion of saints and they are the people who, like *Christ with all his Christians, are priests.*[13]

NOTES

1. For the full list, see the Index of Luther's Works.
2. See chapter 4, at n24 (WA Br: 1:595).
3. Letters to Spalatin and Amsdorf, LW 48:305–312 (WABr 2:387–391).
4. Brecht, *Luther* 3.
5. Susan C. Karant-Nunn and Merry E. Wiesner-Hanks, eds., *Luther on Women: A Sourcebook* (New York: Cambridge University Press, 2003).
6. LW 11:540 (WA 4:401), *Psalm 122:1.*
7. LW 40:179 (WA 12:180), *Concerning the Ministry.*
8. *Sermon on Luke 14:16–17*. Original version in WA 41:281 (1535); revisions in LW 78:82 (WA 22:19), Cruciger's edition of the *Church Postil* (1544).
9. LW 41:358 (WA 54:284), *On the Papacy in Rome.*
10. See Kelly A. Fryer, *Reclaiming the 'L' Word: Renewing the Church from Its Lutheran Core*, Lutheran Voices (Minneapolis, MN: Augsburg Fortress, 2003). While Fryer does not examine the common priesthood in depth (referencing only *The Babylonian Captivity* and *Concerning the Ministry*) she works through its detailed implications for congregational life, the benefit of realising that "everybody has something to offer" (75–92).

11. This concept is used by Luther most clearly as part of his critique of the exclusive teaching claims of the papacy (*To the Christian Nobility, Why the Books of the Pope were Burned, Concerning the Ministry, On the Papacy in Rome*); its use in relation to other teachers is much less prominent.

12. Shauna Hannan, "That All Might Proclaim: Continuing Luther's Legacy of Access," *Dialog* 56, no. 2 (2017), 169–175. https://doi.org/10.1111/dial.12320.

13. LW 76:182 (WA 17/2:6), *Sermon on Romans 12:1–3* (1525/40).

Bibliography

Aland, Kurt. *Hilfsbuch zum Lutherstudien.* Fourth edition. Bielefeld: Luther-Verlag, 1996.
Althaus, Paul. *The Theology of Martin Luther.* Translated by Robert C. Schultz. Philadelphia: Fortress Press, 1966. Originally published as *Die Theologie Martin Luthers*. Gütersloh: Gerd Mohn, 1962.
Anderas, Phillip. "Augustinianism, and Augustine." In OEML, 71–85.
Augustine, Saint. *City of God*, trans. Marcus Dods. New York: Modern Library, 1993.
Australian Lutheran-Roman Catholic Dialogue. *Sacrament and Sacrifice*. Adelaide: Australian Lutheran-Roman Catholic Dialogue, 1985.
———. *Pastor and Priest*. Adelaide: Australian Lutheran-Roman Catholic Dialogue, 1990.
———. *Communion and Mission: A Report on the Theology of the Church.* Adelaide: Australian Lutheran-Roman Catholic Dialogue, 1995.
———. *Living Word, Living Tradition*. Adelaide: Australian Lutheran-Roman Catholic Dialogue: 2011.
———. *The Ministry of Oversight.* Adelaide: Australian Lutheran-Roman Catholic Dialogue, 2007.
———. *The Petrine Ministry in a New Situation: A Joint Statement on the Papacy.* Adelaide: Australian Lutheran-Roman Catholic Dialogue, 2016.
Avis, Paul D. L., ed. *The Oxford Handbook of Ecclesiology*. New York: Oxford University Press, 2018.
Barth, Hans-Martin. *The Theology of Martin Luther*. Translated by Linda M. Maloney. Minneapolis: Fortress Press, 2013. Originally published as *Die Theologie Martin Luthers: Eine Kritische Würdigung* (Gütersloh: Gütersloher Verlagshaus, 2009).
———. *Einander Priester Sein: Allgemeines Priestertum in Ökumenischer Perspektive*. Göttingen: Vandenhoeck & Ruprecht, 1990.
Baudler, Kristian T. *Martin Luther's Priesthood of All Believers: In an Age of Modern Myth*. New York: Oxen Press, 2016.
Bayer, Oswald. *Martin Luther's Theology: A Contemporary Interpretation*. Translated by Thomas H. Trapp. Grand Rapids: W.B. Eerdmans Pub. Co., 2008. Originally published as *Martin Luthers Theologie: Eine Vergegenwärtigung*. Tübingen: J. C. B. Mohr, 2003.
———. "Luther as an interpreter of Holy Scripture." In CCML, 73–85.

Bell, Theo M.M.A.C. "Roman Catholic Luther Research in the Twentieth Century." In OHMLT, 584–597.

Boehmer, Heinrich. *Road to Reformation*. Translated by John W. Doberstein and Theodore G. Tappert. Philadelphia: Muhlenberg Press, 1946. Originally published as *Der junge Luther*. Flamberg Verlag, 1929.

Bornkamm, Heinrich. *Luther and the Old Testament*. Translated by Eric W. and Ruth C. Gritsch. Philadelphia: Fortress Press, 1969. Originally published as *Luther und das Alte Testament*. Tübingen: J. C. B. Mohr, 1948.

———. *Luther's World of Thought*. Translated by Martin H. Bertram. St Louis: Concordia Publishing House, 1958. Originally published as *Luthers geistige Welt*. Gütersloh: Carl Bertelsmann Verlag, n.d.

———. *Luther in Mid-Career, 1521–1530*. Translated by E. Theodore Bachmann. Philadelphia: Fortress Press, 1983. Originally published as *Martin Luther in der Mittes seines Leben*. Göttingen: Vandenhoeck & Ruprecht, 1979.

Bornkamm, Karin. *Christus: König Und Priester: Das Amt Christi Bei Luther Im Verhältnis Zur Vor-Und Nachgeschichte*. Beiträge Zur Historischen Theologie, 106. Tübingen: Mohr Siebeck, 1998.

Braaten, Carl E., and Robert W. Jenson, eds. *Marks of the Body of Christ*. Grand Rapids: W.B. Eerdmans, 1999.

Brecht, Martin. *Martin Luther: His Road to Reformation, 1483–1521*. Translated by James L. Schaaf. Philadelphia: Fortress Press, 1985. Originally published as *Martin Luther: Sein Weg Zur Reformation, 1483–1521*. Stuttgart: Calwer, 1981.

———. *Martin Luther: Shaping and Defining the Reformation 1521–1532*. Translated by James L. Schaaf. Minneapolis: Fortress Press, 1990. Originally published as *Martin Luther: Ordnung und Abgrenzung der Reformation, 1521–1532*. Stuttgart: Calwer, 1986.

———. *Martin Luther: The Preservation of the Church, 1532–1546*. Translated by James L. Schaaf. Minneapolis: Fortress Press, 1993. Originally published as *Martin Luther: Die Erhaltung der Kirche, 1532–1546*. Stuttgart: Calwer, 1987.

Burger, Christopher. "Luther's thought took shape in the translation of Scripture and Hymns." In OHMLT, 481–488.

Cajetan, Tommaso de Vio. *Cajetan Responds: A Reader in Reformation Controversy*. Translated and edited by Jared Wicks. Catholic University of America Press, 1978.

Collver, Albert. "Origin of the Term Laity." *Logia* 19, no. 4 (2010): 5–12.

Congar, Y. *True and False Reform in the Church*. Translated by Paul Philibert. Collegeville, MN: Liturgical Press, 2011. Originally published as *Vraie et fausse réforme dans l'Église* (Paris: Éditions du Cerf, 1950 [Second edition, 1968]).

———. *Lay People in the Church: A Study for a Theology of Laity*. Translated Donald Attwater. Second edition. Newman Press, 1965. Originally published as *Jalons pour une théologie du laïcat*. Second edition. (Paris: Éditions du Cerf, 1950 / 1964).

———. *Martin Luther, sa foi, sa réforme: études de théologie historique*. Paris: Éditions du Cerf, 1983.

Daniel, David. "A Spiritual Condominium: Luther's Views on Priesthood and Ministry with Some Structural Implications." *Concordia Journal* 14 (1988): 266–282.

———. "Luther on the Church." In OHMLT, 333–352.

Daubert, Dave. *Reclaiming the "V" Word: Renewing Life at Its Vocational Core.* Minneapolis, MN: Augsburg Fortress, 2009.

Dictionary of Luther and the Lutheran Traditions. Grand Rapids, Michigan: Baker Academic, 2017.

Doyle, Dennis M. *Communion Ecclesiology: Vision and Versions.* Ossining, NY: Orbis Books, 2000.

Eastwood, Cyril. *The Royal Priesthood of the Faithful: An Investigation of the Doctrine from Biblical Times to the Reformation.* London: Epworth Press, 1963.

Elert, Werner. *The Structure of Lutheranism. Vol. 1, The Theology and Philosophy of Life of Lutheranism, Especially in the Sixteenth and Seventeenth Centuries.* Translated by Walter A. Hansen. St Louis: Concordia Publishing House, 1962. Originally published as *Morphologie des Luthertums.* Munich: Verlag C.H. Beck, c.1931.

Elliott, John H. *The Elect and the Holy: An Exegetical Examination of 1 Peter 2:4–10 and the Phrase Basileion Hierateuma.* Leiden: E.J. Brill, 1966.

Famerée, Joseph. "Yves Congar, lecteur de Luther." In *En 500 Après Martin Luther. Reception et conflits d'interpretation (1517–2017).* Edited by Stéphane-Marie Morgain, 189–201. Turnhout: Brepols Publishers, 2018.

Fischer, Robert Harley. "Another Look at Luther's Doctrine of the Ministry." *Lutheran Quarterly* 18, no. 3 (1 August 1966): 260–271.

Fryer, Kelly A. *Reclaiming the "L" Word: Renewing the Church from Its Lutheran Core.* Lutheran Voices. Minneapolis: Augsburg Fortress, 2003.

Gerrish, Brian A. "Priesthood and Ministry in the Theology of Luther." *Church History: Studies in Christianity and Culture* 34, no. 4 (1965): 404–422.

Goertz, Harald. *Allgemeines Priestertum Und Ordiniertes Amt Bei Luther.* Marburg: N.G. Elwert, 1997.

González, Justo L. "The Universal Priesthood of Believers." *Lutheran Quarterly* 31, no. 3 (2017): 328–329.

Green, Lowell. "Change in Luther's Doctrine of the Ministry." *Lutheran Quarterly* 18 (1966): 174–179.

Haemig, Mary Jane. "The Influence of the Genres of Exegetical Instruction, Preaching, and Catechesis on Luther." In OHMLT, 449–461.

———. "Catechisms." In DLLT, 130–131.

———. "Recovery Not Rejection: Luther's Appropriation of the Catechism." *Concordia Journal* 43, no. 1–2 (2017): 43–58.

Haendler, Gert. *Luther on Ministerial Office and Congregational Function.* Translated by Eric W. and Ruth C. Gritsch. Philadelphia: Fortress Press, 1981. Originally published as *Amt und Gemeinde bei Luther im Kontext der Kirchengeschichte.* Stuttgart: Calwer Verlag, 1979.

Hannan, Shauna. "That All Might Proclaim: Continuing Luther's Legacy of Access." *Dialog* 56, no. 2 (2017): 169–175. https://doi.org/10.1111/dial.12320.

Helmer, Christine. "The Common Priesthood: Luther's Enduring Challenge" in *Remembering the Reformation: Martin Luther and Catholic Theology*, 211–233. Minneapolis: Fortress Press, 2017.

———. *The Medieval Luther.* Spätmittelalter, Humanismus, Reformation / Studies in the Late Middle Ages, Humanism, and the Reformation 117. Tübingen, Germany: Mohr Siebeck, 2020.

Hendrix, Scott H. "The Kingdom of Promise: Disappointment and Hope in Luther's Later Ecclesiology." Luther Congress, Copenhagen, 2002.

———. *Ecclesia in via: Ecclesiological Developments in the Medieval Psalms Exegesis and the Dictata Super Psalterium (1513–1515) of Martin Luther.* Studies in Medieval and Reformation Thought; vol. 8. Leiden: Brill, 1974.

———. *Luther.* Nashville: Abingdon Press, 2009.

———. *Martin Luther: Visionary Reformer.* New Haven: Yale University Press, 2016.

Herrmann, Erik. "Luther's Absorption of medieval biblical interpretation and his use of the church fathers." In OHMLT, 71–90.

———. "Luther's Divine Aeneid. Continuity and Creativity in Reforming the Use of the Bible." *Lutherjahrbuch.* Gottingen: Vandenhoeck & Ruprecht, 2018: 85–109.

Holze, Heinrich. *The Church as Communion: Lutheran Contributions to Ecclesiology.* Lutheran World Federation, 1997.

Hultgren, Stephen, Stephen Pietsch, and Jeffrey Silcock, eds. *Luther@500 and Beyond: Martin Luther's Theology Past, Present and Future.* Adelaide: ATF Press, 2019.

Kärkkäinen, Pekka. "Nominalism and the Via Moderna." In OEML, 2:696–708.

Kärkkäinen, Veli-Matti. *An Introduction to Ecclesiology: Ecumenical, Historical & Global Perspectives.* Second edition. Downers Grove, IL: InterVarsity Press, 2021.

Karant-Nunn, Susan C. and Merry E. Wiesner-Hanks, eds. *Luther on Women. A Sourcebook.* New York: Cambridge University Press, 2003.

Kasper, Walter. *Martin Luther: An Ecumenical Perspective.* New York: Paulist Press, 2016.

Kaufmann, Thomas. "Luther as Polemicist." In OEML, 3:110–127.

Klug, Eugene F A. "Luther on the Ministry." In *Concordia Theological Quarterly* 47, no. 4 (October 1983): 293–303.

Kolb, Robert. *Luther's Treatise on Christian Freedom and Its Legacy [Electronic Resource].* Lanham: Lexington Books/Fortress Academic, 2020.

———. *Martin Luther and the Enduring Word of God: The Wittenberg School and Its Scripture- Centered Proclamation.* Grand Rapids: Baker Academic, 2016.

———. *Martin Luther: Confessor of the Faith.* Christian Theology in Context. Oxford; New York: Oxford University Press, 2009.

Kolb, Robert and Timothy J. Wengert, eds., *The Book of Concord: The Confessions of the Evangelical Lutheran Church.* Minneapolis: Fortress Press, 2000.

Kolb, Robert and James Arne Nestingen, eds. *Sources and Contexts for the Book of Concord.* Minneapolis: Augsburg, 2001.

Kolb, Robert, Irene Dingel and L'ubomir Batka, eds. *The Oxford Handbook of Martin Luther's Theology.* Oxford: Oxford University Press, 2014.

Korányi, András. "Universal priesthood of all believers: unfulfilled promise of the Reformation." In *Reflecting Reformation and the Call for Renewal in a Globalized and Post-Colonial World.* Neuendettelsau: Erlanger Verlag für Mission und Ökumene, 2018.

Kothmann, Thomas. "Luther as Educator: His Vision of Teaching and Learning and Its Significance Today." In *Luther@500 and Beyond: Martin Luther's Theology Past, Present and Future*. Edited by Stephen Hultgren, Stephen Pietsch and Jeffrey Silcock, 221–250. Adelaide: ATF Press, 2019.

Krarup, Martin. *Ordination in Wittenberg: Die Einsetzung in Das Kirchliche Amt in Kursachsen Zur Zeit Der Reformation*. Tübingen: Mohr Siebeck, 2007.

Krause, Gerhard and Gerhard Muller, eds. *Theologische Realenzyklopädie*. 36 volumes. Berlin; New York: W. de Gruyter, 1977–(2006).

Lathrop, Gordon, and Timothy J. Wengert. *Christian Assembly: Marks of the Church in a Pluralistic Age*. Minneapolis: Fortress Press, 2004.

Lehenbauer, Joel. "The Priesthood of All Saints." *Missio Apostolica* 9, no. 1 (2001): 4–17.

Lehmann, Harmut. "New Publications for the Five-Hundredth Anniversary of the Reformation." *Lutheran Quarterly*, 32 (2018): 307–355.

Leppin, Volker. "Luther's roots in monastic-mystical piety." In OHMLT, 49–61.

———. "Luther's Transformation of Medieval Thought." In OHMLT, 115–124.

———. *Martin Luther: A Late Medieval Life*. Grand Rapids: Baker Academic, 2010.

Lieberg, Hellmut. *Office and Ordination in Luther and Melanchthon*. Translated by Matthew Carver. St Louis: Concordia Publishing House, 2020. First published as *Amt Und Ordination Bei Luther Und Melanchthon*. Gottingen: Vandenhoeck & Ruprecht, 1962.

Lindberg, Carter. "Piety, Prayer, and Worship in Luther's View of Daily Life." In OHMLT, 414–426.

———. "Luther's Struggle with Social-Ethical Issues." In CCML, 165–178.

Lindquist, Charles. "The Priesthood of All Believers: Making Room for the Gift." *Missio Apostolica* 17, no. 1 (2009): 31–37.

Lohse, Bernhard. *Martin Luther's Theology: Its Historical and Systematic Development*. Translated by Roy A. Harrisville. Minneapolis: Fortress Press, 1999. Originally published as *Luthers Theologie in Ihrer Historischen Entwicklung Und in Ihrem Systematischen Zusammenhang*. Gottingen: Vandenhoeck & Ruprecht, 1995.

———. *Martin Luther: An Introduction to His Life and Work*. Translated by Robert C. Schultz. Philadelphia: Fortress Press, 1986. Originally published as *Martin Luther—eine Einführung in sein Leben und sein Werk*. Munich: Verlag C.H. Beck, 1980.

Luther, Martin. *D. Martin Luthers Werke*. Kritische Gesamtausgabe. 73 vols. Weimar: Hermann Böhlaus Nachfolger, 1883–.

———. *D. Martin Luthers Werke*. Kritische Gesamtausgabe. *Briefwechsel*. 18 vols. Weimar: Hermann Böhlaus Nachfolger, 1930–1985.

———. *Martin Luthers Werke*. Kritische Gesamtausgabe. *Die Deutsche Bibel*. 12 vols. Weimar: Hermann Böhlaus Nachfolger, 1906–1961.

———. *D. Martin Luthers Werke*. Kritische Gesamtausgabe. *Tischreden*. 6 vols. Weimar: Hermann Böhlaus Nachfolger, 1912–1921.

———. *Luther's Works*. Edited by Jaroslav Pelikan, Helmut T. Lehmann, and Christopher Boyd Brown. 75 vols. St Louis: Concordia Publishing House; Philadelphia: Fortress Press, 1955–.

———. *Sermons of Martin Luther*. 8 volumes. Edited by John Nicholas Lenker. Grand Rapids: Baker Book House, 1983.

Mackenzie, Cameron A. "The 'Early' Luther on Priesthood of All Believers, Office of the Ministry, and Ordination." Accessed 17 October, 2017, http://www.ctsfw.net/media/pdfs/ mackenzieearlyluther.pdf.

McGrath, Alister E. *Luther's Theology of the Cross: Martin Luther's Theological Breakthrough*. Revised edition. Chichester: John Wiley & Sons Ltd, 2011.

McKim, Donald K., ed. *The Cambridge Companion to Martin Luther*. Cambridge: Cambridge University Press, 2003.

Methuen, Charlotte. "'In her soul, a woman is not different from a man': How Scholastic Was Luther's View of Women?" In *Remembering the Reformation: Martin Luther and Catholic Theology*, 75–97. Minneapolis: Fortress Press, 2017.

Meuser, Fred W. "Luther as Preacher of the Word of God." In CCML, 135–145.

Montover, Nathan. *Luther's Revolution: The Political Dimensions of Martin Luther's Universal Priesthood*. Philadelphia: Casemate Publishers, 2012.

Müller, Gerhard. "Luther's transformation of medieval thought." In OHMLT, 105–114.

Nagel, Norman. "Luther and the Priesthood of All Believers." *Concordia Theological Quarterly* 61, no. 4 (1997): 277–298.

Nelson, Derek R., ed. *The Oxford Encyclopedia of Martin Luther*. 3 volumes. New York: Oxford University Press, 2017.

New Dictionary of Theology. Second edition. Edited by David F. Wright. Downers Grove: Inter-Varsity Press, 2016.

Oberman, Heiko A. Heiko Augustinus. *Luther: Man between God and the Devil*. New York: Image Books, 1992.

Oxford Dictionary of the Christian Church. Third revised edition. Oxford: Oxford University Press, 2007.

Ozment, Steven. *Age of Reform*. New Haven: Yale University Press, 1980.

Pelikan, Jaroslav. *Spirit versus Structure: Luther and the Institutions of the Church*. London: Collins, 1968.

———. *Luther the Expositor: Introduction to the Reformer's Exegetical Writings*. St Louis: Concordia Publishing House, 1959.

Peterson, Cheryl M. *Who Is the Church? An Ecclesiology for the Twenty-First Century*. Minneapolis: Fortress Press, 2013.

———. "Ministry and Church." In OELM, 2:542–554.

———. "Church." In DLLT, 145–149.

Pless, John T. *Luther's Small Catechism: A Manual for Discipleship*. St Louis: Concordia Publishing House, 2019.

Posset, Franz. "Our Martin: Catholic Sympathisers of Martin Luther Yesterday, Today and Tomorrow." In *Luther@500 and Beyond: Martin Luther's Theology Past, Present and Future*. Edited by Stephen Hultgren, Stephen Pietsch and Jeffrey Silcock, 51–73. Adelaide: ATF Press, 2019.

Preus, Herman A. "Luther on the Universal Priesthood and the Office of the Ministry." *Concordia Journal* 5, no. 2 (1979): 55–62.

Reumann, John Henry Paul. *Ministries Examined: Laity, Clergy, Women, and Bishops in a Time of Change*. Minneapolis: Augsburg Publishing House, 1987.

Ristau, Harold. *Understanding Martin Luther's Demonological Rhetoric in His Treatise Against the Heavenly Prophets (1525): How What Luther Speaks Is Essential to What Luther Says*. Lewiston: Edwin Mellen Press, 2010.

Roper, Lyndal. *Martin Luther: Renegade and Prophet*. London: The Bodley Head Ltd, 2016.

Rosin, Robert. "Humanism, Luther, and the Wittenberg Reformation." In OHMLT, 90–104.

Schild, Maurice. "Luther's Bible Prefaces and their Contemporary Significance." In *Luther@500 and Beyond: Martin Luther's Theology Past, Present and Future*. Edited by Stephen Hultgren, Stephen Pietsch and Jeffrey Silcock, 167–187. Adelaide: ATF Press, 2019.

Schilling, Heinz. *Martin Luther: Rebel in an Age of Upheaval*. Oxford: Oxford University Press, 2017.

Schurb, Ken. "Church and Ministry." *Logia* 19, no. 4 (2010): 25–29.

Silcock, Jeffrey. "A New Look at the Theology of the Cross." In *Luther@500 and Beyond: Martin Luther's Theology Past, Present and Future*. Edited by Stephen Hultgren, Stephen Pietsch and Jeffrey Silcock, 75–104. Adelaide: ATF Press, 2019.

Silva, Gilberto da. "The Lutheran Church as a Church of Mission against the Background of the Priesthood of All Believers." *Missio Apostolica* 14, no. 1 (May 2006): 21–27.

Smith, Ralph F. *Luther, Ministry, and Ordination Rites in the Early Reformation Church*. Renaissance and Baroque Studies and Texts; Vol. 15. New York: P. Lang, 1996.

Smolinsky, Heribert. "Luther's Roman Catholic Critics." In OHMLT, 502–510.

Spitz, L. W. "The Universal Priesthood of Believers with Luther's Comments." *Concordia Theological Monthly* 23 (1952): 1–15.

Stephenson, John. "Reflections on the Holy Office of the Ministry for the Scandinavian Diaspora." In *Logia* 15 no. 1 (2006): 43–47.

Sundberg, Walter. "Ministry in Nineteenth-Century European Lutheranism." In *Called and Ordained: Lutheran Perspectives on the Office of the Ministry*, 77–92. Minneapolis: Augsburg Fortress, 1990.

Trigg, Jonathan. "Luther on Baptism and Penance." In OHMLT, 310–321.

Webber, David Jay. *Spiritual Fathers: A Treatise on the Lutheran Doctrine of the Ministry, with Special Reference to Luther's Large Catechism*. Second edition. Phoenix: Klotsche-Little Publishing, 2015.

Weinrich, William. "Should a Layman Discharge the Duties of the Ministry?" In *Concordia Theological Quarterly* 68:3 (July 2004): 207–229.

Wendebourg, Dorothea. "The Church in the Magisterial Reformers." In OHE, 217–226.

———. Review of Wengert, "Priesthood, Pastors, Bishops: Public Ministry for the Reformation & Today." In *Lutheran Quarterly* 23 (2009): 348–351.

Wengert, Timothy J. ed. *Dictionary of Luther and the Lutheran Traditions*. Grand Rapids: Baker Academic, 2017.

———. *Martin Luther's Catechisms: Forming the Faith*. Minneapolis: Fortress Press, 2009.

———. *Priesthood, Pastors, Bishops: Public Ministry for the Reformation and Today*. Minneapolis: Fortress Press, 2008.

Wicks, Jared. *Man Yearning for Grace: Luther's Early Spiritual Teaching*. Washington: Corpus Publications, 1968.

Winger, Thomas. "We Are All Priests: A Contextual Study of the Priesthood in Luther." *Lutheran Theological Quarterly* 2 (1992): 129–156.

Wisloff, Carl Fredrik. *The Gift of Communion: Luther's Controversy with Rome on Eucharistic Sacrifice*. Translated by Joseph M. Shaw. Minneapolis: Augsburg, 1964. Originally published as *Nattverd og Messe*. Oslo: Lutherstiftelsens Forlag, 1957.

Wolgast, Eike. "Luther's Treatment of Political and Societal Life." In OHMLT, 397–413.

Yeago, David S. "'A Christian, Holy People': Martin Luther on Salvation and the Church." *Modern Theology* 13, no. 1 (January 1997): 101–120.

Zweck, Dean. "The Communion of Saints in Luther's 1519 Sermon, The Blessed Sacrament of the Holy and True Body of Christ." *Lutheran Theological Journal* 49, no.3 (2015): 116–125.

Index to Luther's Works for Church and Priesthood

Bracketed references give the "Aland number" for each work

Admonition concerning the Sacrament, 1530 (A659), xxv, 99–100

Admonition to Peace. A Reply to the Twelve Articles of the Peasants of Swabia, 1525 (A67), 85

Adoration of the Sacrament, 1522 (A664), 32

Against Henry King of England, 1522 (A280), 64

Against Hanswurst, 1541 (A777), 110–111

Against the Roman Papacy, an Institution of the Devil, 1545 (A550), 111–113, 191

Against the Robbing and Murderous Hordes of Peasants, 1525 (A64), 86

Against the Spiritual Estate of the Pope and the Bishops Falsely So Called, 1522 (A547), 61

Answer to the Book of our Esteemed Master Ambrosius Catherinus, the Keen Defender of Sylvester Prierias, 1521 (A122), 28

Answer to the Hyperchristian, Hyperspiritual and Hyperlearned Book of Goat Emser in Leipzig, 1521 (A190), 45–46, 61, 68–69, 182

The Babylonian Captivity of the Church, 1520 (A120), xx, xxii, xxiii, xxv, 30, 39–42, 44, 60, 68, 182–183, 184, 186

The Blessed Sacrament of the Holy and True Body of Christ and the Brotherhoods, 1519 (A655), xxiii, 26, 30

Church Postil, 1525 / 1544 (A572), 154–161, 182–183

Commentary on Galatians, 1535 (A229), 132,

Concerning the Ministry, 1523 (A575), xx, xxv, 28–29, 50–51, 62, 64, 66, 182–183, 184, 187, 190, 192

Confession Concerning Christ's Supper, 1528 (A2; see also A80:39), xxv, 79–80, 86

To the Councilmen of all Cities in Germany that They Establish and Maintain Christian Schools, 1524 (A676), 83

To the Christian Nobility of the German Nation Concerning the Reform of the Christian Estate, 1520 (A7), xx, xxii, xxiii, xxv, 26, 38–39, 44, 60, 64, 67–68, 182–183, 184, 185

Defense and Explanation of All Articles, 1521 (A114), 28, 68
Disputation on the Church, 1542 (A681), 108n69
Dr Luther's Retraction of an Error Forced upon Him by the Most Highly Learned Priest of God, Sir Jerome Emser, 1521 (A189)

Eine kurze Form des Glaubens, 1520 (A234), 31. *See also* Personal Prayer Book
The Estate of Marriage, 1522 (A178), xxvi
Exhortation to All Clergy Assembled at Augsburg, 1530 (A49), 98
Explanations of the Ninety-Five Theses, 1518 (A638), 25, 29
Exposition of First Peter, 1522 (A563), xx–xxi, 32, 47–49, 59, 61, 70, 182–183, 184, 187

Fraternal Agreement on the Common Chest of the Entire Assembly at Leisnig, 1523 (A241), 49n58
The Freedom of a Christian, 1520 (A227), xx–xxi, 25, 42–43, 58, 61, 64, 132, 156, 182–183, 184, 186

The Holy and Blessed Sacrament of Baptism, 1519 (A714), 26

Infiltrating and Clandestine Preachers, 1532 (A772), xxi, 88–89, 188
Instructions for the Parish Visitors in Electoral Saxony, 1528 (A751), 86, 190

The Keys, 1530 (A670), 99

Large Catechism, 1529 (A364), 78, 83, 89–90, 167

Lectures on 1 John, 1527 (A343), 162n54
Lectures on 1 Timothy, 1528 (A723), 87
Lectures on Deuteronomy, 1525 (A523), 120–121
Lectures on Galatians, 1519 (A228) xx, 10–16, 60
Lectures on Genesis, 1538–1545 (A517), 140–143, 182–183, 190
Lectures on Hebrews, 1517 (A274), 10–16, 60, 63, 65
Lectures on Hosea, 1524 (A294), 121–122, 182, 188
Lectures on Isaiah, 40–66, 1529–1530 (A306), 124–128, 182
Lectures on Joel, 1524 (A312), 121, 182, 188
Lectures on Malachi, 1526 (A449), 122, 182, 188
Lectures on Micah, 1525 (A505), 122, 182, 188
Lectures on the Psalms, 1513–1516 (A593), 1–9, 11, 15–16, 60, 63, 65
Lectures on Psalms 2, 45, and 51, 1532 (A600, 606, 607), 130–133, 184
Lectures on Romans, 1515 (A646), 10–16
Lectures on Titus, 1527 (A726), 86–87, 89
Lectures on Zechariah, 1527 (A654), 122–123, 182, 188
Lectures on Zephaniah, 1525 (A783), 122, 182, 188
Letter to Spalatin, December 1519 (A99.231), 60, 185
Letters to Spalatin and Amsdorf re: Melanchthon, September 1521 (A99.429–430), 185

The Magnificat, 1521 (A444), 61
The Misuse of Mass, 1522 (A503), 46, 59, 61, 64, 65–66, 69–70, 182, 192

On the Councils and the Church, 1539 (A382), xxiv–xxv, 106–110, 182–183, 184
On the Papacy in Rome, 1520 (A548), 27, 44, 58, 62, 183
The Order of Baptism, 1523 (A711), 187

Personal Prayer Book, 1522 (A80), 31
Prefaces to the New Testament, 1522/46 (A83.36), 62, 66–67, 183
Prefaces to the Old Testament, 1523/45 (A83.95), 59, 66–67, 183
The Private Mass and the Consecration of Priests, 1533 (A770), xxv, 89, 101–106, 170, 182–183, 184, 188
Proceedings at Augsburg, 1518 (A51), 58n7
Psalms 1 and 2, 1518–19 (A594), 60, 63
Psalm 82 ("Manual for a Christian Prince"), 1530 (A611), 87–88, 183
Psalm 117, 1530 (A619), 130
Psalm 118, 1530 (A141), 129

Receiving Both Kinds in the Sacrament, 1522 (A663), 28

The Sacrament of Penance, 1519 (A115), xxi, 26, 29–30
Sermon on Acts 6:8–14 & 7:54–60, St Stephen 1522 (A572.24)
Sermon at the Dedication of the Castle Church in Torgau, 1544 (A183), 170–173, 182, 188
Sermon on the First Commandment, 1528 (A366, Pr941)
Sermons on John 14–16, 1537 (A328) xxi, 161–166, 182–183, 189–190
Sermons on John 17, "The Prayer of Christ," 1530 (A333), 166, 189–190
Sermon on John 20:19–23, 1540 (A572.227), 167–170

A Sermon on Keeping Children in School, 1530 (A675), 83, 183, 188
Sermon on Luke 14:16–17, "The Great Supper," 1535 (A438), 79–80, 191
Sermon on Mark 7:31–7, 1522 (A453), xx, xxi
Sermon on Matthew 3, 1544 (A577.1948), 169
Sermon on Matthew 9:2–8, 1522 (A577.246) xxi
Sermon on Matthew 16:13–19, Ss Peter & Paul,1519 (A476), 30
Sermons on Matthew 18, 1537 (A477), xxii, xxvi, 169
Sermon on Psalm 22:23, "On Faith, Love and Good Works," 1522 (A577.208), xxi
Sermons on Psalm 110, 1535 (A616), 133–140, 182–183, 184, 188, 192
Sermon on Romans 12:1, 1525 (A572.34), xx, 158–161, 182
Small Catechism, 1529 (A365), 78, 83
Smalcald Articles, 1537 (A672), 80–81, 89–90

That a Christian Assembly or Congregation Has the Right and Power to Judge All Teaching and to Call, Appoint, and Dismiss Teachers, Established and Proven by Scripture, 1523 (A406), xx–xxi, xxv, 49, 61–62, 64, 70, 182, 187
The Three Symbols or Creeds of the Christian Faith, 1538 (A708)
A Treatise on the New Testament, 1520 (A502), 45, 58, 62, 65, 183

Von der Beichte 1521 (A69), xxii

Why the Books of the Pope and His Disciples Were Burned, 1520 (A545), 58

Index

There is no separate entry for Luther, Martin

Aaron prefigures Christ's priesthood, 58–59, 62–63, 66
Abraham as high priest, 132n93, 141
absolution. *See* confession of sins, forgiveness, office of the keys
Adam and Eve as priests, 140
allegory, 4, 10, 23, 132–133
Althaus, Paul, xv–xvi, xviii–xxv, xxvii–xxviii, 26n20, 29n40, 100n13, 170n106
Antichrist. *See* papacy, pope
apostles, 5, 12, 48 104, 134, 168
Augsburg Confession, 79n10, 105, 129
Augsburg, Diet of, 97–99, 130
Augustine, Saint, xiv, 2, 4, 5, 13n101, 15
Augustinians, 2, 5, 47
authorities, religious, 4–6, 50–51
authorities, secular, 38–39, 51, 85, 187

ban, the (excommunication), 71, 98
baptism, xix, 40, 50, 86, 102–103, 107, 155, 159, 171–172
    as ordination to the common priesthood, 135–136
    subordinated to preaching, 71

See also common priesthood, sacraments
Barth, Hans–Martin, xvi–xxiii, xxv, xxvii–xxviii, 83n34, 89, 186
Bayer, Oswald, xvii, xxii, xxv, xxvi, xxviii, 24, 24n4, 170n106
Bernard of Clairveux, 2, 6, 15
Bible:
    interpretation, 2–4, 10, 23–24, 59, 158, 170, 189
    Luther's biblical theology, 15, 25, 71, 113, 119, 127n56, 188–191
    Luther's creative use, 57, 61, 64, 77, 158, 191
    prefaces, 46, 59, 62, 66–67, 82, 184
    relationship between old and new covenants, 11, 48, 63, 121–123, 125–126, 133, 143–144
    texts (ecclesiology), xxvi, 6, 13–14, 24, 31, 188–189, 191, 196
    texts (ministry), 28, 67–72, 137, 172, 190, 197
    texts (priesthood), 28, 47, 57–72, 159, 161, 164–165, 189–190
    tradition, 1, 5, 40n16, 43, 45, 71, 134, 141, 171

translation, 46, 48, 82, 89, 128, 133n105, 184, 187
Vulgate, Greek, and Hebrew, use of, 60, 83, 133
See also allegory, teaching, word
bishops, 27, 50, 77n1, 86–87, 97–99, 136, 196;
    equal in their office, 81, 112
    failure to preach the word, 49, 63, 67, 102
    servants of the church and the word, as, 9, 67, 79, 81
    terminology, 69, 79, 137
    See also clergy, ministers, public ministry
Bornkamm, Heinrich, xvii, 82n27, 86n33, 120–121, 122n24, 124, 133, 142
Bornkamm, Karin, 57n3, 127n56
Brecht, Martin, xvii, xxi–xxii, xxvi–xxviii, 48, 83n29, 86, 87n58, 124, 129, 132, 140, 188

Cajetan, Cardinal, 29n37, 37, 42n24
call to ministry, xxvii, 15, 41, 49–51, 70, 72, 85, 87–89, 103–104, 105–106, 141, 162, 172, 186, 193
    See also ministry
Cain and Abel, 140
canon law, 58
catechisms, xxii, xxvi, 31, 52, 78–79, 82, 83n31, 90, 101, 126, 183, 187
ceremonies and ritual, 66, 80, 83, 98, 100, 109, 111, 127–128, 133, 142, 159
children, as equal Christians, 80–81, 107, 113, 139, 169
chrism, xiv, 102–107.
    See also consecration, ordination
Christ:
    anointed by God, 59, 126–127
    as Bible's hermeneutical centre, 4, 8, 10, 15, 31, 57, 59, 72, 159
    as example and guide, 10, 24, 131–132
    as first–born brother, 58–59, 61–62, 122, 159
    as head of the church, 7–8, 13, 24–25, 27, 33, 44, 57, 78–79, 81, 113, 132
    as high priest xviii–xix, 8–9, 11, 14–15, 16, 25, 28, 44, 45, 57–59, 60, 64, 103, 125, 134, 136, 138, 157–158, 166, 189, 192, 196
    as intercessor for sin, 158, 165
    as king and messiah, 25, 57–59, 60, 113, 126, 131, 132–133, 134–136, 139, 142, 153, 157–158, 161, 174, 189, 190, 196
    as a "living sacrifice," 66
    as *locus* for worship, 120
    as priest "who teaches the church," 131–132
    as priest "with all Christians," 61, 65, 128, 136, 196
    as prophet, 121, 125n56
    as redeemer, 157–158
    as sacrificial altar, 8–9, 59
    as self–offering for sin, 45, 58–59, 65, 122, 166
    as "true cleric," 103
    as unique sacrifice, 65–66, 122, 132, 138, 199
    circumcised, 156
    commissions and sends his disciples, 162, 168–169, 193–194
    institutes public ministry, 134, 193
    messianic titles, 126–127, 134
    office and work, 42, 113, 126–127, 128, 131
    prays for believers, 165
    preserves the church, 102, 139
    rules by the word, 5, 11, 113, 134
    "sacerdotal" kingdom, 122, 139–140
    shares all his "goods," 29, 32, 48, 156

speaks through his ministers,
126, 169
Christians:
    all hear and speak God's word,
40, 52, 64–65, 124, 126, 131,
138, 162, 168, 192
    as "believers," 15 46, 51, 84,
125, 135
    as Christ's family, 15, 26, 48,
62, 159
    as Christ's voice, 160, 162, 164,
167, 169, 193
    as "father confessors,"
xxiin66, 169
    as one body in Christ, 25, 27,
29, 52, 62, 72, 78–80, 113,
163–166
    as priests (and kings) with Christ,
28, 42, 47, 60, 62, 125,
127–128, 133, 138–140, 156,
159, 165
    as saints, 7, 14, 26, 30, 78, 107,
136, 163, 166, 195
    authority of, 30, 51, 138, 167
    clothed with Christ's holiness, 32,
123, 133, 156, 163
    equality of, xv, 14–15, 27–28, 31,
37, 39–40, 84, 124, 156, 161,
164, 173
    follow Christ's example, 10,
23–24
    highest spiritual status in the
church, 38, 40, 72, 81, 104,
136, 156, 166, 189, 196
    humility of, 3, 8, 9, 11, 24, 132,
159–160, 196
    mutual support and love, xxii,
xxvi, 15, 25, 30–32, 42, 49,
80, 82, 166, 193
    named as Christians, 137, 156
    participate fully in Christ's work,
125, 138, 158, 162, 164, 183
    possess all spiritual blessings, 29,
31, 44, 72, 78, 125, 157, 162
    power to forgive sins in Christ's
name, 167–170, 193
    pray for one another, 60, 111,
139, 162, 165, 193
    represent Christ, xxvii, 126, 162–
164, 169, 193
    right to judge doctrine, 49, 64,
112–113, 155
    sacrificed with Christ, 59, 61,
65–67, 159, 166
    spiritual freedom in Christ, 25,
30–31, 42, 86
    taught by God, 3, 10–11, 24,
62–65, 70, 72, 86, 121, 123,
126, 189
    unity with Christ xviii–xix, 9, 15,
25, 29, 32, 42, 62, 65, 125,
132, 137–138, 156, 164–165,
166, 194
    See also common priesthood,
laity, ministers
Christology. *See* Christ
church:
    apostolic foundation, 10, 110–111,
162, 172
    and preaching, 11, 49, 165, 171
    and leaders, 5, 11, 12, 23, 40, 43,
60, 71, 114, 137, 185, 187,
193, 196, 198
    as any place for worship and
preaching, 27, 142, 154–155,
157–158, 170–173, 188
    as "bride of Christ," 10, 13, 59,
79, 103, 127
    as Christendom, 27–28, 30, 32,
38, 44, 67, 80, 99, 103, 106,
112, 128–129, 135, 162–163,
166, 168
    as communion of saints, xiii,
xviii, 7, 14–16, 24, 29, 31–33,
44, 52, 62, 78, 101, 106–107,
142, 163, 170, 183
    as community, xviii, xxi, xxiii,
24, 26, 32, 51, 78–80, 142–
143, 170

as congregation, assembly, xviii, xxvi, 6, 47, 49, 51, 79, 85, 88, 106, 157, 170–171, 186, 198
as hierarchical institution, xv, 1, 4–5, 9, 12–13, 32, 37, 40, 43, 46, 81, 99, 106, 109, 186, 188, 196
as kingdom of God, 9, 11, 13, 25, 60–61, 64, 104, 122, 125, 134, 135, 137, 139, 142, 168, 171, 174, 197
as "mother" of Christians, 103, 126, 157, 166
as body of Christ, xxvi, 6–9, 10, 13, 15, 23–24, 25–28, 32, 61, 67, 85, 97, 110–111, 137, 160, 184, 191, 194, 197
as (new) people of God xviii, 6, 15, 24, 85, 106, 134–135
as a priesthood xviii, 32, 125, 135, 139–140
as sacramental fellowship, xxiii, 8, 15, 26, 79–80, 101, 105, 190
authority to forgive sins, 167–168, 169–170
corruption and abuses, 12, 37, 38–42, 51, 63, 81, 98–99, 102, 104, 128, 157
defined by its ministry, not the clergy, 81, 108n69
founded on the word, 10, 23–24, 27, 30, 41, 42n24, 49, 78, 81, 90, 105, 112, 140
heretics destroy the church, 4, 5, 8, 12, 110, 112
hidden, except to faith, 14, 105, 109, 111, 114, 140, 196
holiness in Christ's word and faith, 80, 107, 109–110, 110–111, 164, 166
marks of, xxiv, 6, 28, 30, 81, 102, 104–105, 106–110, 114, 184, 196
marriage imagery, 25, 42, 48, 132
medieval church, 5–6, 23, 37, 43, 46, 48, 72, 121, 156, 167
mutual character, xxiii, xxvii, 25, 30–31, 79–80, 82, 170, 171, 193–194
no "spiritual elite," 14, 40, 156, 164, 188, 196
offices, xxi, 84, 125, 128, 137, 192
ordering church and ministry, xxv, 49, 67–71, 71n92, 85, 86–87, 88–89, 105–106, 124, 137, 139–140, 171, 190, 193
papacy, xviin22, 4, 12–13, 27–28, 43, 44, 45, 47–48, 80–81, 102, 111–113
possesses the word and sacraments, 70–71, 100, 105, 107, 110, 126, 171
prefigured in Genesis narratives, 140–143
preserved by the word and sacraments, 102, 104, 110, 162
spiritual community of faith, 5–6, 14–15, 23, 25, 27–28, 44, 78, 102, 114, 156, 163, 173
spiritual possessions held in common, xxii, 31–32, 49, 67–68, 78, 107–110, 112, 160, 184, 18
true and false, 6, 12–13, 51, 110–111, 140, 165
unity of, 7–8, 13, 25–29, 78, 80–81, 106, 112, 165, 194
terminology and definition, 23–24, 27, 31, 78, 106–107, 111, 138
See also common priesthood, ecclesiology, ministry, Reformation
church dialogue, Lutheran–Catholic, xviiin27, 81n18, 134n111
church fathers, influence on Luther, 2. *See also* Augustine, Bernard

clothing, spiritual significance of, 32, 80, 107, 127, 133, 135, 142, 155–156
clergy, 9, 84, 87, 108, 153, 174, 187, 192, 194, 198;
    act *in persona Christi*, 125
    "cleric" a term for all Christians, 103
    control over the sacraments, 27, 39–40, 71, 99, 167, 186
    marriage of, 98
    New Testament, as presbyters or ministers, 42, 50, 68–69, 137
    no unique spiritual status or power, xv, xxvii, 27, 41, 50, 67–68, 72, 80–81, 85, 97–99, 128, 164, 170, 173, 185, 188, 196
    ordination, xxvii, 41, 50, 67, 87, 103, 139
    "Rule" only by common consent, 41, 50, 87
    See also bishops, common priesthood, church, ministers, public ministry
command of God, commandments, 109, 120, 140, 169
common priesthood, xiii–xiv, xix–xxiii, xxvii, 43–44, 51–52, 59–62, 71–72, 119–120, 133–140, 158–159, 165, 173–174, 181–199;
    anointing and consecration 38, 62, 64, 99, 107, 123, 184, 196
    as a Christian's spiritual identity, 42, 52, 60, 72, 82, 88, 104, 131, 184–185, 195–196
    as a product of Luther's biblical interpretation, 59–62, 158, 165
    as a product of Luther's ecclesiology, 71–72, 191, 194
    as Christ's "brethren" and children, 62, 103, 136, 159
    as Luther's "missed opportunity," xxvii–xxviii, 186
    as participation in Christ's priestly work, 42, 45, 47–48, 61, 62, 63, 139–140, 158, 165
    as spiritual gift, not outward status, 62, 159, 164
    authority and dignity rests in the community of believers, 51
    baptism, 38, 48, 62, 99, 103–105, 135–137, 139, 159, 184
    boundaries and horizons xviii, xxix–xxx, 83, 85, 90, 124, 183, 187, 195–199
    both personal and corporate, xxix, 48n51, 52, 60, 108, 130, 132, 161, 184, 193–194, 197
    common to all Christians equally, 50–51, 61, 64, 84, 100, 107–108, 123, 137–138, 161, 183, 194
    communion of saints xvi, xviii–xix, 24, 32–33, 137, 184, 194, 199
    confession and absolution, xx–xxiii, 40, 67–68, 99, 169–170, 183
    consecrated by the word, 164, 169
    established by baptism into Christ, 103, 113, 135–136, 139, 159, 184, 194, 196
    established by Christ's priesthood, xvi, xviii–xx, 44, 45, 57, 59, 136, 138–139, 157–158, 192 164, 193–194, 196
    established by Christ's commission, 169, 194
    established by faith in Christ, 44, 52, 61, 65, 103, 113, 125, 127, 133, 137–138, 164, 196
    faith, 40, 44, 45, 48, 60, 125, 185, 194
    forgiveness, 40, 169–170, 183–184
    individualistic, not, xiii, 130, 173, 193

integral to Luther's reform, 38, 52, 71, 81–83, 165, 183
interpreters of Luther's teaching, xvi–xviii, xxv, xxxiii–xxx, 62n39
judging teaching, 49, 50, 60, 64, 120, 155, 184, 192–193, 198
justification by faith, xvi, xix–xx, 42n24, 52, 120, 128, 132, 144, 183–184, 197
Levitical priests, not, 135–136
mutual encouragement and service, xix, xxvi, 42, 49, 60, 122, 138, 170, 197
offering, 45, 65, 184
offices are sacrifice, prayer and preaching, 48, 66, 125, 128, 131, 136, 138, 184, 192
omission from some key writings, 81, 85, 90, 183–184
ordained by Christ, 165, 169
persistence and integrity in Luther's teaching, xiii–xiv, 52, 77n1, 79, 89–90, 97, 119–120, 158, 161, 173, 182–185, 191–192, 194
prayer, 42, 50, 60, 63, 133, 139, 165, 173
preaching, xx–xxi, 47–48, 69–70, 100, 122–123, 136, 160, 192
public ministry, xvii–xviii, xxiv–xxix, 45, 48, 49, 67–72, 86, 88–90, 124, 133–140, 161–165, 171–172, 183–184, 186, 189, 193–194, 198–199
public ministry, not all priests, 68–69, 87–88, 137, 139
and reform initiatives, 51–52, 183, 185–186
"royal" priesthood, 61
sacrifice, 45, 47, 65–67, 120, 122, 125, 128, 129, 133, 140, 164, 184
teaching, 42, 63–64, 121, 127, 131, 138–139, 140, 184

terminology for, xix, 45, 59–62, 183–185, 187–188, 195
theological development of, xxiv–xxvi, xxix, 1n2, 43, 49, 51–52, 57, 71, 89–90, 129, 136n125, 139–40, 143–145, 161, 165–166, 173–174, 181–182, 184–185, 185–188, 191–192
women as priests, xxix, 69–70, 88, 108, 121, 138–139, 195
worship, 62, 100, 120–123, 125, 129, 184, 192, 194
See also Christ, Christians, church, ministers, office
communion of saints. *See* church, common priesthood
confession of faith, 79n10, 100, 106–107, 127, 129, 130, 135, 143–144, 158, 162, 171, 173.
See also preaching, teaching
confession of sins, xxi–xxii, 8, 28, 30, 40, 50, 167;
absolution, xx–xxii, 28, 40, 67, 98, 167–170, 174
absolution not for sale, 168
See also forgiveness, laity, keys (office of)
Congar, Yves, 42n24, 82n20, 87n62
congregation. *See* church
conscience, 30, 158, 169
councils of the church, 106–107, 111, 120
Creed, Apostles,' xiv, 24, 78–79, 102, 106, 109, 111
cross and suffering, 6, 8, 15, 30, 109, 111, 138–139, 142–143, 164, 167
Cruciger, Caspar, 133, 139, 154, 161, 166, 170

Daniel, David, 2n5, 52n67, 77n1, 78n3

ecclesiology:
Christ's priesthood, significance, 58, 62, 131, 133–140

integral to the common
  priesthood, 1, 24, 27, 32–33,
  43–44, 160–161, 190–194
Luther's formative themes,
  xvi, 24–33, 49, 52, 77–78,
  105–106, 123, 144, 154, 160,
  191, 198
Luther's formative
  themes: community and unity,
  25–29, 156–157, 166, 194
Luther's formative
  themes: equality and
  participation, 29–32, 48, 85,
  124, 128, 139–140, 142, 154,
  156–157, 162, 194
Luther's teaching, development,
  xvii–xviii, xxiv, 1n2, 2–4, 9,
  11, 13, 15–16, 16n112, 23–24,
  33, 52n67, 77–82, 89–90,
  105, 111, 113–114, 129, 166,
  170, 186
Luther's "textual synthesis," 7,
  13–14, 25–26, 28, 29, 31, 38,
  62, 64, 67, 78, 80–81, 101,
  104–105, 112, 137, 160–161,
  190–191
  See also church, common
  priesthood, ministry
Eck, John, 45
education, xxiii, 82, 87
eucharist. *See* Lord's Supper, sacraments
emergency situations ("necessity"),
  68, 71, 85, 87–88, 89, 108, 168–
  170, 193;
  where there are no Christians, 70
Emser, Jerome, 45, 48, 51

faith, 8, 15, 24, 82, 128, 154, 168;
  as *Imitatio Christi*, 24, 30
  as freedom in Christ, 42–43,
    101, 184
  as the true priestly office, 45,
    65, 66
  as true spirituality and worship,
    27, 32, 38, 40, 45, 60, 67, 133
  as union with Christ, 48, 65, 72,
    132, 155, 196
  certainty of faith in God's word,
    3, 24, 29, 129, 169
  examples of, 132–133, 138–139,
    142, 155
  partner of the word, 11, 23,
    25, 32, 40, 68, 82, 84, 108,
    110–111, 130–131, 153, 170,
    173, 192
  "possesses" Christ, 15, 156, 160
  works, 58, 125, 155
  See also Christians, Justification
family. *See* parents
forgiveness of sins:
  authority given to all Christians,
    xxi, 29–30, 50, 99, 167–
    170, 183
  Christ's work as high priest, 126
  not to be bought and sold, 168
  pronounced in Christ's name, 28,
    169, 174
  See also confession of sins, laity,
    keys (office of)

Goertz, Harald, xv, xix, xxv
gospel. *See* word

Hendrix, Scott, xvii, 25n10, 82n27,
  87n58, 143n173, 171n108
Helmer, Christine, 1n2, 38n4
hermeneutics. *See* Bible
Holl, Karl, 3
Holy Spirit, 3, 13, 23, 63, 64, 102, 121,
  141, 160, 168, 193;
  consecrates all Christians in
    baptism, 62, 103, 105, 113,
    123, 135–136, 139, 159
  gathers the church, xiii, 24, 31,
    78, 81, 126, 136, 191, 194, 197
  gifts of, xviii, 47, 66, 112, 123,
    135, 142, 157, 161, 163
  sanctifies the church, 79, 107, 109
  teaches "in the heart," 11, 63
  See also spiritual

Huss, Jan, 50

incense, 133, 173
indulgence controversy, xxii, 25, 29, 40
in persona Christi, xx, 125
Israel as God's people, 121

Jacob as king and priest, 142
judging teaching. *See* common priesthood
justification by faith, 3–4, 10, 23, 31–32, 33, 38n4, 80, 113, 122, 132, 156, 163, 191
    See also common priesthood, faith

Karlstadt, Andreas, xxviii, 87, 120, 126, 131, 186
keys, office of, xxi, 28, 50, 99, 108, 110, 167–170;
    given to all Christendom, 29, 40, 67, 99, 167, 168
    spiritual power only, 167–168
    See also confession of sins, forgiveness
Kolb, Robert, xivn3, xvii, 2n3, 42n25

laity, xiii, xv, xxviii, 14, 26, 31, 99, 141–142, 155, 195–199;
    absolve sins in Christ's name, 68, 168, 169n95
    active participants in worship, 39, 52, 60, 183, 188, 197–199
    Christ "walks like a layperson," 127–128
    learn fundamentals of the faith, 48, 51–52, 79, 138
    not to preach publicly without a call, 86, 88, 155
    robbed of the word and sacraments, 63, 101–102, 186
    spiritual equals of clergy, 27, 40, 52, 68, 82, 103, 123, 127, 156, 164
    See also Christians, clergy, common priesthood
law and gospel, 120, 157, 160
Leipzig Debate, 30, 37, 45
Leppin, Volker, 2, 6n49,
Lieberg, Hellmut, xv, xixn35, xxivn88, xxv
Lohse, Bernard xvii, xxv–xxvi, xxviii, 3, 7, 10, 13, 77n1, 119n1, 186
Lord's Prayer, xxii, xxv, 8, 102, 109, 111, 165, 167, 171
Lord's Supper, xxiv, 39, 41, 50, 100, 107–108;
    as communion, xxiii, 101, 104–105
    as proclamation and worship, 100
    as spiritual sacrifice, 62, 65
    Christ's institution, 26, 68, 101, 104–105
    Christ's presence, 79
    "receiving both kinds," 28, 39, 99
    "testament" is Christ's promise, 65
    see also mass, sacraments
love, xv, 26, 30, 78, 157, 171, 173;
    serves the neighbour, xviii, 42, 163–164, 172

marks of the church. *See* church
marriage, 109, 111, 141
mass, 39–40, 45, 46–47, 99–101, 101–106;
    private, 47, 98, 99, 101–103
    sacrifice, 45, 47, 65, 67, 132, 136, 141, 165, 189
    true mass, 104–105
    See also Lord's Supper, sacraments
Melanchthon, Philip, xxviii, 86, 185
Melchizedek, 8–9, 57–59, 136, 141, 159
ministers:
    as preachers of the word, 15, 63, 79
    as representative of the community, xxv, 105, 139–140

as servants of the church, xxvii,
  27, 108
servants with Christ, 126, 163
terminology for, xxvii–xxviii, 41,
  46, 50, 69, 137
See also bishops, clergy, common
  priesthood, pastors, preachers
ministry:
  as service of God's people, 12,
    15, 40, 68, 108, 126
  authorisation for, xxiv, xxvi, 15,
    48, 49, 50–51, 67–72, 85–86,
    108, 137–138
  Christians, 70, 84, 132, 138, 163–
    164, 167–170, 188, 189, 193
  foundational texts, 68–72
  parents, 83, 138, 163, 190
  participation of both pastors and
    people, xxvi, 114, 126, 138,
    164, 170, 188
  possession of whole church, xxvi,
    50–51, 67, 99, 105, 107–108,
    112–113, 132, 172, 193
  See also church, common
    priesthood, preaching, public
    ministry
Moses as law-giver, reveals sin, 58
Müntzer, Thomas, 87, 120, 126
music and hymns, xxvi, 52, 82, 102, 183
mysticism, 5–6, 65

need, necessity. *See* emergency situation
Ninety-five Theses, 25, 29
Noah as "pontiff," 140–141

offering, 8, 16, 45;
  priestly offering of preaching and
    praise, 130–130, 160
  self-offering of praise and
    thanksgiving, 65, 125
  See also sacrifice
offices in the church, xxvi, 137;
  bishop's office to uphold the
    gospel, 98

Christ works through the public
  offices, 126, 162
Christian's office, to praise God
  and teach others, 127, 163, 167
church's offices are not
  "indelible," xxvii, 50, 137
priest's office to pray and teach,
  64, 128, 192
public, xxiv–xxvi, 39, 48–49,
  83–84, 126–127, 134, 137
require call and appointment,
  87–88, 103, 137
seven offices of the word,
  common to all Christians,
  50–51, 70
spiritual sacrifices are an office,
  66, 128, 160
See also keys (office of),
  ministry, word
orders, holy (church, family,
  government), 86, 163, 166
ordination, xxvii, 59, 103–104, 106,
  135, 139, 170
  "indelible character," no, 67,
    103, 137
  sacrament, not, 41, 50, 67,
    170n102
  See also church, clergy, ministers

papacy. *See* church
parents, 82, 126, 138, 141–142,
  163, 187;
  as household "bishops," xxvi,
    83, 187
pastors. *See* clergy, ministers, public
  ministry
Peasants' War, 85, 126, 186
Pelikan, Jaroslav, 2n3, 50n60, 140n147,
  161n47
penance. *See* confession of sins,
  sacraments
persecution, 140, 165n67
Peter, represents all Christians, 29, 48,
  99, 170, 189
Peterson, Cheryl, xvn13, 25n10, 89n76

polemic, Luther's, xiv, xviin22, 42–44, 45, 47, 51, 80, 111, 112, 165, 171, 195
pope(s), 4, 28, 40, 43, 47, 48, 58, 68, 80, 99, 102, 111, 120, 132, 136, 186;
  as antichrist, 13, 80, 102
  judged by Christians, 112, 155
  high priest, not, 59
  Lord of the church, not, 80–81
  See also bishops, church (papacy)
postils, 46, 82, 154, 158, 173
prayer, 42, 50, 109, 111, 139, 162–163, 173.

See also Lord's Prayer, common priesthood

preaching, 10, 25, 110, 119, 133, 153–154, 161, 168, 181;
  absolution, xxi–xxii, 168–169
  all Christians should "declare God's deeds," 69–70, 124, 130, 138, 157, 171
  as Luther's reformatory task, 26, 48, 51–52, 78, 82, 90, 153, 162, 173–174
  as worship and praise of God, 124–125, 130, 160, 192
  brings people to Christ, 126, 160
  call and authorization, xxv, 49, 69, 70, 87–88, 105–106, 139, 171, 192
  formal or informal, serves God's purposes, 160n39
  highest office, the, xxi, xxvi, 41, 49, 50, 100, 135, 164, 183
  instituted by Christ, 89, 100, 106, 110, 134, 139, 163
  requires "hearers," 100, 124, 131, 164, 171, 192, 198
  Stephen as a lay preacher, 70, 155
  women, 83, 133, 169, 190, 193
  See also church, common priesthood, postils, priests, public ministry, teaching, word

priests and priesthood:
  as teachers and preachers of God's word, 62, 121–122, 127, 140–143, 192
  as ministers, not lords, 12, 39, 41, 50, 79, 127
  false, 41, 47–48, 59, 67, 104, 121, 165
  hierarchical, 37, 45–46, 47, 71
  indelible character, xxvii, 38, 50, 103
  medieval (Roman) orders, xxvii, 30, 65, 67, 121, 135, 141
  new order of priests, 124–125, 128, 135–136
  New Testament, xxvii, 41, 47, 50, 59, 61, 68–69, 103, 122–123, 134–135
  offices of, 136, 192
  Old Testament, 9, 47, 57–59, 62, 120–123, 128, 135–136, 140–143
  patriarchs as priests, 140–143
  See also Bishops, Christ, church, common priesthood, clergy
priesthood of believers, xiii, 191;
  as a metaphor, xv–xvi, 158
  as a slogan, 158, 161, 185
  contested nature of xiv–xv, xxvii–xxviii, 185
  See also common priesthood, priests and priesthood
promise. *See* sacraments, word
prophets, 88, 120–123.
  See also preaching
Psalms:
  Christ's priesthood pre–figured, 57, 133–140
  significance for Luther, 2, 102, 109, 111, 128–129, 133, 139–140, 143
public ministry:
  administers Christ's word for the church, 108, 114, 126, 134, 138, 162, 193

call and consent of the church,
xxvii, 41, 49, 50–51, 67, 70,
105–106, 171, 186, 193
divine institution, xxiv–xxv,
83–84, 108, 134, 162, 193
elected from the baptised priests,
104–105, 137
financial support, 168–169
office transferred or delegated, xv,
xxiv–xxv, 48–49
ordained, xv, xxvii–xxviii, 50–51,
67–72, 103, 139
relationship to priesthood xiv–xv,
xxiv–xxviii, 48–49, 50–51,
67–72, 137–138, 171–172,
188, 193
self-appointed, not, 48, 67, 70, 87,
103, 106, 193
See also bishops, church,
common priesthood, clergy,
ministers, office

Reformation, 26–27, 37–38, 42n24, 44,
50–52, 67, 82n27, 85, 89–90, 97,
127–128;
Bohemia, 50–51, 71
"breakthrough" theology, 1–4,
23–24, 31, 40, 57, 65, 154, 174
continuity with the ancient
church, 102, 110–111
correction of abuses, 42, 51, 98,
99, 102, 121, 156
German, 2, 38–39, 46, 47, 49, 70,
80, 82, 83, 86, 111, 153, 172
major treatises, xx, 33, 37, 43–44,
51, 182, 185–186, 192
Luther's "missed opportunity,"
xxvii–xxviii, 185
positive program of reform, 42,
47–48, 51–52, 79, 81–83,
156, 183
radical reformers, 79, 85, 87, 89,
101, 186
reform, not innovation, 110,
185–186

required preachers, 85, 97
restoration of the gospel, 43, 51,
98, 102
Roman church, xx, 4, 13, 25, 29,
37, 39, 44, 47, 50, 85, 97, 98,
106, 123, 141, 155, 161, 163,
172, 183, 185, 186
social impact, xxiii, 49, 82–83,
85–87, 156, 156n16, 185–187
struggle to implement, xxvii, 32,
46, 48, 78, 82–83, 124, 140,
165, 183, 187, 196
supported by secular authorities,
38–39, 71, 87–88, 172,
185–187
theological character, 23, 27,
30, 52, 67, 78nn2–3, 98, 119,
127–128
See also church
Roper, Lyndal xvii, 26n19, 29n37, 38,
82n22, 86n56, 98n1, 143n173

Sabbath, Jesus' teaching, 171
sacraments, 8, 39, 100, 105;
as marks of the church, 106–110,
110–111
as Christ's promise, received
by faith, 39–41, 43, 65, 80,
99, 104
called pastors administer on
behalf of community, 139
equal possession by all Christians,
15, 27–28, 40, 50, 67–68, 99,
101, 107, 164, 171, 173, 183
foundational texts, 68, 110
instituted by Christ, 39, 41, 47,
67, 101, 104
no unique papal powers, 68,
98–99, 183
person of celebrant, not dependant
on, 28, 68, 105, 164, 183
reformation changes, 39, 67, 99,
183–188

224 Index

See also baptism, Lord's Supper, confession and absolution, word
sacrifice, 8;
    as priestly prayer, praise and worship, 45, 65–67, 83n31, 100, 122, 124–125, 128, 129, 139, 140, 172
    as preaching of God's word, 70, 100, 122–124, 126, 131, 160
    as humility and contrition, 132, 160
    false sacrifice, 45, 47, 130, 132, 189
    "living sacrifice," 8–9, 57, 65–66, 122, 127, 160, 184, 197
    sacrifice of self, 65–67, 138, 159
    spiritual sacrifice, 8, 16, 62, 66, 120, 138, 159–160, 189
    See also cross, common priesthood, offering, priest and priesthood
Schilling, Heinz xvii, 49n58, 71n92, 82n22, 85n33, 98n1, 156n16, 143n173
schools, 82–84, 142
Scripture. *See* Bible, word
sermons. *See* postils, preaching
Smalcald Articles, 80–81, 89–90
Spalatin, George, 60, 185
spiritual, xvi, xix, xxvi, xxviii, 3–4, 5, 6–7, 8–9, 11, 16, 24, 26–27, 29, 41, 45, 61, 78, 89, 108, 144, 162, 193, 196;
    equality of Christians, 14–15, 27, 30–31, 37–38, 42, 44, 50, 52, 60, 67, 69, 85, 123, 156, 164, 166, 184, 186, 195
    spiritual estate, xxiii, 27, 38–39, 67, 83–84, 87, 130
    unity in the word and faith, 27, 80, 130, 155, 166
spirituality of faith, 4, 27, 32, 40, 52, 81, 128, 130, 156, 184, 186

spiritual struggle, Luther's, 2, 15, 28–29, 46, 87, 143
students and colleagues, Luther's, 120, 130–131, 141–143, 161, 195

teaching, xxi;
    apostolic message the norm, 134
    importance of catechisms, 79, 183
    public teaching a called office, 87, 124
    teachers and preachers are true priests, 131
    See also catechisms, preaching, word
temple, 9, 122–123, 128
theology, Luther's:
    development, xxi, xxiv, 3, 10–11, 23, 57, 71–72, 119, 129, 154
    interrelatedness, xiv–xvi, xix, 23, 52, 71, 101, 119, 132, 154, 158, 172, 173–174, 181, 183–185, 191–192, 195
    medieval roots, 1n2, 38n4
Torgau church consecration, 170–173

vocation, xv, 88
vows, 40, 157n26

Wartburg Castle, 46, 154, 158
"we are all priests," xvi, xviii, xxix, 27, 32, 38, 41, 60–64, 123, 128, 133, 161, 171, 184, 185–188, 193, 199
    See also common priesthood
Wendebourg, Dorothea, xvn9, 106n49
Wengert, Timothy xv, 28n29, 83n31
Wicks, Jared, 6, 42n24
Wittenberg, xxii, xxvii, 2, 32, 46, 49, 70, 86, 99, 112, 133, 143, 153, 163, 173, 185, 191
women. *See* common priesthood, preaching
word:
    accessible to all Christians, 63–64, 120, 138, 197

agency, divine / human, 84, 108–109, 121, 126, 141, 162–163, 169
as liberating gospel, 28, 37, 42, 85–86, 186–187
as God's promise, xiv, xv, xvii, 3, 11, 24, 29, 40–42, 45, 51, 80, 99, 104, 109, 120–121, 125, 127, 128, 142, 144, 156, 165, 169–170, 197
Christological centre, 8, 10, 59, 158
early understanding, Luther's, 11–12, 23–24, 63, 126, 192
objective character, 81, 108–109
opposition and conflict, 134, 140
preached external word, 3, 5, 11, 124, 126, 130–131, 136
primary office of church and priesthood, xxi, xxvii, 33, 41, 50, 62–65, 88, 162, 192
reforms the church, 42n24, 67, 90, 102
response of faith and worship, 9, 65, 100, 130, 171, 192
shared power and authority in the church, 41, 51, 138, 170, 193
spoken to the heart, 3, 63–64
suppressed in late–medieval church, 37, 62–63
tradition, 40n16, 45, 134
Trinitarian expression, 126
true holy relic, 107
See also Bible, preaching, teaching
Worms, Diet of, 46
worship, 15, 52, 62, 65, 82, 90, 102, 120, 123, 125, 128, 133, 183;
New Testament, 124–125
Old Testament, 8–9, 122–123, 125
people and pastor worship together as priests, 170
See also church, common priesthood, sacrifice
writings, Luther's:
limited use of, xx, 40n41, 49n53, 97, 101, 119, 143
self-evaluation, 47, 90, 161
variety and unity, 52, 119, 181–185

Zwingli, Ulrich, 101, 131

About the Author

Following retirement from a varied pastoral ministry in England and Australia, **Roger Whittall** is an honorary postdoctoral associate at the University of Divinity, Melbourne, occupying a study at Australian Lutheran College, Adelaide, where he continues to delve into Martin Luther's writings on the church. With Lois he participates in the worship and life of St Stephen's Lutheran Church, Adelaide, blessed to be members of a community that—stretching the boundaries of church order in the LCANZ—has given its women a voice that enables them to join in serving God's people with the word and sacraments, just as Christ intended. Otherwise in the midst of all life's busyness, the very best times are those shared with a family that includes four beloved grandchildren, treasuring every precious moment that God gives.

Milton Keynes UK
Ingram Content Group UK Ltd.
UKHW011315240424
441691UK00006B/42